D1601675

From Politics Past
to Politics Future

From Politics Past
to Politics Future

*An Integrated Analysis of Current
and Emergent Paradigms*

ALAN J. MAYNE

Westport, Connecticut
London

Library of Congress Cataloging-in-Publication Data

Mayne, Alan J. (Alan James), 1927–
    From politics past to politics future : an integrated analysis of
current and emergent paradigms / Alan J. Mayne.
        p. cm.
    Includes bibliographical references and index.
    ISBN 0–275–96151–6 (alk. paper)
    1. Political science. 2. Political science—Philosophy.
3. Democracy. 4. World politics—1945– 5. Right and left
(Political science). I. Title.
JA83.M318 1999
320.9′049—dc21   98–31077

British Library Cataloguing in Publication Data is available.

Library of Congress Catalog Card Number: 98–31077
ISBN: 0–275–96151–6

First published in 1999

Praeger Publishers, 88 Post Road West, Westport, CT 06881
An imprint of Greenwood Publishing Group, Inc.

Printed in the United States of America

The paper used in this book complies with the
Permanent Paper Standard issued by the National
Information Standards Organization (Z39.48–1984).

10 9 8 7 6 5 4 3 2 1

Copyright Acknowledgments

The author and publisher gratefully acknowledge permission for the use of the following
material:

From Brian C. Burrows, Alan J. Mayne, and Paul A. R. Newbury, *Into the 21st Century: A
Handbook for a Sustainable Future* (London: Adamantine Press, 1991). Reprinted by courtesy
of Adamantine Press Limited.

From Alan J. Mayne, *Resources for the Future: An International Annotated Bibliography for the
21st Century* (London: Adamantine Press, 1993). Reprinted by courtesy of Adamantine Press
Limited.

From Alan J. Mayne, "Critical Introduction," to H. G. Wells, *World Brain: H. G. Wells on the
Future of World Education*, edited by Alan J. Mayne (New ed.; London: Adamantine Press,
1995). Reprinted by courtesy of Adamantine Press Limited.

From an e-mail message by Jeremy Geelan to Alan J. Mayne, 8 September 1997. Reprinted by
courtesy of Jeremy Geelan.

Contents

PART III.   POLITICS IN THE TWENTY-FIRST CENTURY

Preface

As the twenty-first century approaches, most global, national, and human problems are escalating into a cluster of interlocking crises. The present world situation often appears to be a battle between good and evil, whose outcome is not yet certain. Both people and governments seem to be more and more overwhelmed and helpless in the face of these problems. More and more people are losing confidence in the ability of governments to solve them. Most governments, even when acting from motives of goodwill, seem to have few clues about how to address the problems. A good many people give up in despair or apathy, but many others are seeking possible ways out.

This book aims to show that the situation is not yet hopeless and that there *are* positive ways of addressing the present human situation, although it will require tremendous efforts by many people even to begin to resolve it. I indicate several possible routes towards finding solutions and bringing about a much more favourable future. I offer an in-depth, integrated analysis that views politics and government from almost all angles and introduces many ideas and various paradigms, both old and new. This analysis and these ideas could help to lay the foundations for the emergence of a positive, new approach to politics and government through the millennial moment and into the early twenty-first century.

The book provides a broad and fairly comprehensive introduction to contemporary and future politics and government. I adopt a holistic and interdisciplinary, indeed, transdisciplinary approach, so that insights from many different fields of knowledge, schools of thought, and viewpoints are brought together. I introduce many different concepts and aspects of politics and the human situation in general that I know about. In this respect, my coverage is broader than that of any other political book that I know; even though it is often preliminary and not detailed, I enable readers to make further explorations for themselves by citing many relevant references.

I have not only compiled this book as an interdisciplinary scholar with many years' experience of research and study, both inside and outside universities, and observation of both local and global events for most of my life. I have also written it as a fairly altruistic and public-spirited person with a radical progressive, 'slightly left of centre' political viewpoint with a 'deep green' tinge, who belongs to no political party. I do not view the present human and global situation as one where more than a few of the answers are already known.

On the contrary, it is a situation where people of goodwill need to work together in mutual cooperation and without dogmatism to seek possible solutions that will be in the ultimate interests of all of us, including those who will live in future generations. These solutions will require changes of lifestyle for many, if not most, people, and it is best that they emerge through mutual discussion and persuasion, not through imposition. For this to happen, democracy in its broadest sense will need to emerge worldwide; at present, there is not one country where it is fully developed.

Despite all the bad news and increasing problems, there are many significant, new positive developments in all fields of life, that could make important contributions to transforming for the better the whole political situation worldwide. There are signs that the rate at which these developments are emerging is steadily increasing. There is plenty of scope for a wide variety of positive and constructive initiatives by individuals, groups, political movements and parties, businesses, nongovernmental organisations, public institutions, government departments, governments, and international bodies.

This book analyses and considers possible approaches to the resolution of the growing and increasingly complex problems threatening humankind and endeavours to integrate these approaches with new, holistic political approaches to their solution. It attempts to provide guidelines for the practical application of these approaches. It presents pictures of three alternative, possible future scenarios facing humanity (pessimistic, piecemeal, and optimistic) and suggests how we could make the emergence of an optimistic scenario much more likely.

Part One presents the facts about the current world situation and some information about its historical background. Chapter 1 gives a brief, but fairly comprehensive, survey of the very wide range of political and human problems and issues that affect all countries in the world. Chapters 2 to 4 examine what kinds of regimes are actually in power and also some earlier regimes, including democratic, authoritarian, totalitarian, and communist regimes. Chapter 5 observes the attempted transition from communism to democracy in the Commonwealth of Independent States (CIS) and Eastern Europe. Chapter 6 assesses the wide variety of political movements currently active or emerging.

Part Two explores existing political paradigms and ideologies and presents many of the elements that seem likely to be used by the emerging new political paradigms. Chapter 7 briefly reviews totalitarianism, dictatorship, and authoritarianism, then has a longer discussion of democracy and how to improve it and make it more participatory. Chapter 8 shows how government may increasingly be distributed between different levels, ranging from the global, through the continental, national, and regional, to local and neighbourhood communities. There could eventually be an element of unified world government, combining federal, functional, and planetary management approaches. Chapter 9 surveys the current political paradigms and ideologies, ranging from authoritarian and democratic schools of thought, through the mainstream political spectrum, to a variety of alternative political paradigms and ideologies. Chapter 10 shows how paradigms for other aspects of human life and most other fields of knowledge are becoming more and more relevant to contemporary politics. It discusses mainly paradigms from different social sciences and areas of human affairs but includes examples from the natural and mathematical sciences. Chapter 11 discusses ethical, religious, and spiritual approaches to politics.

Chapter 12 starts outlining and putting together some possible components for a new political paradigm, which would be *holistic* in several different ways. This paradigm would adopt an integrated approach to policy-making responding sensibly to various human needs, replace confrontation by cooperation, and make democracy genuinely participatory. It would apply a 'unified practical philosophy', encourage 'win-win' cooperation and 'stakeholder partnership', and unify the policy-making process. It would provide a framework for synthesising ideologies into 'unity in diversity'. It would allow the evolution of a collective World Brain/World Mind/World Heart that would achieve constructive and caring government on behalf of ourselves and our planet.

Part Three examines the consequences of the alternative approaches to politics in all parts of the world in terms of three scenarios resulting from blind continuation of existing trends, attempting to solve problems in isolation, or a holistic, altruistic, spiritual approach. Chapters 13 to 15, respectively, describe these pessimistic, piecemeal, and optimistic scenarios. Chapter 16 presents the conclusions of the book and shows that the holistic, altruistic, spiritual approach is the only way in which we can hope to solve our increasing man-made problems. The epilogue shows how important it is for us to ACT NOW, because we could soon reach the 'point of no return'. Our future existence depends on the very delicate interactions between many factors. We have a choice between changing our motives and activities to preserve this balance or entering a catastrophic situation. I suggest several specific guidelines for achieving an optimistic scenario.

This book is intended to be a starting point for exploration in greater depth of the complex web of human and planetary problems and of the human actions, policies, and political approaches that could lead to their eventual resolution. As such, it can usefully be read by academics, researchers, students, politicians, policy makers, and intelligent, concerned citizens. It includes an annotated bibliography of considerably more than 200 important, sometimes key books and several periodicals, some of which present a more comprehensive view of interrelated problem areas and most of which provide more details of specific problems, issues, and topics.

In addition, each chapter ends with notes that provide annotated references to relevant literature, including items in the annotated bibliography, then suggests specific subproblems or aspects of problems that can be investigated further by groups of readers or, sometimes, by individual readers. I would be most interested and grateful to receive information about the results and findings of readers' investigations so that I could assess the ideas and information and pass them on to those best able to use them. Because of limited space, I have been able to use only a small fraction of the relevant material that I found while preparing this book. Larger selections from this material will be cited or indicated in a subsequent book, whose provisional title is *Multimedia Resources for the Future: A Global Directory of Web- and Print-Based Reference Sources*, and at much greater length on the Internet and other nonprint media.

I would like to thank the many friends who have provided information and encouragement for this book and the many politicians of various viewpoints whom I have met or with whom I have corresponded. I am especially grateful to Jeremy Geelan, Publishing Director of Adamantine Press and Chairman of 21st Century Studies Limited (New York and London), for his continual practical support and valuable advice from the start of this project, to James T. Sabin, Director of Academic Research and Development, Greenwood Publishing Group, for his continuing encouragement, to Rebecca Ardwin, Production Editor, for her helpful collaboration, to Carol Lucas, who copyedited the book with commendable speed and thoroughness, and to Jason Pearce for his invaluable help in the final makeup and design of this book. I take responsibility for any imperfections that remain in this book despite these people's help.

Prologue—Humanity at the Crossroads

From 7 to 13 October 1995, I attended an important international conference at Findhorn, Scotland, on the theme "Eco-Villages & Sustainable Communities: Models for 21st Century Living". At this remarkable gathering, attended by people from almost all parts of the world, ideas were exchanged, and practical projects were presented that *could* play a decisive part in human affairs during the twenty-first century, especially for politics in the twenty-first century. They concern the evolution and design of new patterns of living, sustainable development, and fulfillment of human needs within a broad framework of spiritual values. They range even wider than that, by being expressed within the context of the total human situation.

One part of the conference discussed new ways of living, based on community and sustainability, that have already been tested and found to work in a considerable number of intentional communities in various parts of the world. Together with eco-villages, they provide prototypes of new paradigms of practical living, human settlements, governance, and politics that may well become widespread in the twenty-first century. Many of the presentations covered the experience of specific intentional communities. At a more theoretical level, Robert Gilman discussed the basic concepts of eco-villages and the reasons for their existence. An eco-village is a full-featured human settlement on a human scale in which human activities are harmlessly integrated into the natural world in a way that supports healthy human development and can be successfully continued into the indefinite future. It is a unified system whose biosystem, built environment, economy, and governance are integrated by applying spiritual, emotional, and cultural 'spiritual glue'.

Those who attended the conference were also well aware that there are many serious human and global problems to be addressed and many destructive trends, some of which could go out of control unless decisive action is taken to stop them within a few years. There is thus a race between escalating trends that could destroy human civilisation and seriously damage our planet and an upsurge of constructive, creative, altruistic endeavours and projects world-wide. The nature and root causes of these problems and trends are outlined in Chapter 1 of this book. Some of them were also made very clear at the conference.

Helena Norberg-Hodge pointed out how the inexorable spread of the lowest forms of Americanised 'Western' culture were eroding the formerly sustain-able ways of life of even quite remote communities in the Third World, for example, in Ladakh, North India, and other parts of the Himalayas. Rashmi Mayur, director of the International Institute for Sustainable Futures, em-phasised the need to reverse *fast* the alarming trends resulting from human attempts to master the Earth; instead, we must protect and give back to the Earth. Every citizen of the world should have a decent place to live and an adequate diet. Today, he said, humanity faces the same challenge as Arjuna, in the Mahabharata, when he feared that he was about to lose his fight against seemingly overwhelming forces of evil. Krishna said that the important thing was to continue to wage a war against evil. The same is true today in the pres-ent human situation. We should be in the battle against all evil trends. The day we win, just as Arjuna won, the sun will shine again for the children, people, and wildlife of the world.

Robert Muller, a former assistant secretary-general of the United Nations (UN) who is now chancellor of the University for Peace, showed strong aware-ness of some of the frightening problems facing the world but was nevertheless more optimistic today than he had been many years ago as a young man. He pointed to the many hundreds of international initiatives that have been preparing for, and will prepare for, the twenty-first century and that are begin-ning to address the whole range of human and planetary problems. Added to all these, there are many thousands of positive, worthwhile projects being conducted by nongovernmental organisations (NGOs) and other bodies all over the world. Here are just some of the many further steps forward that he recommended:

Create a world association of eco-villagers as an accredited UN NGO.

Create a world ecological university at Findhorn.

Recommend to the United Nations Educational, Scientific and Cultural Organization (UNESCO) that it hold a conference on long-term evolutionary sciences.

Demilitarise the Earth, as had already been done in Panama, Costa Rica, and Haiti and would soon be done throughout Central America.

Set up a World Commission on the Oceans.

Celebrate the UN World Days, especially World Environment Days; we need more of these days, for example, a World Water Day.

- A whole strategy for humankind from the eco-self through the eco-family, eco-village, eco-neighbourhood, eco-city, eco-region, eco-nation, eco-Earth, eco-atmosphere and outer space, eco-solar system, to eco-Universe.
- A World Commission on People's Associations; already there are well over 1,000 UN-accredited NGOs.
- A World Conference on Philanthropy, which would address priorities.
- All of us should write down ideas for the year 2000; *ideas change the world.*

Robert Muller summed up his speech as follows: "Never had humanity such an opportunity to prepare itself well for a new century and millennium. We seem to be doing it". Those at the conference echoed this statement by affirming out loud: "We *are* doing it".

Jonathon Porritt, a leading ecological thinker and writer, outlined the emerging *ecocommunitarian approach*, which adds green ideas to the principles of community. He viewed it as the most astonishing collection of ideas that the world has ever seen, which should be presented to *all* people. Yet too many greens talk about it only among themselves, as if they felt that other people would not listen! We need a model of ecocommunitarianism in the *real world*, engaging with people in *partnership*. This will be really difficult to achieve and require really hard work. Jonathon Porritt urged us to do this work, strengthened by our core of spiritual values, love, and compassion. Then we would see things change for the better.

I

POLITICS TODAY

1

Political Problems and Issues

'Politics' can be defined as "the art and science of government" or as "public life and affairs as involving government". Government is concerned with authority and with the control, management, and administration of an organisation or grouping of people. Such groupings range from local neighbourhoods and communities, through nations, to the whole population of human beings living on Earth. Political problems and issues arise for all these groupings and for almost every different aspect of their life. Indeed, they can be equated with human and global problems and issues, *all* of which now need to be addressed by politicians and governments. This chapter provides a broad overview of the most important types of problems and issues[1] and begins with a brief discussion of the distinction between problems and issues. It ends by indicating some approaches to their possible resolution.

As most countries in the world today either have more or less democratic regimes or aspire to become democracies, one fundamental contemporary issue is the *future of democracy*. It is not possible to achieve an adequate democracy or a good regime without respecting human rights and recognising the need for human responsibilities, in appropriate balance with each other. *Economic* problems and issues arise from attempts to provide adequate material standards of living and livelihood for people and fair distributions of resources between them. *Environmental* problems and issues arise from various human impacts on the environment and the needs to conserve resources, achieve a sustainable way of life, and avoid excessive pollution. A wide range of *social* problems and issues arise from the variety and complexity of different ways in which people interact with each other. Important problems arise from the *rapid advance of science and technology*. All these categories are brought together in the problems and issues of *sustainable development*.

Problems and issues also arise from the mechanisms and processes of *government and administration*, from *international relations*, and from the whole range of *human conflict*, from wars to personal disputes.

In addition, none of these problems and issues or their different categories are isolated from each other. All of them mutually interact and overlap. None of them can be addressed adequately by themselves. The whole complex web of global and human problems and issues is known as 'the human *problematique*'. The similarly complicated array of contributions towards their resolution is known as 'the human *resolutique*'. One of the most striking characteristics of the human problematique is that it is becoming more intricate and complex so rapidly that the human resolutique is finding it increasingly hard to 'catch up'. Any 'solution' that is applied all too often leads to other problems that could become even more serious. The other very evident characteristic is that there are many harmful trends as well as many beneficial trends in the human and global situation, so that there often seems to be a closely run race between them. *Our world seems like an arena on which a great battle is being fought between good* [2] *and evil.* [3]

PROBLEMS AND ISSUES

Dictionary definitions of 'problem' include "doubtful or difficult matter requiring a solution" and "something hard to understand or accomplish or deal with". There are many meanings of the word 'issue', but the dictionary definitions most relevant to its use in politics and government are "an important subject of debate" and "a subject of contention". White, Little, and Smith (1997, Chapter 1) discuss the relationships between problems and issues in unusual detail, in the context of world politics. An issue attracts the attention of those who engage in world politics and of those who wish to understand it. It requires the expenditure of resources in some form, even if only of human resources such as diplomatic resources. To understand an issue, one needs to go beyond knowing its associated facts and figures; the issue must also be put into context. Issues are liable to become more or less important on the political agenda as circumstances change. More important, they usually represent one 'face' or aspect of a more persistent problem or group of problems arising in world politics.

White et al. go on to discuss issues in relation to political agendas and agenda setting, issues and the media, the classification of issues, the significance of issues in world politics, the management of issues in world politics, and the selection of which issues to view as having key importance. For example, issues can be classified according to their extent or scope, their urgency or intensity, their salience or visibility, and their centrality or locality.

THE FUTURE OF DEMOCRACY

The concept of 'democracy' originated in the city-state of ancient Athens, but the ancient world was mostly dominated by empires and kingdoms. Democracy did not begin to reemerge until the Renaissance in the fifteenth century, which brought republican regimes in the Italian city-states that could be viewed as an intermediate step. From the mid-seventeenth century on, democracy gradually evolved, mainly in Western Europe and North America. Since World War II, democracy began to spread to many countries of the Third World, as they were liberated from colonial rule. From 1989 on, the communist regimes of the USSR and Eastern Europe began to be transformed and then to collapse, and a transition towards democracy took place in most of these countries, although some serious conflicts also emerged. Many problems have arisen in all regimes that aim to be democratic, and they are sometimes so severe that democracy seems to be in a crisis. For example, a high proportion of voters in many democracies are disillusioned with party politics, many people are losing their sense of purpose and sense of community, and a small, but significant, minority is alienated from society. It seems probable that, even in democracies like the United States and the UK, only about 25% to 30% of democracy's potential is yet achieved, and, in the best democracies in small countries, only about 50%. Almost everywhere, party politics seems to be dominated by old paradigms; none of the main parties yet seem to have taken on board a genuinely radical new approach of the type that I attempt to outline in this book.

HUMAN RIGHTS AND
HUMAN RESPONSIBILITIES

'Basic human rights' are concerned with the needs of human beings to live lives of a decent quality as well as survive physically. Very broadly, human rights can be classified into political rights, associated with individual liberty, and economic rights to have a reasonable livelihood for oneself and one's family. In the late eighteenth century, the newly formed United States already had a Bill of Rights associated with its Constitution. During the mid-twentieth century, entitlements to human rights for human beings worldwide began to be codified in 'declarations of human rights', of which the most notable were the Wells-Sankey and United Nations Declarations. There was also a European Declaration of Human Rights. Although serious breaches of human rights have occurred throughout human history and occasionally occur in even the most advanced democracies, human consciousness of these breaches and campaigns against them have grown enormously during the twentieth century.[4] It is not realised sufficiently that higher proportions of women and children than of men are victims of human rights violations.

However, there has been a danger that some sections of the population tend to overemphasise their rights and pay too little attention to their duties and responsibilities. This has overcompensated for earlier tendencies to emphasise only human responsibilities, although these do need to be properly stated. It is thus very important to link human rights with human responsibilities in the most appropriate and best-balanced way. There has not yet been an adequate 'Declaration of Human Rights and Human Responsibilities', but a preliminary version of a 'Declaration of Human Responsibilities' has already been drafted.[5] All too often, people not only have too few human rights but are also given too few opportunities to contribute responsibly to society.

ECONOMIC PROBLEMS AND ISSUES

The dominant economic paradigms today are *capitalism*, which has been evolving for over five centuries, and *collectivism*, which emerged in the nineteenth century. Both capitalism and collectivism have had very severe problems. Capitalism has been liable to recession and sometimes even depressions and is often accompanied by serious unemployment and gross inequalities between rich and poor, which often (as today) increase.

In their most rigid form, in the Soviet Union and parts of Eastern Europe, collectivist economies became so inefficient that they eventually collapsed and were replaced by various forms of market economy. It is still an open question how far less rigid 'socialist' forms of collectivism can be viable.

Capitalism has now become very powerful worldwide through the process of globalisation, where worldwide financial institutions and networks and multinational companies are becoming increasingly dominant. These very strong vested interests are largely 'ruling' Third World development and international 'free' trade, leading to extensive Third World debt. The global capitalist economy may face further crises in the near future. It only just succeeded in saving itself from the Great Depression of the 1930s and has again suffered from severe recessions and unemployment in many parts of the world during the 1980s and 1990s. Instabilities in its financial structure became more evident during 1997 and 1998 and could lead to extensive financial collapse. The gap between rich and poor countries and individuals has been widening so much that many of the underprivileged may decide to tolerate it no longer; grassroots movements, especially in the Third World, are beginning to assert themselves more.

From the 1970s on, forms of 'new economics' and 'new business' have begun to emerge, that provide the main hope for resolving these problems.[6] When sufficiently well developed and formulated, they will be able to transform the world economy into a 'world cooperative economy', which would combine the best features of market and planned economies and provide a 'win-win' and 'stakeholder partnership' environment of creative and constructive work for all those who wish to participate.

ENVIRONMENTAL PROBLEMS AND ISSUES

Environmental problems and issues relate to conservation and resources; pollution and other environmental hazards; energy; and the urban and rural environments. Many tropical rain forests and temperate forests are still being cut down too fast. Sustainable forest management, including replanting and new planting, is needed and would do much to counter global warming and save natural ecosystems.[7] More needs to be done to conserve wildlife, protect threatened species, and preserve biodiversity. Exhaustible materials need to be conserved and recycled, and their use needs to be replaced by renewable materials or materials with long times to depletion. The most severe resource shortage in the near future could be lack of fresh water;[8] the problem of desertification also needs to be addressed. The United Nations Conference for Environment and Development (UNCED) at Rio in 1992, followed by its subsequent treaties and by Agenda 21, was a useful first step towards correcting the worldwide environmental crises.

The most serious environmental threats are the *greenhouse effect*, which could bring excessive global warming and undesired climate changes and flooding risks, and *ozone layer depletion*, caused by the emission of chlorofluorocarbons (CFCs) and other halocarbons into the atmosphere. While the latter problem is being addressed relatively well, the former gives rise to increasing concern, especially after the disappointing results of the Kyoto Conference on Climate Change in December 1997. Many other forms of pollution and environmental hazards also need to be addressed.

Much can be done to conserve energy and increase the efficiency of its use. For the longer term, the extensive use of appropriate forms of renewable energy, especially solar energy and biomass energy, will become increasingly extensive, at a cost that will fairly soon become reasonable. However, it may be difficult to produce sufficient energy to meet world needs during the next few decades.

Other urgent environmental problems and issues include urban and rural planning and regeneration and severe urban transport problems.

SOCIAL PROBLEMS AND ISSUES

Social problems are so severe and so extensive, not only in the Third World but also in the less well-off people in all parts of the world, that they have become evident to almost everyone. One reason for this is the widening gap between rich and poor. Poverty, all too often accompanied by hunger and homelessness, is appalling in large parts of the Third World and disgracefully extensive in most of the 'affluent' countries. At present, hunger is caused mainly by poor people's inability to pay for food and inadequate distribution of food, *not* by insufficient world food production.

Whereas it was thought that unemployment had been banished from many countries, for over thirty years after World War II, it returned with a vengeance, and too many governments, businesses, and economists feel unable to reduce it effectively. As a result, far too many people are denied constructive work opportunities and are unable to achieve decent livelihoods for themselves and their families, and too many others lose the inclination and aptitude to work.

In many countries, social security provisions have been severely, if not drastically, reduced under the influence of capitalism and also because of the aging of populations in many, if not most, of the richer countries. Health services all over the world are under increasing pressure as new illnesses appear to replace old illnesses that have been conquered, as the stresses of contemporary civilisation take their toll, and as many populations age.

The population problem itself remains serious, as populations are still increasing very rapidly in some countries, for example, in much of Africa, although population growth rates have decreased dramatically in many other parts of the world. Migration is becoming increasingly important, partly because many poor people seek better economic opportunities and partly because many refugees flee from oppressive regimes. Special policies are needed for indigenous people, who are all too often the innocent victims of global economic expansion; their ways of life should either be protected or gradually guided towards acceptable alternative cultures that respect their human dignity.

The welfare state, which was so widespread in the decades after World War II, has come under severe strain in almost every country where it operated and has even collapsed in some of the former communist countries. It is nonexistent in most Third World countries. Its future prospects are being widely questioned by many people in many parts of the world. However, continuing rises in economic productivity have been so great that, with appropriate planning, sufficient resources should fairly easily be found to meet all reasonable future welfare and social service needs. When better new economic and business systems emerge, it should also be possible to abolish the welfare dependency culture.

More and more people are becoming alienated, especially in the more 'affluent' countries, and this alienation and its accompanying lack of purpose and lack of social responsibility are becoming more and more prevalent among young people. This is leading to less law and order and more conflict and to an escalating global drugs problem.

The need for human community is all too often not being met under contemporary conditions, and too many of the previously existing community structures are under strain or are even being swept away.

Media play a vital part in informing, influencing, and entertaining the public. The ownership of most of the high-circulation media is concentrated among relatively few, very rich people; this constitutes a potential, if not actual, danger to democracy, because it could seriously restrict the range of facts and opinions communicated to most people. The rapid expansion of the number of Internet users should reduce this danger by greatly increasing the number of people with an opportunity to transmit their news and views worldwide.

A wide range of problems and issues arise in education, which should ideally be concerned with the development of the individual and social potential of all people. All too often, it is seriously failing to do this, so that far too many children going to school do not leave it with a sense of purpose, a coherent idea of citizenship, or an appropriate range of working and living skills. They are just not being prepared for modern life.[9]

THE EFFECTS OF ADVANCES
IN SCIENCE AND TECHNOLOGY

Almost every scientific discovery and new technology can be applied for both good and evil purposes. As science and technology advance, their power for both good and evil increases. Therefore, it is especially important today to maximise the potential for good of science and technology and minimise their bad applications and impacts.[10] The book *Factor Four* (von Weizsäcker et al. 1997) shows that science, technology, and skillful management can be used to double the production of wealth while halving the use of resources. Although computing and information technology seems to be predominantly beneficial, it could also lead to 'Big Brother' and increase the dangers of a police state. Although ethical guidelines have been formulated for biotechnology and genetic engineering, the possibility of their dangerous misapplications has been increased greatly by their extensive commercialisation.[11] Psychotechnology could have dangerous impacts on human integrity, especially when used by dictatorships. Improved policies are needed for science and technology, allocating more resources to research and development for peaceful purposes, Third World needs, and environmental problems. The potential for applying scientific method to improve government policies and political decision making should be properly explored.

THE REQUIREMENTS OF
SUSTAINABLE DEVELOPMENT

Sustainable development is urgently needed worldwide, especially in the Third World, if humanity is going to have a good future. It will require to be conducted in a holistic way, because it involves many interacting problems, issues, and aspects of life to be addressed simultaneously. The limitations of the prevailing First World approach to development need to be overcome, and its outdated paradigms need to be replaced.[12] Typically, development is planned in the Third World, in a situation where poverty needs to be removed, and a reasonable standard of living should be sought. Economic progress and increased productivity should be achieved at the grassroots level in a way that provides fair terms of trade and viable markets for the developing economy. This should be done in a way that meets the needs of the local people, with reasonably equitable distribution of wealth, educates them, and helps them to help themselves. This should be done in a way that makes good use of material and human resources, in a way that sustains and conserves the material and human environment as far as possible. If applied correctly, this process gradually increases quality of life, begins to reduce population growth, and assists the harmonious development of the developing country or community as part of a unified human community. If applied wrongly, as is usually the case, many of these principles are thrown overboard in a scramble for indiscriminate economic growth and, all too often, exploitation of the poor by the rich. If this happens, quality of life for most people falls, the poor are trapped in vicious cycles of debt, welfare and education services are often decimated, rural environments are degraded, urban slums emerge, and the population explosion often continues almost unchecked.

PROBLEMS AND ISSUES OF GOVERNMENT

Many, if not most, citizens of most countries are, in several ways, highly dissatisfied with the effects of government and specific government regimes on their lives. This is true even among the large sections of the population who more or less favour or even support the specific governments under which they live. But many other people, including many who feel alienated and excluded from citizenship, are much more critical of their governments and of politicians, civil servants, and lawyers in general. Sometimes, they refuse to vote or otherwise to participate in their local form of 'democracy', perhaps because they feel it does not offer them any real democratic choice. Even if they do participate, they often feel that their governments ignore their grievances and ideas for improving public policies. To them governments seem to be arrogant and often seem to act as if they already know all the answers.

The causes of this situation arise from a whole range of governmental issues, including the concepts of government, aspects of specific forms of government, structures of government, constitutional problems and issues, government departments and bureaucracy, problems and issues of scale, consent and consultation, participation, and policy-making and decision making. These problems and issues are addressed in later chapters. Even in 'advanced' democracies, many people feel dissatisfied or even outraged by how government fails to meet their needs or opposes them outright. For example, the legal systems and bureaucracies in at least some of these countries have so many defects and so often work badly in practice that many people of goodwill view the whole institutional system as a travesty of justice.

Governments could react positively in several ways by listening carefully to these criticisms, then endeavouring to address them constructively.

INTERNATIONAL PROBLEMS AND ISSUES

Shortly after World War II, many people had genuine hopes that the whole international world order would become vastly better than it had ever been before. World wars and all other major wars would be abolished. However, the postwar international scene has continued to be turbulent. The defeat of Nazi Germany and militarist Japan left in place the very strong power blocs based in the United States and the USSR.

The American power bloc soon expanded into the North Atlantic Treaty Organization (NATO) alliance, and the Soviet bloc comprised most of Eastern Europe as well as the USSR itself, and for a time, communist China. The spheres of influence of both these blocs spread much wider, and new conflicts between the blocs had become evident as early as 1946. The Cold War began and continued as an intense, mostly nonmilitary conflict until the mid-1970s. It then eased off, and it suddenly ceased with the collapse of Soviet communism in 1991. The accompanying nuclear deterrents, applied by both blocs, did at least prevent the outbreak of World War III.

Nationalism was very powerful in the Third World, as many countries there gained their independence from European colonial rule, and as the influence of Islamic fundamentalism increased. However, violent nationalist conflicts were suddenly unleashed in many parts of Eastern Europe and the former USSR. Western Europe moved steadily towards closer unity, first as a European Community but more recently as a European Union, but this process has not been without many problems.

It is still not clear whether a truly federal 'United States of Europe' will ever come about. Other multinational groupings include the British Commonwealth, whose roots go back for over a century, the nations of North America and Latin America, the countries of the Pacific Rim, the Arab countries, and most of the African countries. None of these groupings have anything even remotely approaching the elaborate intergovernmental mechanisms and institutions of the European Union. However, some of the groupings, which are often called 'regional' because they consist of geographically neighbouring nations, have acquired considerable significance in their own right, so that their study is already of special interest to political scientists.[13]

Ever since its formation in 1945, the United Nations (UN) has developed steadily as an association of nations that are theoretically cooperating with each other according to the UN Charter and other well-recognised principles. The UN Assembly and the Security Council are playing more positive parts, now that the Cold War is over, and UN peacekeeping operations have expanded significantly, but they still face severe problems. The UN specialised agencies have done much good work but could make much better contributions to human welfare. There is much room for improvement in the UN, and many important constructive criticisms of the UN have been made by those who are its true friends.

World governance is still a very important issue, although it is still not very clear how best to implement it.

HUMAN CONFLICT

Many wars and other human conflicts are still widespread in many parts of the world. Although there has not yet been a Third World War and hopefully never will be, there has been a considerable number of extensive and vicious wars since World War II, which have together killed and injured many millions of people. There have been years of war in the former Yugoslavia, where even now there are threats to lasting peace. The incidence of terrorism and the number of terrorist groups have both increased worldwide, as has the incidence of violent crime, drug-related crime, and most other forms of crime. Human nature has all too often led to human conflict, although it may be possible to find ways in which to reduce this effect drastically.

Many causes of human conflict have now been identified, both for individual and social conflict and for serious misunderstanding and violent conflicts between nationals and quasi-national groupings. Approaches to conflict resolution include creative conflict, peace education, peace studies, peace research, and specific techniques of conflict resolution. In the long run, conflicts could also be dramatically reduced by the evolution of a new politics of cooperation, whose nature is discussed in some of the later chapters of this book.

THE HUMAN PROBLEMATIQUE

As far back as 1937, H. G. Wells was aware of the human problematique, the complex web of intricately interrelated human and global problems as a whole. He knew that humanity needed to adapt to this situation by applying sufficient clear thinking.[14] The problems were made more difficult by the expanding scale of the community in which we live and the immense increase of power in our hands. What Wells said then is even more true now.

The first part of *The First Global Revolution* (King & Schneider 1991) sees world problems as a complex, interconnected whole, so that they can be solved only by viewing them as a whole, with all the complex links between them. It considers many of these problems, provides subtle insights into the relationships between them, and presents the global challenge that humankind now faces.

The *Encyclopedia of World Problems and Human Potential* (Judge 1995)[15] is the most comprehensive source of information on world problems, on how they are perceived to be interrelated, and on the human resources and strategies that can be used to address them. Volume 1 describes about 12,000 world problems, clustered into 320 overlapping hierarchies and linked by about 120,000 relationships of seven types. It pays special attention to the search for vicious cycles of problems.

The Worldwatch Institute's *State of the World* series of reports on the human and global situation, of which the latest book is Brown et al. (1998), provides extensive surveys of a wide range of world problems and their possible solutions and is concerned especially with progress towards a sustainable society.

The latest edition of *The State of the World Atlas* (Kidron & Segal 1995) translates key political, economic, and social indicators into full-colour maps and charts; it reveals international trends and differences in an easily understandable form.

THE HUMAN RESOLUTIQUE

H. G. Wells also realised that the human resolutique, the process of reshaping human affairs to work towards a resolution of the human problematique, would draw together an increasing number of human minds.[16] Not only would new solutions, using new paradigms, be needed. The problematique was far too complex to allow the application of a set of 'panaceas' and simple 'solutions'. We needed to know more and have more reliable relevant facts. *Our minds were not equipped for the job, and we needed to think again.* This was the starting point for Wells' development of the concept of a World Brain/World Mind, capable of providing a human resolutique.[17] A very good way of realising this concept would be to set up a worldwide network of citizens who would, together, consciously and conscientiously collaborate to develop the resolutique. This idea was also foreseen by Wells in his concept of an 'Open Conspiracy'.[18] The governments of the world should help to establish and empower this network, tune into it, work with it, and learn from it but in no way attempt to dominate it.

The second part of *The First Global Revolution* responds to the challenge that humankind now faces, by discussing what approaches might be adopted to resolving the problems and taking effective action.

The inspiring fifty-minute documentary video *Life on Earth: A True Civilisation* (GVN 1996) presents extracts from the State of the World Forum held at San Francisco, interviews with some of its participants, and scenes illustrating some of the most critical global problems. The forum brought together some of the best minds of humanity from many walks of life and many nationalities, ranging from Mikhail Gorbachev, former president of the USSR, to representative young people and children from around the world. Between them, they showed the urgency of the human problematique but, through their moral determination, vision, and creative thinking and ideas, demonstrated that they were making significant contributions to the human resolutique. The forum is an increasingly global network of imaginative and influential people seeking innovative methods and approaches for global change.

Volume 2 of the *Encyclopedia of World Problems and Human Potential* contains the most comprehensive available description of the variety of approaches to human development. Volume 3 outlines over 9,200 strategies currently used by international bodies in response to world problems or to enhance specific values or modes of development. It also identifies mutually reinforcing strategic cycles, which are especially valuable in responding to vicious problem cycles.

The Report of the Independent Commission on Population and Quality of Life (de Lourdes Pintaçilgo et al. 1996) examines the challenges facing all countries during the 1990s. It includes powerful personal testimonies from hearings of the commission in all parts of the world. Its radical agenda to address today's economic, human, and environmental crises includes

1. targets and timetables to improve worldwide standards of health care and education
2. a tax on international financial transactions to raise the required funds
3. a rejection of excessive reliance on free-market economics
4. giving priority to women's rights in the effort to stabilise the world's population.

In *Into the 21st Century*, Burrows et al. (1991: ch. 21) present their conclusions about the most important human and global problems, and possible approaches to their solution. Before presenting their more detailed findings, they begin as follows:

1. These world problems cannot be solved in isolation. They must be viewed as a unified whole, taking full account of their complex mutual interactions.
2. The most important root cause of these problems is human nature. Too many people, especially but not only among those in positions of power and influence, are selfish, greedy, power-seeking, and cruel.
3. The second most important root cause is the prevalence of inappropriate economic systems, whether capitalist or collectivist. There is an urgent need for an economics of sustainable development, and for a world cooperative economy. Fortunately, there are signs that they are emerging.   (pp. 354–355)

In his key book *Crucial Questions About the Future*, Allen Tough (1995: 50–51) states five priorities that humanity must pursue vigorously to achieve a reasonably positive future for human civilisation. (1) Humanity's knowledge of world problems and social change must increase much faster than the problems themselves and should include a threefold increase in future-oriented research and allied activities. (2) This knowledge, as soon as it is obtained, should be disseminated to political leaders, other key decision makers, and people of all ages through education, books, mass media, and new methods. (3) Governance must be improved, including planning, policies, government structure, and public administration. (4) Avoid the worst catastrophes. (5) Promote positive directions and improvements.

At the same time, it should be realised that each worldview, or system of new paradigms, that emerges to provide a new 'resolutique', creates its own serious problems. Thus, there will be a continuing evolution of both human 'problematique' and human 'resolutique'.[19]

NOTES

1. This chapter takes account of the analyses of problems and issues made by Burrows et al. (1991: pt. 1), White, Little, and Smith (1997), *The New Internationalist* (January/February 1997), and Kennedy (1993), for example.

2. The spiritual teachings of Alice Bailey state that human evolution is being guided by a spiritual hierarchy, which is helping to inspire millions of world servers, in all walks of life, who are helping the divine plan for human evolution to unfold. One of her many interesting ideas on this theme is as follows (Bailey 1996). As goodwill develops in the human consciousness, it first reveals the cleavages that are present in political, religious, social, and economic life everywhere. This revelation is always accompanied by efforts along all possible lines to bridge or heal the cleavages.

3. Conspiracy theories, such as those presented in Vankin and Whelan (1997) and Icke (1996), suggest that the scales are at present tilted towards evil. They postulate that world events are orchestrated by a sinister conspiracy behind the scenes, to whose 'strings' the world's political leaders are attached like puppets. Outlandish as these theories may seem, their possibility cannot be ruled out. The actual events of the Watergate conspiracy, uncovered in the United States in 1994 (Krieger 1993: 970–971), show how difficult it can be to prove the existence of conspiracies that actually occur. Conspirators can easily 'arrange' events so that the existence of their conspiracy seems highly implausible! Icke suggests that the present 'ruling conspirators' can be defeated by people becoming aware of their plot and deciding to empower themselves.

4. Amnesty International is a leading international network conducting such campaigns. It has carefully documented reports of many atrocities and other extreme violations of human rights in all parts of the world and finds that they occur, not only in dictatorships and authoritarian regimes but sometimes also in many 'democracies'.

5. See the documentation of the draft declaration, prepared by the InterAction Council.

6. See the subsections on new economics and new business in Chapter 10. As far as I know, the phrase 'world cooperative economy' was first used by Bernard Zamaron.

7. This problem is by no means new. Some early human societies were ecologically sound, but some were definitely not, usually through ignorance (Wilber 1996: 47). Some practise slash and burn, and some were responsible for making many species extinct. The Maya culture in Mexico disappeared largely through depleting the surrounding rain forests.

8. The threatened global water crisis is not as well known as it should be. Rees (1997) discusses its urgency and reports the emerging consensus that the management of water resources and water-based services requires radical change.

9. See Wells (1995: 39–44, 125–143).

10. The book *Science for the Earth* (Wakeford and Walters 1995) provides many

valuable insights into the nature of science and the need to reform it radically to enable it to be applied with maximum benefit. It should be read by as many politicians, civil servants, scientists, technologists, business executives, and other professionals as possible. For my review of this important book, see Mayne (1996).

11. Ho (1998) has emphasised these dangers of genetic engineering, as well as the potentialities. See also the mutual discussion of Ho et al. (1997), which presents three different viewpoints on the benefits and dangers of biotechnology.

12. See the penetrating critique of this approach in Sachs (1992), which examines many of the concepts arising in development and includes annotated bibliographies about them.

13. See White, Little, and Smith (1997: ch. 4), for example.

14. See Wells (1995: 97–98).

15. This is now being updated by additional material on the Internet Web site http://www.uia.org/uiademo/, whose files include integrative concepts, profiles of methods of human development and modes of awareness, and a virtual reality demonstration.

16. See Wells (1995: 99–103).

17. Wells (1995) reprints H. G. Wells' own ideas on a 'World Brain', summarises subsequent scholarly commentary on his ideas, and includes an annotated bibliography of relevant literature. Work is still in progress to develop, extend, and implement these ideas.

18. See Wells (1928), its later version published in 1933, and its new edition (Wells 1998) with a critical introduction by Warren Wagar.

19. This point is explained clearly by Wilber (1996: 68).

SOME TOPICS FOR FURTHER INVESTIGATION

1. Examine recent trends in the development of capitalist economics and of business, both globally and in your local community. Note the ways in which they are becoming *less* as well as *more* green. In each case, try to decide which of these two trends seems to be gaining the upper hand, or whether they are both about equally balanced.

2. How can sustainable development be achieved? How can the output of essential goods and services worldwide be obtained with minimal environmental degradation? In what ways can economic growth be sustainable?

3. Which is the more promising route for improving the human situation: improving business methods or reforming politics? What is the best way of combining both these approaches?

4. How far is it practicable and desirable to achieve some form of world federalism?

5. How far could the UN evolve into an effective functional arm of world government? How far could it broaden into an organisation and organism working for the *peoples* of the world? Note that the UN Charter does begin with the words "We the people".

6. Discuss how far the governments of your nation, state, and local community could be made more responsive to the needs of the people.

7. How can you increase awareness of the human problematique in yourself and in other people, including those whom you know?

8. What contributions can you make to the human resolutique?

2

British Politics and Government

This chapter describes in some detail the democratic regime in the UK. I devote special attention to the UK for three reasons. It is a regime that I know very well, as a lifelong British citizen. It has many unusual and distinctive features that set it apart from most other democratic regimes; its differences from the U.S. regime are especially notable. Although it ceased to be a Great Power shortly after World War II, the UK still has great international influence and, in my view, will continue to have it. Good surveys of contemporary British politics include the books *Contemporary British Politics* (Coxall and Robins 1998), *The British Polity* (Norton 1994), *British Politics in Focus* (Roberts 1997), *Politics UK* (Jones et al. 1998), *The New British Politics* (Budge et al. 1998), Jones and Kavanagh (1998), and Hunter (1997: 1290–1368). Books on recent British political history include *British Political Facts* (Butler and Butler 1994), *British Politics since the War* (Coxall and Robins 1997), *Britain since 1945* (Childs 1997), *British Politics since 1945* (Dutton 1997), *Half a Century of British Politics* (Robins and Jones 1997), *Intelligent Person's Guide to Post-War Britain* (Sked 1997), *Post-War Britain* (Sked and Cook 1993), and *British Social Policy since 1945* (Glennerster 1995). Jones (1994) discusses contemporary British issues, Barker (1997) describes current political ideas in Britain, and Berrington (1998) examines the striking changes in British politics. Dickson (1996) discusses various aspects of British political culture. *Turning the Tide* (McKinstry 1997) analyses the state of modern Britain. Halsey (1995) reviews changes in British society during the twentieth century. For several years, the ongoing series *Developments in British Politics* has been published by Macmillan. For briefer surveys, see Derbyshire (1996: 517–523) and Krieger (1993: 89–92).

THE EVOLUTION OF BRITISH DEMOCRACY[1]

From Monarchy to Parliamentary Government

British democracy evolved gradually from the absolute monarchies that were in power from the Anglo-Saxon times, through the Middle Ages, and into the seventeenth century. Parliament had already played a representative and financing role from the thirteenth century on and later divided into two Houses, Commons and Lords. A conflict and struggle with the monarchy emerged, with Parliament gradually gaining more powers. This eventually led to the English Civil War in the early seventeenth century against King Charles I and his Royalist supporters. In 1649, Parliament won and set up a Commonwealth under Oliver Cromwell. Although the monarchy was restored in 1660 under King Charles II, it again become unpopular under his successor, James II, who was deposed. This was followed by the 'Glorious Revolution' of 1688, where England was ruled by a 'constitutional monarchy', no longer by an absolute monarchy.

Rule by a Sovereign Parliament

After the passage of the Bill of Rights in 1689, the sovereignty of Parliament was established. Since then, further executive powers were gradually withdrawn from the monarch, who became increasingly dependent on ministers, specially selected members of Parliament (MPs), on whom he or she became more and more dependent for advice. During the eighteenth century, the office of first lord of the Treasury gradually became transformed into that of prime minister, the leader of the British government, which had to govern by consent of the House of Commons as a whole. A two-party system was well-established by the mid-nineteenth century, with Conservatives and Liberals as the two dominant parties, each of which offered itself as the potential party of government, whenever a general election was held. At first, only a small minority of the people could vote in general elections, but, after a sequence of reform acts in the nineteenth century and early twentieth century, almost any male or female citizen, aged at least eighteen, became entitled to vote. During the 1920s, the Liberals were replaced by Labour as one of the two main parties. During World War II, there was a Conservative–Labour coalition government.

1945–1979: Postwar 'Consensus Politics'[2]

In 1945, a Labour government was returned to power with a massive majority. The welfare state was established during the 1940s and greatly extended by that government, with the foundation of the National Health Service especially and with a much wider range of social services. This form of welfare state was for over thirty years accepted by subsequent governments, whether Labour or Conservative, and contributed to postwar 'consensus' politics. The rise of the 'consensus' was strengthened by the fact that there was virtually full employment, with a proportion of unemployed workers typically around 2% and only rarely exceeding 5%. Although the 1945 Labour government's programme of extensive public ownership ('nationalisation') of key industries was very controversial at the time, it led to the establishment of a mixed economy in the UK, whose general mixture of public and privately owned industries remained intact, even though a few industries, like steel, alternated between the two forms of ownership and control several times, as governments changed. From 1951 to 1964 and from 1970 to 1974, there were periods of Conservative government. There were Labour governments from 1964 to 1970 and 1974 to 1979.

1979–1997: 'Confrontation Politics'[3]

In 1979, the Labour government of the late 1970s was replaced by a Conservative government with Margaret Thatcher as prime minister. Its political policies were so radical and divisive that a new era of 'confrontation' began. Conservative governments remained in power for about eighteen years, until some people began to wonder whether they might not be a permanent feature of the British political landscape! The new Conservative 'subideology' of 'Thatcherism', which was very different from the 'one nation' Conservatism of the 'consensus' period, became well established. It emphasised self-reliance, enterprise, drastic cuts in public spending and social services, partial dismantling of the welfare state, and systematic privatisation of industries, even some public services, previously in public ownership and control. The gap between rich and poor steadily widened, and poverty became much more widespread. For all its emphasis on individual freedom, the government was amazingly authoritarian in some respects and dramatically increased its powers over local governance by steadily eroding the powers and finances of local authorities. Mutual controversies and attacks between different political parties, on the whole, became more and more acrimonious. After public reaction against Thatcherism became evident, Conservative MPs *themselves* ousted Margaret Thatcher as leader of their party, so that she was succeeded as prime minister by John Major in 1990. He was, at first, fairly popular, so that he unexpectedly won the general election of 1992. It was not long before his government and his own record became increasingly unpopular. In the general election of 1 May 1997, another Labour government was elected, this time with a large majority, giving rise to hopes of a possible return to 'consensus' politics, taking more account of the true wishes of the people.

BRITISH POLITICAL PARTIES[4]

The British political system has been dominated by two main political parties for almost all its history during the last three centuries, although the identity of these parties has occasionally changed. For the nineteenth century into the early twentieth century, the two dominant parties were Conservative and Liberal, but this grouping had shifted to Conservative and Labour by 1940. However, what was left of the original Liberals remained an important 'centre party', even though the nature of that party changed. These three parties can be viewed as the 'main' British political parties; it is interesting to note that, for each of them, there is a wide range of viewpoints and even political ideologies among their supporters. Their positions in mid-1997 are presented in their election manifestos and in their *Why Vote?* books (Willetts 1997; Wallace 1997; Wright 1997). The Scottish and Welsh Nationalist Parties are important in Scotland and Wales, respectively. In Northern Ireland, as opposed to Great Britain (England, Scotland, and Wales), there is a totally different set of political parties. There is very limited popular support for various other parties, of which the Green Party is the most important.

The Conservative Party

Since the end of the eighteenth century, Conservatism has contained two important strands, which are still present in today's Conservative Party, although with varying relative importance from one decade to another. The first strand is libertarian and individualist, supports the free market, and opposes government intervention in it. It dates back to Edmund Burke, the founder of modern Conservatism, who strongly opposed the French Revolution but *also* had a strong sense of *community*. The second strand is paternalist (with a concern for people who are worse off) and 'collectivist' and favours a considerable amount of state intervention, even in aspects of the market economy. The second strand was strong in the mid-nineteenth century under the influence of Benjamin Disraeli's 'one nation' Conservatism and again became strong during and after World War II. The first strand was fairly strong between World Wars I and II and became transformed into the 'New Right' and 'Thatcherism' from the late 1970s on. However, even Thatcherism had a strong authoritarian streak, which derived more from the second strand. Although Thatcherism is now less strong in the Conservative Party, another dichotomy of viewpoints has become very important: the division between those who strongly favour Britain's active membership of the European Union and the 'Eurosceptics', who more or less strongly oppose it. The Conservative vision for Britain, as presented in its 1997 election manifesto, emphasised the UK as the 'Enterprise Centre of Europe', opportunity and ownership for individuals and families, 'world-class' health and public services, a safe and civil society, and a confident, united, and sovereign nation.

The Centre Parties

The Liberal Party in its modern form succeeded the Whigs in the 1860s and was at first based mainly on advocacy of individual freedoms and limitation of constraints on individual freedoms. It was thus concerned with controlling the powers through constitutional checks and balances, and it favoured a free-market economy and free trade. By the late nineteenth century, this emphasis on 'negative' freedom was complemented by increasing promotion of 'posit-ive' freedom, enabling self-realisation or development of individual potenti-alities. Thus, the Liberal government of 1906 advocated a more interventionist state, to provide a decent education and some security against unemployment and old age; in this way, it was helping to relieve the considerable poverty and social deprivation that had resulted from unconstrained economic liberalism. Although the Liberal Party began to decline in the 1920s, its major thinkers, Beveridge and Keynes, played a major part in shaping the concepts of the welfare state and a more managed economy, which became important from the 1940s on. Despite this, very few Liberal MPs were elected; the numbers between 1945 and 1979 ranged from six to fourteen.

In March 1981, four former Labour Cabinet ministers led the formation of the Social Democratic Party as a breakaway from the Labour Party. This party wanted to change the pattern of British politics by moving away from adver-sarial politics towards consensus politics representing the centre of British politics. It favoured decentralisation of government, electoral reform (also ad-vocated by the Liberals), equality, a prices-and-wages policy; like the Liberals, its members especially supported the UK's membership of the European Community. By the end of 1981, it had formed an Alliance with the Liberal Party, which soon constituted a major threat to the dominance of the Con-servative and Labour Parties. Although some of its early support was lost, the Alliance was able to obtain 26% and 23% of the votes in the 1983 and 1987 general elections, respectively, although winning only twenty-three and twenty-two seats. In 1988, most members of both parties agreed to their merger into what finally became known as the Liberal Democrat Party, which won forty-five seats in the 1997 general election. Some members of the minorities who voted against the merger formed the remainder of the Social Democratic Party, which eventually closed down in 1990, and a tiny Liberal Party, which still exists. The Liberal Democrat 1997 election manifesto pre-sented a practical, forward-looking programme to modernise Britain, with the widening of opportunities as its central theme. Its vision was to create a nation of self-reliant individuals living in strong communities and supported by an active, enabling government. It had the courage to accept the need for some tax rises to achieve its policies.

The Labour Party

The Labour Party has always been a coalition of separate interests. Its predecessor, the Labour Representation Committee, was founded in 1900 by representatives of two socialist parties, the Fabian Society, which believed in gradual socialism, and sixty-five trade unions. It was renamed the Labour Party just after the 1906 general election, when twenty-nine Labour MPs were elected. In 1918, it adopted a new Constitution and its 'Socialist Commitment'. Soon afterwards, it adopted a conference programme, *Labour and the New Social Order*, on which its policy was to be based for over thirty years. This policy contained a commitment to full employment and a national minimum wage, the democratic control of industry, financing of social services through more taxation of higher incomes, and using surplus wealth for the common good. After Labour formed minority governments in 1923 and 1929 and participated in a wartime coalition government from 1940 to 1945, it won a decisive victory in the 1945 general election; the resulting Labour government conducted a radical programme of social reform to strengthen the welfare state, including the formation of the National Health Service (NHS), and placed several key industries under public ownership and control. Since then, UK governments have been either Conservative or Labour, being Conservative for most years, but, in 1997, a new Labour government was formed, with a large majority, as in 1945. To achieve this victory, Labour had to transform its policies radically while attempting to maintain most of its core principles; thus, the programme of public ownership was dropped, but commitment to a strong welfare state continued, though requiring some rethinking. The Labour Party's 1997 general election manifesto had many similarities to the Liberal Democrat manifesto, though also some significant differences. It was a radical programme for modernisation whose objectives included giving top priority to education, promoting personal prosperity for all, helping to create successful businesses, aiming to bring the unemployed from welfare to work, being tough on crime and the causes of crime, and putting concern for the environment at the heart of policy-making.

The Nationalist Parties

The Scottish National Party and Plaid Cymru, the nationalist parties in Scotland and Wales, advocate full independence for their countries as members of the European Union. In the 1960s, they began to have some electoral successes and to become important. Since then, both of them have had a few MPs each. The Scottish Nationalists are supported by a considerable proportion of Scottish voters, while Plaid Cymru is strong only in those parts of Wales with especially active Welsh culture. Both parties favour the Labour government's policy for setting up local Parliaments in Scotland and Wales, but, unlike the government, see it as a stepping-stone towards independence.

Other British Parties

The Green Party is best known for its radical environmentalist policies but has a wide range of policies, some of them also radical, on other political issues. It was founded in 1973 as the People Party, was renamed the Ecology Party in 1975, and took its present name in 1985. Because its supporters are normally fewer than 5% of voters and fairly evenly distributed throughout Britain, it has never won a parliamentary seat and only very occasionally won a seat in local government. Its greatest success was in the 1989 European Parliament election, when it obtained nearly 15% of the votes; even then, it won no seat, because of the first-past-the-post electoral system.

The Referendum Party was formed shortly before the 1997 general election to give the people of Britain an opportunity to say whether they wished to be governed by the European Union or the UK. Its only objective was to secure a referendum that would allow them to decide Britain's future in Europe. It presented the alternatives as being a European family of sovereign nations, cooperating for their mutual advantage, or a federal European superstate governed by officials in Brussels. Although it obtained only about 1% of votes in the election, its influence was sufficient for all the main parties to promise to hold a referendum on the future of Europe, if returned to power.

Other parties in Great Britain include the following. The Natural Law Party has a programme with some remarkably progressive elements that is based on the spiritual teachings and 'vedic sciences' of the Maharishi Mahesh Yogi. The Communist Party represented the British far Left, until most of its members moved into other political orbits after the collapse of Soviet communism. The Socialist Party of Great Britain still valiantly proclaims a genuinely socialist programme. The National Front and British National Party represent the tiny minority of voters on the far Right. The fringe Loony parties add a colourful and picturesque element to British election campaigns!

Northern Ireland Politics[5]

Party politics in Northern Ireland is totally different from that in Great Britain; *none* of the British mainland parties are active there, other than the Conservative Party to a limited extent. Instead, the parties are split predominantly on religious and cultural lines. Protestant voters almost all favour the continuance of union between Northern Ireland and Great Britain, to form the United Kingdom of Great Britain and Northern Ireland (UK). They bitterly oppose union between Northern Ireland and the Republic of Ireland into a United Ireland, which has, until very recently, been the main objective of most Catholic voters and is still strongly supported by many of them. The Protestants are represented mainly by the Ulster Unionists, which until the 1970s had a close link with the Conservative Party, and the more extreme Democratic Unionists. The Catholics have been represented mainly by the

Social Democratic and Labour Party (SDLP), but a considerable minority of them vote for Sinn Fein. The Alliance Party, a nonsectarian party attempting to bridge the gap between the Protestant and Catholic communities in Northern Ireland, is supported by about 10% of voters.

For most of the past thirty years, politics in Northern Ireland has been marred by conflict between the two communities, and especially by many acts of terrorism by their most extreme elements, but a process of peaceful negotiations progressed gradually towards a political settlement, which was at last agreed on 10 April 1998. On 22 May 1998, it was ratified by 71% of the 81% of those who voted in a referendum of the people of Northern Ireland. On the same day, nearly 95% of the 55% voting in a referendum in the Irish Republic agreed to renounce the republic's 'claim' to the territory of Northern Ireland.

BRITISH POLITICAL INSTITUTIONS

Good general descriptions of British political institutions are given, for example, in the books by Birch (1998), Hennessy (1996), Coxall and Robins (1998: pt. 2), and parts of Norton (1994) and Jones et al. (1998). Bogdanor (1997b) and Barnett (1997) discuss some possibilities for their reform. Hennessy (1997) discusses politics and the quality of government in postwar Britain. Jackson and Lavender (1996) provide a comprehensive review of UK policy, finance, and management. Books about policy-making in UK government include James (1997), Rose and Davies (1994), and Hogwood (1992); see also Jones (1994: pt. 7). Books on British policy research institutions ('think tanks') include Denham (1998), Kandiah and Seldon (1996), and Blackstone and Plowden (1988).

This section describes the most important British political institutions and considers their roles in the process of politics and governance in the UK.

The Constitution[6]

Unlike most other countries, the UK has no written Constitution, but only a few documents representing fragments of what such a Constitution might contain. Effectively, the British Constitution has the single principle that what the British monarch enacts through Parliament is law. This situation dates back to the Glorious Revolution of 1688, followed by the establishment of relations between the Crown and Parliament in the 1689 Bill of Rights, which effectively established the 'sovereignty of Parliament' over a unitary state under a rule of law in England and later on in the UK. This is basically parliamentary government under a constitutional monarchy. As a result, the UK is still one of the most centralised democracies in the world. Since 1689, the major elements of the Constitution have been built up, sometimes explicitly but also largely implicitly, through successive parliamentary legislation and conventions, 'common law', which is basically case law and custom, authoritative interpretations by constitutional experts, and, from 1987 on, European Union law.

In his Dimbleby Lecture "The Elective Dictatorship", Lord Hailsham (1976) concluded that the defects of the UK Constitution are beginning to outweigh its merits. The Constitution confers absolute powers on the sovereign body, Parliament, which can be removed only by change of government as the result of a general election usually held at intervals of four or five years; these powers are concentrated in an executive government formed from one party that does not necessarily represent the popular will. Although Lord Hailsham is a distinguished Conservative, the Labour and Liberal Democrat Parties proposed a package of constitutional reforms in 1996, after some years of campaigning by Charter 88, formed in 1988. Constitutional reform in the UK aims to renew the outdated conventions of the political system and attempts to form a new relationship between government and citizens and between political power and the people. Bogdanor (1996) considers why the UK Constitution is a subject of continuing political debate. Klug et al. (1996) discuss human rights and freedoms in the UK, and argue that they have been weakened by British political and legal institutions.

The Monarchy[7]

The British monarchy is a 'constitutional monarchy', a system of government where the monarch is 'head of state' but constrained by the provisions of a Constitution. The 1689 Bill of Rights defined the relationship between Crown and Parliament and imposed extensive restrictions on the monarch's power, which have gradually increased since then. However, the monarch does still possess a few important *royal prerogatives* and other powers to influence the British government. By the mid-nineteenth century, a leading constitutional expert[8] had explicitly stated that, during the continuance of governments, the Crown had the right to be consulted, the right to encourage, and the right to warn. Today, as then, these rights remain and provide an important source of influence, especially as the monarch has a continuous political experience of a form that professional politicians lack, due to the vagaries of general elections. In addition, to become an act of parliament and thus part of the law of the land, any parliamentary legislation in the UK must not only be passed by both houses of Parliament but also receive the Royal Assent, which the monarch can *theoretically* withhold, although no monarch has refused it in practice since Queen Anne vetoed a Scottish Militia Bill in 1707; indeed, Queen Victoria once considered withholding it but was persuaded not to.[9]

The other royal prerogatives are the right to appoint a prime minister and the right to agree or refuse a dissolution of Parliament. Both of these need to be exercised on advice of ministers and party leaders, but their use would probably be more extensive if a proportional representation (PR) electoral system were to come into effect, as now seems possible. The sovereign has generally been guided by two principles when forming governments. (1) Politicians should resolve the process of forming a new government themselves, as far as possible, with the sovereign intervening only as a last resort. (2) The sovereign's use of a prerogative depends entirely on the circumstances in which it is used. The sovereign has discretion in its use, when it is *not* possible to be guided by past precedents. Such cases have been rare in twentieth-century UK politics.

The Prime Minister[10]

The prime minister of the UK has a formidable concentration of power, which is probably almost unprecedented for a modern democratic regime. Whereas a U.S. president can often be hampered by a hostile Congress, it is relatively rare for the prime minister not to command an absolute majority in the House of Commons. He or she is head of both legislature and executive by being responsible for forming and dissolving a government, appointing members of the Cabinet and other ministers, directing and coordinating the government through the Cabinet, and generally supervising the Civil Service. He or she has many additional functions and is generally recognised as the UK's national leader, and is normally leader of the political party that won most votes in the previous general election. Some of the prime minister's powers are fixed, including several prerogatives gained from the Crown, and others are variable. His or her functions can be divided broadly into constitutional and procedural, appointments to ministerial and other senior posts, conduct of Cabinet and parliamentary business, the organisation and efficiency of government, the Budget and other economic decisions, and special foreign and defence functions.

The Cabinet[11]

The Cabinet is the supreme directing authority of the British government and the key link between its legislature and executive. It consists of about twenty of its most senior ministers, including the prime minister. One view, perhaps more strongly held in the nineteenth century than in the twentieth, is that members of the Cabinet should have comparable power and status to those of the prime minister, who should be primus inter pares, first among equals in the Cabinet. However, in contrast to this view, some prime ministers, notably, Sir Winston Churchill and Margaret Thatcher, have been more dominant than that. The Cabinet is the location of the most important decisions by a British government, and its members take *collective responsibility* for them. Most of the decisions by Cabinets are taken by Cabinet Committees, specialising in specific areas of policy. It plans the business of Parliament, usually about a week in advance, arbitrates in disputes between government departments, helps to coordinate government policies, and provides political leadership. Jones et al. (1998: 409–411) outline some criticisms and proposed reforms of Cabinet government.

The Civil Service[12]

The Civil Service is responsible for executing and running the policies of the government of the day. It is divided into government departments, each directed by ministers who are responsible to Parliament. Civil servants advise ministers on policy and implement government decisions. In contrast to the situation in the United States, civil servants are career officials whose tenure is usually permanent and who are required to be politically neutral; they also offer their advice to ministers anonymously. The Civil Service has functions of economic management, political management, management of national integration, policy management, and service provision. Its management was reformed during the 1970s and 1980s, and a new Civil Service Code has been drafted by the House of Commons Treasury and Civil Service Select Committee. The most powerful government department is the Treasury, which has extensive influence on the detailed financing of government policies.

Parliament[13]

Since 1689, the concept of the *sovereignty of Parliament* has been the central part of the British Constitution. Of its two chambers, the House of Commons has become much more powerful than the House of Lords. The House of Commons currently has 659 MPs, each elected by the voters in a constituency. The House of Lords consists mainly of hereditary peers, mostly Conservative and most of whom only rarely attend but also of law lords, bishops, and a large number of appointed life peers. Through the distribution of MPs between different parties, the House of Commons determines which party or, occasionally, which coalition of parties forms the UK government. Any government must retain the confidence of the House to be able to continue to govern effectively. Parliament, especially the House of Commons, passes most, though not necessarily all, of the government's proposed legislation. It scrutinises and influences the conduct and administration of government policy through parliamentary questions and discussions by its Select Committees. It is also supposed to examine European Union legislation and policy. It votes funds to finance those government activities that it supports. It transmits citizens' grievances, concerns, and opinions to the government. Through its members' activities, it facilitates democratic interchange of views between the government and politicians, on one hand, and various interests, groups, and individuals, on the other. The powers of the House of Lords are now strictly limited and are mainly to amend and sometimes delay legislation passed in the House of Commons; the Lords cannot oppose the passage of financial legislation from the Commons. Bogdanor (1997b: ch. 4) discusses some possibilities for the reform of the composition and powers of the House of Lords but points out that no satisfactory proposals have yet been formulated.

Electoral Politics[14]

General elections are held at irregular intervals, which are usually between four and five years long but can occasionally be much shorter, usually because the preceding election gave an indecisive result. Each time that there is a general election, the House of Commons is dissolved, the government resigns, and MPs for a new House of Commons are elected by a first-past-the-post voting system. There is a strong difference of opinion in the UK about the merits of this system. Its defenders point out the advantages of having one MP representing each constituency and its tendency to provide strong British governments. Its opponents deplore the unfairness of its party representation, whereby the Liberals, Social Democrats, and Liberal Democrats have had very much less than their fair share of seats during recent years. The Conservatives have traditionally opposed a change of electoral system, and the centre parties have all strongly supported it, favouring a change to the single transferable vote (STV) proportional representation (PR) system that is used in the Irish Republic. The new Labour government adopts an intermediate position and has already authorised PR for the Scottish and Welsh Parliaments, to be set up in 1999, and for the next European Parliament election in the UK. It has appointed a commission to investigate possibilities for a new system for electing the House of Commons. Although it has agreed to hold a referendum to ratify the recommendations of the commission, it is by no means clear yet what new electoral system the commission will recommend or even if it will be a form of PR, rather than the alternative vote (AV) system. Referenda are used only occasionally in the UK,[15] but there will in due course be another referendum to decide whether the UK agrees to adopt a single European currency and European Monetary Union. Bogdanor (1997b: ch. 6) discusses the question of how political parties should be funded.

Quasi-Governmental Bodies[16]

The scope of UK government activity had already begun to increase during World War II and grew further under postwar governments until 1979. A great variety of quasi-governmental bodies has been set up to administer this expanded public sector. At first, most of them were nationalised industries or public services, but later many *'quangos'* with more specialised functions were set up. These bodies have been widely criticised for being undemocratic, because they are appointed, not elected, excessively bureaucratic, and insufficiently accountable to both Government and people. The Conservative governments from 1979 to 1997 privatised all the nationalised industries and many of the quangos, but with results whose merits are still controversial.

Devolution[17]

The government of the UK has hitherto been very centralised, compared with that of most other democracies. The devolution of Ireland from the United Kingdom, at a time when it covered the whole British Isles, was attempted and almost achieved by 1914, but World War I prevented it. As a result of an Irish rebellion in 1916, Ireland became independent in 1921, and a devolved Parliament, Stormont, was set up in Northern Ireland in 1921. By the 1970s, devolution again became an important topic in the UK, and separate bills for the devolution of Scotland and Wales were enacted in 1978, but they were not ratified by the subsequent referenda. In 1997, the Labour government passed legislation to set up a Scottish Parliament with fairly extensive powers and a Welsh Assembly with much more limited powers; this time, the devolution of Scotland and Wales was ratified by referenda, though by only a narrow margin in Wales. In 1972, Stormont was dissolved by the UK government, so that Northern Ireland was no longer devolved. A new Assembly is being set up as a result of the ratification of the Northern Ireland peace settlement of 10 April 1998 by referenda. Devolution of the English regions is a difficult question, but some de facto devolution has already occurred with the regional offices of various UK government departments; the boundaries of these regions often differ for different departments but are beginning to be harmonised. One possible route to English devolution is 'rolling devolution', as practised in Spain, where regions themselves choose the rate and extent of their devolution.

Local Government[18]

Local government in its modern form, with local authorities for large cities and counties as well as smaller towns and rural localities, began to be developed extensively in the UK in the nineteenth century. Further local government reforms were made in the 1960s and 1970s, with the creation of the Greater London Council, six metropolitan counties, and redrawn local authority boundaries in many areas. Under the Conservative governments from 1979 to 1997, the powers of local authorities were progressively restricted, indeed, invaded, by national government, which, in particular, imposed harsh limits on local authorities' ability to spend or even raise money. Further reorganisation of local authority boundaries occurred. Some restoration of local authority powers seems likely under the new UK government, though it is not yet clear how much.

The People

Bogdanor (1997: ch. 8) argues that the political reforms discussed in his book, which basically represent the constitutional reform agenda of the

Labour and Liberal Democrat Parties, would redistribute power away from the parties and widen the range of people involved in decision making. Although he thinks that this constitutional reform agenda alone is probably not enough to satisfy popular aspirations, he considers that constitutional reform could also point to a redistribution of power between politicians and people that would make the British people much less disenchanted with politicians. We need to go beyond the constitutional reform agenda to create a new relationship between people and politicians, aiming to replace government by the political professionals with government by the people. Only this would bring a real transfer of power from government to the people.

THE FUTURE OF BRITISH POLITICS AND GOVERNANCE

There are now so many serious problems in the UK that there have been some doubts about the future of the democratic system in the UK. It is certainly in need of fairly extensive reform.

On 2 May 1997, a new Labour government,[19] the first for eighteen years, came into power after a decisive Labour victory in the 1997 general election. Many people had great hopes of what it would achieve in the future, but it also faced enormous problems because of the inadequate policies of previous governments. In a speech on 7 May, the new prime minister, Tony Blair, said, "There is great excitement and there is hope in Britain today. Even greater is our sense of humility and responsibility in not disappointing those hopes. . . . We are not the masters. The people are the masters. . . . This is the chance to build a new coalition of support—let us use it." This gave rise to renewed hopes that the UK would soon become much more democratic and also meant that the government would have to achieve a very high standard of effective policy-making and implementation to avoid later disappointment and disillusion.

As of October 1998, there were considerable doubts about how far the new government had lived up to its own expectations, even among its own supporters. On one hand, it has ambitious plans for the improvement of education and the health service, a stronger British economy, more constructive uses of funds from the National Lottery, devolution and constitutional reform, the formation of a Social Exclusion Unit to meet the needs of those least well-off in society, and the reform of social services by enabling more of their beneficiaries to return to work. It has plans for increased spending on school education, the National Health Service (NHS), the National Endowment for Science, Technology and the Arts (NESTA), and research and development. On the other hand, its policies are hampered by its adherence to a more capitalist approach to economics, which it adopted to win over support from more middle-class and business voters.

As a result, except for the 'windfall tax' on excess profits of some of the privatised industries and utilities, it refused to impose higher taxes on richer people and thus could not allow sufficient increases in public expenditure to finance its reforms properly. This has already led to an increase in waiting lists for many types of hospital treatment, the imposition of fees on British as well as overseas higher education students, and erosion of some social benefits. Too many of the altruistic principles of 'old Labour' seem to be sacrificed, and it is largely the Liberal Democrats and 'rebel' Labour MPs who are endeavouring to retain them.[20] However, it is true that new proposals for 'simple government', involving reorganisation of the Civil Service and the application of information technology, are now being considered, which could reduce the cost of administering government departments and social services and thus release more funds for the public benefit.[21]

In February 1998, the Labour government outlined its proposals for reform of the welfare state in a consultation document, based largely on the ideas of the then minister for welfare reform, Frank Field.[22] In the same month, the Nexus Third Way Debate[23] on the Internet,[24] in which I took part, was part of a consultation process with the prime minister to discuss which principles should underlie the UK political economy and welfare state during the next ten years. Twenty-five participants from across the UK were invited to the Nexus 10 Downing Street Seminar, convened by the prime minister on 7 May 1998. He also invited the public to visit his Internet Web site.[25] In *The Observer*'s feature "Third Way? Which Way?", published on 10 May 1998, McSmith (1998) reviews the seminar, and Leadbeater (1998b) summarises one of its most important papers. *New Economy* (June 1998) has a feature on a 'Third Way' for the welfare state.

The Conservative Party is beginning to formulate a new approach to its policy, now that it is in Opposition, and has a new leader, William Hague. In a recent interview,[26] Hague said that it is vital for the Conservatives to be shown to be compassionate, tolerant, and inclusive. These are fine ideals but seem to many people to be far removed from the *actual* performance of the Conservative governments of 1979 to 1997.

The UK's future role in Europe and worldwide is at present somewhat uncertain. Both the Labour government and the Liberal Democrats favour a more active involvement of the UK in the European Union, including entry into a Single European Currency and European Monetary Union, subject to approval by a referendum. Most, though by no means all, of the Conservatives fear that this would erode British national sovereignty too much. Being so closely engaged in trading and finance, the UK economy is also very dependent on the terms of trade and the state of financial markets worldwide. British policies are still vulnerable to the vast influence of multinational corporations.

There are possibilities that the UK will gradually move towards more open and democratic government, which will genuinely be in the interests of the British people, with their consent and participation.[27] During recent years, there have been an increasing number of public consultations about specific areas of proposed future government policies, including social justice, freedom of information, transport, education, and science, where citizens, as well as experts and members of the 'establishment', are invited to contribute their views. More publicity is also being given to such consultations. The Labour government has adopted the concept of 'stakeholder partnership', where as many stakeholders as possible in a society—sectors of society, institutions, groups, or individuals—share responsibility for a socially valuable project, so that they complement each other's abilities. Stakeholder partnerships, using this concept, have been set up in several British local authorities, such as Milton Keynes Council in the city where I live. In these and other ways, participatory democracy can slowly, but surely, become more of a reality.

The Human Rights Bill, published in October 1997, aims to bring the European Convention on Human Rights (ECHR) into British law; it is due to become law, as the Human Rights Act, in the current parliamentary session. A report by the Institute for Public Policy Research (Spencer and Bynoe 1998) argues that a Human Rights Commission will be essential in Britain, as in Northern Ireland, if this new law is to become effective. It would help to promote a culture of awareness of human rights, help to advise individuals how to obtain redress against abuses of rights in the UK, and select test cases in whose outcome there would be a wider public interest. Therefore, it would begin to make inroads into the large backlog of civil rights cases that urgently need attention. Amnesty International, Charter 88, and Oxfam cosponsored an important conference, "Beyond the Human Rights Act", in London on 30 May 1998; the interest and concern that it aroused could lead to the development of a new British human rights movement, reaching out widely into the public.

NOTES

1. See also Norton (1994: ch. 8).
2. For more details, see Sked and Cook (1993: chs. 1–12), Coxall and Robins (1997: 17–36, 49–60; 1998: 19–28), Roberts (1997: 37–45), and Jones et al. (1998: 23–29).
3. For more details, see Kavanagh (1997, 1990), Jenkins (1996), Sked and Cook (1993: chs. 13–15), Coxall and Robins (1997: 36–48, 60–68; 1998: 28–32), Roberts (1997: 45–68), and Jones et al. (1998: 29–33).
4. For more details, see Robins et al. (1997), Fisher (1996), Peele (1995: chs. 6–7), Coxall and Robins (1997: ch. 7; 1998: ch. 7), Jones et al. (1998: chs. 8, 14), and Norton (1994: ch. 6). Robinson (1992) discusses how green thinking has influenced the ideas and policies of British political parties. See also the series *British Elections and Parties*, published by Frank Cass, London.
5. For more details, see Coxall and Robins (1998: 354–360), Jones et al. (1998: ch. 30), Roberts (1997: 82–92, 533–536) and Krieger (1993: 651–653).
6. For more details, see Bogdanor (1996, 1997b: ch. 1), Peele (1995: ch. 1), Hennessy (1996: ch. 2), Coxall and Robins (1997: ch. 6; 1998: ch. 12), Jones et al. (1998: ch. 15), Norton (1994: ch. 4), and Roberts (1997: ch. 4).

7. For more details, see Bogdanor (1997a, b: ch. 7), Hennessy (1996: ch. 2), Jones et al. (1998: ch. 16), Norton (1994: ch. 12), and Roberts (1997: 93–96).

8. This statement was made by Bagehot (1867) and used by King George V as guidance, even before he became monarch; see Hennessy (1996: 47).

9. See Jones et al. (1998: 232), and Norton (1994: 61, 67).

10. For more details, see Hennessy (1998, 1996: ch. 3, especially pp. 86–90), Thomas (1998), Coxall and Robins (1998: 249–257), Jones et al. (1998: ch. 19), Norton (1994: 176–183, 312–313), and Roberts (1997: 344–354).

11. For more details, see Kaufman (1997), James (1992), Hennessy (1990, 1996: ch. 4), Peele (1995: ch. 3), Coxall and Robins (1998: 257–272), Jones et al. (1998: ch. 19), Norton (1994: 184–188), and Roberts (1997: 355–370).

12. For more details, see Barberis (1997), Hennessy (1990, 1996: ch. 5), Peele (1995: ch. 4), Coxall and Robins (1998: ch. 15), Jones et al. (1998: ch. 20), Norton (1994: 166–198, 202–206), Roberts (1997: ch. 13), and Kaufman (1997).

13. For more details, see Silk and Walters (1998), Hennessy (1996: ch. 6), Peele (1995: ch. 5), Coxall and Robins (1998: ch. 16), Jones et al. (1998: ch. 17, 18), Norton (1994: ch. 11), and Roberts (1997: ch. 4). Searing (1994) discusses eight political roles of the House of Commons. Longley and Davidson (1998) show how parliamentary committees have acquired new roles within the political system. Dixon (1996) gives an insider's view, emphasising the need for change, and McCloughry (1996) includes interviews with leading MPs. Riddell (1998) discusses the current relevance of Parliament and its future.

14. For more details, see Hennessy (1996: ch. 3), Peele (1995: chs. 8, 9), Coxall and Robins (1997: ch. 8; 1998: chs. 8, 9), Jones et al. (1998: ch. 11), Norton (1994: ch. 5), and Roberts (1997: ch. 7, 9). Butler and Kavanagh (1997) give full coverage of the UK general election of 1997, in the latest in a series of definitive guides. Crewe et al. (1998) also cover it fully. Bogdanor (1981) discusses electoral reform in British politics. See also the series *British Elections and Parties*, published by Frank Cass, London.

15. Bogdanor (1981 & 1997b: ch. 5) discusses the role of referenda in British politics and some possible ways of increasing it.

16. For more details, see Coxall and Robins (1998: ch. 17), Jones et al. (1998: 479–480), Norton (1994: 214–222), and Roberts (1997: 496–502).

17. For more details, see McNaughton (1998), Bogdanor (1997b: ch. 2), Peele (1995: 394–397, 416–422), Jones et al. (1998: 221–222, 290–291), Coxall and Robins (1998: ch. 18), Norton (1994: 222–230, 234–235), and Roberts (1997: 83–86).

18. For more details, see McNaughton (1998), Bradbury and Mawson (1997), Leach (1998), Peele (1995: ch. 11), Coxall and Robins (1998: ch. 19), Jones et al. (1998: ch. 21), Norton (1994: 214–222), and Roberts (1997: ch. 16).

19. Definitive guides to the likely politics, policies, and personalities of the Labour government include Anderson and Mann (1997), Blair (1996), Layard (1997), Mandelson and Liddle (1996), Perryman (1996), and Radice (1996). Hutton (1996, 1997, 1998) and Hall et al. (1997) discuss some of the issues arising. *Time* (27 October 1997) includes a special report on the prospects of the new government from an American viewpoint. Driver and Martell (1998) give details of the ideology of 'New Labour'.

20. The Liberal Democrat peer Shirley Williams (1998) considers that the Liberal Democrats are now probably to the left of Labour. She gives the following marks out of 10 for the Labour governments early performance: constitutional reform 9, handling the trade unions 7, Europe 6, decentralisation 5, but social justice only 2.

21. The proposals in Liam Byrne's (1997) Fabian Society pamphlet *Redesigning the State* are intended as a basis for discussion about such a reform.

22. See Frank Field's book *Stakeholder Welfare* (Field et al. 1996) and his 1998 Beveridge Memorial Lecture to the Royal Statistical Society, to be published in the society's *Journal*.

23. This is part of a much wider Third Way Debate on both sides of the Atlantic, seeking a middle way between traditional forms of social democracy and democratic socialism, on one hand, and right-wing ideologies and policies, on the other. Published contributions by its leading British participants include Giddens (1998a, b), Holtham (1998), Le Grand (1998), and Leadbeater (1998a). The BBC 1 television programme *On the Record* on 3 May 1998 interviewed some of them, giving examples of the wide range of opinions expressed. The contributors to *Tomorrow's Politics* (Hargreaves and Christie 1998) offer a far-reaching contribution to the Third Way Debate. Views on how the Third Way might develop in the United States include those of Corera (1998) and White (1998).

24. Active British Internet forums on politics include Nexus and UK Citizens Online Democracy (UKCOD). Prime Minister Tony Blair considers that Nexus has a crucial role in progressive politics and government in the UK.

25. This Web site is at http:///www.number-10.gov.uk. It includes information sections and has discussion forums on the themes of health, welfare, international affairs, the economy, and education, to which Internet users are invited to contribute brief ideas if they wish. Blair (1998) sets out the prime minister's vision of the Third Way as a modernised social democracy.

26. See the interview of William Hague by Steve Richards (1997b).

27. However, Marr (1995) considers that the *real* sources of power in the UK provide a serious threat to the future of British democracy. He suggests several ways of preventing the occurrence of this dangerous situation.

SOME TOPICS FOR FURTHER INVESTIGATION

1. Comparing and contrasting the UK and U.S. Constitutions and models of government, outline your own formulation of a possible approach and framework that would combine the best features of both.

2. From your observations of the British political scene, assess the prospects for the gradual emergence of a more participatory, less confrontational approach to politics in the UK.

3. Discuss why such a high proportion of British people, especially young people, are so disillusioned with modern politicians and political parties. What prospects, if any, do you see for the emergence of new political parties in the UK?

4. What roles do you see for the British monarchy in the future? Considering that the power of Royal Assent has not been used for 290 years, should it be abolished? Alternatively, should it be retained, with a convention that it could be used to indicate a policy issue that should referred to a national referendum?

5. Discuss the problems of work overload faced by the prime minister and members of the Cabinet. Should ministers continue to be constituency MPs, or should those two roles be kept separate, to enable full attention to be given to both functions? Should

ministers be appointed from outside Parliament, analogous to the practice of U.S. administrations?

6. Discuss what electoral system seems to be most appropriate for the election of members of the House of Commons (MPs). In what other ways would you reform the House of Commons?

7. Outline your proposals for the reform of the House of Lords, including the electoral procedures, if any, that you would use.

8. What framework for devolved regional and local government do you consider most appropriate for the UK?

3

Other Democratic Regimes

This chapter briefly surveys the democratic regimes in the world other than the UK, while pointing out that they are still far from achieving the full potential of democracy. It considers governance in the United States in moderate detail, then outlines the situations in Western Europe, the British Commonwealth, and other parts of the world. It ends by describing briefly the work of the United Nations, which, to some extent, acts as a democratic forum for the nations and peoples of the world. The emerging democracies in the former USSR and Eastern Europe are discussed in Chapter 5.

THE UNITED STATES[1]

The U.S. Democratic System

The United States has nominally been a democracy since its Declaration of Independence from the UK in 1776. It is a federation that currently has fifty states and the District of Columbia;[2] there are also eight U.S. dependencies[3] with their own democratic local governments and a variety of relationships with the United States. The U.S. Constitution was ratified in 1787 and became effective in March 1789. The Bill of Rights[4] consisted of the first ten amendments to this Constitution, especially the first eight, which identify specific individual rights; it was proposed in 1789 and took effect in December 1791. Since then, seventeen further amendments have been made to the Constitution. It provides for the sharing of the powers of government between the federal and state governments and, inside the federal government, between the executive, legislature, and judiciary. The executive is led by a president,[5] assisted by a vice president.

The president is elected every four years in a national contest by universal adult suffrage; votes are counted at the state level by a first-past-the-post system, and each state is assigned a block of seats in the 538-member electoral college, which formally elects the president. The vice president is the vice-presidential candidate in the party or slate to which the president belongs. The executive function of federal government is conducted by the federal administration, consisting of the president, vice president, and a cabinet selected by the president subject to the Senate's approval. As cabinet members are forbidden to serve in the legislature, they are normally specialists who concentrate on the work of their government departments and often have business or academic, rather than party political, experience. The president is also served by a large White House Office.

Congress,[6] the federal legislature, has two equally powerful chambers, the Senate, which has two elected members per state and thus now has 100 members, and the House of Representatives, which now has 435 elected members, allocated in approximate proportion to state population. Senators are elected for six-year terms, one-third of them being elected at a time every two years. Representatives are elected for two-year terms.

The judiciary is headed by the U.S. Supreme Court,[7] which interprets the written U.S. Constitution to ensure that a correct balance is maintained, is the final arbiter over federal laws, and is also the top court of appeal in the United States. It consists of nine judges who normally serve for life and are appointed by the president, subject to Senate approval, whenever a vacancy arises.

The United States has two dominant political parties, the Democratic Party, which tends to be more liberal and to support the underprivileged, and the Republican Party, which tends to be more conservative and to support big business and other privileged interests. However, both parties are coalitions of members with very varied political views; their relative absence of party discipline is largely due to the separation of powers in the U.S. Constitution. For the same reason, there is no guarantee that Congress will favour the policies of the president; the president normally has great difficulty with Congress, even when his party controls both houses of Congress, and even more difficulty when Congress is dominated by the other party, as happens quite often. No significant left-wing or socialist party has emerged in the United States, partly because of its dominant free-enterprise culture and partly because of Americans' deep distrust of government intervention. Rather unusually, the independent presidential candidate Ross Perot achieved considerable proportions of the votes in the 1992 and 1996 presidential elections.

A Brief History of the United States

Despite its democratic Constitution, the United States in practice did not give rights to its black slaves, most of whom were freed only after the end of the American Civil War (1861–1865). Even then, it still took a long time for the

African Americans,[8] Hispanic Americans,[9] and Native Americans[10] to gain anything approaching proper recognition of their rights. President Abraham Lincoln introduced the concept of democracy as "government of the people, by the people, for the people" in his famous Gettysburg Address of 1863. The next really notable U.S. president was Franklin Roosevelt,[11] whose radical administration from 1933 to 1944 successfully introduced the economic reforms of the New Deal[12] to counter the disastrous effects of the Great Depression of the 1930s and then led the United States during most of World War II. On his accession, Roosevelt was faced by the United States' greatest crisis since its Civil War and was granted considerable additional powers by Congress, especially in the first 100 days of his presidency.

The postwar U.S. administrations, both Democrat and Republican, retained and adapted many of the New Deal provisions and gradually extended civil rights for over thirty years. For example, President Lyndon Baines Johnson[13] introduced many social and economic reforms under the Great Society programme[14] of the 1960s. In contrast, his immediate predecessor, John Fitzgerald Kennedy,[15] concentrated on foreign policy,[16] and Johnson, too, became deeply involved in the war with Vietnam, which began under Kennedy's presidency. U.S. democracy was almost brought into disrepute by Watergate,[17] the most serious political scandal in its modern history, which occurred under Richard Nixon's presidency and culminated in his resignation in August 1974. The scandal was very well concealed and remarkably difficult to uncover, but its lessons now seem to have been well and truly learned. In 1980 President Ronald Reagan[18] was elected, and U.S. politics swung sharply to the right, with much more emphasis on laissez-faire and monetarist economics and on high military expenditure against the threat of communism; yet he achieved a notable agreement in May 1988 with the Soviet Union, which was by then under the control of President Gorbachev. The Bush administration from 1989 to 1992 continued most of the Reagan policies.

A partial reversal of this trend occurred in November 1992, when Bill Clinton was elected president by a large majority; nevertheless, the Clinton administration has been weakened seriously by a hostile Congress that began to acquire a Republican majority. As a result, many of the policies that Clinton intended to introduce were prevented or seriously diluted, but he was reelected in November 1996. As in the UK, many citizens have serious doubts about the future of the democratic system in the United States. Many of them voted in 1992 and 1996 for the third presidential candidate, Ross Perot, and an even larger proportion did not vote at all. Despite all these problems, the Clinton administration *does* have important ideals that it is endeavouring to apply. In his book *Between Hope and History*, President Clinton (1997) presents his vision for the United States as it enters the twenty-first century; he shows how the broad values of opportunity, responsibility, and community can play a critical part in helping the American people to meet the challenges ahead. The people must go forward together, to fulfill a vision grounded in their core values and in America's founding principles. The United States has a Third Way debate, which is in many respects like that in the UK described at the end of Chapter 2; this debate is reviewed by Corera (1998) and White (1998) and discussed more briefly by Walker (1998) and Lloyd and Bilefsky (1998).

Reinventing American Government

The bureaucratic model of government worked very well in the United States during the first half of the twentieth century, especially during its times of crisis in the two world wars and in the depression of the 1930s. This top-down, command-and-control approach worked well when aims and objectives were clear and widely shared, and people were willing to work together for a common cause. By the 1980s, it had been replaced by a much more laissez-faire, market-oriented approach, with a much smaller role for government, but this, too, worked well only for a limited time. Today, most government institutions have to address increasingly complex tasks in competitive, rapidly changing environments where citizens want quality and choice. As a result, there has been enormous stress in government in the United States and many other countries.

In their best-selling book *Reinventing Government*, David Osborne and Ted Gaebler (1993) present case histories to show how a new paradigm of *entrepreneurial government* has been emerging gradually to meet these needs, first at the local level, then in several U.S. states and in federal government. Further details are given in the new book *Banishing Bureaucracy* (Osborne and Plastrik 1997). This paradigm has influenced many leaders in both the Democratic and Republican Parties, especially the Clinton administration,[19] although much work still needs to be done before it dominates American governance. As an American *perestroika*, it focuses not on *what* government should do but on *how* it should work. Its *third* way of government differs from both the bureaucratic and the laissez-faire approaches and aims to combine positive and caring government with high efficiency and effectiveness.

Osborne and Gaebler spent five years investigating how governments at all levels in the United States were changing their modes of operation. They found ten common principles[20] used by these new, innovative, entrepreneurial organisations that are appearing in American government. (1) They promote *competition* between service providers. (2) They *empower* citizens by moving control from bureaucracy into the community. (3) They measure the performance of their agencies by focusing on *outcomes*. (4) They are driven by their *missions*, not by rules and regulations. (5) They call their clients '*customers*' and offer them choices between options. (6) They try to *prevent* problems before they emerge. (7) They concentrate on *earning* rather than spending money. (8) They *decentralise* and encourage participation. (9) They prefer *market* to *bureaucratic* mechanisms. (10) They *catalyse* all sectors—public, private, and voluntary—into action to solve the problems of their communities. These principles can be implemented by thirty-six service delivery options.[21] Policy research institutions and think tanks, such as the Brookings Institution in Washington, D.C., have also helped to transform American politics.

The new entrepreneurial paradigm of government has already begun to influence the approaches adopted by governments in the UK, New Zealand, and other countries.[22] However, the influential British political think tank Demos has criticised the paradigm for not being broad enough; it should also address collaboration *between* government agencies and between government and the public.

WESTERN EUROPE

West European Democracies[23]

Democracy evolved later in most of the countries of Western Europe than it did in the UK. France[24] was governed by an autocratic monarchy until the French Revolution of 1789, which attempted to introduce elements of democracy but was soon replaced by the Napoleonic empire. Between 1815 and 1871, there were alternations of monarchies and republics, followed by parliamentary democracy, which has lasted since then except for five years of German occupation. The present regime is governed by the Constitution of the Fifth Republic, adopted by popular referendum in September 1958. As a result of the previous period of indecisive parliamentary government, it greatly increased the power of the executive, headed by a president with extensive powers who is elected by the people every seven years. There is a two-chamber Parliament, with a National Assembly, elected directly by a second ballot system, and a Senate, one-third of which is elected indirectly for nine-year terms every three years. A Constitutional Council can review certain governmental actions. France is a unitary state, with twenty-two regions for national development, planning, and budgetary policy and ninety-six departments within the regions. French politics is dominated by one socialist and two right-wing parties, but there are over thirty minor political parties, of which only two, the Communists and the extreme right National Front, are important.

Germany[25] was ruled by an emperor until its defeat in World War I in 1918. After the brief interlude of the Weimar Republic, the totalitarian Nazi regime was in power from 1933 until Germany's defeat in World War II in 1945. Since then, a full parliamentary democracy evolved in the Federal Republic of Germany, which was formed in West Germany in 1949[26] and was extended to the whole of Germany after German reunification[27] in 1991. The Federal Republic has a president and a two-chamber Parliament with a dominant Bundestag, with a combination of elected constituency and party-list members, and a Bundesrat, representing the Land governments; each of the sixteen

Lände is a state with fairly extensive powers. The dominant German parties are the moderate conservative Christian Democrats and the centre-left Social Democrats. The Christian Democrats have led most of the governments, and the Social Democrats a few of them, until recently with the liberal Free Democrats usually holding the balance of power and being minor coalition partners. The other important party is the German Greens, who became co-alition partners with the Social Democrats in the new German government, as a result of the September 1998 general election.

Parliamentary democracies have flourished in Scandinavia[28] during recent decades, and have mostly had social democratic regimes, with more highly developed welfare states than anywhere else in the world. Switzerland,[29] a federation of twenty-three cantons, has an exceptionally high degree of local democracy and holds referenda more frequently than any other country in the world; it has maintained a policy of international neutrality for over 400 years. The other West European countries are now all parliamentary democracies, although Italy and Spain had fascist regimes for long periods, and there were also dictatorships in Portugal and Greece.[30]

The Evolution of the European Union[31]

Just after World War II, six West European countries—France, Germany, Italy, Belgium, the Netherlands, and Luxembourg—decided to contribute to the creation of institutions that would make another war in Europe almost impossible. They established the European Coal and Steel Community in 1951 and the European Economic Community (EEC) in 1957 under the Treaty of Rome. The treaty aimed to develop an even closer union between the peoples of Europe, improve their living and working conditions, progressively aboli-tion restrictions on trade between them, and develop the prosperity of other countries. In 1986, the Single European Act prepared for the establishment of a Single European Market in 1992, with extensive freedom of movement between member states. The 1991 Maastricht Treaty on European Union, eventually ratified by all member states by 1993, made the *European Union* (EU) a reality. Its specific objectives included the eventual establishment of a Single European Currency and European Monetary Union (EMU) and a more positive and united international presence. The number of member states rose from six to nine in 1973, ten in 1981, twelve in 1986, and fifteen in 1995, so that most West European countries are now also members of the EU. The EU is now actively exploring the possibility of its gradual extension, to include at least some of the East European countries.[32]

However, there are now considerable controversies about the appropriate nature of the EU. Many Europeans are said to favour a move towards a polit-ical federation of EU countries,[33] while many others would prefer to retain extensive amounts of national independence, preferring a confederation of freely cooperating nations.[34] There are also strong criticisms of the Common

Agricultural Policy, Common Fisheries Policy, and the extent of EU bureaucracy and vigorous controversies about the feasibility and desirability of EMU and a Single European Currency.[35] Northcott (1995) examines the underlying, long-term developments, which will influence the future shape of Europe and the UK's role in it.

During the preparations for the EU Summit at Cardiff in mid-June 1998, near the end of the UK's presidency of the EU, there were strong indications of a move towards a climate of much greater openness in the EU. The People's Europe 98 (PE98) Conference was held on 5–7 June in London, as 'the European Summit for everyone', and those addressing it included EU commissioner Neil Kinnock, European Parliament vice president Ursula Schleicher, and UK foreign secretary Robin Cook, as well as representatives from many European countries and from a wide range of nongovernmental organisations (NGOs) and grassroots activities. It initiated what will probably become an increasingly important People's Europe movement, which will gradually make the EU more democratic and accountable. The principal findings of its parallel discussions were conveyed to the EU Summit itself.

The important Demos report *Rediscovering Europe* (Leonard 1998) was launched one day later, on 8 June, and revealed new data about how Europeans *really* feel about Europe and how a *real* People's Europe could emerge. The extensive surveys, whose results the report presents, found that there has been a widening gap between Europeans and the institutions of the EU; most people living in the EU member states *feel* European but also consider that the institutions are too remote from them and do not respond sufficiently to their needs. The report goes on to make many proposals about how this situation could be corrected and addressed in a positive way. It is very significant that, at the launch, Neil Kinnock praised the project that had given rise to the survey and agreed with many of the report's findings, although disagreeing with some of them. He stressed the urgency of providing Europeans with impartial information about the EU, because, on their own admission, most of them know far too little. Here, as at PE98, he stated that the EU is *not* an emerging 'superstate' or even state but a framework for mutual cooperation between member nations in problem areas that are too large for nations alone to handle. He emphasised that the diversity of Europe is as important as its unity; indeed, both these aspects are complementary.

The Council of Europe[36] was established in 1949 as a forum to obtain greater unity between the European countries, by discussing their common interests and problems and seeking new methods and areas of cooperation. Its members include all EU member states and many other European countries, some from Eastern Europe. It has a Consultative Assembly, meeting each year in Strasbourg, France, and a Standing Committee. It has been especially active and effective in the field of human rights, where it established the European Convention on Human Rights, the European Commission on Human Rights, and the European Court of Human Rights.

THE BRITISH COMMONWEALTH[37]

The former British Empire gradually became the British Commonwealth. First, Canada,[38] Australia,[39] New Zealand,[40] and South Africa[41] became independent, self-governing dominions, each with its own parliamentary system. Canada, Australia, and South Africa, but not New Zealand, were set up as federations. Shortly after World War II, independence was granted to India,[42] Pakistan, and Sri Lanka on the Indian subcontinent. In subsequent decades, almost all the remaining British colonies achieved independence, in the Caribbean, Southeast Asia, and large parts of Africa. Although all these newly independent countries were supposed to be democracies, many of them were not, and some had more or less dictatorial regimes.

In South Africa, which was not fully democratic, because it offered full rights only to its white citizens and not to those who were Asiatic, coloured, or black, a regime of 'apartheid', racial separation, was introduced by the incoming National Party government in 1948. Extensive interracial conflict, much of it violent, occurred as a result. Eventually, by a 'miracle', a Government of National Unity was formed in South Africa in 1993, after the first multiracial elections ever. Since then, South Africa has had a transition back to democracy and rejoined the Commonwealth.

Although the British Commonwealth has no formal institutions for international government, it nevertheless has considerable moral power as a free association of over fifty mutually cooperating nations, many of which are loyal to the British monarchy. It seems likely to continue such a role in the future, even though some of its members sometimes fail to live up to its ideals and standards. In 1995, Mozambique became the first 'non-British' country to join the Commonwealth; it has six other Commonwealth countries as neighbours.

OTHER DEMOCRACIES[43]

Until its defeat at the end of World War II in 1945, Japan[44] had an emperor, the mikado, who nominally had absolute power; the actual power was held by a militarist regime. In 1947, Japan was given a new Constitution, which pledged support for peace and democracy, guaranteed human rights, and made the mikado head of state with symbolic powers only. From then on, Japan's parliamentary democracy gradually evolved. Its dominant political party, which has almost always held power, is the Liberal Democratic Party, which applies a broad range of ideas in a pragmatic and corporatist way; it believes in a private enterprise economy, a welfare state, and the United States–Japan alliance.

After the Holocaust during World War II, where millions of Jews were murdered, most of their survivors emigrated to Palestine, which was at that time still ruled by the UK. Palestine was already inhabited by a considerable number of earlier Jewish settlers and many Palestinian Arabs. The new state of Israel[45] was formed as a parliamentary democracy in 1948 but was immediately in conflict with the surrounding Arab countries. This conflict had several short periods of warfare but has gradually eased during recent decades. A settlement was achieved with Egypt, and relationships with some other Arab countries have improved. Most notably, an initial settlement was recently negotiated with the Palestinian Arabs to give them limited self-government in some of their territories although this settlement is still fragile.

There are also some other Asian[46] and African[47] democracies and semi-democracies outside the British Commonwealth, but their degrees of democracy are generally considerably and quite often much lower than those of the democracies in Western Europe, North America, and Australasia. In Latin America,[48] which used to have many dictatorships, most countries are now more or less democratic, although their degrees of democracy still vary considerably from one country to another.

THE UNITED NATIONS[49]

Between World Wars I and II, the League of Nations was formed, in an attempt to prevent the outbreak of any further world war, but it totally failed to achieve this objective. The United Nations (UN) was originally the informal association of nations that were allies in World War II against Nazi Germany, fascist Italy, and militarist Japan.

In 1945, the UN was formally established as an association of collaborating nations, which replaced the League of Nations and had much broader terms of reference under the UN Charter. Its main bodies were the UN General Assembly, where each member nation has one seat, and the UN Security Council, which has five permanent national members and over a dozen temporary national members. The UN can be viewed as a form of democracy between the nations of the world, because almost all nation states are now UN members, and because UN members have voting rights. The General Assembly is essentially a parliament of nations with limited powers that passes broad resolutions relating to the activities of the UN as a whole. The Security Council uses its influence to attempt to settle disputes between member nations when they threaten the peace of the world. It has often sent UN peacekeeping forces and very occasionally approved military intervention on behalf of the UN.

There are also many UN specialised agencies, with very specific international functions, which were mostly founded after the UN itself, although a few were taken over from the former League of Nations. They include the International Monetary Fund (IMF), the International Bank for Reconstruction and Development (IBRD, World Bank), the World Trade Organization (WTO), the International Labour Office (ILO), the Food and Agriculture Organization (FAO), the World Health Organization (WHO), and the United Nations Educational, Scientific and Cultural Organization (UNESCO). There are also the UN Development Programme (UNDP) and the UN Environment Programme (UNEP).

The UN has also held many very important international conferences,[50] which have more recently provided forums for nongovernmental organisations (NGOs) as well as nation states. The UN Conference for Environment and Development (UNCED), otherwise known as the Rio Earth Summit and held in June 1992, was perhaps the most important of these conferences,[51] as it led to several significant international treaties and agreements and to the international Agenda 21 programme aiming to achieve sustainable development worldwide, at all levels from the local to the global. It was followed by Earth Summit II (UNGASS) in New York in June 1997.[52]

NOTES

1. The many books on the United States' political system include Edwards et al. (1998), McKay (1997), McKenna (1997), Patterson (1997), Grant (1997), Danenberg (1996), Hames (1996), Lasser (1996), and Bowles (1998). See also Krieger (1993: 936–943), Derbyshire and Derbyshire (1996: 456–464), and Hunter (1997: 1390–1438). Critiques of the current U.S. system include Esler (1998), Fishkin (1997), Greenberg and Skocpol (1997), Nye et al. (1997), Sandel (1998), and Morgan (1994). Sargent (1997) documents the history of U.S. political thought. Parenti (1996) discusses U.S. politics and political economy. Bok (1998) surveys the major social changes in the United States since 1945.

2. Hunter (1997: 1438–1562) details the regimes in all the U.S. states.

3. See Hunter (1997: 1562–1573).

4. See Krieger (1993: 79–81).

5. See Krieger (1993: 742–744).

6. See Krieger (1993: 181–183).

7. See Krieger (1993: 888–891).

8. See Krieger (1993: 5–9).

9. See Krieger (1993: 389–392).

10. See Krieger (1993: 621–622).

11. See Krieger (1993: 799–802).

12. See Krieger (1993: 624–626).

13. See Krieger (1993: 493–495).

14. See Krieger (1993: 363–365).

15. See Krieger (1993: 500–502).

16. For U.S. foreign policy in general, see Krieger (1993: 23–26).

17. See Krieger (1993: 970–971). Robert Williams (1998) discusses U.S. political scandals in general.

18. See Krieger (1993: 769–771).

19. See Holman (1997), who notes that Osborne and Gaebler are both associated with the Alliance for Redesigning Government.

20. These principles are summarised by Osborne and Gaebler (1993: 19–20) and discussed in the first ten chapters of their book. Their last chapter, Chapter 11 presents a synthesis of their new paradigm.

21. These thirty-six options are explained in Osborne and Gaebler (1993: app. A).

22. See Osborne and Gaebler (1993: 328–331) and Holman (1997).

23. For further details, see Derbyshire and Derbyshire (1996: 465–524, 286–288), and also entries for the relevant countries in Krieger (1993) and Hunter (1997).

24. See Derbyshire and Derbyshire (1996: 477–485), Krieger (1993: 316–320), and Hunter (1997: 495–513).

25. See Derbyshire and Derbyshire (1996: 486–494), Krieger (1993: 353–355), and Hunter (1997: 547–581).

26. See Krieger (1993: 353–355).

27. See Krieger (1993: 351–353).

28. See Krieger (1993: 817–818), for example.

29. See Krieger (1993: 894–895).

30. See Chapter 4.

31. Bainbridge and Teasdale (1998) and Wallace and Wallace (1996: chs. 1, 2) provide introductory surveys of EU politics, policies, and institutions. Recent books on the politics of Western Europe and the EU include Budge and Newton (1997), Colomer (1996), Hackett (1996), Hancock and Conradt (1998), Lane and Ersson (1996), McCormick (1995a), and O'Neill (1996). Stavridis et al. (1997) discuss policies and policy-making in the EU. Middlemas (1995) provides an insight into how the EU works in practice, as well as in theory. Krieger (1993: 285–287) and Derbyshire and Derbyshire (1993: 648–649) provide brief introductions to the evolution of the EU. For discussions of the future prospects of Europe and the EU, see De Smijter (1997), Feld (1998), Gowan and Anderson (1997), Cortada and Cortada (1997), Kramer and Kimball (1997), and Edwards (1996).

32. The possible expansion of the EU is discussed by Croft and Redmond (1998), Mayhew (1998), Laurent and Maresceau (1997), and Redmond and Rosenthal (1997).

33. The section on continental government in Chapter 8 discusses in some detail the nature of the EU system of government and shows that it is by no means federal.

34. The book *Europe of Many Circles* (Body 1990) considers how to reshape the European Community into a confederation large enough to serve the people of all Europe but 'small' enough to allow the peoples of its nations to enjoy both democracy and individual freedom. It introduces the concept of 'overlapping circles' of integrated, common interests between nations; each specific 'circle' would be a grouping of nations that *voluntarily* agree to cooperate in a specific functional area. Body (1998) envisages that new technology will enable the EU to become more democratic.

35. The book *The Rotten Heart of Europe* (Connolly 1998) is an exceptionally outspoken critique of how the EU is run, by someone who used to be a senior Eurocrat. Other strong critiques of the EU include Jenkins (1998) and Laughland (1998). Goldsmith (1994), a former Member of the European Parliament (MEP), argues that something fundamental has gone wrong with the development of the EU, and Goldsmith (1995) answers the critics of his arguments. However, defenders of the EU refute such criticisms as misunderstandings, exaggerations, or even fantasies. Very recent discussions of the European Monetary Union (EMU) and the Single European Currency include the feature in *Time* (10 May 1998) and the article by Browne (1998), which shows that there are still very wide disagreements about how well the EMU will perform; forecasts range from very beneficial to catastrophic.

36. The Council of Europe should not be confused with the European Council, which is the council of heads of governments of EU member states. For brief descrip-

tions, see Derbyshire and Derbyshire (1996: 649–650) and Krieger (1993: 203). Body (1990: ch. 9) gives a more detailed but less up-to-date description. Coleman (1999) also covers the Council of Europe in every aspect, including its role in the twenty-first century.

37. See Krieger (1993: 158–159) and Derbyshire and Derbyshire (1996: 691) for brief descriptions and also entries for the relevant countries in Krieger (1993) and Hunter (1997).

38. See Krieger (1993: 109–111), Derbyshire and Derbyshire (1996: 452–455), and Hunter (1997: 279–328).

39. See Krieger (1993: 57–59), Derbyshire and Derbyshire (1996: 526–530), and Hunter (1997: 107–167).

40. See Krieger (1993: 634–635), Derbyshire and Derbyshire (1996: 539–541), and Hunter (1997: 962–978).

41. See Deegan (1998), Krieger (1993: 845–847), Derbyshire and Derbyshire (1996: 399–402), and Hunter (1997: 1157–1175).

42. See Krieger (1993: 416–418), Derbyshire and Derbyshire (1996: 138–144), and Hunter (1997: 640–707).

43. Derbyshire and Derbyshire (1996) has entries for countries in Asia, Central America and the Caribbean, Central and Southern Africa, the Middle East and North Africa, and South America on pp. 113–210, 211–245, 337–417, 418–451, and 560–584, respectively. See also entries for the relevant countries in Krieger (1993) and Hunter (1997).

44. See Krieger (1993: 481–488), Derbyshire and Derbyshire (1996: 147–153), and Hunter (1997: 768–776).

45. See Krieger (1993: 476–478), Derbyshire and Derbyshire (1996: 430–433), and Hunter (1997: 743–752).

46. See Maidment and Goldblatt (1998).

47. See Ottaway (1997) and Deegan (1996).

48. See Lowenthal and Treverton (1994).

49. See Daws and Taylor (1997), Whittaker (1997), Krieger (1993: 932–935), Derbyshire and Derbyshire (1996: 635–641), and Hunter (1997: 3–28). The sections on world government and international functional cooperation in Chapter 8 give further details and references, especially on possibilities for reforming the United Nations.

50. See Grubb et al. (1993).

51. Dodds (1997) reviews the successes and failures of the developments after the Earth Summit, including Local Agenda 21, and indicates a possible way forward beyond Agenda 21.

52. See Osborn and Bigg (1998).

SOME TOPICS FOR FURTHER INVESTIGATION

1. Discuss the relative advantages and disadvantages of the American and British systems of government. How would you modify them to provide a more appropriate form of government for the country where you live?

2. Consider the actual performance and experience of the American and British regimes to decide whether or not the presence of a full written Constitution provides a

better form of government. Extend your assessment by allowing for the experience of other countries with written Constitutions.

3. Assess the performance to date of entrepreneurial approaches to governance in American governments at the federal, state, and local level. What modifications to the entrepreneurial paradigm of government do they suggest to you? If you do not live in the United States, answer the corresponding questions for the country where you live.

4. How far do you think that the entrepreneurial paradigm is appropriate to government in other countries, such as the UK? What allowance should be made for cultural differences between those countries and the United States?

5. In what ways could the future evolution of the EU into a true People's Europe be facilitated? Do you favour a closer, more federal style of union or a looser confederation? How would you ensure that the citizens of the EU were properly consulted in this process and encourage them to participate in it more actively?

6. What changes most urgently need to be made to the treaties, institutions, and policies of the EU? What obstacles do you see to the practical implementation of the changes that you recommend?

4

Other Regimes

In the ancient world and the Middle Ages, most governments were *authoritarian* and ranged from empires, through kingdoms, to local duchies and feudal estates. From the Renaissance onwards, traditional authoritarian regimes gradually lost their powers. During the twentieth century, *dictatorships* emerged, which were very different from all but the most tyrannical of earlier regimes. Some of these dictatorships were *totalitarian* in the sense that they attempted to supervise many, if not most, aspects of people's way of life, attitudes, opinions, and even thoughts. The most notable totalitarian regimes were in Nazi Germany and communist Russia. Many other dictatorships have existed since World War II, and some are still in power. They have arisen especially in Eastern Europe, Latin America, the Middle East, and Africa but also occasionally in Asia and Western Europe.

AUTHORITARIAN REGIMES

Before the rise of modern democracies in the mid-nineteenth century, almost all governments and political regimes were authoritarian. They were conservative and 'right wing' in the sense that they supported the 'status quo' and traditional ways of life. They did not envisage the possibility that an existing regime might eventually evolve into a different type of regime. In their dictatorial form, where the ruler had more or less absolute power, they took the form of empires and monarchies. In some cases, where some of the absolute power of the ruler was lost to other powerful people, they took the form of aristocracies and oligarchies. Even in the earlier forms of democracy, votes and decision-making powers were available only to a limited section of the population and almost always only to males. After aristocratic and oligarchic regimes gradually gave way to democracies or were transformed into them, authoritarian regimes of the traditional type became extinct, except in a few, very small localities. Authoritarian regimes continued to appear from time to time.

During the latter part of the twentieth century, most nondemocratic regimes have been dictatorships or totalitarian regimes. There are still authoritarian monarchies in seven Arab countries and in Bhutan and Brunei. There are several authoritarian nationalist regimes in Asia and Africa, including Indonesia and Kenya.

The National Party regime of South Africa,[1] which held power from 1948 to 1993, was authoritarian in many respects but was also nominally a parliamentary democracy. Its most unusual feature was that it was run on racist lines, with official policies of white supremacy and apartheid, which imposed artificial separation between the white, African, and coloured peoples. Full democratic rights were available to white people only, although the Africans were given partial self-government in limited areas of the country away from the main centres of population. The Africans, especially in the urban townships, bore the brunt of the oppressive apartheid policies and their restrictive regulations. South Africa was a white-dominated British dominion from 1910 on, and the new regime came into power after the general election of 1948, open to white voters only, which the pro-apartheid National Party won decisively. Probably as a result of intense international pressure on South Africa for many years, President F. W. de Klerk announced a five-year plan for 'constitutional reform'. This led to negotiations with Nelson Mandela, the previously imprisoned leader of the African National Congress. In February 1993, de Klerk and Mandela agreed to the formation of a government of national unity, after free elections, with citizens of *all* races being entitled to vote.

DICTATORSHIPS

There have been many right-wing dictatorships that have not generally been totalitarian and have often been militarist dictatorships, put into power by coups by the armed forces of their countries. Regimes of this sort have included the vast majority of the numerous Latin American dictatorships, which used to be widespread but now seem to be dying out. These regimes were sometimes quite long-lived, like Pinochet's sixteen-year-long dictatorship in Chile[2] from 1973 to 1989, which he termed 'authoritarian democracy'. Sometimes, they alternated with more democratic regimes, as in Argentina[3] but more often had rather brief lives, especially in those countries that had fairly frequent revolutions.

In Europe, there were four well-known, nontotalitarian dictatorships. In 1926, a military dictatorship was set up in Portugal[4]; in 1932, it appointed António de Oliveira Salazar, a Roman Catholic economics professor, as prime minister. In 1933, he introduced the 'New State', an authoritarian, corporatist political regime that lasted for forty-one years; Salazar stood down in 1968 and was succeeded by Marcello Caetano, who attempted political liberalisation but was overthrown in 1974.

In Spain,[5] General Francisco Franco rebelled against the left-wing Second Republic of Spain in July 1936 and won the resulting Spanish Civil War, finally gaining full power in March 1939. Although Franco received some military support from Nazi Germany and fascist Italy, and although the Falange, the Spanish fascists, became the regime's official political party, the regime was not particularly ideological. It began as a military dictatorship but later adopted a civil structure, largely based on conservative, middle-class, Catholic, and military support; it had limited political pluralism. Franco stood down in 1973 and died in 1975. His regime was followed by a peaceful transition to monarchy and then to parliamentary democracy, which was fully established in 1977.

Greece[6] had military dictatorships under General Ioannis Metaxas, from 1936 to 1941, and under a group of colonels, dedicated to protecting Greece from communism, from 1967 to 1974. A new parliamentary system, more democratic than its predecessors, was established in 1975.

The authoritarian and dictatorial regimes of the Middle East[7] have been strongly motivated by Arab nationalism and often also by Islamic fundamentalism. The most durable and totalitarian of these regimes is Saddam Hussein's dictatorship of Iraq,[8] based on the Arab Ba'ath Socialist Party, which built up remarkably strong armed forces and quite advanced weapons and military technologies. It is still in power, despite being worn down by a long war with Iran, followed by a major military defeat in the Gulf War.

For a considerable number of years, after the overthrow of its monarch, the shah, Iran[9] has had an authoritarian regime dominated at first by the Islamic fundamentalist leader Ayatollah Khomeini.

Several other Middle-East, Asian, and African countries, such as Syria,[10] Nigeria,[11] and Myanmar,[12] have dictatorial regimes.

TOTALITARIAN REGIMES

The totalitarian nation-state is characterised by dictatorial rule by one political party claiming to speak for the whole nation. The first regime incorporating significant elements of this type of government was Mussolini's[13] fascist dictatorship of Italy from 1922 to 1943. Benito Mussolini, a former revolutionary socialist, founded the fascists in 1919 as a politically heterogeneous group of war veterans and radicals that played on middle-class fears of a socialist revolution and committed acts of violence against communists and others. In October 1922, the Italian king invited Mussolini to form a coalition government, after the fascists threatened to 'march on Rome'. Mussolini became dictator of Italy in January 1925, and his regime was violent, repressed civil liberties, and aspired to become a totalitarian state. At home, it also attempted rather unsuccessful programmes of land reclamation, economic self-sufficiency, and population growth. Its foreign policy was aggressive, including conquering Ethiopia in 1935–1936, annexing Albania in 1939, helping Franco in the Spanish civil war of 1936–1939, and joining the German side in World War II in June 1940. After the defeat of the Italian armed forces by the Allies, Mussolini's regime was overthrown in July 1943, but a remnant of it was rescued by the Germans and continued in North Italy until April 1945.

In 1919, Adolf Hitler[14] joined and soon led a small political party that he renamed the 'National Socialist' ('Nazi') Party. It rapidly expanded, and he attempted a coup against the German government, but the coup was poorly planned and soon failed. While in prison for nine months, he wrote his famous book *Mein Kampf* (My Struggle). He resumed the development of the Nazis as a subversive party, using the methods of street violence, vicious propaganda, and continual electioneering. The party's fortunes began to rise in 1930 as a result of the Great Depression, and he was appointed chancellor of Germany in January 1993, after the Nazis won the most votes in the Reichstag elections. Hitler lost no time in systematically introducing a totalitarian dictatorship by eliminating his opponents and converting institutions into Nazi bodies. He gradually solved the mass unemployment problem by starting large building and rearmament programmes and for some years gained the support of even more of the German people. His aggressive foreign policy began with the reoccupation of the Rhineland in 1936 and the peaceful take-over of Austria and Czechoslovakia in 1938. However, his invasion of Poland in September 1939 started World War II when challenged by the UK and France. For a few years, Nazi Germany had a succession of dramatic military victories but failed to conquer the British Isles in 1940 and overreached itself by invading Soviet Russia in June 1941. Military defeat, after a tremendous struggle, led to the sudden end of the regime in May 1945. Especially evil features of the regime were its racialism, leading to the mass extermination of most Jews still living on the continent of Europe, and its systematic persecution and often torture of political opponents and of various minority groups.

The other totalitarian regimes have mostly been communist regimes, described in the next section, although some of those regimes have not been totalitarian. The dictatorships described in the previous section have almost all not been totalitarian; the most significant exception is Saddam Hussein's regime in Iraq.

COMMUNIST REGIMES

The communist regimes in Russia and Eastern Europe arose as the result of revolution or military takeover by adherents of the communist political ideology, which was, in turn, strongly influenced by the thought of Marx,

Engels, and Lenin. The communist regimes in China and some of the countries around China were also strongly influenced by Mao Zedong; the Chinese communism that he helped to develop has been and is in several important respects different from Soviet communism.

Soviet Communism

The former Russian Empire under the tsars was overthrown by the successive stages of the Russian Revolution.[15] Early in 1917, the liberal or political revolution brought in a provisional government under Kerensky. In October 1917, this government was, in turn, removed by the workers' revolution led by the Bolsheviks. A Soviet government, the world's first communist regime, was established under Lenin,[16] although there was civil war in parts of the country, so that the Russian Empire was replaced by the *Soviet Union.*[17] After Lenin's death in 1924, Stalin[18] gradually built up his power, which eventually became almost absolute. After Stalin's death in 1953, there was a series of post-Stalinist communist regimes in the USSR, which gradually became less totalitarian. The last of these regimes, under Mikhail Gorbachev,[19] paved the way for the transition towards democracy and a free-market economy, described in the next chapter.

The formation and functioning of the Soviet Union were influenced mainly by the inheritance of the Russian Empire and the ideology of revolutionary communism. The empire's territories, taken over by the Soviet Union, had many national and ethnic groups besides the Russians, so that the Soviet Union developed as a federation, the *Union of Soviet Socialist Republics* (USSR). The Communist Party of the Soviet Union (CPSU)[20] grew out of the Bolshevik section of the Marxist Russian Social Democratic Labour Party, which was led by Lenin and gained a mass following. Lenin had not intended to lead a fully autocratic regime, but the pressure of events and especially the regime's struggle for survival forced him to apply more and more dictatorial measures. Thus, Lenin interpreted the Marxist concept of 'dictatorship of the proletariat' as meaning a dictatorship of the Communist Party. This dictatorship was at first an oligarchy, became a personal dictatorship under Stalin, then again became an oligarchy. The ideology of the CPSU was at first *Leninism,*[21] which set up a vast 'democratic centralist' network of mass organisations and associations, including the system of *soviets* (councils) for the country's administration. It extended democratic centralism over the whole system of government, gave priority to economic growth (though introducing a semicapitalist New Economic Policy for the time being), introduced a cultural revolution, and was willing to apply terror through the secret police (Cheka).

Under Stalin, Leninism evolved into the much more totalitarian and centralised *Stalinism.*[22] During the 1930s, this led to ruthless programmes of very rapid industrialisation, forced collectivisation of farms, and much stricter control of a much wider range of human activities. There was a much more widespread terrorisation of large sections of the population, with millions of people who were alleged to be 'enemies of the people' being deported to the notorious 'gulags' (labour camps), where a large proportion of them died. This terror extended right up into the top ranks of the communist leadership, as Stalin became more paranoic about possible threats to his dictatorship.

After Stalin's death in 1953, the apparatus of terror was gradually dismantled, and the regime on the whole became progressively less totalitarian during subsequent decades, although there were phases, as under Brezhnev, when it become more conservative and resistant to change. Dissidents, opposing the regime, suffered much for many years.[23]

During the history of the USSR, Soviet foreign policy had several successive phases.[24] Some foreign countries intervened in the civil war in 1918, and there was much Soviet distrust of foreign governments for a long time after that. In 1939, Germany and the USSR signed a Non-Aggression Pact, and the USSR took over eastern Poland with German agreement and also parts of Finland. In 1940, it seized the three Baltic Republics. In June 1941, it was invaded by Germany but won the subsequent very violent war with the help of the Allies. After the Allied victory, the USSR established a strong Soviet sphere of influence, which led to most East European countries becoming communist,[25] as discussed in the next section. Because the United States and its West European allies feared the Soviet invasion of Western Europe, they increased their defence preparations and formed the North Atlantic Treaty Organization (NATO)[26] in 1949. The *Cold War*[27] began as a military confrontation between the two 'superpowers', the United States and the USSR, though without actual fighting between them. In 1995, the USSR and its East European 'satellite' countries formed the Warsaw Treaty Organization (Warsaw Pact).[28] There were occasional military interventions by the USSR outside its borders, two of them in Eastern Europe in 1956 and 1968 (see next section) and one in Afghanistan[29] from 1979 to 1988. However, the Cold War gradually eased from the early 1970s on, when the policy of 'détente' (East-West cooperation) began to emerge, though its progress had its ups and downs.

In his memoirs, Mikhail Gorbachev (1997) provides some interesting insights into what it was like to live under the successive communist regimes in Soviet Russia. He was born in 1931 in a rural area of south Russia. His grandparents were arrested under the Stalin purges, though later released (pp. 25–27), yet one of them was convinced that Stalin knew nothing about the evils committed by the secret police. There was much genuine grief among the people when Stalin died in 1953 (p. 47). Looking back to when he was a student at Moscow University, Gorbachev admits that the massive ideological brainwashing there affected the minds of the students and that the whole educational system was designed to prevent them from developing a critical mind (p. 45). Nevertheless, he joined the CPSU in 1952. He emphasises the very low level of the standard of living in the USSR for many years after 1945;

this was due to the low level from which the regime started in 1918 and was made far worse by the massive destruction in much of the USSR during World War II.

When he was in the Politburo, he perceived, and was frustrated by, the stultifying effects of many of the rigid ways in which the Soviet command-and-control bureaucracy worked; it sometimes laid down strict rules for determining the minutest local detail of a plan or procedure. It strongly *dis*couraged innovative behaviour on the job and gave no real incentives for extra effort and enterprise above a very mediocre norm. He found much manoeuvring for more power among different factions inside the Politburo. The advancement of his own career was helped enormously because he happened to know people in high positions, especially Yuri Andropov, who were aware of his abilities and willing to back him.

East European Communism

Towards the end World War II, the Red Army passed through, and occupied, most of Eastern Europe to invade Germany and contribute to its final defeat. Usually, 'democratic' regimes were installed there immediately but gradually made more pro-communist. A parliamentary democracy was restored in Czechoslovakia in 1945, only to be overthrown by a communist coup in 1948. As a result, there were by then more or less Stalinist regimes in East Germany, Poland, Czechoslovakia, Hungary, Romania, Bulgaria, and Albania. There was also a communist regime in Yugoslavia under Tito, who had been an effective resistance leader against the German occupation from 1941 to 1944. Stalin unsuccessfully plotted Tito's overthrow in 1948, and Tito then adopted an independent variant of communism.

During the years after Stalin's death, there were considerable variations in the pattern of evolution of different East European communist regimes. In Hungary,[30] the communist regime was overthrown by a people's revolution in October 1956, which was soon crushed by the Red Army of the Soviet Union. Although the communist dictatorship was restored under Janos Kádár, it very gradually became more liberal and introduced some elements of a market economy in 1968. In January 1968, Alexander Dubček became the new leader of the Communist Party in Czechoslovakia[31] and rapidly introduced new freedoms as ordinary citizens began to press for changes. Unfortunately, Dubček failed to reassure the leaders of neighbouring countries, including the USSR, so that their troops invaded the country and a hard-line communist regime was restored under Gustáv Husák. Despite this, Czech dissidents remained active and formed Charter 77 as a focus for their activity in 1977. Poland's variant of communism[32] generally provided steady economic growth, a large free-enterprise farming sector, and a more liberal regime than usual, with a somewhat better standard of living. In 1978, Carol Woytila, archbishop of Kraków, was elected Pope John Paul II. His official visit to Poland in 1979 stimulated the rise of the *Solidarity* movement under Lech Wałęsa. Although the communist Party at first reacted by imposing martial law, it introduced some political and market economic reforms during the 1980s. In contrast, the German Democratic Republic,[33] the communist regime in East Germany, maintained a hard-line policy, closely based on that of the Soviet Union. In Romania,[34] the Stalinist trend intensified under the brutal dictatorship of Nicolae Ceauşescu, which began in 1965.

Chinese Communism[35]

The *Chinese Communist Party*, founded in 1921, ruled parts of China from 1937 to 1949 and took power over the whole of China, apart from the island of Taiwan and the colonies of Hong Kong and Macao, in 1949, after defeating the Kuomintang government of Chiang Kai-shek. The party's leader, Mao Zedong,[36] stayed in power until his death in 1976. He rejected Stalinist orthodoxy and emphasised the importance of the continuous socialist transformation of human beings and their social relations, which he considered essential to ensuring that modern economic development had a socialist outcome. This approach was partly responsible for the extraordinary policies of the Great Leap Forward and the Cultural Revolution, which brought enormous death and suffering. Mao Zedong was succeeded by Hua Guofeng for a few years, but Deng Xiaoping[37] was firmly in power by 1980 and ruled China until his death in 1997; he was succeeded by Jiang Zemin. During recent years, the Chinese communist regime has introduced considerable elements of a market economy, but, politically, it has remained autocratic and resisted pressures from several sections of the Chinese people to become more democratic. Nevertheless, there have been considerable changes in the Chinese communist regime during recent years.[38] In July 1997, the former British colony of Hong Kong became a part of China, with its own special regime, under a treaty between the UK and Chinese governments. Although Chinese communism has always been rather different from Soviet communism, it can, in several respects, be described as Leninist. It seems possible that, after its present generation of leaders, there could in the future be trends towards a more open economy and a freer polity, perhaps towards democratic socialism or social democracy. However, while discussing China's upsurge and future prospects, Dick Wilson (1996) points out that most of the Chinese do not understand what Western-style democracy means or involves. Chris Patten (1998) discusses the role of China and future prospects for its political and economic liberty, and considers what East and West can learn from each other.

Other Communist Regimes

There are communist regimes in the republics of Vietnam,[39] Laos,[40] and (until fairly recently) Kampuchea,[41] which were formerly part of the French colony of Indochina. These regimes have been influenced by both Soviet and Chinese communism. Ho Chi Minh,[42] who was both a nationalist and a communist, set up a communist regime in Vietnam on the defeat of the Japanese in 1945, but France unsuccessfully tried to overthrow it. In a cease-fire in 1954, the country was partitioned into the communist North Vietnam and the Diem regime in South Vietnam. Guerrilla warfare between the two halves followed, and the United States became involved in what then became the Vietnam War. A new Socialist Republic of Vietnam was proclaimed in 1976, after the U.S. defeat in 1975. In December 1978, Vietnam overthrew the murderous Khmer Rouge communist government in Kampuchea and replaced it by a regime that is now in transition to democracy. After having a variety of regimes since 1945, Laos became communist in 1975, but its regime became more liberal in the late 1980s under the influence of Gorbachev.

The Democratic People's Republic of Korea,[43] also known as North Korea, has a 'hard-line' communist regime derived from both Stalinist and Chinese communist influences. Its first leader, Kim Il Sung, died in 1995.

From 1921 to 1985, Mongolia,[44] as a neighbour of the USSR, had communist regimes that were very similar to the corresponding Soviet regimes. Its regime then began to liberalise under the influence of Gorbachev. In 1992, Mongolia became an emergent democracy.

The Cuban revolution of 1959,[45] which overthrew the Batista dictatorship, was led by Fidel Castro[46] but was originally nationalist. After hostility from the United States and the unsuccessful United States-sponsored Bay of Pigs invasion in 1961, Castro declared the Cuban revolution to be socialist, and his regime evolved a local version of communism, extensively influenced by Soviet communism. It had some impressive achievements in building up health and education services but also gave much revolutionary support for Latin American guerrilla movements during the 1960s. It is still in power but suffers severely from external and internal economic problems and continued hostility from the United States.[47]

In the Nicaraguan revolution of 1979,[48] the Sandinista Front[49] overthrew the Somoza dictatorship and set up a regime that was in some respects communist but at first had broad national support. However, it was weakened economically by the strain of fighting the counterrevolution by the Contras and by a U.S. economic embargo. In 1990, it was defeated in a general election by a twenty-party coalition of opposition parties.

There are a few examples of 'communist' regimes that are, nevertheless, democratic. Kerala state in India had such a regime, which was elected democratically and stayed in power for some years. San Marino,[50] a tiny, independent state inside Italy, had democratically elected communist-led Coalition governments from 1945 to 1957 and 1978 to 1986, and has had a Communist-Christian Democrat Coalition government since 1986.

NOTES

1. For further details, see Derbyshire and Derbyshire (1996: 401–402) and Krieger (1993: 845–847).
2. See Krieger (1993: 126–128).
3. See Krieger (1993: 46–48) and Derbyshire and Derbyshire (1996: 564).
4. See Krieger (1993: 731–733).
5. See Krieger (1993: 320–321) and Derbyshire and Derbyshire (1996: 513).
6. See Krieger (1993: 363–365) and Derbyshire and Derbyshire (1996: 287).
7. See Chehabi & Linz (1998).
8. See Krieger (1993: 405–406, 469–471) and Derbyshire and Derbyshire (1996: 428–430).
9. See Krieger (1993: 464–467, 506–507), and Derbyshire and Derbyshire (1996: 426–428).
10. See Krieger (1993: 895–896) and Derbyshire and Derbyshire (1996: 444–445).
11. See Derbyshire and Derbyshire (1996: 175–178).
12. See Derbyshire and Derbyshire (1996: 388–390).
13. See Krieger (1993: 609–610).
14. See Krieger (1993: 392–395).
15. See Krieger (1993: 806–808).
16. See Krieger (1993: 534–536).
17. See Krieger (1993: 861–867) and Derbyshire and Derbyshire (1996: 313–315).
18. See Krieger (1993: 874–876).
19. See Krieger (358–360). For more detailed accounts, see Brown (1997) and Gorbachev's *Memoirs* (1997).
20. See Krieger (1993: 165–167).
21. See Krieger (1993: 536–538).
22. See Krieger (1993: 876–878).
23. See Krieger (1993: 850–856).
24. See Krieger (1993: 857–861).
25. See Krieger (1993: 167–169).
26. See Krieger (1993: 650–651).
27. See Krieger (1993: 351–353).
28. See Krieger (1993: 969–970).
29. See Krieger (1993: 3–5).
30. See Krieger (1993: 403–405).
31. See Krieger (1993: 213–215).
32. See Krieger (1993: 707–709).
33. See Krieger (1993: 349–351).
34. See Krieger (1993: 797–799).
35. See Krieger (1993: 128–136), Derbyshire and Derbyshire (1996: 131–138), and Hunter (1997: 348–359).
36. See Krieger (1993: 561–565).
37. See Krieger (1993: 227–229).
38. See Li (1996), Pei (1998), and Blecher (1997).
39. See Derbyshire and Derbyshire (1996: 206–210), Krieger (1993: 955–956), and Hunter (1997: 1593–1597).
40. See Derbyshire and Derbyshire (1996: 164–167) and Krieger (1993: 524–525).

41. See Derbyshire and Derbyshire (1996: 127–131) and Krieger (1993: 106–107).

42. See Krieger (1993: 395–396).

43. See Derbyshire and Derbyshire (1996: 155–158) and Krieger (1993: 512–514).

44. See Derbyshire and Derbyshire (1996: 172–174) and Krieger (1993: 600–602).

45. See Derbyshire and Derbyshire (1996: 221–223), Krieger (1993: 206–211), and Hunter (1997: 400–405).

46. See Krieger (1993: 116–118).

47. *New Internationalist* (May 1998) describes and discusses the current situation in Cuba. See also Centeno and Font (1996) and Cole (1998).

48. See Derbyshire and Derbyshire (1996: 237–238) and Krieger (1993: 637–638).

49. See Hoyt (1997) and Krieger (1993: 814).

50. See Krieger (1993: 814–815).

SOME TOPICS FOR FURTHER INVESTIGATION

1. Using frequently updated reference books that contain details of the political regimes of different nations, find out which countries had autocratic, dictatorial, and totalitarian regimes in different years. How far do you detect trends for progressive democratisation of regimes in different parts of the world? How often are they interrupted by coups that temporarily impose nondemocratic regimes?

2. How many of the conditions that led to dictatorships earlier in the twentieth century are still present in certain countries today? In the light of this answer, assess which countries, if any, seem to be at risk of having coups that could lead to dictatorship.

3. Following your investigation of question 2, what measures would you advocate for minimising the risk of new dictatorships occurring?

4. How far has the influence of powerful countries tended to encourage or discourage the origin and continuance of authoritarian or dictatorial regimes outside their jurisdiction? What comparable influences have been exercised by multinational companies?

5

The Transition from Communism to Democracy

By the time that Mikhail Gorbachev became general secretary of the Communist Party of the Soviet Union (CPSU) in 1985, the USSR was already suffering severe economic strain. Gorbachev introduced his concepts of *glasnost* (public openness and transparency) and *perestroika* (reconstruction) in his government's attempts to remedy this situation and reform the economy. However, it was not possible to prevent the collapse of communism or even the breakup of the former Soviet Union.[1] In effect, a revolution occurred, which led to the introduction of a free-market economy and more democratic general elections, together with enhanced parliamentary institutions. The *Commonwealth of Independent States* (CIS) was formed, of which Russia emerged as by far the most powerful country. During the late 1980s, revolutions or other rapid changes of regime occurred in the formerly communist countries in Eastern Europe, and most of them had more democratic regimes as a result. However, this transition had many problems. Extensive and prolonged armed conflicts broke out in the former Yugoslavia, and there were also wars in several parts of the former Soviet Union. The economic and social problems of transition to capitalism have also been considerable. The future prospects for Russia, the CIS, and parts of Eastern Europe are still uncertain.

GLASNOST AND PERESTROIKA[2]

When Mikhail Gorbachev became general secretary of the CPSU and thus leader of the USSR, one of the most dramatic changes in Soviet and Russian history began. The radical political and economic reforms that he put on the

Soviet agenda made the communist regime in the USSR much more liberal and much more democratic, but they eventually led to the collapse of the Soviet communist system and the disintegration of the USSR. Gorbachev soon started applying 'new political thinking' to both foreign and domestic policy. The new foreign policy allowed much more autonomy to the countries of Eastern Europe and even accepted free elections there, without Soviet intervention. The new domestic policies increased civil liberties, freed dissidents, and allowed much freer expression. Gorbachev called for further democracy and glasnost in the media and in public life. Glasnost intended that citizens should be well-informed and that they should become more aware of the real state of affairs. The term 'perestroika', introduced early in Gorbachev's regime, came to mean the comprehensive reform of the Soviet political and economic system.

Perestroika had arisen from dissatisfaction with the performance of the Soviet Union during the early 1980s, but it was stimulated much more by an awareness that the potential of socialism had not been fulfilled.[3] It became an urgent necessity because of the profound problems of development of the socialist society of the Soviet Union, which included a slowing down of economic growth, a gradual erosion of the ideological and moral values of the people, and the regime's increasing resistance to new ideas and to attempts to examine constructively the problems that were emerging.[4] The energy for revolutionary change had been accumulating in the people and the CPSU for some time. Perestroika was a carefully prepared programme, drawing on the ideas of Lenin and closely connected with socialism as a system.

It had several successive stages.[5] (1) Society was put into motion as perestroika gained momentum, based on the principles that there are no ready-made formulas for solutions and that new ideas should be developed in a spirit of glasnost. (2) A new programme of economic reform was introduced at the June 1987 Plenary Meeting of the CPSU Central Committee, replacing predominantly administrative methods by mainly economic methods, developing a new concept of 'democratic centralism', and addressing questions of scientific and technological progress. (3) Reviving a sense of responsibility for the future of the Soviet Union among its people and proceeding along the road to increasing democracy. (4) Examining how perestroika is regarded in the West and discussing it with Western leaders. An essential part of perestroika was to apply new thinking to Soviet foreign policy and to improving the relationships between the Soviet Union and the rest of the world.[6]

In introducing more democracy, Gorbachev favoured competitive elections but at first aimed at linking electoral choice to democratisation of the Communist Party. In 1990, he accepted the need to legalise other political parties, but several of the elections in the republics of the USSR produced noncommunist majorities. Because he was faced by increasing problems, he attempted to increase his personal power in 1990 in a new state presidency and acquired the power to rule by decree.

Gorbachev also saw the need for a 'radical reform' of the Soviet economy, due to the steady decline of its growth rates from the mid-1950s on. At first, he introduced a much more decentralised economic and industrial management. Then, in 1990, he presented a vision of 'humane democratic socialism' and human development, but against a background of economic shortages, rising prices, and social inequalities. Perestroika attempted to find a 'middle way' between a capitalist market economy and the Stalinist form of 'socialism' or collectivism, while at the same time avoiding the social inequalities of the market. However, this 'ideal' version of perestroika was widely agreed to have failed by the early 1990s, and it rapidly lost its influence after 1991.

RUSSIA AND THE COMMONWEALTH
OF INDEPENDENT STATES (CIS)[7]

During 1990 and 1991, Gorbachev attempted a more radical approach to relations between the republics of the USSR. In mid-1991, an attempt was made to agree on a new union treaty between Russia and nine other republics willing to remain in a decentralised federation. The Russian republic became much more powerful after Yeltsin was elected its president in June 1991. In August 1991, an unsuccessful coup against Gorbachev was attempted by more 'conservative' elements of the Soviet 'establishment'. Although Gorbachev was not overthrown, he rapidly lost power, and the coup also accelerated the breakup of the Soviet Union, which was replaced by the Commonwealth of Independent States (CIS) at the end of 1991. Gorbachev resigned as president of the USSR and handed over his powers as commander-in-chief of the Soviet armed forces to President Yeltsin of Russia. Just before its end, the USSR recognised the independence of the Baltic Republics in August 1991.

In his closing televised "Address to the Soviet Citizens" as president of the USSR on 25 December 1991,[8] Gorbachev summarised the achievements of the reform process so far. (1) Most important, society had been freed politically and spiritually. (2) The totalitarian system had been dismantled. (3) Important democratic reforms had been achieved, including free elections, freedom of the press, freedom of worship, representative legislatures, and a multiparty system. (4) Reforms towards a pluralistic economy were in progress, including the equality of all forms of ownership, land reform, the elements of a market economy, and privatisation; at the same time, these reforms should be done to ensure the social protection of individuals, especially old people and children. (5) The Cold War and arms race had been ended, and everything possible was being done to ensure a safe control over nuclear weapons. Gorbachev emphasised the vital importance of sustaining the democratic achievements of the last few years and thanked those who had participated in them and supported them. Though he left his post with concern, he was convinced that, sooner or later, the common efforts of the people would bear fruit and that they would live in a prosperous and democratic society.

Since then, the Republic of the Russian Federation (Russia)[9] has continued to be led by President Boris Yeltsin. It is by far the largest of the former republics of the Soviet Union, covers most of its area, and has about 150 million inhabitants, of whom about 83% are Russian. Although most of Russia has eighty-nine administrative regions, ruled directly from Moscow, there are also twenty-one constituent republics inside it, with populations ranging from nearly 4 million to under 200,000 and a total population of about 25 million. The Russian federal government has powers over socioeconomic policy, the budget, taxation, energy, foreign affairs, and defence. Other powers are jointly managed by the federal , republic, and local governments. The federal government has an elected president as head of state, with considerable powers, a Federal Assembly, and a prime minister and Council of Ministers (Cabinet) appointed by the president. The Federal Assembly has a 450-seat lower house, the State Duma, consisting of elected constituency MPs and MPs elected by proportional representation from party lists, and a 178-seat upper house, the Federation Council, with two members each elected by first-past-the-post from Russia's administrative regions and republics. The assembly is relatively weak compared with the president. Of about 250 political parties, there are about ten significant political blocs, arranged into three groupings of comparable power: (1) conservative ex-communist; (2) radical right-wing nationalist and populist; and (3) liberal centre or right-of-centre pro-market and pro-pluralist. In 1994 and 1995, the Our Home Party, Forward Russia Party, and leftist Accord bloc also became important.

The Commonwealth of Independent States (CIS)[10] is a very loose grouping of twelve of the former fifteen republics of the Soviet Union, of which Russia is by far the largest. Of its other eleven members, the Ukraine, Belarus, Moldova, Georgia, and Kyrgyzstan are emerging democracies, and Armenia, Azerbaijan, Kazakhstan, Tajikistan, Turkmenistan, and Uzebkistan have authoritarian nationalist regimes. The three Baltic Republics of Estonia, Latvia, and Lithuania again became independent democracies.

THE TRANSITION IN EASTERN EUROPE

The collapse of the communist regimes in Eastern Europe, which began in mid-1989, was both unexpected and contagious.[11] Successive regimes fell one after another, like a house of cards, within months of each other. The process was helped by Gorbachev's decision, as leader of the Soviet Union, not to intervene.

In October 1989, Honecker resigned as leader of the German Democratic Republic (GDR),[12] otherwise known as East Germany. On 9 November 1989, the communist government of the GDR itself began to dismantle the Berlin Wall, in response to a large exodus of GDR citizens to the German Federal Republic (GFR, West Germany). Free elections in the GDR in March 1990 led to a coalition government pledged to reunite Germany. A formal treaty between the GFR and GDR to reunite Germany was signed on 31 August 1990.[13] Both Parliaments ratified the reunification treaty on 20 September 1990, and Germany was reunified on 3 October 1990. Reunification brought many problems as well as great new resources to Germany. The rapid economic union caused a collapse of much of East Germany's economy and severely strained the German economy as a whole.

During the 1980s, Solidarity was already a very powerful social movement in Poland.[14] Poland's variant of communism was already considerably milder than that of the Soviet Union. A series of Solidarity-led strikes during 1988 led to the 'roundtable agreement' of April 1989, followed by partly free elections in June 1989 and a commitment to far-reaching reforms in all areas of life. Solidarity won the elections, and its leader, Lech Wałęsa, was elected president in December 1990, although he was defeated in a later presidential election. Poland had become a democracy with a limited presidential political system and a two-chamber assembly.

Czechoslovakia,[15] which had been a democracy between World Wars I and II and briefly from 1945 to 1948, almost became a democracy again with the Dubček reforms of mid-1968. However, a hard-line communist government was reimposed by the USSR in August 1968. In 1977, Charter 77 was formed by an underground opposition movement as a focus for independent activity and thought. After massive public demonstrations in Prague in November 1989, the old communist regime was rapidly swept from power, and Václav Havel, leader of Charter 77, became president of Czechoslovakia in late December 1989. The new democratic regime of Czechoslovakia faced many problems, including ethnic issues. In September 1992, it split up into the Czech Republic[16] and Slovakia,[17] both of which have their own democratic governments with a two-chamber and a one-chamber Parliament, respectively.

The attempted Hungarian revolution in 1956 was suppressed, but the policies of the communist government in Hungary[18] began to relax gradually in the early 1960s. In May 1988, a reformist group took over the communist leadership, and, in October 1989, the Hungarian Constitution was amended to guarantee full political and civil rights and allow for free elections. All the new parties advocated a democracy and a market economy with social justice. After the elections of spring 1990, a noncommunist coalition government was formed in Hungary. There are a president with some executive powers and a one-chamber Parliament, elected by a mixture of direct and proportional representation.

From 1965 on, Romania[19] was governed by the increasingly ruthless dictatorship of Ceauşescu. In December 1989, this regime was overthrown in a brief, violent revolution by the Romanian people, with the help of the army. However, the resulting new regime was not completely democratic and included some authoritarian elements. Romania now has limited presidential government, with an elected two-chamber Parliament, but there are still some Western concerns about the future prospects of democracy there. It has had a deteriorating economy and especially bad social conditions, which largely result from its previous regime.

In Bulgaria,[20] the communist regime seemed to govern relatively well and provide a relatively prosperous economy until 1983, after which political discontent began to rise. President Zhivkov fell from power after thirty-five years in office but left a partial political vacuum. There have been several governments after the parliamentary elections of June 1990. Bulgaria now has a president with very limited powers, an elected, one-chamber assembly, and a prime minister and Cabinet.

The Stalinist dictator Enver Hoxha ruled Albania from 1945[21] until his death in 1985. His successor, Ramiz Alia, was forced by growing popular pressure to bring in a wide range of reforms during late 1989 and 1990, and the first free elections were held in March 1991. The country is still unstable and has many problems, as its new leaders attempt to set up a market economy. It has a multiparty democracy with an elected, one-chamber assembly, which elects the president.

THE BREAKDOWN OF THE FORMER
YUGOSLAVIA AND SUBSEQUENT CONFLICTS

Yugoslavia[22] had a relatively stable communist federal government under Marshal Tito's rule from 1945 to his death in 1980. Whereas Tito had been strong enough to hold Yugoslavia together, conflicts between the separate nationalities and regions of Yugoslavia reemerged after his death. In the 1990 elections, the communists won in Serbia, but noncommunist government coalitions came into power in other Yugoslav provinces and called for a looser federation. These calls were resisted by President Slobodan Milosevic. In February 1991, the republics of Croatia[23] and Slovenia[24] gave notice of their intention to secede from the rest of Yugoslavia and by June 1991 declared independence; in the meantime, Yugoslavia's collective presidency had broken down. Fighting between Serbians and Croatians broke out, and there was a devastating war until an uneasy peace settlement was reached in 1992. By October 1991, the Yugoslav federal government had collapsed, and the remaining 'Yugoslavia' soon consisted only of Serbia (as its dominant republic), Montenegro, and the regions of Kosovo and Vojvodina. Bosnia-Herzegovina[25] had declared its independence in October 1991, and Macedonia[26] in January 1992.

The Serbs in Bosnia did not wish to separate from Yugoslavia, and a Serbian Republic of Bosnia and Herzegovina was set up in March 1992. In April 1992, civil war broke out between the Serbian, Muslim, and Croatian communities of Bosnia-Herzegovina, with even more disastrous results and even higher loss of life. Although continuous attempts at mediation were made by UN representatives, and UN peacekeeping forces were able to provide humanitarian relief with very limited success, a reasonably successful peace settlement in Bosnia-Herzegovina was achieved only in December 1995, and it is still too early to be sure how long it will last.

To this day, there is considerable confusion about what *really* happened in Yugoslavia and to what extent different parties in the conflicts were to blame. In her remarkable, but controversial, book *Yugoslavia: An Avoidable War*, published soon after her death, Nora Beloff (1997) presented an unusual view of the conflicts that contradicted a large part of the conventional views about them prevalent in Europe and the United States but could well be largely true. Nora Beloff was a distinguished foreign correspondent for many years and had extensive experience of Yugoslavia. She argued against the conventional view that Yugoslavia collapsed from within and claimed that the violent conflicts there could have been averted, and a complete nation-state could have been preserved in some form. The main reason this did not happen, in her opinion, was the ignorant and arrogant intrusion of outside countries, especially certain member states of the European Union, which had their own set views of what Yugoslavia should be like and their own agenda for achieving it. She considers that peace would have been more, not less, likely if the Yugoslav Federation had been allowed to use its own armed forces to preserve Yugoslavia as *one* nation-state. She also argues strongly against the view that the Serbs were the bad national community in the conflicts, while the Croatians and Muslim Bosnians were innocent. In fact, all three nationalities shared the blame.

Although there have been underlying conflicts between the different nationalities of Yugoslavia throughout the twentieth century, it is nevertheless true that, before the recent conflicts, in large parts of Yugoslavia, especially in Bosnia, people of all three nationalities lived peacefully side by side in the same local communities; quite often, there were marriages between people of different nationalities. Tragically, that all seems to have been lost. In the view of Michael Ignatieff (1993: 16), the vicious ethnic hate that he observed firsthand during his visit to Serbia and Bosnia not long after the fighting resulted from the terror that arises when legitimate authority disintegrates. Tito created an intricate ethnic balance that contained local nationalisms, but this balance depended on his personal dictatorship. If Tito had allowed a citizens' politics in the 1960s or 1970s, Yugoslavs might have begun to feel a nonethnic loyalty to Yugoslavia as a whole, while mutually respecting each other's nationalities and cultures.[27]

Of the five national regimes now in place in the former Yugoslavia, all are nominally emerging multiparty democracies. The remaining 'Federal Republic of Yugoslavia' and Republic of Croatia are, in practice, probably rather autocratic, with Presidents Milosevic and Tudjman still in power. The situation in Bosnia-Herzegovina still seems very unstable, but NATO is continuing its protection. During 1998, there was much violent conflict in the Yugoslav province of Kosovo, which has a large Albanian minority. By the beginning of October, this crisis had escalated, but the UN Security Council had passed a stronger resolution and NATO was standing by for possible air strikes. Macedonia has had considerable internal difficulties. Only Slovenia seems well set on a course towards political and economic normality, with hopes of becoming an associate member of the European Union.

CONFLICTS IN THE CIS

In the former USSR, there have also been several serious armed conflicts. Fighting between the Republics of Armenia[28] and Azerbaijan[29] over the disputed territory of Nagorno-Karabakh began in 1988 and continued intermittently until May 1994. There were insurrections and civil war in the Republic of Georgia[30] from mid-1990 to May 1994. In Russian itself, the Republic of Chechnya[31] declared its independence in November 1991. In September 1994, civil war broke out there, and, in December 1994, the Russian army invaded Chechnya in an attempt to reimpose central control. A cease-fire was signed in July 1995. Fighting also broke out in several parts of Central Asia formerly in the USSR.

ASSESSMENT AND FUTURE
PROSPECTS OF TRANSITION[32]

The most serious problems of transition in the CIS and Eastern Europe have been the nationalist problems of transition, already discussed, which have all too often led to armed conflicts and which have seriously worsened relationships between different national and ethnic groups. Most governments interfere excessively with their media. The economic problems of transition have also been severe, especially in Russia but also in many other countries. In most of these countries, they have included poor economic growth and, in many cases, economic decline, high inflation and unemployment, falling standards of living for the majority of the population, rapidly rising wealth for the minority of rich people, and the severe problems of an overly sudden transition to a form of capitalism that is usually extreme and totally inappropriate. Although standards of living tended to be drab in the latter days of the former USSR and communist East Europe, at least a minimum standard of living that was not too bad could be guaranteed in most of these countries, and there was usually 'full employment'. Today, in most of these countries, welfare and healthcare systems are overloaded and usually grossly inadequate, leading to lower life expectancies; what was a considerable welfare state has been very seriously eroded and damaged. Crimes of violence have escalated; a new, very dangerous 'Russian Mafia' has emerged, which is not only operating within the CIS but also has overseas influence.

Tismaneanu (1998) traces the intellectual struggle between liberals and authoritarians in Eastern Europe since the collapse of the USSR. He warns that authoritarian nationalists pose serious threats to democratic forces and shows that nationalist and authoritarian thought has been influential in Eastern Europe for much of the twentieth century, while liberalism has only shallow roots there. It is wrong to assume that liberalism will necessarily triumph. Nationalist intellectuals have encouraged ethnic hatred in Russia, Yugoslavia, and other countries by reviving patriotic myths, which have been welcomed by ordinary people desperate for some form of 'salvation' from political and economic uncertainties.

In his book *Post-Communism: An Introduction*, Leslie Holmes (1997) introduces a fourteen-point model that elaborates three factors common and unique to the postcommunist states of the CIS and Eastern Europe. (1) They had a similar starting point and legacy of Soviet communism. (2) They had a comprehensive revolution, attempting a simultaneous, very rapid transition from a centralised, largely nationalised, state-run command economy and a centralised, relatively closed society with almost no 'bourgeoisie', towards a privatised market economy with a powerful capitalist class and a pluralist democracy. (3) These attempts were made in a context where global capitalism was dominant, and the Cold War was over.

At least the following stages occurred during the transition.[33] (1) Several countries had leadership crises. (2) Several countries had roundtable talks between government and opposition representatives. (3) The communist parties lost their leading role. (4) Opposition parties became legal. (5) The communist parties changed significantly, often abandoning Marxism-Leninism and moving towards social democracy. (6) Parliamentary elections were held, with a genuine choice between parties. (7) Several nation-states changed their name. (8) New or extensively modified constitutions were adopted.

Though possibly by no means without hope, the futures of Russia, the rest of the CIS, Eastern Europe, and the former Yugoslavia are now all in the balance. Some of their economies and parliamentary democracies are not particularly stable. The nationalisms unleashed by the fall of communism are still highly dangerous and could, for example, viciously reemerge in Russia. The stocks of nuclear weapons in the former USSR, which used to be under the control of one authority, are now under several separate governments and could become a threat if obtained by unscrupulous people. Fortunately, it is not that easy for terrorist groups or nation-states with small resources to make effective use of nuclear weapons or materials.

Clark (1995) considers that Russian power has never been gentle before and is unlikely to be become gentle now, to its own citizens or anyone else; its democratic procedures might be one of the first things to go if the situation becomes too difficult. Mikhail Gorbachev (1997: 695) predicts that the crisis in Russia will continue for some time, perhaps leading to even greater upheaval. In his view, nevertheless, Russia has irreversibly chosen the path of freedom and cannot now again become totalitarian; only democracy can bring the Russian people a life of dignity and eventual prosperity in the community of other civilised nations.

NOTES

1. The collapse of the Soviet regime is discussed by Cox (1997), Pei (1998), and Longworth (1998: ch. 1). Service (1998) considers the whole question of the rise and fall of the Soviet state. Petrie (1997) is a reader on the fall of communism.

2. The best description of the new approach of glasnost and perestroika is in Gorbachev's (1987) book *Perestroika*. Gorbachev's (1997) *Memoirs* includes his subsequent assessment of this approach and an invaluable description of how events actually unfolded in the Soviet Union while he was still in power and afterwards. For other assessments, see, for example, Brown (1997) and Krieger (1993: 358–360, 693–695).

3. See Gorbachev (1987: 10).

4. See Gorbachev (1987: ch. 1).

5. These stages are described in Gorbachev (1987: ch. 2).

6. This aspect is discussed in Gorbachev (1987: pt. 2) and, in retrospect, in Gorbachev (1997: pt. 3).

7. Gorbachev (1997: pt. 4) describes in detail the dramatic changes that occurred during 1991. Boris Pankin was the Soviet Union's last foreign minister and relates its final three months; his view is that Russia was concentrating on choosing its future during that period (Pankin 1995). Gorbachev (1997: 673–695) discusses subsequent events up to July 1996. Krieger (1993: 864–867) and Derbyshire and Derbyshire (1996: 316–320) outline the transition from the Soviet Union and the USSR to the emergence of the CIS with Russia as its dominant nation-state.

8. A transcript of this speech is given in Gorbachev (1997: xxvi–xxix).

9. Hunter (1997: 1078–1089) and Derbyshire and Derbyshire (1996: 311–313) describe the current regime in Russia. White et al. (1997b) and Petro (1997) discuss recent developments in Russian politics. Sakwa (1996) covers the major issues in the development of postcommunist Russian politics and society. Handelman (1997) describes the organised crime and corruption that plague Russian society today.

10. Hunter (1997: 1089–1098) and various articles in Krieger (1993) describe the current forms of government in the CIS republics other than Russia.

11. See East and Pontin (1997) and Krieger (1993: 640–642).

12. See Krieger (1993: 349–351).

13. See Krieger (1993: 351–353).

14. See Derbyshire and Derbyshire (1996: 302–306) and Krieger (1993: 707–709, 841–843, 961–962).

15. See Krieger (1993: 213–215, 383–384).

16. See Derbyshire and Derbyshire (1996: 276–280) and Hunter (1997: 414–419).

17. See Derbyshire and Derbyshire (1996: 320–323) and Hunter (1997: 1141–1145).

18. See Derbyshire and Derbyshire (1996: 288–292), Hunter (1997: 625–632), and Krieger (1993: 403–405).

19. See Derbyshire and Derbyshire (1996: 306–310), Hunter (1997: 1070–1077), and Krieger (1993: 797–799).

20. See Derbyshire and Derbyshire (1996: 267–270), Hunter (1997: 250–256), and Krieger (1993: 95–96).

21. See Derbyshire and Derbyshire (1996: 253–255), Hunter (1997: 73–78), and Krieger (1993: 15–16).

22. See Derbyshire and Derbyshire (1996: 331–336), Hunter (1997: 1608–1617), and Krieger (1993: 997–1000).

23. See Derbyshire and Derbyshire (1996: 270–274) and Hunter (1997: 395–399).

24. See Derbyshire and Derbyshire (1996: 323–325) and Hunter (1997: 1146–1149).

25. See Derbyshire and Derbyshire (1996: 263–267) and Hunter (1997: 228–231).

26. See Derbyshire and Derbyshire (1996: 247–249) and Hunter (1997: 857–860).

27. The book *Burn This House: The Making and Unmaking of Yugoslavia* (Udovicki & Ridgeway 1998) represents the critical, nonnationalist voices inside the former Yugoslavia.

28. See Derbyshire and Derbyshire (1996: 257).

29. See Derbyshire and Derbyshire (1996: 259–260).

30. See Derbyshire and Derbyshire (1996: 285).

31. See Derbyshire and Derbyshire (1996: 319). Gorbachev (1997: 688–690) suggests how the Chechnya tragedy could have been avoided.

32. Recent books on the transition in the CIS and Eastern Europe and its future prospects include East and Pontin (1997), Pogany (1998), and OMRI (1998), which is the latest in an ongoing series. Henderson and Robinson (1997) describes the democratic political systems in the East European countries. Redington (1994) discusses the new legislative processes in the CIS and Eastern Europe. Yergin and Gustafson (1994) present four scenarios for possible Russian futures. Skidelsky (1996) and Burgess (1997) provide critical assessments. Hall (1997) shows how relations between Russia and the European countries need to improve.

33. See Holmes (1997: ch. 6)

SOME TOPICS FOR FURTHER INVESTIGATION

1. By the early 1990s, most commentators on perestroika considered that its original attempt to introduce a form of humane democratic socialism, somewhere between communist and capitalist extremes, had failed. Discuss how far this situation might have been prevented. How far could more economic aid from the West have helped?

2. How far would the course of perestroika and the transition from communism to democracy in the former USSR and Eastern Europe have been improved if their decision makers and intelligentsia had had access to ideas about possible new forms of economics?

3. Discuss the possible futures of Russian politics. Assess what types of regime could emerge and estimate the approximate probabilities of their occurrence.

4. Discuss the prospects for reducing nationalist and ethnic violence in the former Yugoslavia and in the CIS. What are the best ways of beginning to reconcile different national and ethnic communities there?

5. In what ways will the Chinese economy become more capitalist during the next few years? How will the Chinese takeover of Hong Kong affect this process?

6. Discuss the prospects for the emergence of democracy in China.

6

Political Movements

Many political movements have been developing in various parts of the world during recent decades that are mostly outside the mainstream of contemporary party politics. There are movements for nationalism and devolution of local nationalities within larger nation-states, for and against greater European unity, for federalism and federalist world government, and for constitutional reform, peace, and human rights. There are feminist movements, several other types of liberation movements, green movements, and a range of religious and spiritual political movements. Grassroots, nongovernmental organisations (NGOs) and other movements are emerging that often address several of these issues together, and there are also many types of social movements.[1]

NATIONALISM AND NATIONALIST MOVEMENTS

Although the older nation-states had been evolving gradually from the late Middle Ages on, newer nationalities and nationalisms began to emerge in the late eighteenth century. The United States declared independence in 1776, and the Latin American countries started to break away from Spain and Portugal in the early nineteenth century. From 1820 to 1920, approximately, a whole range of new European nation-states became independent, and several European countries, especially Germany, showed extreme forms of nationalism that were largely responsible for World Wars I and II. After World War II, many countries in Asia and Africa became independent as a result of liberation from colonial rule, following the emergence of nationalist movements there.

From 1885 on, the Indian National Congress campaigned for the greater

autonomy and eventual independence of India. The Indian nationalist movement became much more extensive and radical from the 1920s, and Mahatma
Gandhi and Jawaharlal Nehru led a series of civil disobedience campaigns
for Indian independence. The All-India Muslim League was founded in 1906
to campaign for specifically Muslim interests in India and, from 1940 on,
campaigned for a separate Muslim state there. In 1948, the UK granted
independence to India, Pakistan, Burma, and Sri Lanka in the Indian subcontinent.

During the same period, there have been new nationalist movements in
Western Europe, proposing new nation-states or devolved subnational governments in regions like Scotland and Wales in the UK, Brittany and Corsica
in France, and Catalonia in Spain. In the Middle East and North Africa, many
nationalist movements, some of them violent, emerged under the influence of
Arab fundamentalism. Violent ethnic and nationalist conflicts have been especially severe and prolonged in the former Yugoslavia[2] and parts of the former
Soviet Union.[3] There are national movements for formerly independent nations
now governed by other countries, for example, Tibet by China. There are also
national movements for national groups whose peoples live in several different
countries, for example, the Basques in Spain and France and the Kurds in
Turkey, Iraq, Iran, and Syria. The extraordinary revival of nationalisms in the
1980s encouraged remarkably many theoretical and comparative studies of
nationalism and descriptions of its manifestations in various parts of the
world.[4] Then several cultural historians and anthropologists interested in
history made powerful contributions to studies of deep nationalist feelings
and passions.[5]

The Fourth World movement[6] represents the interests of small nations,
small communities, and the human spirit and strongly advocates that people
should be governed in relatively small communities on a human scale. It
publishes *Fourth World Review* several times a year and holds occasional international conferences. John Papworth's (1995) book *Small Is Powerful* presents
its outlook well.

PRO-EUROPEAN AND 'EUROSCEPTIC' MOVEMENTS

Movements for a more united Europe arose out of the ashes of World War
II, when many people felt it *imperative* to ensure that an armed conflict between
European nations never again occurred. The European Economic Community, founded in 1957 with six member nations that signed the Treaty of
Rome, extended into the European Community (EC), which now has fifteen
member nations. The Maastricht Treaty, signed in December 1991 and ratified
by member states within two years, set up a framework for a closer European
Union (EU). Several political movements have emerged, cutting across normal
party political boundaries, that have reacted to these European developments
in different ways.

Some pro-European movements mainly emphasise *broader* European unity and the gradual admission of East European nations, including several from the CIS, to the EU, until the whole continent of Europe belongs to the EU. Some of them mainly emphasise *deeper* European unity, political as well as economic, usually aiming for an eventual 'United States of Europe' with a federal structure. Others mainly emphasise the consolidation of the EU, concentrating on ensuring the firmness and stability of the present structure of the EU and reforming and extending it *gradually*.

In contrast, the 'Eurosceptic' movements strive for *less* European unity and *more* national independence, because they fear that the EU in its present form already has excessive bureaucratic powers and has already excessively and unacceptably eroded the national sovereignty of the EU's member states.

FEDERALIST AND WORLD GOVERNMENT MOVEMENTS

The concept of *federalism* was apparently invented in the late eighteenth century by the authors of the American Constitution. The United States was the first country in the world that had a truly federal government. Federalist movements, advocating the federal union of various groupings of states, including the federal government of all countries in the world by a federal world state, emerged from the early twentieth century on. From the 1920s on, H. G. Wells developed his ideas for a functional type of world governance[7] and for an 'Open Conspiracy'[8] of intelligent, thinking people worldwide.

Contemporary movements for world government mostly emphasise the federal approach. The organisations that belong to them include the United World Federalists, the Association of World Federalists, the Parliamentary Association for World Government, and the One World Trust. The United Nations movement, with its United Nations Associations and associated bodies in different countries, aims to strengthen and reform the United Nations and its associated institutions, thus, in effect, enhance the functional approach to world governance.

CONSTITUTIONAL REFORM MOVEMENTS

The Czech civil rights movement, Charter 77, chose to fight political repression by publicising how the Czech government violated the provisions of the Czech Constitution. Its members felt that the movement would gain legitimacy at home and abroad by expressing their criticisms in constitutional terms.[9]

Charter 88 is the principal British constitutional reform movement, whose charter was signed by thousands of leading people and others from all walks of life and publicised widely in the national press. It campaigned vigorously for a written Constitution and a Bill of Rights for the UK. Its discussions and activities stimulated strong interest in constitutional reform in the UK in the Liberal Democrat Party and then in the Labour Party.

PEACE MOVEMENTS[10]

The roots of peace movements are to be found in expressions of pacifism and conscientious objection, which began in the nineteenth century. The early peace movements convened a great series of International Peace Conferences at The Hague from the 1890s onwards, The Women's International League for Peace and Freedom, founded in 1915, tried to end World War I. By the end of World War II, artists, writers, academics, and politicians were ready to explore a vision of a worldwide culture of peace, and UNESCO was created against this background in 1946.[11] From the 1950s on, the modern peace movement first concentrated on nuclear disarmament but later extended its concerns to include general humanitarian and environmental aims. There are over 1,400 peace groups worldwide, with many millions of supporters. They include the Society of Friends, Women's International League of Peace and Freedom, Nuclear Freeze, the Campaign for Nuclear Disarmament (CND), European Nuclear Disarmament (END), Women's Action for Nuclear Disarmament, and groups of various professional people working for peace, such as the Pugwash movement among scientists. In 1987, the Global Challenges Network was set up as part of a World Peace Initiative, which was envisaged as eventually having a similar scale to that of the U.S. 'Star Wars' Strategic Defense Initiative (SDI).[12]

In his statement "An Agenda for Peace" and in a statement on 10 September 1994 to the forty-seventh Annual Conference of NGOs, the former UN secretary-general Boutros Boutros-Ghali[13] stated that organising the UN for peace would demand the concerted attention and effort of the whole UN system, nation-states, regional organisations, and NGOs. Indeed, NGOs will need to be involved at every stage and will play an especially important part in drawing the attention of governments to impending conflicts and emerging crises, because of their familiarity with the situation on the ground.

Nonviolence movements, including those led by Mahatma Gandhi and Martin Luther King, have effectively used a variety of peaceful techniques, including marches, sit-ins, strikes, and civil disobedience.

HUMAN RIGHTS MOVEMENTS[14]

Amnesty International[15] is a movement trying to help, support, and liberate 'prisoners of conscience' who are held in captivity by a wide variety of governments in all parts of the world. It aims to release prisoners of conscience, work for fair and prompt trials of all political prisoners, and oppose the imposition of the death penalty, torture, or other cruel or inhumane treatment on *any* prisoner.

The Human Rights Information and Documentation Systems, International (HURIDOCS), is a global network in which several hundred human rights organisations participate.[16] It aims to improve access to, and dissemination of, information on all types of human rights. Many groups worldwide are working for women's rights, because women are especially underprivileged and oppressed in many parts of the world.[17] Many more groups are working for children's rights.[18] Survival International is a worldwide movement to support tribal peoples.[19] Seventh Generation Fund (SGF) was created by North American Indian community activists to provide direct funding and technical assistance to their local communities.[20]

Liberty is the principal organisation in the UK for human rights in general and held an important international conference in London in 1997. Many other countries also have human rights movements.

An international movement for human responsibilities is also beginning to emerge. As a result of the recent call by the InterAction Council for a Universal Declaration of Human Responsibilities, a high-level expert group presented its conclusions and recommendations about such a declaration at a meeting in Vienna on 20–22 April 1997. On the evening of 7 November 1997, a meeting convened by the One World Trust at the House of Commons, London, presented a preliminary draft of such a declaration.[21] The principles of the draft declaration include truly humane treatment of every person, non-violence and respect for life, justice, and solidarity, truthfulness and tolerance, mutual respect, and partnership.

FEMINIST MOVEMENTS[22]

Feminist movements have aimed primarily to end men's systematic domination of women and eliminate inequality between the two genders. Individual feminists began to make their views known in the late eighteenth century, and the concept of a modern women's movement began to emerge in the nineteenth century. Late nineteenth-century and early twentieth-century women's movements focused mainly on education; political rights, including voting; legal rights, including property rights; and women's special needs, including those of motherhood. Different types of feminist movements have included the following. (1) There have been various types of politically oriented feminists, including liberal, radical, socialist, Marxist, and anarchist feminists. (2) Women's liberation movements first appeared in the 1960s. (3) Women's movements in the Third World emerged even later and have played an important part in local grassroots movements there. (4) Women's rights movements have already been mentioned in this chapter. (5) Ecofeminist movements are beginning to emerge that pursue green aims as well as feminist aims. In their book *Ecofeminism*, the internationally respected feminists and environmental activists Maria Mies and Vandana Shiva (1993) construct their own ecofeminist epistemology and methodology. Describing the work of movements such as the Chipko Women in India and the Seikatsu Club in Japan, they show the potential of grassroots and ecofeminist movements, especially in the Third World, that advocate consumer liberation, subsistence production, sustainability, and regeneration. Nelson and Choudhury (1994) analyse women's political participation and political goals worldwide and consider how women should mobilise for change.

LIBERATION MOVEMENTS

Many movements work for various specific types of 'liberation'; they are often associated with different forms of 'liberation ideologies' (see Chapter 10). Feminist and women's liberation movements are discussed in the previous section.

The gay liberation movement and ideology emerged in the mid-twentieth century and began to be significant from 1969 on.[23] The International Lesbian and Gay Association (ILGA) was founded in 1978, aims to exchange information and coordinate action, and has helped to produce many reforms. Gay liberationists aim to repeal discriminatory laws against gays, gain opportunities previously denied to gays, and overcome mistaken beliefs about, and attitudes to, gay people.

'Black liberation'[24] aims to end the racism that oppresses black people. In the United States, it had two approaches. (1) The Civil Rights movement,[25] with a basically liberal outlook, emerged in the Deep South in the mid-1950s, was for a time led by Martin Luther King, until his tragic assassination in 1968, and became one of the most important freedom struggles in the twentieth century. It was noted for its use of nonviolent methods. (2) The black liberationist variant attempts to remove insidious forms of racism that are liable to affect and damage the minds of coloured people themselves. It gave rise to the 'black power' and 'black pride' movements in the United States in the late 1960s and 1970s. The African National Congress has been a significant black liberation movement in South Africa, where its leader Nelson Mandela is now president.

Animal liberationists[26] tend to be more militant than other liberationists and more willing to take personal and political risks for their beliefs. Although they aim to liberate animals, they present their ideology to people. Specifically, they address their appeals to people who oppress or abuse animals, benefit from animal oppression to some extent, and do little or nothing to prevent further oppression of animals. They also oppose 'speciesism', the belief that humans are superior to animals and thus entitled to exploit them.

GREEN MOVEMENTS

Conservation movements began in North America in the mid-nineteenth century. Environmental concerns beyond the conservation of nature led to the green movements of the 1970s. The Stockholm Conference of 1972 was the first international conference on the environment. Green consumerism began to have an important effect on large companies and other businesses in the 1980s. Green approaches to business began to emerge in the 1980s as part of a wider movement for new forms of ethical business; they are discussed in the subsection Business and Management Paradigms in Chapter 10. Green business clubs began to be formed in the 1990s.

Green political movements and parties[27] began to be formed in the 1970s. The most successful of them, the German Greens, was the first to obtain seats in a national parliament and in October 1998 negotiated with the Social Democrats to become a partner in Germany's new coalition government. Other European green movements, including the Green Party in the UK, have had much less electoral success but have nevertheless strongly influenced some 'mainstream' political parties to take environmental issues more seriously and include some green ideas in their political platforms. It is possible that a green socialist movement could emerge in the UK.[28] North American green movements range from the long-established Sierra Club, which lobbies actively for laws to protect the natural environment, to the militant Earth First! movement, which advocates 'ecotage' (ecological sabotage). There are various Third World green movements active at the grassroots level, together with various environmental NGOs in most parts of the world.[29] There are also international environmental movements, like Greenpeace and Friends of the Earth, that are mainly concerned in spreading awareness about specific green issues and taking effective action on them.

At least in the United States, strong opposition to the environmental movement has also emerged.[30]

RELIGIOUS MOVEMENTS[31]

There is a very wide range of politically active religious movements. The Arab fundamentalists strongly influence various nationalist movements in Arab and other Middle East countries, often in rather fanatical ways. Christian fundamentalists are especially strong in the United States, where they influence certain forms of right-wing politics. Christian Democrats[32] have been an important, moderate, somewhat right-of-centre political grouping on the continent of Europe. Christian socialists have had some influence in the UK especially.

Liberation theology[33] emerged as a radical political approach in the 1960s. It was developed by progressive Roman Catholics in Latin America especially and aims to call attention to the plight of the poor and promote the economic and social rights of underprivileged people in the Third World. It endeavours to inspire people, including the poor themselves, to do something effective to help end their poverty. It calls for political, even revolutionary action on behalf of the poor.

SPIRITUAL MOVEMENTS

Several spiritual political movements are becoming important today. World Goodwill is a globally oriented humanitarian movement[34] promoted by followers of the spiritual teachings of Alice Bailey. One of its offshoots is *The New Humanity* journal,[35] which is the platform of 'pneumatocracy', which aims to apply spirituality to politics. Some *New Age* movements have important influences on politics, though not always in the same political direction. Especially important examples are the movements influenced by the New Age spiritual communities at Findhorn, Scotland,[36] and at Shutesbury, Massachusetts (Sirius Community). The *creation spirituality* movement, as developed by Matthew Fox and others, emphasises God Immanent and the need for practical applications of spirituality, just as New Age movements usually do. Its members work to empower individuals, support human rights, and honour the sacredness of planet Earth. *Green spirituality* extends the main concepts and concerns of more altruistic parts of the green movement by linking them with ethical values and spirituality. Its advocates include the well-known green thinker Jonathon Porritt. Some of the modern ethical business movements are spiritually based and often also use green ideas.

NOTES

1. Ekins (1992) provides much useful information about movements, organisations, and individuals involved in policy and action at the grassroots level. The areas where they work include peace and security, human rights, economic development, the environment, and human development. Bryant and Bailey (1997: 174–183) and Korten (1996: ch. 3) also give some examples of grassroots movements. Willetts (1995) discusses the already extensive influence of grassroots organisations in the United Nations system. Button (1995) is an extensive guide to radical movements and leading individuals involved in them. Giddens (1997: 511–516) briefly discusses social movements in general, including Aberle's (1991) classification of them into four types. Zirakzadeh (1997) is a comparative study of social movements in politics, and Markoff (1996) discusses social movements in relation to political change; see also Bronner (1996: pt. 4). Escobar and Alvarez (1992) survey social movements in Latin America. Andrews and Chapman (1995: pt. 3) discuss democratic movements. Schedler (1997) explores modern 'antipolitical' movements, and Lawson and Merkl (1988) survey a wide range of organisations emerging as alternatives to political parties. Richardson (1993) discusses the role of pressure groups in politics.
2. See Cranna (1994: ch. 7) and the section on the former Yugoslavia in Chapter 5.
3. See the section on conflicts in the CIS in Chapter 5.
4. The many books on nationalism and ethnic politics include Alter (1994), Calhoun (1997), Connor (1993), Dahbour and Ishay (1995), Diamond and Plattner (1994), Gellner (1994, 1997a, and 1997b), Hutchinson and Smith (1994, 1996), Ishiyama and Breuning (1998), Kedourie (1993), Lake and Rothchild (1998), Nairn (1997), Smith (1995), Smith (1998a, b), and Wicker (1997). See also Krieger (1993: 614–619). Petrie (1997) is a reader on the rise of nationalism.

5. See the books cited in Krieger (1993: 614–619). Ignatieff (1993) gives a striking account of his observations of nationalist feeling in various parts of the world, especially of the virulent ethnic hatred that had emerged in parts of Yugoslavia. Ignatieff (1998) explores modern warfare, including ethnic war, and the rise of moral interventionism. Robins and Post (1997) show how nationalist movements, such as Nazism and *some* contemporary movements, can give rise to paranoia and hatred.

6. Fourth World has its headquarters at 24 Abercorn Place, London NW8 9XP, England.

7. The most important books on this theme by H. G. Wells are Wells (1954), originally published in 1931, and Wells (1942).

8. See Wells (1928) and its later version Wells (1933). Adamantine Press published a new edition in 1998, edited by Warren Wagar and including his critical introduction.

9. See Krieger (1993: 189–190).

10. See Barnaby (1988: 156–158) and Ekins (1992: ch. 3).

11. See Mayor (1995: 9).

12. See Ekins (1992: ch. 4).

13. See Willetts (1995: app. C).

14. See, for example, Willetts (1995: ch. 6–ch. 8) and Ekins (1992: ch. 4).

15. See Willetts (1995: ch. 6), Ekins (1992: 68–69), and Krieger (1993: 26).

16. See Ekins (1992: 71–73).

17. See Willetts (1995: ch. 6). Ekins (1992: 73–80) describes two particular organisations working for women's rights. Krieger (1993: 782–785) discusses the politics of women's reproductive rights.

18. See Willetts (1995: ch. 8).

19. See Ekins (1992: 81–84).

20. See Ekins (1992: 85–86).

21. See the documentation of these activities and of the draft Declaration prepared by the InterAction Council.

22. See, for example, Goodin and Pettit (1995: 269–271), Ball and Dagger (1995b: 212–217), and Krieger (1993: 297–299).

23. See Ball and Dagger (1995b: 217–219) and Krieger (1993: 333–335).

24. See Ball and Dagger (1995b: 209–212).

25. See Krieger (1993: 140–143).

26. See Ball and Dagger (1995b: 224–227).

27. Dobson (1995) includes an explanation of the aims and strategies of green movements; see also Garner (1995: ch. 4). Bramwell (1989) gives a history of the green movement during the twentieth century. McCormick (1995b) discusses the global environmental movement from 1945 on. Bramwell (1994) and Pearce (1990) discuss later developments from about 1970 on. Porritt and Winner (1988) examine how green thinking, including that of green movements, began to influence all aspects of Western society during the 1980s. Rüdig (1990, 1992, 1995) and Doherty and de Geus (1996) survey green movements in relation to politics worldwide. Krieger (1993: 365–366) discusses green parties. Jacobs (1996) discusses the new politics of the environment that is now emerging. Merchant (1995) discusses women's roles in environmental movements.

28. Red-Green Study Group (1995) summarises the ongoing discussion of this theme up to 1995.

29. See Bryant and Bailey (1997: ch. 6), Willetts (1995: ch. 5), Ekins (1992: ch. 7), and Ghai and Vivian (1995).

30. See Switzer (1996) and Rowell (1996).

31. Reference is made to various religious movements with an influence on politics in Krieger (1993: 778–782).

32. See Krieger (1993: 136–137).

33. See Ball and Dagger (1995b: 219–224) and Krieger (1993: 542–544).

34. World Goodwill has premises at (1) 120 Wall Street, 24th Floor, New York, NY 10005; (2) Suite 54, 3 Whitehall Court, London, SW1A 2EF, England; and (3) 1 Rue de Varembé, (3e), Case Postale, 1211 Geneva 20, Switzerland.

35. *The New Humanity* is obtainable by subscription from Johan Quanier, 51A York Mansions, Prince of Wales Drive, London SW11 4BP.

36. See Riddell (1990).

SOME TOPICS FOR FURTHER INVESTIGATION

1. Describe any political movement or group in which you are involved or that you otherwise know that is in any of the categories described in this chapter. What relation, if any, does it have to other movements or groups mentioned here?

2. How effectively and in what ways have political movements, of the types considered in this chapter, influenced local opinion and lifestyles in the area or local community where you live?

3. If you have formed a new political movement or group or are actively considering forming or becoming involved in one, how does it relate to the types of movements and groups described in this chapter?

II

POLITICAL PARADIGMS

7

Forms of Government

This chapter surveys those paradigms that are concerned with different forms of government, ranging from the most restrictive to the most liberating. Forms of government reflect partly the requirement to keep under control the potentially conflicting activities of more or less individualist citizens and partly the motivations for expression of power by members of governments and other political players. They range from the totalitarian form, which tries to control the lives of citizens very extensively, through dictatorships and authoritarian regimes, to the wide variety of more or less democratic regimes, which attempt to provide at least moderate scope for the expression of individual freedoms. However, even the most democratic forms of government require the exercise of civic duties and responsibilities as well as freedoms. Important lessons can be learned from totalitarian, dictatorial, and authoritarian regimes to help achieve more democratic regimes or protect existing democracies, whose freedoms need to be guarded with 'eternal vigilance'.[1]

TOTALITARIANISM

'Totalitarian' and 'totalitarianism' describe regimes, ideologies, political parties, and leaders that aim for the total transformation and control of a nation-state or society or at least of everything actually or potentially significant there.[2] Somewhat paradoxically, 'totalitarianism' can also be defined as 'participatory despotism', a tyranny that is applied on behalf of all citizens and with their active participation, whether voluntary or coerced.[3] The term was originally used in the early twentieth century, mainly in association with the fascist and communist ideologies, which had strong totalitarian strands. Its intention was to provide a contrast with earlier dictatorships and authoritarian regimes that only rarely attempted to exercise such complete control over the lives of their subjects.

Totalitarianism has not been restricted to fascist and communist regimes, nor did it first appear in the twentieth century. In practice, among various fascist regimes, the Nazi regime was most totalitarian, and the Franco regime was much less totalitarian, with Mussolini's fascist Italy somewhere in between. Soviet communism was most totalitarian under Stalin's very dictatorial rule. There have also been several examples of totalitarian rule by military dictatorships in various parts of the world and by some Middle East dictatorships, such as that of Saddam Hussein in Iraq.

Totalitarian approaches to governance are quite different from other forms of dictatorship and from authoritarianism in two respects. They advocate a much more thorough and total control by government over many or most aspects of people's lives, and they usually arise as natural parts of certain specific ideologies. Totalitarian regimes are usually strongly nationalist, always place the requirements of the 'state' first, far ahead of individual needs, and attempt to control more or less completely most aspects of the lives and thoughts of their subject peoples. They tend to use ideological themes to try to unite their citizens against real or imaginary 'common enemies', partly because their founders may promise to change the world according to some utopian ideal.

Friedrich (1965) lists five factors characterising the totalitarian concept of the nation-state:

1. an official ideology, focused on a perfect, eventual utopia, to which everyone is required to conform
2. a single mass party usually subordinate to one leader
3. a technologically advanced, almost complete monopoly of military weapons by the regime's party and bureaucracy
4. a similar, almost complete monopoly of mass communications media
5. a system of physical or psychological control by terror.

Shapiro (1972) argues that the presence of one dominant leader is most characteristic of a totalitarian regime, although it is also strongly supported by its political ideology and party. He suggests that totalitarianism is not a fixed model of government but has a spectrum, with various degrees of totality.

DICTATORSHIP

I would like to suggest, more generally, that this subspectrum is the beginning of a wider spectrum of 'dictatorship', a type of regime where a single leader, perhaps in collaboration with a small 'cabinet' of colleagues, makes at least almost all the decisions about government policies and actions. The most extreme and restrictive dictatorships are totalitarian, but there are also 'milder' forms of dictatorship, which have much less than total control over the lives of their subjects. These, in turn, merge into 'authoritarian' regimes, which still impose control from the 'top' but where the 'top' consists of one group of people, an 'oligarchy', or may even consist of several groups. The distinction between dictatorial and authoritarian regimes tends to be blurred and is, indeed, not made at all by some political scientists. However, I use it in this chapter.

Arguments for and against dictatorship, whether as a permanent regime or as a temporary form of emergency government, need to be understood well, to achieve better understanding and protection of democracy itself. They are presented later in this section.

Different Types of Dictatorship

Most of the larger ancient civilisations were ruled by empires, which were ruled, more or less absolutely, by emperors or kings. However, the concept of 'dictator', as opposed to emperor or king, arose originally in ancient Rome as a national leader who was *temporarily* given unrestricted powers to resolve an emergency situation faced by the Roman Republic.[4] In the late first century B.C., the Roman Republic collapsed and was replaced by the Roman Empire. In the ancient world, 'tyrant' was used to denote a ruler who *deliberately* sought to impose absolute power.

In the Middle Ages, most of Europe was divided into kingdoms, each of which had a king or other more or less absolute monarch. Some, but by no means all, of these monarchies were dictatorships. Many were oligarchies or other forms of authoritarian regime. After the Middle Ages, fewer and fewer European monarchies were dictatorships. From 1796 to 1815, Napoleon was dictator of France and emperor of much of Europe.

In the twentieth century, the first modern dictatorship was the Soviet communist regime of the USSR, set up by Lenin in 1917 and made more totalitarian by his successor, Stalin. In 1922, Mussolini took power in Italy, with a semitotalitarian fascist regime, and, in 1933, Hitler's Nazi regime became the German government after a general election in which it won more seats than any other party but very rapidly became totalitarian. There have been many other subsequent dictatorships during the twentieth century. Some were communist, like the Soviet 'satellite' regimes in Eastern Europe from 1944 on, the Chinese communist regime, and a few other dictatorships. In most, but not all, cases, the communist regimes gradually became less totalitarian and eventually became authoritarian rather than dictatorial, before revolutions led to their ultimate overthrow. Since the rise of fascism, most of the other dictatorships were military dictatorships, only some of which were similar to fascism, which were widespread in Latin America for several decades but also appeared in Africa, the Middle East, and Southeast Asia.

Arguments for Dictatorship

The empires and kingdoms of ancient civilisations were implicitly accepted by their subjects as being 'just there'. In the Middle Ages, European monarchies tended to be justified by the 'divine right of kings' to rule absolutely. The original argument for dictatorship in ancient Rome was that a temporary dictatorship was needed to avoid the breakdown of society. Other arguments for dictatorship have been that it is decisive, that it is efficient and 'gets things done', and that a good dictatorship could provide the best regime. The latter argument tends to become more widespread when democracies show signs of not working very well and where many citizens begin to fear that they will never be able to provide sufficient quality of life. During the 1930s, a remarkable number of people in the UK and United States, for example, referred to the regimes of Mussolini, Hitler, and Stalin in surprisingly favourable terms. This was before the real horrors of those regimes become really widely known. However, it *is* true that there were occasionally some remarkably enlightened regimes among the emperors of the ancient world.

Arguments against Dictatorship

The arguments against dictatorship are, on the whole, stronger than those for it. It is well known that absolute power corrupts,[5] that dictatorship often, if not usually, destroys human rights, and that dictatorial regimes are usually bureaucratic and inefficient. Above all, most dictatorships are or have been bad regimes, and the most appalling regimes are or have been dictatorships. As Sir Winston Churchill once said, contemporary democracy is a bad system, but its alternatives are much worse.[6]

AUTHORITARIANISM

In the ancient world and Middle Ages and during the subsequent gradual transition to modern democracy, authoritarian ideologies, advocating rule by 'oligarchies' or *groups* of people on power at the top, were generally closely associated with the prevailing traditional philosophies of life of those times, which generally assumed that the 'status quo' was static or at least relatively static and that every person had his or her appointed place in society. From time to time, there were also dictatorial tyrannies, motivated mainly by lust for power, without explicit associated ideologies.

Plato's *Republic* was the first known attempt to formulate an authoritarian political philosophy and paradigm, and Plato was one of several ancient Greek thinkers who had considerable misgivings about the course taken by Athenian democracy. The concepts of 'tyranny by the majority' and 'elective dictatorship' have been introduced by defenders of democracy who wish to warn that it may nevertheless degenerate into less than democratic forms of

governance. Insofar as authoritarian regimes have had ideologies, these ideologies have tended either to be traditional, status quo approaches to governance that have been parts of wider traditional social paradigms, worldviews,
and philosophies of life or to be reactionary ideologies that advocate a return
to more traditional approaches and philosophies.

Plato's Republic

In his Socratic dialogue *The Republic*, Plato (c. 400 B.C.) introduced the concept of an 'ideal republic', governed by an elite that was brought up for this
task from birth. Plato was strongly critical of the Athenian democracy of his
time. Plato's *Republic* has been strongly criticised by many people for being too
authoritarian or even as helping to lay the foundations for totalitarianism.
Nevertheless, it has several useful ideas and considerable contemporary relevance for the future of democracy. For example, there is an important sense in
which contemporary democratic regimes should have 'Guardians of the Constitution', and the quality of democratic governance would also be increased if
there were a requirement that every important decision-making body, for
example a cabinet, had sufficient skills, knowledge, and experience among its
members.

Tyranny by the Majority and Elective Dictatorship

The concepts of tyranny by the majority and 'elective dictatorship' are
important. For example, John Stuart Mill and others in the early nineteenth
century expressed concerns that inappropriate majority votes could, in fact,
decrease the amount of democracy. Lord Hailsham[7] was one of those who
expressed concern about 'elective dictatorship' in the 1970s. Elective dictatorship is liable to arise in practice in countries where the same political party is
repeatedly elected in successive general elections and especially in 'first-past-
the-post' electoral systems, where it is all too easy for governments with strong
policies or even extreme policies to be elected by minorities of those entitled to
vote or even by minorities of those actually voting. Thus, policies highly
unacceptable to most citizens can be imposed on them against their will. It
should not be forgotten that Hitler was *voted* into power in the German
general election of 1933, though not by an absolute majority of voters.

DEMOCRACY

Most citizens who think about contemporary politics have some sort of
belief in democracy, and a considerable number of books discuss the theory of
democracy.[8] Most regimes today, whether or not they are actually democratic,
claim that they support some form of democracy. However, they do not all
have the same definitions of democracy, and some regimes alter the usual

definitions of democracy to suit their own purposes and to enhance their propaganda. Therefore, this section first presents various definitions of 'democracy' in common use and introduces concepts of 'full democracy' and of 'degree of democracy', a measure of how fully a given regime has achieved democracy in practice.

Although the original forms of democracy in Athens and some other city-states of ancient Greece were *direct*, because they expected the active participation in decision making of all people who were viewed as citizens, it is not practicable to run modern nation-states along these lines, as their populations are much too large. Democratic nations today use various forms of *representative* democracy instead, but this approach introduces further problems, such as how to distribute different powers and functions of government to avoid tyranny and how best to elect representatives. During the latter part of the twentieth century, there have been much public pressure and some actions by various governments to reintroduce some form of directness into governance by consulting citizens and inviting them to express their views on certain issues and by enabling them to participate in various governmental processes if they so wish and to make their representatives more responsive to their ideas, opinions, and needs.

In practice, most nation-states are too large to rule as monolithic units, so that most of them delegate some of their powers to various levels of regional and/or local government. Similarly, many nation-states have important relationships between each other at a continental level, and, through the United Nations, almost all nations have some mutual interactions at the global level. Because of this and because of increasingly complex international and intra-national relationships, the concepts of multilevel government and democracy are becoming important from the global level downwards. They are indicated at the end of this chapter and discussed fully in Chapter 8.

Definitions of Democracy

'Democracy' was originally defined by the ancient Greeks as rule by the people, and most people have defined it in a very similar way ever since. It is often equated with rule by the majority, but that is an oversimplification that can lead to the problems of tyranny by the majority and elective dictatorship. The best definition of democracy that I know is Abraham Lincoln's famous phrase "government of the people, by the people, for the people".[9] Although this definition seems to be widely ignored today, even in books on politics and governance, it does bring out clearly what a true democracy actually needs to do. It needs to govern effectively by being a government *of* the people. As far as possible, it should be government *by* the people, that is, with participation by the people and contributions to decision making by the people, with as much consent as possible by as many of the people as possible. It needs to be government *for* the people, in the sense that it benefits as many of the people as possible and minimises the harm done to people by its decisions, policies, and actions. It needs to balance conflicting interests among the people as fairly as possible. The main forms of democracy include direct democracy (where every citizen is entitled to participate in a decision-making assembly and vote on every issue), 'votocracy' (with exceptionally heavy reliance on people's votes), representative democracy, political democracy, economic democracy, liberal democracy, social democracy, and people's democracy. 'People's democracy' is a phrase that tends to be used by totalitarian and dictatorial regimes to pretend to the world at large and to their own subjects that they are democracies when, in fact, they are not. These different types of democracy are often overlapping, as they express different aspects of democracy.

Degrees of Democracy

It is an observed fact that all democracies rather imperfectly achieve the full objectives implied by Lincoln's definition. If a 'democratic' government is not really stable, it fails to fulfill the aim of government *of* the people. If it is not sufficiently participatory, and if its citizens do not sufficiently meet their responsibilities, it is not truly government *by* the people. If it does not meet as fairly as possible the political, social, economic, and cultural rights and other legitimate interests of its citizens or sufficiently ensure that all its 'players' act responsibly, it is not truly government *for* the people.

It is thus at least theoretically possible to define and measure the 'degree of democracy' of a democratic regime. This can be done by identifying all the characteristics that are important for obtaining a good regime, weighting them according to their relative importance, and measuring what proportion of its potential maximum each characteristic actually achieves. It is especially important to require that the interests of less privileged people are duly addressed, so that the presence of serious injustices to such people would attract large negative scores when calculating the degree of democracy, especially if these injustices persist despite extensive protest, as is liable to happen all too often.

As far as I know, nobody has yet constructed adequate 'degree of democracy' indexes nor attempted to assess degrees of democracy objectively for specific countries, but both these exercises urgently need to be done. Personally, I doubt if more than a few democracies would have indexes above 50%; perhaps Switzerland and the Scandinavian countries would. I would estimate that the United States and the UK both have indexes below 30%. These figures show how very far the degree of democracy still needs to be improved even in nominal 'democracies'.

Representative Democracy

Nation-states need some form of representative democracy, because direct democracy is far too cumbersome for governing communities of more than a few thousand people. Even in small communities, direct democracy requires a high degree of commitment to succeed, and such commitment is relatively unusual in contemporary life. Historically, various forms of representative democracy have emerged where government is coordinated and, to some extent, conducted by politicians who directly or indirectly represent the people. The principles of representative democracy vary somewhat from one nation-state to another but have several common features. In a typical parliamentary system, members of Parliament are elected by voters in given constituencies, which are usually specific geographical localities in the nation-state. In addition, some members of Parliament also represent specific interest groups. In most democracies, they almost always belong to specific political parties.

Approaches to representation range between delegation, where representatives are supposed to follow the known wishes of their constituents, and trusteeship, where representatives use their independent judgment on behalf of their constituents. One of the main functions of the representatives is to formulate and implement policies and legislation on behalf of the citizens of their nation. This can be done by the members of Parliament, in turn, selecting representatives from among them to form a government, led by a prime minister, either from among members of that party that has a majority of members or from a coalition of parties that between them have a majority. Alternatively, if the nation has a presidential system, the nation's citizens vote directly or indirectly for the president of its government.[10]

Representative government needs various checks and balances to ensure, as far as possible, that the elected government and the representatives themselves do not exercise excessive power and depart too far from the wishes of the people. The first principle of such checks and balances is the division of powers between legislative, executive, and judiciary functions.

Electoral and Voting Systems

An electoral system specifies how and on what basis to conduct an election of representatives at some level of government. It includes:

1. specification of which offices are to be elected (whether members of Parliament or holders of specific offices such as president)
2. who is to be entitled to vote
3. the specific voting system, by which votes are to be converted into seats in a Parliament or into holders of specific offices.

Voting systems[11] for parliamentary or local government representatives include *majority representation* systems, where a candidate with a majority of voies is eventually elected, and *proportional representation* (PR) systems, which endeavour to elect numbers of candidates for a party that are approximately proportional to the votes cast for that party. The principal majoritarian systems are:

1. *simple majority* ('first past the post'), where the candidate receiving most votes is elected, whether or not supported by a majority of voters or of those actually voting
2. *absolute majority—alternative vote* ('preferential vote'), where voters, each with one vote, rank candidates, the bottom candidate is eliminated, the votes for that candidate are redistributed according to preferences, and the process is repeated until one candidate has a majority
3. *absolute majority—second ballot*, where the first two candidates face a second vote, if no candidate has a majority on the first ballot.

The principal PR systems are:

1. *list system*, where a vote is cast for a party's list of candidates, but electors can usually also express support for individual candidates on the list
2. *single transferable vote* (STV), a form of proportional representation where voters, each with one vote, rank candidates to elect several members in one constituency in approximate proportion to their support for their parties.

The chief merit of 'first past the post' is that one member of parliament (MP) represents all the citizens in a given local area, the MP's constituency, so that he or she can work more effectively on their behalf and address their problems better by knowing his or her constituency in depth, and the system usually provides stable governments. However, a very serious defect is that governments can be elected that are grossly *un*representative of the people, because the proportions of MPs elected for different parties may differ greatly from the proportions of people who voted for those parties. This system is especially unfair on small parties, which may have *no* MPs representing them, and tends to perpetuate a two-party system, because even the party with third-most votes may receive very few seats. In contrast, in PR systems, the proportion of MPs elected for a party is usually roughly proportional to the national votes received by the party, but the result can be more unstable government. With STV, constituencies tend to be too large, so that they represent citizens less well, but voters are also given a choice of MP whom they can consult. Various attempts have been made to find electoral systems that combine the advantages of both approaches.[12]

Participatory Democracy

Direct democracy has only rarely been practised, although it was used in one the earliest democracies to exist, the city-state of Athens in ancient Greece in the sixth and fifth centuries B.C. Even there, it was only partially democratic, because women and slaves were not given votes. Even in nondirect

democracies, there are several other ways, besides voting and the opportunity
to belong to an assembly, in which citizens can participate in a democracy. The
more opportunities that a citizen has for participating in a democracy, the
more participatory that democracy is. Participatory democracy gives citizens
a better sense of being consulted by their government, recognises that the right
to participate properly is an important human right, even though relatively
few people might choose to take it up seriously, and is an important protection
against the abuse of power by politicians and bureaucrats.

There is considerable scope for democratic dialogue between citizens and
their representatives, ranging from citizens meeting or writing to their constituency MPs about specific issues and grievances, to citizens writing to
members of the government or to leading Opposition politicians about policy
issues of concern to them. At least in the UK, governments and government
departments quite often invite consultation about their proposed policies and
collect considerable amounts of written and spoken evidence from many
interested citizens, which is relevant to consideration of those policies and
possible alternatives. For a local or national community to be truly democratic, it should provide good scope for participation in different areas of life,
not only in politics but also in local community affairs, the conduct and
operation of community services, working life, education, and culture.

Deliberative democracy[13] is an aspect of participatory democracy that
encourages citizens to deliberate publicly on issues that are best understood
through open deliberative processes. Its participants not only put their cases
for promoting their specific interests but also learn to meet each other's needs
and influence each other through reasoned argument, evidence, evaluation,
and reasonable persuasion. They listen to presentations of the main different
approaches to the problems and issues being discussed and to their own viewpoints. The process respects their autonomy and capacity for self-government.
The resulting decisions are often, if not usually, much better and better
informed than they would otherwise be.[14]

Multilevel Democracy

Contemporary governance has become so complex that it is becoming
essential to introduce the concepts of 'levels of government' and of 'multilevel
democracy'. The tasks of governing a nation and, even more, of governing the
human species as a whole need to be subdivided into different groups, with the
tasks in each group being conducted at the appropriate levels. These concepts
are discussed in detail in Chapter 8.

NOTES

1. *Democracy and the Global Order* (Held 1995) shows how the future of democracy is becoming increasingly uncertain. Different sources of social and economic power and dense networks of global and continental connectedness are undermining some key assumptions of democratic thinking and practice. Nation-states and national societies are becoming increasingly limited by international conditions and processes, such as globalisation and the activities and power of multinational and transnational companies. *The Collapse of Democracy* (Moss 1977) shows how democracies can and sometimes do drift into situations where they are confronted with authoritarianism or even dictatorship and totalitarianism. He examines several historical examples of where this happened (Germany between the wars, Czechoslovakia, Portugal, and Chile) and assesses the danger that it could also happen to the UK. Cortada and Cortada (1997) considers whether democracy can survive in Western Europe, and Ostrom (1997) discusses the vulnerability of democracies.

2. This is the definition used by Eugene Kamenka in his article on totalitarianism (Goodin and Pettit 1995: ch. 38).

3. This is the definition favoured by Alfred G. Meyer in his article on totalitarianism (Krieger 1993: 916–917). He also gives examples of totalitarian regimes *before* the twentieth century.

4. See Heywood (1997: 363).

5. Lord Acton said, "Power tends to corrupt, and absolute power corrupts absolutely".

6. Winston Churchill expressed his view that "democracy is the worst form of government except all the other forms that have been tried from time to time" in a speech in the House of Commons in 1947 (Heywood 1997: 65).

7. This idea was first expressed in Lord Hailsham's (1976) famous Richard Dimbleby Lecture *Elective Dictatorship*.

8. *Models of Democracy* (Held 1996) provides a wide-ranging survey of the historical development and present state of democratic theory and its many varieties. It explores the context, nature, and limits of each major development in democratic theory. *Prospects for Democracy* (Held 1993) provides a comprehensive overview of current debates about democracy worldwide. *Democracy and the Global Order* (Held 1995) assesses traditional conceptions of democracy, discusses the rise and displacement of the modern nation-state, explores the theoretical bases of democracy and democratic states, and advocates a 'cosmopolitan' model of democracy for a new world order. See also *New Forms of Democracy* (Held and Pollitt 1986) and Held's article about democracy (Krieger 1993: 220–224). *The Terms of Democracy* (Saward 1998) offers a single integrated theory of democracy. Other examples of books on democracy are given in the section on Democracy in the Annotated Bibliography. Guttman's article (Goodin and Pettit 1995: ch. 19) gives a good outline of different forms of democracy.

9. President Abraham Lincoln made this remarkable statement in his Gettysburg Address of 1863. In his Foreword to Jenkins (1998), Frederick Forsyth interprets it as meaning that power belongs to all of the people and that their governments should exercise it to maximise their security, prosperity, freedom, and contentment.

10. Lijphart (ed.) (1992) compares and contrasts the parliamentary and presidential forms of democratic government. Bogdanor (1985) discusses how representative of the people parliamentary government is in various Western democracies.

11. Books on electoral politics and electoral systems include *Democracy and Elections* (Katz 1997), *Comparing Electoral Systems* (Farrell 1996), *Principles of Electoral Reform* (Dummett 1997), Kavanagh (1992, 1995), and Bogdanor and Butler (1983). Hain (1986) and Bogdanor (1981) discuss electoral systems in the British context. Lijphart (1995) presents a study of the electoral systems and party systems in twenty-seven democracies from 1945 to 1990.

12. Chapman (1997a, c, d) has explored several possibilities for fairer new electoral systems. In 'Territorial PR', the existing single-member constituencies are retained, but a candidate is allowed to stand in any cluster of adjacent constituencies; this enables small parties to have a few elected MPs, each of whom is an MP for a cluster, and also gives voters a choice of representative. 'Preference-Score Representation' (PSR) gives the three main parties a strong incentive to converge towards moderate centre positions. In 'Consensus PR', the election of MPs of many different parties is avoided by providing incentives for 'allied' parties to merge. Chapman (1997b) discusses the role of suitably reformed electoral systems in the resolution of ethnic conflict, for example, in Northern Ireland. Hain (1986) assesses the arguments for and against PR and suggests radical electoral and other reforms that would make the British political system more representative and participatory.

13. Deliberative democracy is discussed in detail in *Democracy and Deliberation* (Fishkin 1993), *The Voice of the People* (Fishkin 1997), and *Deliberative Democracy* (Bohman and Rehg 1998) and briefly by Gutmann (Goodin and Pettit 1995: 417–420).

14. Books on other aspects of participatory and direct democracy include *Referendums around the World* (Butler and Ranney 1994), *Participation and Democratic Theory* (Pateman 1990), *Putting Power in Its Place* (Plant and Plant 1992), *The New Challenge of Direct Democracy* (Budge 1996), and *Power to the People* (Schaeffer 1997).

SOME TOPICS FOR FURTHER INVESTIGATION

1. Discuss the possibility that democracy could deteriorate or be destroyed in your own country and suggest some positive ways of preventing this from happening.

2. Choose an example of a totalitarian regime or other dictatorship and find out what citizens' rights it violated but also what rights it maintained. Analyse how far it operated with the consent of its subjects (especially what sections of the population) and how far it had to oppress them (especially what sections). Examine also how far it had effective control over people's lives, activities, and thoughts.

3. Answer a similar question for an authoritarian, but nondictatorial, regime of your choice, from present or past history.

4. If you live in a democratic nation-state, answer a similar question for that state to disclose how far democratic practice falls short of democratic ideals.

5. Compare your answers to questions 2 to 4 to find out what interesting patterns, if any, emerge.

6. Discuss how well the political system of the country in which you live represents the interests and viewpoints of different groups of people in the country. Which groups are well, moderately well, and badly represented?

7. Discuss the problems that are liable to arise with typical systems of constitutional 'checks and balances' operating in democracies toady. For example, how are nonelected civil servants and judges, who belong to the executive and judiciary, respectively, made accountable to the people?

8. Discuss which electoral systems you would favour for the different types of elections in which you can vote in the country in which you live. Explain the reasons for your choices and discuss their advantages and disadvantages.

9. Discuss specific ways in which you would like to see the regime in your country become more participatory. How would they improve your own opportunities for democratic participation and the extent to which you *actually* participate politically.

10. Attempt to design an approximate index for the 'degree of democracy' of a regime and estimate roughly what it is for your own country.

8

Levels of Government

Because of the size and complexity of many nation-states, and because of the increasingly intricate nature of the interactions between them, it has also become more and more important during the twentieth century to devise and implement various forms of 'multilevel government'. The principles of 'subsidiarity', 'devolution', and 'federation' play a decisive part here. The principle of subsidiarity[1] states that public functions and services should be provided at the lowest practical level of government. In addition, there need to be appropriate communication and feedback between the different levels of government. It is best expressed in federal nation-states or federations.

A federation is typically divided into states or regions, each with its own democratic government, which is ideally responsible for aspects of government that are specific to that state or region and best carried out at that level. The national government of a federation performs functions, such as foreign policy, defence, and national finance and budgeting, that are most appropriately performed at the national level, but it devolves many other functions to states or regions. The state government or regional government should in turn devolve more local functions to various forms of local government, including urban councils and (largely rural) county councils and district councils. Ideally, there should be an effective level of neighbourhood government below local government that would provide a range of services and functions for the citizens of small local communities, such as villages and urban housing estates. There are already good working examples of federal nation-states, but concepts of federation also need to be built from the nation-state upwards.

Working upwards from the nation-state, it is possible to have supranational federations. The European Union (EU), which has evolved gradually from the

European Community (EC), has the potential of becoming such a federation. In its present form, the EU at least nominally adopts the principle of subsidiarity, though it is doubtful how far it applies in practice. The EU is not yet a federation, although many, but by no means all, European politicians and citizens would like to see it evolve into one; however, it is by no means clear how many of them know the true meaning of 'federalism'.

For many decades, there have been advocates of world federal government, although opinions about its practicality in the near future diverge. Nevertheless, it is not impossible that a world federation could eventually evolve by building on current structures such as the organisations of the United Nations (UN) and of continental groupings of which the EU is the most advanced example. The UN has taken important additional steps towards 'international functional cooperation' but needs much improvement, as well as more merging of its concepts with those of federalism. Various concepts of 'planetary management' have been formulated, but they need to be extended and applied in ways consistent with the development of global democracy.

NATIONAL GOVERNMENT[2]

The whole of the inhabited area of the Earth's surface is now subdivided into about 200 independent nation-states. Yet the concept of the 'nation-state' is relatively recent and originated only a few centuries ago. Two hundred years ago, there were fewer than twenty countries recognisable as nation-states by today's criteria, and the rest of the world was divided between a few empires, many very small principalities and city-states, and large areas of tribal communities without fixed boundaries. The government of a nation-state has authority over all people living within its borders. Concepts arising in connection with a nation-state include 'nationalism', 'national identity', 'national integration', and 'national government'. Many of the problems of national government arise because nation-states are inhabited not by homogeneous masses of people but by many communities and groupings of people that have arisen historically through social, ethnic, cultural, special interest, political, economic, and commercial forces.

Approaches to national government adopted by different nation-states include:

1. *centralised*, where there is a very strong central government of the nation-state supported by a large central bureaucracy, which devolves relatively little power to more local organs of government

2. *decentralised*, where the national government is mainly a coordinating body, devolving much, if not most, of its power to more local organs of government

3. *federalist*, a special form of more or less decentralised government, where there is a well-defined structure of more local organs of government and their interactions with central and other levels of government

4. *nationalist*, which allows more or less explicitly for the nationalist feelings of different groupings of people living in the nation-state.

It is a fact of modern life that nation-states are more and more becoming subject to pressures from levels above and below their own. This is especially true of the larger nation-states, so much so that there is now quite a strong 'Fourth World' political movement, which is campaigning vigorously for smaller nation-states and limits to the maximum sizes of nation-states and other units of government and administration. See, for example, the books by Papworth (1995) and Kohr (1974) and the magazine *Fourth World Review*, edited by Papworth. The rest of this chapter discusses some ways in which nation-states can address these pressures from above and below.

SUBSIDIARITY AND DEVOLUTION

In its original form, the 'principle of subsidiarity' states that, inside an overall framework of multilevel government, public functions and services should be provided at the lowest practical level of government. In other words, an authority at a given level should perform only tasks that cannot be performed effectively at a lower level. For example, in Germany, the principle has been applied to provide welfare at the lowest practical level. In practice, the principle means that an attempt should be made to make decisions of specific types as close as possible to the level at which they are most effectively implemented. Subsidiarity provides a framework for efficient allocation of responsibilities of multilevel government between all its different levels. However, the version of the principle used in the European Union is rather vague and has various, sometimes conflicting interpretations; it is described in more detail later in this chapter in the section on continental government. For more details see Begg et al. (1993: ch. 3).

'Devolution' means the delegation of power at a given level to at least one lower level. It refers most usually to the delegation by central or national government to bodies of elected representatives at the regional or the local level. The structure and configuration of levels of government inside a nation-state vary considerably from one nation to another.

Usually, especially for larger countries, the first level below national government is regional government, although the regions are given different names in different nations, for example, 'states' in the United States, 'Länder' in Germany, and 'regions' or 'provinces' in some other countries.

The level of government below regional government is usually called 'local government',[3] although the pattern of local government areas may be quite complicated and may even itself have more than one level. Local government areas range from conurbations, through cities and towns, to 'parishes' within urban areas, and may include counties, districts, and 'parishes' within rural areas.

In the UK, the pattern of local government is especially confusing, partly because there is no regional level operating across the country as a whole. There are special regional structures in place in Scotland, Wales, and Northern Ireland, and as yet *no* regional level elsewhere in the UK. Northern Ireland used to have its own elected assembly under the UK government, before civil disorders started there in 1979, and it will again soon have one as a result of the Northern Ireland Peace Settlement of 10 April 1998. Proposals for the devolution of Scotland and Wales under the UK government were extensively discussed in the 1970s, although then rejected, but they later returned to the political agenda (Norton 1994: 227–230; Bogdanor 1979; Drucker & Brown 1980). In 1997, devolution for both these nations of the UK was approved by popular referenda, and preparations are being made for the formation of a Scottish Parliament and a Welsh Assembly in 1999. There used to be a regional government for the conurbation of London as a whole. This was abolished by the UK government under the Thatcher administration, but, on 7 May 1998, the people of London voted by a large majority for its restoration and for having an elected mayor of London, with jurisdiction over the London area.

There is a strong case for the further devolution of local government to a new level of neighbourhood government, which would be based on natural local communities, such as housing estates or large blocks of flats in urban areas and villages in rural areas. Sufficiently large and effective intentional communities, such as the Findhorn Community in Scotland, should also be treated as units of neighbourhood government. The purposes of the neighbourhood level would be to revive a full sense of community in each neighbourhood and to ensure the provision of especially useful local services that could appropriately be provided at that level. Some possibilities in this connection are considered, for example, by Plant and Plant (1992) and Gibson (1984, 1996).

FEDERAL GOVERNMENT[4]

Most nation-states with several tiers of government can be divided into:

1. highly centralised *unitary* systems, such as the UK, with authority concentrated in central government
2. relatively decentralised *federal* systems, where authority is shared fairly evenly between national and lower levels
3. very decentralised *confederal* systems, where the central government has little authority.

In its modern form, the concept of federalism was developed by the authors of the U.S. Constitution just over 200 years ago. Under the U.S. Constitution, each American citizen is a citizen of the national government of the United States and also of his or her local U.S. state at the regional level.

At any one time, only a minority of the world's nation-states have been federations, although they have included some of the most important countries in the world. There are less than 20 federal nation-states today. They can be grouped as follows:

1. the United States itself, where federalism originated[5]
2. Latin American federal states, such as Argentina, Brazil, Mexico, and Venezuela, whose form of federalism is influenced by the American model
3. federal dominions in the British Commonwealth, including Canada,[6] Australia,[7] India, and Malaysia, and, formerly, several African countries
4. European federal nation-states: Austria, Germany, and Switzerland, together with an evolving federation in Belgium[8]
5. federations in former countries that had communist regimes: the USSR, Yugoslavia, and Czechoslovakia.

In a functioning federal system, the nation-state has several governments at the regional level in addition to its national government. It has a written constitution that specifies the responsibilities, functions, and roles of the national and regional governments and the rights of citizenship at each level of government. The central government is generally responsible for foreign affairs, defence, immigration, and some domestic functions such as national budget, currency, and interest rates. Regional governments have quite a wide range for domestic functions, though they may share some of them with the central government. A federal country also has a constitutional court, such as the Supreme Court of the United States, whose functions include arbitration of disputes between governments at different levels by referring to the Constitution. In addition, a federation has a bicameral assembly, one of whose chambers contains elected national representatives, while the other chamber has elected regional representatives. Each region is also largely governed by its own elected assembly.

Federalism basically aims to reconcile unity with diversity. For example, many nations have adopted it as a way to balance the interests of different ethnic and linguistic groups.[9]

There have been several debates about federalism among political scientists (Krieger 1993: 296–297). One school of thought stresses its amorphous nature and its operational complexity. Some members of this school consider that it 'inevitably' progresses towards centralised unitary government. A second school emphasises the distinctive role of regional governments in federal systems, with their powers, relative to those of central government, perhaps sometimes increasing and then decreasing in cycles.

CONTINENTAL GOVERNMENT

Fairly early in the twentieth century, shortly after World War I, people began to think of various possibilities for supranational government, to remove the possibility of terrible and devastating wars between nation-states that were sometimes already too strong and were becoming even more powerful. This movement of thought became even stronger after World War II. Most advocates of supranational government viewed it in terms of federations of nation-states. Such federations would be set up either at the continental level or at the global level. The latter possibility is considered in the next section. In the former case, a continent, such as Europe, is set up as a federation, with a continental government at the continental level and national governments at the level below, that of the nation-state.

Very soon after World War II, the European Community (EC) began to evolve, very strongly motivated by a concern to end war between European nation-states. In practice, it developed among 'West European' democracies only, because most countries of Eastern Europe were in the communist bloc and effectively controlled by the Soviet Union.

In 1957, the Treaty of Rome established the European Economic Community (EEC) with six member nations and formed the constitutional basis for mutual cooperation between the member nations of the EC, into which the EEC later evolved. The Treaty established the European Commission, the Council of Ministers, and the European Parliament as decision-making bodies at the EC level and also set up a European Court of Justice to interpret EC law. However, it was *not* a federation of its member states.

In 1992, the New Treaty of European Union (Maastricht Treaty), which came into effect on 1 January 1993, began to transform the EC (which by now had twelve member nations) into the European Union (EU).[10] Although it reflected the EC's wish to expand the scope of economic and monetary union and establish a framework for a common defence and foreign policy, and although it attempted to set up a framework for closer political union, it still did not set up a European federation.

Indeed, it is doubtful whether West European public opinion would yet support a federation. Despite the many politicians who strongly advocate a 'federal' Europe, many other politicians equally strongly oppose it, and many people who already genuinely concerned that existing institutions in the EU have already excessively eroded the national sovereignty of their countries and threaten to do so even more.

One part of the problem is that many people have insufficient knowledge of what 'federalism' means. Another part is the lack of a true federal structure within the EU. There is *no* European federal government that is *directly* elected by the citizens of the EU and *directly accountable* to them. The relationships between the EU and its member nations are also much less tidy and well formulated than they would be in a genuine federation of nations. Nor have the structures of the Council of Europe, which was established in 1949, been properly integrated with those of the EU. An additional difficulty is that few of the EU member nations are themselves federations; the best-developed federation among them is the Federal Republic of Germany.

Ideally, a federation of nations should have a federal structure running through *all* its levels of government, and it should also generally apply the principle of subsidiarity. At least in theory, this principle is supposed to be used in the EU to make and implement decisions at lower levels wherever possible, but it is very doubtful how far this is true in practice.

The version of the principle of subsidiarity, that was introduced for the EU in the Treaty of Maastricht in 1992 is *not* an overall recommendation to decentralise but only a presumption in favour of decentralisation that operates in the *absence* of a clear case for centralisation. It is thus an incomplete guide to decisions about the exact level where power should be exercised within the EU, which depends very much on the specific areas and situations for decision making. By laying the burden of proof on centralisers, the principle of subsidiarity in the EU recognises the initial sovereignty of member states in the EU and acknowledges that excessive centralisation brings loss of accountability. It implies that certain categories of power should be decentralised wherever possible, thus exercised at a lower level of government by more local jurisdictions, unless convincing reasons can be found to assign them to higher, more central levels.

The onus of proof is placed on the advocates of centralisation. The relevant powers are:

1. levying taxes
2. undertaking expenditure on providing public funds and resources
3. regulating the behaviour of private sector agents.

In the Treaty of Maastricht, the principle of subsidiarity applies only to matters not within the EU's exclusive competence and only if the objectives of the proposed action cannot be achieved sufficiently by member states or better at the European level. This position represents a compromise between the different views about subsidiarity held by the governments of different member states.

There is much talk of a 'Europe of the Regions', with a few commentators even suggesting that 'regions' might increasingly take over the role of member states. However, by no means do all West European nationalities, which do not themselves have their own nation-states, yet feel adequately represented at the regional level inside the EU. The eventual integration of Eastern Europe and possibly also at least a large part of the CIS is another issue that must be faced in relation to a possible European Federation.

Despite all its problems and deficiencies, the European Union nevertheless is by far the most advanced structure of attempted continental government

that has yet been formed.[11] Indeed, no other paradigms of continental government, other than the present EU paradigm and the continental federation
paradigm, seem to have been formulated yet. There are no other continental
groupings of nation-states as yet that in any sense constitute the embryo of a
continental government. There are several groupings of national governments
at a less formal level than in Europe that represent the nation-states of the
continents of Africa and Latin America. The United States, Canada, and
Mexico have set up a North American Free Trade Agreement (NAFTA), but
there is no attempt to set up a governmental structure for this area. The British
Commonwealth is an informal grouping of mutually cooperating nations,
consisting almost entirely of nation-states from the area of the former British
Empire, but again no supranational framework of governance is envisaged,
nor does the Commonwealth cover any specific continental area. It is not yet
clear how any continental federations could emerge outside Europe or, indeed,
whether they will be formed, even in Europe.

WORLD GOVERNANCE AND WORLD GOVERNMENT[12]

The concepts of world governance can be subdivided broadly into those
of world government[13] and those of effective mutual cooperation between
'independent' nation-states.[14] Theoretically, it might seem that the strong
arguments for government by a nation-state, originally formulated by Thomas
Hobbes and John Locke, should also apply at a global level. If the inhabitants
of a country mutually agree to be ruled by a government of a nation-state
established in their country, why should not the governments of the nation-
states of Planet Earth or the people of the world similarly mutually agree to be
ruled by a world government? At first sight, they would receive similar
benefits. The situation is, in fact, much more complicated than this!

In the world of the twentieth century, there have already been many
appalling tyrannies, especially among totalitarian nation-states, and modern
technology has provided progressively more terrible and deadly weapons
systems and methods of political oppression. Thus, many people consider that
the advantages of living in a contemporary nation-state are all too easily
outweighed by its disadvantages. Most people are similarly terrified of the
prospects of a world government that could all too easily become a totalitarian world tyranny.

For reasons like this, the only form of direct world government that could
even begin to seem tolerable would be a federal world government. Serious
advocates of world government today are mostly, if not entirely, advocates of
federalism at the global level. There was considerable interest in federal world
government in the late 1940s, just after World War II, and several good books
were written about it then, but the idea never gained general acceptance.
However, several associations were formed to promote world unification, each
advocating different approaches. Most progress was made by the World

Constitution and Parliament Association (WPCA), which drafted an agreement in 1958 to call a World Constituent Assembly and circulated it worldwide, with invitations to national governments and peoples to send delegates. The fourth and latest session of its World Constituent Assembly was held in 1991. In 1977, the WPCA prepared *Constitution for the Federation of Earth*, whose text is included as an Appendix to Harris (1993), which also discusses its principles and content.

This Constitution specifies in detail a federation providing for a world government at the global level, acting above nation-states operating at the national level. It provides no continental level of government, presumably because of the absence of effective continental institutions in all continents of the world other than Europe. However, it does provide for twenty world electoral and administrative regions, grouped into at least five continental divisions.

Its proposed organs of world government are:

1. the World Parliament
2. the World Executive
3. the World Administration
4. the Integrative Complex
5. the World Judiciary
6. the Enforcement System
7. the World Ombudsmus, in effect providing a global system of ombudsmen.

The World Parliament would contain three chambers:

1. the House of Peoples
2. the House of Nations
3. the House of Counsellors.

The authorities and powers of the world government would be limited to "problems and affairs transcending national boundaries", while national governments would retain jurisdiction over their internal affairs, consistent with the world government's authority to protect universal human rights as defined in its Constitution.

The WPCA and its Constitution both address the question of how to set up the world government through a gradual process. Whether or not the world government in this form or any other similar form is ever actually established depends on the decisions of the national and international politicians to whom this proposal is put, as well as on the decisions of various citizens worldwide. A possible weakness of the proposal is that it seems to provide no method of transition between existing United Nations and European Union institutions and the proposed eventual structure of world government.

However, the WPCA Constitution does contain many useful ideas that should be taken into account when considering appropriate forms of global governance for the future.

THE UNITED NATIONS (UN)[15]

The United Nations (UN), set up in 1945, provides an alternative approach to international relations that depends on extensive voluntary cooperation between the nations of the world. It fairly recently celebrated its fiftieth anniversary, and this has been the occasion for extensive reassessments of its achievements and shortcomings. Its 'Parliament' is the UN General Assembly, which has one delegate for each nation-state that belongs to the UN; almost every country is now a member of the UN. The UN also has a Secretariat, headed by the UN secretary-general, a Security Council, sixteen specialised agencies, and many other closely associated intergovernmental organisations. The UN has a mixed record in attempting to handle the many wars and other conflicts and crises since 1945; Parsons (1995) discusses UN interventions from 1947 to 1995. However, its peacekeeping operations have not been entirely without success, although they could also have been very much more effective. The UN specialised agencies and the UN's international conferences on many different subjects of global concern have had many important achievements, though they could also have done much better. Despite its weaknesses, including a continual shortage of funds, the UN has become the first genuinely global international organisation that brings almost all countries together under a single set of principles, those of the UN Charter.

Challenges to the United Nations (Childers 1995) is an outspoken, but carefully documented, challenge to people who despair about the UN. It defends the UN's achievements, explains its failures, and presents a feasible agenda for UN reform. It discusses the UN's record with respect to:

1. economic and social responsibilities
2. human rights and humanitarian challenges
3. peace and security
4. a 'United People's' approach, which addresses the questions of collaboration between the UN and NGOs and of public participation in the UN.

Perhaps the greatest problem that the UN faces is that national governments too often do not enable the UN to work effectively and take far too little action against the root causes of global problems.

In particular, national governments should ensure that the UN is equipped with a Rapid Response Force, instantly available to the secretary-general. Far more vigilance and resolution is required to ensure that decision makers behave according to the high moral principles of the UN Charter. There should be determined pressure on the 'citadels of economic power' to collaborate with the UN system, equip it with adequate resources for macroeconomic policy formulation, and overhaul its machinery. Only thus can the problems of world poverty be solved. There should be a UN Parliamentary Assembly, whose directly elected representatives could monitor and assist national governments' contributions to international affairs. It is now vital to proceed with the gigantic enterprise of building a democratic United Nations that will make the world safe, just, and sustainable for all its people.

In his book *The Birth of a Global Civilization*, Robert Muller (1991), who was a former assistant secretary-general of the UN and is now Chancellor of the University for Peace, makes various proposals for a new political system for planet Earth. He outlines four approaches to achieve this goal:

1. extending and strengthening the European Community
2. a dramatic reform and strengthening of the United Nations and its specialised and associated agencies
3. the creation as soon as practicable of a federal world government, which could be called the United States of the World or the United Nation of the World
4. the appointment of a committee of the most eminent and original thinkers of the world to propose and consider new ideas for the governance and good management of planet Earth.

All these approaches should be be pursued simultaneously, to enable all possibilities to be explored, and help the world to enter an entirely new civilisation and world order, instead of continuing in its present wasteful, costly, and bloody chaos.

Our Global Neighbourhood presents the findings of the 1995 Report of the Commission on Global Governance (1995). The Commission is an independent group of twenty-eight leaders with varied experience and responsibilities whose members were set the task of suggesting ways in which the global human community could better manage its affairs into the tweny-first century. Their report projects a strong, people-centred world vision and emphasises the need for shared values, a global civic ethic, and progressive and well-informed leadership to guide people and nations worldwide.

It explores the challenges facing humanity and offers carefully considered proposals to:

1. promote the security of people and the Earth
2. manage the global economy
3. reform the United Nations
4. strengthen the rule of law worldwide.

It suggests an important additional process through which the world community could consider its proposals and other similar recommendations: the

UN General Assembly should agree to hold a carefully prepared World Conference on Governance in 1998, with its decisions to be ratified and put into effect by the year 2000.

Baratta (1987: ch. 4) has an extensive bibliography of earlier proposals for reforming the UN, including proposals of limited world government.

INTERNATIONAL FUNCTIONAL COOPERATION

'International functional cooperation' is another approach that is committed to building peace in relatively small, but useful, steps performing very specific practical tasks of international importance. However, it can be viewed as complementary to the federal approach, not only as an alternative to it. It began as early as the nineteenth century with the formation of the Rhine River Commission in 1804 and the Danube River Commission in 1857. The first examples of 'global functional cooperation' were the formation of the Red Cross in 1862, the International Telegraphic Union in 1865, and the International Postal Union in 1874. Between World War I and World War II, the League of Nations established the International Labour Organisation and the Committee on Intellectual Cooperation. The former still exists, and the latter was replaced by UNESCO in 1948. The transnational organisations implementing this approach emphasise the sharing of sovereignty instead of its surrender. Advocates of the functional approach see technical and professional experts, not politicians and diplomats, as the best people to achieve effective international collaboration.

It is significant that H. G. Wells, as one of the first people who openly proposed some form of world government, supported the functional approach to it. For example, in *The Work, Wealth and Happiness of Mankind* (Wells 1931b [1954]), he spoke favourably of these and other, then existing forms of global international functional cooperation, and also introduced concepts of 'functional economic planning' at the global level. He saw no hope for recovery of the great economic depression of the early 1930s except through cosmopolitan action, and he hoped that the Bank for International Settlements of the 1930s might develop into one such agency. He also considered that an International Conservation Board was urgently needed to protect against the waste of natural resources and the extinction of many species of wildlife.

After World War II, global functional cooperation formed an integral part of the approach of the newly formed United Nations, which implemented it through its specialised and associated agencies. As already mentioned, it has been only partially successful in this respect, and there is great scope for its improvement and reform. Kegley and Wittkopf (1997, pp. 508–509) briefly discuss some possible variants of functionalism and criticise them on the ground that functionalism ignores several important political realities. They then (509–510) outline and assess 'neofunctionalism', a 1950s reconstruction of functionalism that attempted to address directly the political factors that dominate the process of merging formerly independent states.

PLANETARY MANAGEMENT[16]

One of the most helpful approaches to the study of organisations and their management and performance is the 'systems approach', in which organisations are seen as open systems with a greater interaction between their members. 'Dynamic systems modelling', which is discussed in Sections 10.4 and 16.1 of *Into the 21st Century* (Burrows et al. 1991), can be used to 'prepare the ground' before policies are formulated in an integrated way. The process of integrated policy formulation, using such a systems approach, is outlined on pp. 187–191. In his book *Platform for Change*, Stafford Beer (1994) presents in detail the principles and practice of 'cybernetic management', which can be applied at the level of government. The new culture of 'business networking', that is emerging in the business community, in terms of social and environmental issues, could transform the present harsh climate of global capitalism and help the Third World to become integrated with the developed world. It will also be an essential facility for the systems models and cybernetic systems that will be used for planetary management in the future. A good example of such a combined approach is now being developed by the Royal Society of Arts (RSA) working group on *The Company as a Living System*, of which I am a member.

Although at least a large part of the conceptual basis for planetary management has now been indicated, its implementation is the most challenging task in human history. The key factors have been described well in *The Gaia Atlas of Planet Management* (Norman Myers 1994), which is an important pioneering contribution to the solution of this huge problem. A complementary approach is 'ekistics', the science of human settlement developed by Doxiadis (1968, 1977), based on the development of a grid system of all the factors in the human settlement and its surrounding environment. This process can be performed in great detail in a very structured way. Although this approach is challenging and difficult, it can provide much of the information needed to develop a planetary management system.

To study how a planetary management system is to be funded, it is necessary to examine wealth creation in the private sector, but this must be complemented by appropriate public sector activities. For example, extra revenue from environmental taxes like a carbon tax could be levied according to how far businesses damage the environment and then applied to environmental protection and the conduct of 'green audits'. Green audits will not only reduce the harm being done to the environment but result in more efficient management, contribute to wealth creation, and provide a basis for a philosophy of planetary management. Governments still do not sufficiently realise that planetary management needs funds, to which especially extensive contributions should be made by the wealthiest industrial countries and companies, both because they can easily afford to pay and because they contribute most to pollution and other environmental problems.

The Commission on Global Governance (1995) made far-reaching proposals for managing global economic interdependence, especially the establishment of an Economic Security Council (ESC) within the UN. The ESC would provide leadership and promote consensus on international economic issues, and on balanced, sustainable development, while endeavouring to obtain consistency in the policy goals of multilateral economic institutions. The IMF, the World Bank, and the World Trade Organization should be invited to report regularly to the ESC, while the Commission on Sustainable Development and some other institutions should report to it on specific matters.

Various options for financing planetary management should be explored, including

1. an international tax on foreign currency transactions
2. an international corporate tax base for multinational companies
3. charges for the use of common global resources, such as: flight lines for aircraft, sea-lanes for ships, ocean fishing areas, and the electromagnetic spectrum.

The September 1989 Special Issue of the *Scientific American*, entitled *Managing Planet Earth*, makes important contributions of ideas and proposals that will help to develop an overall global management system. However, much more research needs to be done to explore in depth the linkages between all the different aspects and problems of managing planet Earth. It will not be easy to achieve an appropriate planetary management system because of the fragmented structure and built-in inertia within existing national and international governmental organisations and policy-making bodies and within national and multinational companies.

It will also be necessary to address the legitimate feelings of many people that they do not want their lives run by any overriding world authority. It is essential to be clear that the introduction of an appropriate planetary management system will not interfere with people's lives beyond the minimum of environmental taxation and regulation that will be necessary and that such a system will provide the basic infrastructure needed to enable people to achieve and maintain a satisfactory quality of life.

NOTES

1. The book by Begg et al. (1993) discusses the principle of subsidiarity with special reference to its application in Europe. Devolution is discussed in detail by Bogdanor (1979) and Drucker and Brown (1980). Bradbury and Mawson (1997) and, more briefly, Norton (1994: 224–230) make special reference to devolution within the UK especially to Scotland and Wales.

2. For an especially extended discussion of the evolutionary and revolutionary changes in the nature of the nation-state, see Part 2 of *Comparative Government and Politics* (Hague et al. 1998). Chapter 3 of this book considers liberal democratic, communist, and postcommunist nation-states, together with the politics of economics. Chapter 4 considers revolutions and other political changes in nation-states, with special reference to ideologies. Chapter 5 discusses the increasing interdependence between nation-states.

3. See Keen and Scase (1998) and King and Stokes (1996).

4. Books on federal government and federalism include Elazar (1987) and Wheare (1963). Katz and Tarr (1995) discuss federalism in relation to rights. For briefer discussions, see, for example, the article on federalism in Krieger (1993: 296–297). Knop (1995) explores issues of citizens, markets, and governance in the light of federal ideas and experience, especially in the United States. Harris (1993) gives extensive details of how federalism might operate in relation to world government especially. Lister (1996) discusses the possibility of reviving voluntary, confederal associations between nations as a means of improving prospects for world peace.

5. For experience of federalism in the United States, see Anton (1989), Vile (1973), and also Mathews (1976).

6. For experience in Canada, see Vile (1973) and also Mathews (1976).

7. For experience in Australia, see Vile (1973) and Mathews (1976).

8. For experience in Belgium, see Fitzmaurice (1996).

9. Smith (1995) examines federalism's successes and failures as a method of managing ethnic conflict.

10. Duff et al. (1994) and Church and Phinnemore (1994) discuss the Maastricht Treaty and subsequent developments and their implications. Armstrong et al. (1996) consider successive stages of European Union up to and including the Maastricht Treaty.

11. Key issues of European government are discussed, for example, by Baum (1995), Begg et al. (1993), Colomer (1996), Kourvetaris and Moschonas (1996), and McCormick (1995a). See also Archer and Butler (1996), Bainbridge and Teasdale (1998), Close (1994), and Pinder (1995).

12. For a general discussion of global politics and its future, see the book *World Politics* by Charles W. Kegley, Jr. and Eugene R. Wittkopf (1997), especially Part V "Toward the Twenty-First Century".

13. For discussions of world government, especially federal world government, see, for example, the book by Errol Harris (1993) and the periodical *World Federalist*. Zolo (1997) provides a critique of the idea of 'global government'. Baratta (1987) is an extensive bibliography of earlier literature on possibilities for world federation.

14. For other approaches to global governance, emphasising especially the reform and further development of the United Nations system to include more direct participation by the people of the world, see, for example, *Our Global Neighbourhood*, a report by the Commission on Global Governance (1995) and its summary (Ramphal 1994).

15. Proposals for reforming the UN include Childers (1994) and its summary (Childers 1993), Childers with Urquhart (1994), Muller (1991), Taylor et al. (1997), and De Marco and Bartolo (1996). White (1996) examines the functions and powers of intergovernmental organisations (IGO), including those of the UN. Schacter and Joyner (1995) explains and appraises the relationship between the UN and the international legal order.

16. Planetary management is discussed in more detail in Chapter 20, "Planetary Management", of *Into the 21st Century* (Burrows et al. 1991). For a fuller survey, see the September 1989 Special Issue of the *Scientific American, Managing Planet Earth*. Beer (1994) presents a scientific approach that can be applied to planetary management. Doxiadis (1968, 1977) presents the fundamental concepts of ekistics.

SOME TOPICS FOR FURTHER INVESTIGATION

1. How far is it desirable and feasible for nation-states to try to resist or reduce the tendency for them to lose their independence under the influence of global economic forces? For example, should they do this by trying to reduce their dependence on international trade? How far can they be proactive despite such forces?

2. Discuss what functions could appropriately be used by government at the neighbourhood level. How could such a neighbourhood government most easily evolve in the locality where you live?

3. Describe how you would like to see multilevel government develop within the nation-state where you live. What is the most likely way in which your vision for it could be achieved?

4. Formulate the arguments for and against the evolution of the European Union towards a European federation or United States of Europe. If such a federation were to evolve eventually, how would its pattern of multilevel government differ from the present pattern of the EU? What lessons can be learned from the process by which the United States was transformed from a confederation to a federation in the years up to 1788?

5. What prospects are there for the emergence of genuine government at the continental or subcontinental level outside Europe, for example, in North America, Latin America, Africa, and Southeast Asia?

6. What are the prospects for a democratically reformed United Nations to evolve into a form of world federal government that would also have strong organs of functional government?

7. Outline what forms of planetary management should be adopted in addition to government institutions at all levels from global down to neighbourhood. How far could the democratic nature of the whole framework of planetary management be ensured?

8. Outline a possible plan, with budgets, for financing the implementation and operation of a planetary management system, including its organs of government at all its different levels.

9

Political Ideologies

This chapter presents the ideologies that are used in a wide variety of political discussions by politicians or members of the general public interested in, or concerned with, political problems and issues. It first introduces various definitions of the concepts of 'ideology' and 'ideologies' and discusses the nature and classification of ideologies. It then outlines several types of social attitudes that people can hold. After that, it discusses a 'main spectrum of political ideologies', running very roughly from right to left: nationalism, the 'far Right', conservatism, liberalism, social democracy, democratic socialism, the 'far Left', and anarchism. It finally considers the wide range of 'alternative' political ideologies, which have been emerging during recent decades and can be grouped broadly into nonviolence ideologies, liberation ideologies such as feminism, and green ideologies.

THE NATURE OF POLITICAL IDEOLOGIES[1]

A typical ideology has many variants and usually several distinctive schools of thought. The boundaries between different ideologies tend not to be hard and fast, and ideologies often overlap, in the sense that adherents of different ideologies can sometimes have very similar combinations of political viewpoints.

The word 'ideology' was invented by the French scholar Antoine Destutt de Tracy, who attempted to found a systematic scientific study of the sources and origins of ideas in the 1790s and early 1800s. He also claimed that this science could be used to reform and improve society, by enabling false ideas to be identified and removed, so that people could be taught the right kind of ideas to lead to a rational and happy society. Not surprisingly, the Roman Catholic

Church, the nobility, and some powerful political figures attacked ideology and 'ideologues' as dangerous. Although Napoleon at first supported ideology, he then, when he needed the support of the church and the nobility, attacked it as a mask to cover subversive political plans and ideas. Marx continued to use the term 'ideology' in this latter sense and came to use it to refer to a set or system of ideas to justify and legitimate the rule of a dominant class in society. Since then, 'ideology' has remained a pejorative term to many, if not most, people.

In *Ideology and Utopia*, Karl Mannheim (1936) distinguished between the 'particular conception' of ideology to refer to the ideas of particular groups of people whom 'we' oppose, and the 'total conception' of ideology to refer to the characteristic ways of thinking of a whole class or society or historical period. In this latter sense, Mannheim extended the meaning of 'ideology' to something like a system of beliefs about the social world, a social worldview, or a social paradigm. Although this latter definition has not yet been very widely adopted, it is similar to the one that I use in this book.

Ball and Dagger (1995b) use a more precise definition of 'ideology', whereby it performs explanatory, evaluative, orientative, and programmatic functions for its adherents; it also includes, implicitly, a set of basic beliefs about human nature and a conception of freedom. According to this approach, political 'ideologies' perform these functions, because they attempt to link ideas and beliefs to action. Each of them provides a picture of the social and political world as it is, and a vision of what it should be. An ideology is thus not a scientific theory, as it is also normative by having ideas about how people should live. It should be noted that, on this definition, 'democracy' is an idea, not an ideology, because it does not offer any explanations. However, most ideologies advocate various forms of democracy, at least in principle. Goodwin (1997), Morrice (1996), and Needler (1996) discuss ideology in relation to political thought.

Vincent (1995) also has a fairly complicated definition of 'ideologies', which expresses several of their functions and aspects. To sum up this definition, they claim both to *describe* and to *prescribe* for humans.

Eatwell's definition of 'ideology' (Eatwell and Wright 1993: ch. 1) is also complex but not dissimilar; in addition, ideologies are considered to be essentially the product of collective thought.

Walford (1979), building on the thought of Harold Walsby in the 1930s and 1940s, defines an 'ideology' as "a system of assumptions", where the assumptions may or may not be explicit; very often, the assumptions are held subconsciously but nevertheless decisively influence the behaviour of those who hold the ideology. On this view of ideology, which Walford calls 'systematic ideology', Walford views ideologies as being more than systems of ideas, worldviews, or paradigms; they are also associated with specific attitudes and patterns of behaviour, and their scope extends beyond political parties and movements into all our social activities.

Systematic ideology claims to explain the broad patterns of support for different political views that are actually observed. After 1945, Walsby and Walford used it to develop their classification of ideologies according to their perception of the main groupings of assumptions held by most people. Walford (1979) distinguishes six main ideologies, in order of decreasing proportion of supporters:

1. 'nonpolitical' or *protostatic*, displaying the ethos of expediency, adapting their conduct to the circumstances, and accepting society
2. 'conservative' or *epistatic*, displaying the ethos of principle, patriotic, loyal to the political status quo, responsible
3. 'liberal' or *parastatic*, displaying the ethos of precision, seeking exact specification and implementation of principles, wishing to improve society without basic changes
4. 'socialist' or *protodynamic*, displaying the ethos of reform, seeking the peaceful achievement of a different society
5. 'communist' or *epidynamic*, displaying the ethos of revolution, seeking the replacement of society by a new social order
6. 'anarchist' or *paradynamic*, displaying the ethos of repudiation, seeking the elimination of authority and coercion in society.

The first three ideologies, said to be held by the vast majority of people, are *eidostatic*; the other three, held by only a minority, are *eidodynamic*. The commitment to economic-material freedom decreases from strong for the first ideology to weak for the sixth. The commitment to political-intellectual freedom increases from weak for the first ideology to strong for the sixth. Beyond the six ideologies is a seventh, *metadynamic*, ideology, the 'ideology of systematic ideology' itself, which accepts all seven major ideological groups as functional constituents of a developed society, so that all of them have important parts to play. Whereas each of the first six ideologies identifies positively with some assumptions and negatively with others, the seventh, *metadynamics*, takes no assumptions for granted, questions all assumptions, and studies all assumptions in relation to each other. The seven ideologies are held by progressively smaller groups of people, so that the proportion of people holding the first ideology is highest, and the proportion holding the seventh is lowest.

This classification is, on the whole, similar to the 'main spectrum' of political ideologies discussed in this chapter, which consists of:

1. nationalism
2. the 'far Right'
3. conservatism
4. liberalism
5. communitarianism
6. social democracy

7. democratic socialism
8. the 'far Left'
9. anarchism.

Nationalism and the 'far Right' are both variants of the protostatic ideology, but in most countries most people with protostatic assumptions are 'non-political', so that, according to some definitions of ideology, they hold no ideological position at all! Conservatism is clearly epistatic, and liberalism and communitarianism are clearly parastatic. Social democracy has a position somewhere between the parastatic and the protodynamic and can be closely allied to either position. Democratic socialism is clearly protodynamic, the far Left is clearly epidynamic, and anarchism is clearly paradynamic.

SOCIAL ATTITUDES

Sample surveys during the late 1980s have revealed major shifts in the patterns of attitudes held by different categories of the population (McNulty 1989; Kinsman 1990). The surveys were carried out in several countries by the Taylor Nelson Group Ltd./Applied Futures Ltd., using questionnaires and in-depth interviews.

As a result of the surveys, people can be classified into three major groups:

1. *Sustenance-Driven*, whose prime concerns are the needs for a secure daily life and belonging to a supportive group
2. *Outer-Directed*, whose main motivation is the search for esteem and status and who are concerned by what other people think of them
3. *Inner-Directed*, who are basically self-actualised people and are largely unconcerned by how other people view them.

These groups are based on values and motivations, and they cut across the usual boundaries of class and income level. Further analysis reveals that, in the UK at that time, there were seven subgroups:

A. *Self-explorers* (15%), motivated by self-expression and self-actualisation, socially concerned but nondoctrinaire
B. *Social resisters* (14%), motivated by fairness, including carers, political idealists, and single-issue campaigners
C. *Experimentalists* (11%), keen to try out new experiences, highly individualistic
D. *Conspicuous consumers* (22%), striving to succeed and be seen as successful
E. *Belongers* (17%), conservative, conventional, pragmatic, devoted to the family
F. *Survivors* (15%), hardworking, class-conscious, strong community spirit
G. *Aimless* (6%), either old and apathetic or young, after short-term pleasure and liable to show mindless violence.

The inner-directed (36%) consist of A, B, and part of C; the outer-directed (35%) consist of D and parts of C and E; the sustenance-driven (29%) consist of F, G, and part of E. The percentage figures are those observed in the UK in 1987.

It is interesting to compare and contrast systematic ideology with the study of social attitudes. In contrast to systematic ideology's view that the proportions of adherents to different ideologies change only slowly, the attitude surveys of the 1980s point clearly to fairly rapid changes in the proportions of the three major attitude groups and the seven subgroups, with a marked shift towards more inner-directed people. Both approaches are needed to understand fully the shifting patterns of political support; further empirical research is needed to find out how accurate they are.

THE 'MAIN SPECTRUM' OF POLITICAL IDEOLOGIES

Deeper analysis shows that this is a considerable, if not gross, over-simplification, and a second approximation, which is attempted later in this chapter, reveals a much more complex picture.

Nationalism[2]

Although there have been nations in some form for several millennia, nationalism as an ideology has arisen only during the last 200 years or so, but it has been very widespread throughout the twentieth century. Its driving force is the sense of belonging to, and serving, a perceived national community. Nationalists attribute to their nation a distinctive cultural identity, which sets it apart from other nations, usually making it 'superior' to other nations and giving it a special role in history. The more moderate forms of nationalism, in the form of 'love of one's country' or patriotism, can make positive contributions to the political stability and social cohesion of a democratic nation-state. However, nationalism as a modern political ideology is too easily liable to take extreme forms, where it becomes too intense and becomes vulnerable to exploitation by demagogues or state oligarchies. Extreme nationalism is liable to 'legitimate' hatred of foreigners (xenophobia) or ethnic discrimination (racism) and leads to military aggression against neighbouring nations. Many authoritarian and totalitarian regimes have built up and used extreme nationalism to make their own nations more powerful and united and then more prepared to follow the regimes' own purposes. Both liberal and illiberal nationalist theories have emerged, and nationalism also has a very important dimension as a sociopolitical myth. Several new nation-states appeared just after World War I, and the former colonies achieved national independence in the decades after World War II. Since the end of the Cold War around

1990, nationalism has achieved a new lease of life, with the breakup of the former Soviet Union and the liberation of Eastern Europe from communist domination. There have been extreme manifestations of nationalism in parts of the Middle East, partly under the influence of Islamic fundamentalism, and also in the former Yugoslavia.

Many ethnic minorities and subnationalities of existing nation-states are expressing their nationalist feelings more strongly in many parts of the world. They include:

1. the Kurds, who should have been given a nation-state in the Treaty of Versailles (1919) but whose territory was divided between Turkey, Iraq, and Iran
2. the Basques, whose territory is shared by Spain and France
3. Scotland, which was independent of England until the Act of Union of 1707, when it was effectively 'merged'
4. Wales, which was a collection of Celtic principalities until its conquest by England in the Middle Ages.

The 'Far Right'[3]

Until the end of World War I, the 'far Right' included authoritarian and reactionary regimes whose ideologies were based mainly on the traditional cultures in their nation-states. Later in the twentieth century, authoritarian regimes, as opposed to totalitarian states, had little formal ideology. Such ideological principles as there were included:

1. the right of those in power to govern and not to be displaced by elections
2. the lack of freedom for citizens to create their own political parties or other groups and organisations to compete for power or question the rulers' decisions.

In contrast, totalitarian regimes have almost always had strong, sometimes fanatical, though not always well-defined, ideologies, and fuel, and are fueled by, strong nationalist feelings. On the 'far Right', the most important totalitarian ideologies have been fascism and Nazism. All forms of these ideologies attempt to win mass support by appealing to people in the simplest and most emotional language. 'Fascism' originally referred to the political system by which Mussolini ruled Italy from 1992 to 1943. It has since then been widely applied to a variety of other right-wing totalitarian and authoritarian regimes, including Franco's Spain and several Latin American dictatorships. In his version of fascism, Mussolini not only appealed strongly to the nationalist feelings of Italians but also claimed to synthesise 'still vital' elements from the 'ruins' of liberal, socialist, and democratic doctrines. His regime adopted a corporatist approach to economics and an imperialist approach to foreign policy. Under Hitler, Nazism was not only strongly nationalist, imperialist, and militarist but also especially characterised by its vicious brand of racism, which upheld the supremacy of white 'Aryans' and first attacked, then tried to exterminate all Jews. Curiously enough, the Nazi approach to nature and the environment in some ways foreshadowed the ideas of later 'green' ideologies. Although the many variants of contemporary neofascism often either look back with nostalgia to fascist Italy and Nazi Germany or deny that they committed their worst atrocities, they are ideologically rather different in some respects, and there is perhaps no hard-and-fast line between them and 'far Right' viewpoints such as those of Le Pen's Front National in France.

Conservatism[4]

Although all 'conservatives' wish to conserve or preserve some important features of their social environment, usually the traditional way of life of their societies, they do not all wish to conserve the same things. This makes 'conservatism' difficult to define, because there are many different forms of conservatism. Conservatives tend to resist change and to be especially pessimistic about the ability to change human nature for the better. In the eighteenth century, early or classical conservatism was largely attempting to preserve or restore a traditional aristocratic society from liberalism or from the French Revolution. It naturally evolved into traditional conservatism, which attempts to conserve what its followers consider to be the best features of contemporary society. The distinctive form of conservatism developed by Edmund Burke in the late eighteenth century had an organic conception of society, where individuals are viewed as interdependent members of a living social organism. The social organism of a nation should be a partnership between all its individuals, not only between those at present living but also between them and past and future generations. Burke favoured representative government but not yet democracy in the full sense; he advocated 'natural aristocracy'. Enlightened representatives from the aristocracy should defend private property and the common good. However, power should also be spread throughout society, so that the 'little platoons', the ordinary people, should also have their share of power and empowerment. This version of ideology evolved into what was later called 'one-nation conservatism' or Tory democracy, which also gave considerable support to various parts of the welfare state. A totally different form of conservatism, individual conservatism or capitalist conservatism, arose out of classical liberalism in both the United States and the UK, and favoured a more or less 'laissez-faire' market economy. This form of conservative ideology dominated the Reagan administrations in the United States from 1980 to 1988 and also the Thatcher governments in the UK from 1979 to 1990; it still has a very strong influence on conservative politics in both the United States and the UK. Although it tends to minimise the role of the state in economic and business affairs, it upholds strong national government in various other areas of life; the Thatcher governments were remarkably authoritarian and centralist in several respects, for example, in the ways in which they imposed the very unpopular Poll Tax, and interfered with democratically elected local authorities and severely cut back their powers and finances.

In the United States, two other forms of conservatism have also emerged:

1. neo-classical conservatism, which is, in several respects, intermediate between one-nation conservatism and individual conservatism
2. the 'religious Right', which is largely supported by Christian fundamentalists.

Liberalism[5]

The earliest forms of 'liberalism', like all its later forms, attempt to promote 'liberty', although there is much disagreement between liberals about how to define 'liberty' and how best to promote it. Liberalism traditionally views individuals as typically rational, self-interested, and competitive and also believes that everyone should have equal opportunity, an equal chance to succeed within a tolerant society. The Declaration of Independence, declared in 1776 just before the foundation of the United States, was based on traditional liberalism by claiming that "all men are created equal" and by defending the rights and liberties of individuals against government. It was followed by the U.S. Constitution, which was drafted in 1787, ratified in 1788, implemented in 1789, and amended on various later occasions. Liberal ideas also played an important part in the French Revolution, from 1789 on. Other important strands of thought were introduced into liberalism by the 'utilitarianism' of Jeremy Bentham, based on the principle of utility that everyone should do whatever will produce the greatest happiness of the greatest number, and by the concern of John Stuart Mill, who was also a utilitarian, to extend individual liberty, including women's rights. He strongly supported representative democracy on the grounds that it would make the government more responsive to the wishes of the people, but he was also very concerned to avoid 'elective dictatorship' and the tyranny of the majority. In the early nineteenth century, all liberals supported 'laissez-faire liberalism' and capitalism, which was developing rapidly as a result of the Industrial Revolution. This variant of liberalism developed into neo-classical liberalism, which argued that government should be as small as possible to provide full scope for the exercise of individual freedom. The more extreme neo-classical liberals advocated social Darwinism, whereby the 'survival of the fittest' should apply to social and economic life as well as to wildlife. A later variant of neo-classical liberalism is libertarianism, which supports an exceptional degree of individual freedom, indeed, so much that it advocates minimal interference by the state, even where the freedom of different individuals clashes severely. From the mid-nineteenth century on, another strand of liberalism split off from 'laissez-faire' liberalism, which began to argue that the government should rescue people from the worst forms of poverty, ignorance, and illness, which had become widespread through the effects of the Industrial Revolution. This gradually developed into welfare liberalism, which progressively evolved more and more of the concepts of the modern welfare state and eventually advocated considerable public expenditure and other government intervention to support the welfare state. John Rawls (1973) and Derek Phillips (1986), as political philosophers, made important contributions to theories of social justice and a just social order, which could help to guide welfare liberalism. Some variants of welfare liberalism, especially in the UK, also devote much attention to the development of local communities and local, grassroots politics.

Communitarianism[6]

During the 1980s, 'communitarianism' arose as a school of thought in political philosophy that gives community, or fraternity, a role comparable to that of liberty and equality. Communitarians believe that liberal theories of justice and the public culture of liberal societies do not sufficiently recognise the value of community in society. Although Marxists also recognise the value of community, they view it as achievable only through revolution. In contrast, communitarians believe that community already exists, as common social practices, community spirit, shared social understandings, and cultural traditions, and they see it as needing respect and protection, rather than needing to be built afresh.

They agree that traditional liberal principles of justice and rights need to be modified but have different views on how to do this. Here, Kymlicka in Goodin and Pettit (1995: ch. 15) distinguishes three strands of communitarian thought, the beliefs that:

1. principles of community replace principles of justice
2. community should be seen as the source of principles of justice
3. community should influence the principles of justice more, with justice giving more weight to the 'common good' and less to individual rights.

The best-known presentations of communitarianism are *The Spirit of Community* (Etzioni 1995) and *The New Golden Rule* (Etzioni 1996). In the first book, Etzioni argues that the 'Western' democracies' passion for individualism should be balanced by a new sense of social responsibility. To him and his associates, communitarianism is a social movement aiming to support the moral, social, and political environment. It is concerned partly with changing people's hearts, partly with renewal of social bonds, and partly with reform of public life. Individual rights should be matched by individual responsibilities. The "Responsive Communitarian Platform: Rights and Responsibilities" (Etzioni 1995: 251–267) was drafted by Etzioni, endorsed by seventy leading

Americans, and issued on 18 November 1991. Communitarians do not claim to have 'all the answers' but are engaged in a genuine shared project and believe that many of the answers must evolve from give-and-take between those in the communitarian movement.

Etzioni (1996) presents and develops the theme of a 'new golden rule', where social order, based on moral values, and autonomy, concerned with liberty, are in equilibrium, as the next logical development from communitarianism. To be effective, a communitarian society requires a core of shared values and a voluntary agreement to accept responsibility from its members. Etzioni (1996: 7–10) also suggests a redrawing of the 'intellectual-political map', which he reluctantly considers necessary. The old map, corresponding roughly to the 'main political spectrum', has, as its main dimension, the authority of the state or government (left-wing) versus that of the individual or private sector (right-wing). The new map has a new dimension, concerned with the relationship between the community and the individual, and between order and freedom. Here, the communitarian advocates a finely balanced middle position, departure from which leads to an approach that is either too libertarian or too authoritarian.

Allied to communitarianism is the concept of 'stakeholding', which began to emerge in business during the 1980s. It identified within a business organisation several groups of interested parties, the 'stakeholders', each with appropriate rights and interests. The stakeholder model of a company views an organisation as a community rather than a property. In the mid-1990s, the Labour Party in the UK generalised the stakeholder model to the whole of society. It used a concept of 'stakeholder partnership', where as many stakeholders as possible in a society—sectors of society, institutions, groups, or individuals—share responsibility for a socially valuable project. In this way, stakeholders complement each other's abilities, and the whole exceeds the sum of its parts.

Communitarianism has already strongly influenced the views of many leading politicians, with ideologies ranging from conservative, through liberal, to social democratic. These leaders are said to include President Bill Clinton and Vice President Al Gore in the United States, Prime Minister Tony Blair and Liberal Democrat leader Paddy Ashdown in the UK, former European Commission president Jacques Delors, and several German politicians (Etzioni 1995: ix).

Social Democracy[7]

'Socialism' originated in the early nineteenth century as various attempts were made in Europe to impose a more egalitarian and cooperative social order on the new economic order that was evolving as a result of the Industrial Revolution. By the mid-twentieth century, it had evolved into three main forms:

1. 'social democracy', which is basically concerned with the organised reform of society
2. 'democratic socialism', which advocates the democratic transformation of the current political system
3. 'Marxism', which advocates more radical, often revolutionary transformation of the political system.

In the UK, social democracy was greatly influenced by Fabian socialism, which began at the end of the nineteenth century and envisaged society as reforming itself on collectivist, not individualist, principles, through a gradually unfolding series of specific reforms. In this process, social democratic politics was to use the state to reform capitalism into socialism by the extension and evolution of existing society. Between World War I and World War II, social democracy in the UK was especially influenced by the thought of R. H. Tawney, who presented a powerful moral case against competitive individualism and contrasted it with the benefits to be obtained in a national community with practical equality, solidarity, and a common culture. This form of social democracy was ethical and based on firm moral values and a view of a decent society, combined with a flexible approach to techniques of implementation. In Sweden, Ernst Wigforss also emphasised the need to state a distinctive set of social democratic values as the basis for a politics of reform. He presented the ideals of freedom, equality, democracy, security, solidarity, and economic efficiency as core values. Thus, social democracy emerged basically as an extension of welfare liberalism. It provided the basis for the welfare states that emerged in Sweden and other Scandinavian countries in the mid-twentieth century and have lasted there ever since, although they are now beginning to experience various challenges and problems. Social democracy also combined with welfare liberalism to formulate the original version of the welfare state in the UK, which began to be prepared during World War II, and was then developed along more explicitly socialist lines after 1945.

Although the earlier forms of socialism strongly emphasised public ownership and control of the means of production and thus explicitly opposed capitalist economics, social democracy gradually departed from this approach, as experience of nationalisation and other forms of public ownership and economic planning was found to be rather disappointing and sometimes revealed serious difficulties. For socialist thinker Anthony Crosland, this meant reaffirming socialism as an ethical doctrine, rooted in social equality and emphasising social policy, rather than public ownership, as the main approach to achieving socialist goals. Eventually, social democracy strongly advocated the 'mixed economy', a combination of capitalism and socialism where some key enterprises are placed under public ownership or subjected to greater or lesser degrees of public control, while the rest of the economy is conducted by private businesses and enterprises. Different types of 'market socialism' emerged to describe various ways in which market dynamics and socialist objectives could be reconciled in advanced economies. In one version of market socialism, workers own their factories, but resources are allocated by markets. In another variant, markets are viewed as being able to operate without capitalism and can be used thus to promote socialist aims, bringing about equality, welfare, ethics, and economic efficiency. Concepts of 'social market' also arose to complement those of 'economic market'.

Democratic Socialism[8]

The best-known definition of 'socialism' is that it is a political and economic approach to social organisation that advocates that the 'community as a whole' should own and control the means of production, distribution, and exchange. This definition itself has several variants, because 'community as a whole' is sometimes defined as nation-state, leading to 'command socialism', where the state or specific government departments run a nation's collectivist economy. In practice, only communist regimes have attempted to implement full command economies. Alternatively, 'community as a whole' can mean local authorities, local communities, cooperative enterprises, or businesses owned and/or controlled by their workers. The very first form of socialism, 'Utopian socialism', beginning with Sir Thomas More's (1516) book *Utopia* in the sixteenth century, attempted to outline or describe in detail a possible 'ideal' form of human society and human life corresponding to 'true human nature'. Socialism as a movement arose originally to achieve a much more equal distribution of resources between the members of a society or nation and to achieve equality of opportunity for all people. It also recognised that the capitalism of the early nineteenth century could not achieve these objectives. Thus, it considered that the early liberals' advocacy of equality of opportunity was not practicable within the liberals' own conceptual framework or under any form of capitalism. Thus socialists then advocated public ownership and control as the best method that they could envisage for achieving socialism.

During the late twentieth century, the shortcomings of state ownership became so obvious that democratic socialists, as well as social democrats, began to become less enthusiastic about nationalisation and often also about other forms of public ownership, although there is still an appreciable, perhaps significant minority of socialists who advocate them. However, democratic socialists, as distinct from social democrats, propose a radical transformation of contemporary capitalist society, although by democratic and not revolutionary means.

Several other forms of socialism have been significant in the past and strongly influence certain specific groups of socialists today. 'Pluralist socialism' does not regard the state as an appropriate device for introducing or extending socialism. It views socialism as arising only from many groups of self-organised workers, producer associations that would gradually take over administrative and welfare functions previously performed by the state. 'Guild socialism', as advocated by William Morris and others, is a variant of pluralism. Fabian socialism was described briefly in the previous section and was originally more allied to democratic socialism, as it at first strongly advocated the widespread use of nationalisation as a form of public ownership. The tradition of Fabian socialism is still continued vigorously in the Fabian Society in the UK, but most Fabians are now probably social democrats rather than democratic socialists. 'Ethical socialism' or 'Christian socialism' is strongly motivated by ethical values, usually by Christian values. Most of its adherents have been active Christian reformers and have included both social democrats and democratic socialists.

The 'Far Left'[9]

The term 'communism' originated among revolutionaries in Paris during the 1830s, with two meanings:

1. a political movement of, or on behalf of, the working class to overthrow the emerging capitalist society
2. the kind of society that this movement wished to inaugurate.

The 'classical' expression of communism was the 1848 *Communist Manifesto* of Marx and Engels. During the latter half of the nineteenth century, Marxism arose as the first communist ideology, under their influence, but at first the terms 'communism' and 'socialism' were used almost synonymously, while the communists were viewed as the leading section of the late nineteenth-century socialists. It was only later, during the twentieth century, that communism and the other forms of socialism split apart. Marxism also introduced the concept of the 'withering away of the state', which would occur when socialism had evolved into true communism. The basic concepts of early Marxism included:

1. 'dialectical materialism'
2. the materialist interpretation of history
3. the Marxist theory of production and its material forces and social relations
4. the concept of class struggle between the capitalist class, the bourgeoisie, and the working class, the proletariat
5. the concept of an 'ideological superstructure' for every society, a set of ideas, ideals, and beliefs that legitimates and justifies its arrangements and institutions
6. the view of religion as the 'opiate of the people'
7. Marx's critique of capitalism.

Added to these ideas was a whole theory of how communist revolutions would be achieved against capitalist regimes through the 'dialectic of change'.

The revolutionary sequence in capitalist, industrialised countries was predicted to be:

1. economic crises of capitalism in the form of recessions and depressions
2. immiseration of the proletariat
3. development of revolutionary class consciousness among the proletariat
4. seizure of state power by the proletariat during their revolution
5. establishment of the revolutionary dictatorship of the proletariat, which would be a 'socialist' regime
6. eventual transformation of the socialist regime through the 'withering away of the state'
7. the final establishment of a 'communist' regime as an open and democratic society.

The first national communist regime was established in the Russian Empire in October 1917 and was called the USSR or Soviet Union. Communist ideology worldwide was then dominated by the successive versions of the ideology of communism as established in the USSR:

1. Leninism
2. Stalinism
3. post-Stalinist versions.

Trotskyism became a major variant after Trotsky had an unsuccessful contest with Stalin for the leadership of Soviet communism and then left the USSR. As the Chinese communist movement achieved success under the leadership of Mao Zedong, a distinctively Maoist variant of communist ideology evolved, which was succeeded by further versions of Chinese communist ideology after Mao's death. When the communist regimes of the USSR and Eastern Europe collapsed in 1989 and the early 1990s, very radical shifts occurred in the ideologies of the remaining communists and Marxists in Western Europe, North America, and most other countries; they no longer thought in terms of removal, let alone overthrow, of the capitalist regimes of the world.

Anarchism[10]

'Anarchism' believes that the state has no legitimate authority to govern, so that the state either may or should be ignored, resisted, or undermined. Many different interpretations and variants of anarchism have arisen. It arose with this name in the mid-nineteenth century under the influence of Pierre-Joseph Proudhon. Its main principles are the primacy of the individual and the virtue of moral autonomy. The anarchist theories and schools of thought include:

1. 'individualist anarchism', with 'conservative' and 'liberal' variants, which goes beyond individualism as held by conservatives and liberals

2. 'communitarian anarchism', which advocates the efficient and humane organisation of social life by cooperative communities for the collective good

3. 'collectivist anarchism', which believes in collectivising the means of production, determining distribution of goods and services by criteria of work

4. 'communist anarchism', which is committed to common ownership, often proposes distribution according to need, and also stresses social solidarity and cooperation

5. 'mutualist anarchism', which envisages the gradual disappearance of states and governments and their replacement by economic organisation

6. 'anarcho-syndicalism', devoted to overthrowing both capitalism and the state, opposed to democracy, and advocating class war and violent revolution.

'ALTERNATIVE' POLITICAL IDEOLOGIES

This section discusses some important ideologies that are outside the 'main spectrum' and have mostly become important during the twentieth century, although some of them have much earlier roots. As human affairs have evolved during the late twentieth century, the 'main spectrum' view of political ideologies, presented in the previous chapter, has become more and more incomplete, as new political movements, ideologies, and paradigms have emerged. An outline is given of what seem to be the most important of these new approaches, especially those perspectives that could contribute important ideas and insights to the more constructive and cooperative forms of politics that will be needed so urgently in the twenty-first century.

'Basic needs paradigms', concerned with meeting basic human needs and common human aspirations, are discussed in Chapter 10. Such concerns have generally motivated most of the new movements and their accompanying ideologies, most of which began as single-issue movements and ideologies. During recent decades, some of them have been showing signs of cooperating with each other and beginning to dissolve the boundaries between them. The relevant ideologies include nonviolence ideologies, feminism and other liberation ideologies, green ideologies, and 'spiritual politics' (which is discussed in Chapter 11).

Today, more and more people are considering how to extend this process of mutual cooperation and coalescence even further, hence, the emergence of 'holistic politics', which was the theme of an important conference held at Findhorn, Scotland, in 1988. Hopefully, holistic politics will play a key part in the twenty-first century, and this theme is developed further in Chapter 12.

Nonviolence Ideologies[11]

Pacifism is a code of conduct, rather than an ideology, but it includes theories about the moral status of war. Its most important philosophical rival is the traditional doctrine of the 'just war'. The book by Teichman (1986) describes and analyses the principles and theories of pacifism and of the 'just war' doctrine, compares them with each other, and considers objections that have been or might be made against them.

'Pacifism' in its modern form is a concept dating from 1902. It has different variants, although all pacifists have in common their opposition to war. Pacifist beliefs have been held by religious sects, such as the Society of Friends (Quakers) and the Mennonites, but also by some nonreligious groups, for example, anarchists who refuse to accept the right of the state to conscript people for war.

Pacifism can be distinguished from:

1. love of peace
2. opposition to all forms of violence as such
3. pursuit of pragmatic attempts to abolish war.

Many people who are not pacifists accept at least some of these ideals, but pacifism goes beyond them by involving a moral judgment and a personal commitment.

Pacifism has been adopted by a small, but quite influential, minority of people in many countries during the twentieth century. Although it does not have a comprehensive political ideology, its strong principles include:

1. the principle of nonviolence
2. the belief that all war and violent conflict are crimes against humanity
3. belief in the responsibility of all pacifists to oppose war-making policies in their own countries
4. a commitment not to support any war in any way
5. a commitment to strive for the removal of all causes of war.

The main approaches used by pacifists include:

1. *civil disobedience*—the open, deliberate, nonviolent breaking of laws and regulations—where this is considered to contribute to the fulfillment of pacifist principles and the promotion of pacifist objectives.
2. *nonviolent action*, which is a general technique of political and social action, applied through symbolic protests, noncooperation, and nonviolent intervention, by a variety of methods.

Pacifist viewpoints have been classified in several different ways. For example, Brook (1972) distinguished:

1. three variants of pacifism held on religious grounds

2. *integrational pacifism*, which combines an ethic of peace and peacekeeping with participation in reform movements opposed to war and having other aims

3. *goal-directed pacifism*, advocating the use of nonviolent techniques to achieve specific aims.

Integrational pacifists do not reject government or the use of force by government but only the injurious use of external force in international relations. Goal-directed pacifists include Gandhi and his followers, who used nonviolent methods in the struggle for India's independence from British colonial rule up to the mid-1940s, and many protesters against nuclear weapons.

Yoder (1971) classifies pacifism according to its motivations and identifies ten partly overlapping categories with the following beliefs and approaches:

1. *Christianity*, which, as a universal religion has a basis for the absolute rejection of war

2. *just war pacifism*, which examines each instance of armed conflict to see if it conforms to the conditions of justice in and for war

3. *absolute pacifism*, which views all deliberate killing of humans as evil

4. *Gandhian nonviolence*, as a generalised form of political pacifism, which sees nonviolence, peaceful resistance techniques, and conscientious objection as a way of solving not only the problem of international wars but also other political problems, such as colonialism, racism, and abuse of police powers

5. absolute rejection of *war* but without rejection of all violence or even all killing

6. some forms of *Christian pacifism*, based on the New Testament's new standard of righteousness

7. *utopian pacifism*, which considers that the rejection of violence is essential for the achievement of 'utopia'

8. the *pacifism of a categorical imperative*, the theory that one is bound to adopt a maxim of behaviour that one can will to be a universal law of nature

9. forms of pacifism based on an appeal to an *absolute conscience*, which tend to be rather vague

10. forms of pacifism based on the belief that really desirable political change is impossible and only personal change should be sought.

This classification emphasises the wide variety of different religious or moral beliefs that can lead to characteristic pacifist responses and nonviolent actions and resistance.

Liberation Ideologies[12]

'Liberation ideologies' have several common characteristics. Like mainstream democratic ideologies, they stress the importance of liberty. But they also seek liberation from types of domination and oppression that have been largely ignored or underemphasised by the main ideologies. They also propose new and distinctive approaches to overcoming or ending oppression. Each of them addresses a particular group of people. Each of these groups is alleged to be mistreated or oppressed by some dominant group. Each liberation ideology aims to remove an oppressed group from 'internal' as well as 'external' restrictions. It aims to 'raise the consciousness' and change the outlooks of people who have somehow participated—unwillingly, unwittingly, or unconsciously —in their own oppression or victimisation. It also aims to liberate the oppressors, by freeing them from illusions of their own superiority and helping them to recognise the humanity of their former victims.

Feminism[13]

Feminism and *women's liberation* have a long history, dating back to the late eighteenth century. For a long time, suffragettes in the UK and United States campaigned for women's right to vote and eventually succeeded. There are several variants of the feminist ideology, including liberal feminism, socialist feminism, anarchist feminism, and ecofeminism (described near the end of this chapter). From the 1960s on, the women's liberation movement has pursued several strategies for fighting sexism. It tends to emphasise differences between men and women, unlike liberal feminists, who tend to emphasise equal rights, equal opportunities, and similarities of both sexes.

Feminism's primary aim is to end what feminists perceive as men's systematic domination of women. Feminist theory aims to understand, explain, and challenge that domination, to help end it. Different feminist schools of thought and strands of opinion result largely from feminists' different individual experiences and from differences of interpretation.

The central position of 'modern liberal feminism' is that women are reasonable people entitled to full human rights; therefore, they should be free to choose their role in life and to compete equally with men in politics and paid work. It has been attacked not only by antifeminists but also by some other feminists who consider that it cannot provide a strategy for women's liberation because it does not understand women's true interests.

'Modern radical feminism' arose from women's experience in various political and 'alternative' movements in the 1960s, including those against war and for civil rights. It is essentially an ideology of, by, and for women, viewing the oppression of women as the most universal and fundamental form of domination. Thus, the interests of women as a group are opposed to those of men as a group, and politics must be redefined to overcome patriarchal domination.

Another strand of feminism is associated with 'postmodernism', a vague concept that different people tend to define in different ways but that very roughly challenges the once-widespread faith in rationalism and the inevitability of 'progress'.

Other Liberation Ideologies

Some of the strands of feminism, especially those related to women's liberation, can be viewed as a feminist liberation ideology.

The gay liberation movement and ideology emerged in the mid-twentieth century and, in the United States, began to be significant from 1969 on. Gay liberationists aim to:

1. repeal discriminatory laws against gays and gain opportunities previously denied to gays
2. overcome mistaken beliefs about, and attitudes towards, gay people.

Animal liberationists tend to be more militant than other liberationists and more willing to take personal and political risks for their beliefs. Although they aim to liberate animals, they present their ideology to people. Specifically, they address their appeals to people who:

1. oppress or abuse animals
2. benefit from animal oppression to some extent
3. do little or nothing to prevent further oppression of animals.

They also oppose 'speciesism', the belief that humans are superior to animals and thus entitled to exploit them.

Black liberation aims to end the racism that oppresses black people. In the United States, it has two approaches:

1. a civil rights variant, with a basically liberal outlook
2. a black liberationist variant, which seeks to remove insidious forms of racism that are liable to affect coloured people themselves.

The African National Congress has been a significant black liberation movement in South Africa, where its leader, Nelson Mandela, is now president.

Liberation theology has emerged during the last thirty years or so. Developed mainly inside the Roman Catholic Church, it aims to call attention to the plight of the poor, especially in Third World countries, and inspire people, including the poor themselves, to help to end their poverty. It calls for political, even revolutionary action on behalf of the poor.

Green Ideologies[14]

Green ideologies, together with other environmentalist and ecologist viewpoints, have roots going back as far as the late eighteenth century, when the Industrial Revolution and Romantic poetry movement both began. The first strand of green ideology was conservationism, which started in the mid-nineteenth century and was concerned with the conservation of wildlife, nature, and natural resources. By the early 1970s, there was additionally great concern about the far-reaching effects of various forms of pollution and about the dangers of exceeding the 'limits to growth'. Green political parties, with various shades of green ideology, began to appear at about the same time.

To a first approximation, green ideologies can be subdivided into 'moderate green' ideologies and 'deep green' ideologies. The former advocate participation in the democratic political process, together with adoption of a lifestyle that is at least partly green and a variety of direct environmental actions. The latter seek a total transformation of worldviews in general and political paradigms in particular; they advocate a shift from anthropocentric to ecocentric perspectives.

Green ideologies have no natural position on the main political spectrum from right to left, as 'greenness' is a distinct political dimension. It is, in fact, found that green sub-ideologies correspond to each position on the main spectrum. Thus, there are conservative, liberal, and socialist variants of green ideology. In addition, the main political parties today usually claim to have adopted some of the specific ideas from moderate green political ideologies, although it is not fully clear how far this claim corresponds to actual party politics; to a considerable extent, it could be used to attract the support of the many voters who adopt environmentalist and green viewpoints to lesser or greater degrees.

'Ecosocialism' is one of the most significant variants of green ideology and has emerged from a critical dialogue between various strands of Marxism, democratic socialism, social democracy, and the radical environmental movement. It generally argues that the state must play a key part in the shift towards a more egalitarian conserving society and views ecological policies as part of a larger struggle to overcome capitalism and obtain social justice for all. It views the 'environment' as an essentially human context that is socially determined rather than wholly external. It considers that human autonomy can be realised fully within a safe and healthy physical environment and a cooperative democratic social environment.

'Ecofeminism' combines green and feminist principles in various ways. Various versions of its ideology have been formulated in several recent books. In their book *Ecofeminism*, Maria Mies and Vandana Shiva (1993), as internationally respected feminists and environmental activists, offer a thought-provoking critique and analysis of many current environmental, development, and other political issues from a unique North-South perspective. In constructing their own ecofeminist epistemology and methodology, they examine the potential of movements, often at the grass roots, that advocate consumer liberation, subsistence production, sustainability, and regeneration. They argue for the acceptance of limits to growth and reciprocity and the rejection of exploitation, the commoditisation of needs, and violence.

In *Breaking the Boundaries: Towards a Feminist Green Socialism*, Mary

Mellor (1992) advocates bringing together elements of deep ecology, eco-feminism, radical feminism, spirituality, and revolutionary socialism in a new synthesis to offer an exciting political vision for the twenty-first century.

In *From Apocalypse to Genesis: Ecology, Feminism and Christianity*, Anne Primavesi (1991) presents an original reevaluation of Christianity that is opposed to its traditional, but damaging, concept of human domination over the rest of creation. She argues for the essential interrelatedness and inter-dependence of all creation, on the basis of an ecofeminist paradigm of humankind and nature.

'Ecocommunalism' comprises a wide range of utopian, visionary, and largely anarchist green theories that attempt to show how to develop human-scale cooperative communities that enable the balanced mutual development of people, while respecting the integrity of the nonhuman world. As mentioned at the end of the Prologue, Jonathon Porritt, a leading ecological thinker and writer, has begun to outline a similar emerging 'ecocommunitarian' approach that combines green ideas with the principles of community.

'Ecophilosophy' has been formulated in several books by Henryk Skolimowski. In *Living Philosophy* (Skolimowski 1992), he presents a detailed argument for a new 'ecological consciousness', concerned as much for our inner environment as our outer environment. He criticises existing political systems, proposes a new approach to living, and outlines his comprehensive ecological worldview on which this approach is based.

NOTES

1. Important books on political ideologies include *Political Ideologies and the Democratic Ideal* (Ball and Dagger 1995b), *Contemporary Political Ideologies* (Eatwell and Wright 1993), *Modern Political Ideologies* (Vincent 1995), *A Companion to Con-temporary Political Philosophy* (Goodin and Pettit 1995: pt. 2 "Ideologies"), *British Po-litical Ideologies* (Leach 1996) (which includes classifications of specific ideologies), *Political Ideologies* (Heywood 1998), *Ideologies* (Johnston 1996), *Political Ideologies* (Eccleshall et al. 1994), *Political Ideologies* (Funderburk and Thobaben 1994), *Ideo-logies and Their Functions* (Walford 1979), and *Beyond Politics* (Walford 1990). See also Heywood (1997: ch. 3). Lent (1998) reviews both established and emerging ideologies. For surveys of political ideologies in the United States, France, and Latin America, respectively, see Schwartzmantel (1998), Flood and Bell (1997), and Bethell (1996). *Ideals and Ideologies* (Ball and Dagger 1995a) is a sourcebook of original readings on various ideologies and can be studied in conjunction with Ball and Dagger (1995b). Donald and Hall (1986) is a reader with examples of readings from ideological theory and specific ideologies.

2. Descriptions of nationalism are given in Gellner (1998a), Smith (1995), Alter (1994), Kedourie (1993), Eatwell and Wright (1993: ch. 7), Vincent (1995: ch. 9), Leach (1996: ch. 8), Krieger (1993: 614–619), and Ball and Dagger (1995b: 18–20). Readers on nationalism and ethnicity include Hutchinson and Smith (1994, 1996). Canovan (1996) argues that it is naive to choose either nationalism or internationalism and

ignore the other and that the concept of 'nationhood' is both complicated and, to some extent, contradictory.

3. Descriptions of far-Right ideologies, including fascism, are given in Ball and Dagger (1995b: ch. 7), Eatwell and Wright (1993: ch. 8), Vincent (1995: ch. 6), Leach (1996: ch. 7), Goodin and Pettit (1995: 263–266), and Krieger (1993: 294–296).

4. Descriptions of conservatism are given in Ball and Dagger (1995b: ch. 4), Eatwell and Wright (1993: ch. 3), Vincent (1995: ch. 3), Goodin and Pettit (1995: ch. 9), Leach (1996: ch. 5), and Krieger (1993: 538–542). Gray and Willetts (1997) discuss the future of conservatism. Galbraith (1993) includes a critique of conservative ideologies.

5. Descriptions of liberalism are given in Rawls (1996), Ball and Dagger (1995b: ch. 3), Eatwell and Wright (1993: ch. 2), Vincent (1995: ch. 2), Goodin and Pettit (1995: ch. 11), Leach (1996: ch. 4), and Krieger (1993: 538–542). Kautz (1995) and Kymlicka (1991b) discuss liberalism in relation to the community.

6. Full presentations of communitarianism are given by Etzioni (1995, 1996) and Tam (1998). Other descriptions are given in Goodin and Pettit (1995: ch. 15), Kymlicka (1991a: ch. 6), Ball and Dagger (1995b: 87), and Leach (1996: 171). Etzioni (1998) is a reader of communitarian literature. Critiques of communitarianism include Avineri and de-Shalit (1992), Bell (1993), and Phillips (1993).

7. Descriptions of social democracy are given in Eatwell and Wright (1993: ch. 4), Vincent (1995: ch. 4), Goodin and Pettit (1995: 335–337, 416–417), Leach (1996: 137, 167–170), Krieger (1993: 832–839), and Ball and Dagger (1995b: 256). Pierson (1995a) discusses the closely related 'new market socialism'. See also Crouch and Marquand (1995) and Driver and Martell (1998).

8. Descriptions of democratic socialism are given in Wright (1996), Ball and Dagger (1995b: ch. 5, ch. 6), Eatwell and Wright (1993: ch. 4), Vincent (1995: ch. 4), Goodin and Pettit (1995: ch. 13), Leach (1996: ch. 6), and Krieger (1993: 832–839). Stiglitz (1996) discusses the future prospects of socialism. Little (1998) considers postindustrial socialism. Crouch and Marquand (1995) aim to stimulate new debate about the emerging left and centre-left. Wainwright (1994) presents arguments for a new left viewpoint in answer to the free-market Right.

9. Descriptions of far-Left ideologies, including Marxism and communism, are given in Ball and Dagger (1995b: ch. 5, 6), Eatwell and Wright (1993: ch. 5), Vincent (1995: ch. 4), Goodin and Pettit (1995: ch. 8), Leach (1996: ch. 6), Krieger (1993: 165, 569–575). Panitch and Leys (1998) assess the contemporary significance of the Communist Manifesto. Smith (1996) discusses several ways in which Marxists have misunderstood Marx's own concepts. Polychroniou and Targ (1996), Itoh (1995), and Van Parijs (1993) explore some possible new directions for Marxism.

10. Descriptions of anarchism are given in Eatwell and Wright (1993: ch. 6), Vincent (1995: ch. 5), Goodin and Pettit (1995: ch. 8), Leach (1996: 185–187), Krieger (1993: 26–27), and Ball and Dagger (1995b: 20, 168–170).

11. A description of the approach of nonviolent action is given in Krieger (1993: 647–650).

12. A description of liberation ideologies is given in Ball and Dagger (1995b: ch. 8), and of liberation theologies in Krieger (1993: 542–544).

13. Descriptions of feminism are given in Eatwell and Wright (1993: ch. 9), Vincent (1995: ch. 7), Goodin and Pettit (1995: ch. 10), Leach (1996: ch. 9), Krieger (1993: 297–300), and Ball and Dagger (1995b: 212–217). Phillips (1991) considers democracy from a feminine perspective.

14. Important books on green political ideologies include Eckersley (1992), Merchant (1992), Paehlke (1991), Pepper (1993), Hayward (1995), Dobson (1995), Dobson and Lucardie (1995), and Goodin (1992). Wall (1993) is a reader on environmental literature, philosophy, and politics. Jacobs (1998) presents the new politics of the environment. Ecosocialism is discussed especially by Eckersley (1992) and Pepper (1993) but also in Red-Green Study Group (1995). Merchant (1995), Mellor (1992), Mies and Shiva (1993), and Primavesi (1991) present ecofeminism from partly different, but, in some ways complementary, viewpoints. For formulations of different versions of ecophilosophy, see Naess (1990) and Skolimowski (1992). Other descriptions of green ideologies are given in Ball and Dagger (1995b: ch. 9), Eatwell and Wright (1993: ch. 10), Vincent (1995: ch. 8), Goodin and Pettit (1995: ch. 24), Leach (1996: ch. 10), and Krieger (1993: 267–271). For a fairly controversial, but carefully researched, critique of various environmental ideologies and of environmentalism in general, see North (1995). Beckerman (1995) criticises much of the environmental 'conventional wisdom', including the 'precautionary principle' and the concept of 'sustainable development', but admits the existence of serious environmental problems.

SOME TOPICS FOR FURTHER INVESTIGATION

1. Comment on existing classifications of political ideologies and suggest some possibilities for improved classifications.

2. If you can find any significant political ideologies that are not mentioned in this chapter or elsewhere in this book, describe them briefly.

3. Explain how far your own political ideological position does or does not include elements of the political ideologies described in this chapter.

4. How far does your voting behaviour reflect a correspondence between your own political ideology and that of the candidates for whom you vote? How far do other factors, such as your perception of the performance of an administration or the competence of its team, affect your voting behaviour? Do these factors influence you more than your ideological position?

5. What are the best ways of reviving a spirit of local community in your country and in the locality where you live?

6. What forms of nonviolent action, if any, do you consider appropriate, that go *beyond* the normal democratic processes of voting, contact with political representatives, activity in and for political parties, and expressing political views in writing and in speech?

7. What further developments can you envisage in some form of liberation ideology in which you are especially interested?

8. What extensions do you consider should be made to contemporary green ideologies to enable them to have a wide, popular appeal? Or do you consider that most people will *never* adopt a green lifestyle? If so, why?

10

Paradigms and Politics

Paradigms from other aspects of human life and most other fields of knowledge are becoming increasingly relevant to contemporary politics, and their influence will become much more important during the twenty-first century. Different areas of human affairs are interacting with each other more and more, science and technology now have very important impacts, and coherent holistic, philosophical, and ethical paradigms are urgently needed to enable both politicians and people to make better sense of life as a whole.

One of the principal tasks of a democratic regime is to endeavour to fulfill as far as possible the basic human needs of all people under its jurisdiction and, indeed, to contribute as best it can to meeting the needs of all people worldwide. Basic needs paradigms provide a framework for assessing what human needs should be meet and provide a good idea of their relative priorities. Political science paradigms, supported by paradigms from psychology, sociology, and the other social sciences and the humanities, provide conceptual frameworks that can help politicians to formulate their approaches to government and political action. Paradigms from economics, business, and management address areas of great concern to policy-makers and provide their own insights into policy-making. Paradigms from all the sciences and technologies—social, biological, physical, and mathematical—contain analogies that can provide valuable insights to political scientists and politicians if used with discrimination. The 'consciousness paradigm' and other spiritual paradigms are presented in Chapter 11. Some holistic philosophical paradigms, providing guidelines for a future 'unified, practical philosophy' and including systems concepts, are outlined in Chapter 12.

An adequate description of the political implications of all these paradigms, taken together, would itself require a whole book. Therefore, this chapter

88888888

provides only a broad-brush outline. For a more extensive, but much less up-to-date, coverage of paradigms, see Burrows et al. (1991: pt. 2).[1]

BASIC NEEDS PARADIGMS

Many, if not most, people have a whole range of wishes that they would like to see fulfilled. The aspirations commonly held by large numbers of people include:

1. meeting their basic human needs
2. the achievement of freedom and individual liberty
3. the availability of adequate choice
4. adequate encouragement for their enterprise
5. fulfillment of their human potential
6. the ability to live in genuine local and national communities
7. the ability to live peacefully and harmoniously with each other in a global community covering the whole of planet Earth.

The psychologist Abraham Maslow[2] was one of the first people to realise that human individuals have a whole hierarchy of basic needs:

1. the *physiological needs*: food, drink, shelter, clothing, sleep
2. the *safety needs*: physical safety, security, family life, physical health
3. the *belongingness and love needs*: giving and receiving love, affection, friendship, belonging
4. the *esteem needs*: self-respect and other *self-esteem needs*: status, appreciation, and other needs for others' esteem.
5. the *need for self-actualisation* and individual fulfillment of talents and aims
6. the *desires to know and understand*
7. the *aesthetic needs*.

On the whole, the lower needs usually require to be satisfied first.

Most people in 'Western' democracies consider that their freedom and individual liberty are essential, but politicians and political scientists differ considerably on how to interpret them or even on what they are. I personally take a broad view about them by considering that both political freedom and economic freedom are vitally important. I also realise that, to achieve a harmonious society, it is essential to have limits to these freedoms and balance human rights and freedoms with human responsibilities, to ensure that the exercise of freedom by individuals minimises interference with the freedoms of other individuals and to guarantee that all the essential tasks of the community are performed as completely and as well as possible.

Individuals are very diverse in their characteristics, abilities, needs, and tastes; 'unity in diversity' is the essence of a good community. It is thus important to provide both individuals and groups with as much choice as is reasonably possible. Important constraints on freedom of choice include availability of the resources that are required to implement them and the need to minimise conflicts between individuals. For example, it is important for a democratic regime to be flexible enough to ensure that its institutional arrangements respect the values, choices, and preferences of different citizens.

Encouragement of enterprise is one of the keys to a successful economy with successful businesses that generate products and services to meet the varied needs of many different people. Enterprise is also one of the fruits of human creativity, and its successful exercise can give great individual satisfaction, as well as many benefits to the community. However, enterprise needs to be exercised with responsibility, so that the goods and services that it generates are valuable to other people and do not exploit them.

The full release and harnessing of creative talents and human potential are most likely to be fulfilled if the human needs at all levels are properly met. It is very important for individual talents to be fully developed and provided with adequate channels for their expression. It is one of the tragedies of the present work situation in most parts of the world that far too many people have totally inadequate opportunities for constructive and fulfilling work, both through extensive unemployment and through inappropriate work patterns and excessive workloads for too many of those who do work.

Modern trends in most parts of the world have seriously eroded the extent to which most people are able to live in community today, but the already significant influence of communitarianism has begun to reverse this trend. Urban areas in all parts of the world are now largely social deserts, with only pockets of local communities still present among them. Many villages even have lost much, if not most, of their previous community spirit. Indigenous peoples who used to live in genuine tribal communities have all too often had their communities eroded by external political and economic forces or even forcibly destroyed. Successful intentional communities, such as at Findhorn in Scotland, have already been established in various parts of the world. They set good examples for community living by many more people.

The greatest challenge to humanity today is for its people to live together on Earth in peace and friendship. This requires the progressive reduction and resolution of all human conflicts that can be identified and extensive efforts to foresee and prevent further human conflicts before they arise. In addition, communities should begin to regrow from the grass roots up, in all areas of life, networking into communities of communities, and communities of communities of communities, and so on, until a genuine global community emerges.

POLITICAL SCIENCE PARADIGMS

The best discussion of social science paradigms relevant to politics, that I have yet found is Michael Haas' remarkable book *Polity and Society* (1992). Its author aims to find a common framework for discussion of these paradigms and schools of thought and assumes that all theories about reality are metaphysically based. He argues that discussions of each theory's claim to truth have been diverted to ideology and methodology, instead of directly attempting to identify the ontological nature of political and social reality. He explains some of the many debates that have concerned political scientists and sociologists during the latter half of the twentieth century, by presenting theories in terms of their ontological assumptions. He classifies theories of metaphysics into (1) *monistic* theories (materialism, idealism, and double aspect theory), (2) *dualistic* theories (parallelism and interactionism), and (3) other theories (skepticism and positivism). He shows how social scientists make metaphysical assumptions all the time in their research and classifies some of their paradigms metaphysically. He assumes an instrumentalist methodology, as it enables the correction of scientific theories by a combination of logic and human observations, so that systematic inquiry remains open to new evidence. His epistemology is fundamentally antipositivist. He hopes to show how scholars might develop a scientific agenda for testing alternative verbal theories.

Haas' theorising focuses on seven areas of research with which he has been concerned at one time or another:

1. paradigms of development
2. paradigms of community power
3. paradigms of U.S. presidential voting
4. paradigms of ethnic voting
5. paradigms of civil strife
6. paradigms of international violence
7. paradigms of international community.

Both American and international political and social issues are addressed. For each area explored, comparative tables are given of the characteristics of the different paradigms being applied, and each of these paradigms is analysed and criticised in the context of the area. Haas concentrates on theories that have been discarded or ignored, exposes some fallacies of existing theories, and identifies several new directions for research. He selects some, but not all, of the central theories of political science and sociology but covers them deeply enough to uncover their basic philosophical assumptions.

In writing this book, Haas has a political and social agenda:

I believe that human societies are insufficiently organized to provide the good life for their people today. . . . The dialectical tension between material realities and ideas of how to govern awaits a synthesis that will simultaneously provide economic development, political democracy, social justice, and world peace for all. I believe that it is the task of the social sciences to hasten the day when power will be shared, economic attainments will be much less stratified, and building peace will be easier than preparing for war. These are the proper goals of social science. (xiii–xiv)

Although my own agenda and views are in many ways similar, the approach of my book is mostly complementary to that of *Polity and Society*. In it, I am much more concerned about political paradigms that have been, are, and could in future be held by citizens in general, politicians, governments, and civil servants. In this context, the paradigms held by political and social scientists usually play a fairly minor part, though exceptionally, as with the paradigms originated by Adam Smith and Karl Marx, they can have a wide influence. Again, as Haas has shown, these theorists are often strongly influenced by widely held popular or elite political paradigms.

A New Handbook of Political Science (Goodin and Klingermann 1998) is a successor to the eight-volume *Handbook of Political Science* (Greenstein and Polsky 1975). It examines what has happened to the discipline of politics since that handbook, and its scope is considerably more international. It is also conspicuously organised around subdisciplines chosen to represent the dominant configurations of political science as it is today. Its editors state that it is inevitably incomplete. For each subdiscipline, a lead chapter surveys recent developments as well as possible, but inevitably with considerable omissions. Other chapters provide additional material about a selection of specific perspectives in the subdiscipline and compare old with new approaches in the subdiscipline.

The first part of *A New Handbook* considers the discipline of political science as a whole, and subsequent parts consider the following subdisciplines:

1. political institutions
2. political behaviour
3. comparative politics
4. international relations
5. political theory
6. public policy and administration
7. political economy
8. political methodology.

The handbook's editors express the hope that they have covered most of the main currents in the discipline of political science.

The handbook is well complemented by *Contemporary Political Philosophy* (Goodin and Pettit 1996), which contains thirty-eight seminal passages from postwar political philosophy. The themes of these essays are state and society, democracy, justice, rights, liberty, equality, and oppression.

Goodin and Klingermann (1996: 7) characterise 'politics' as the constrained use of social power, and characterise the study of politics, by academics or politicians, as the study of the nature and sources of political constraints, and the techniques for using social power within those constraints. Young et al. (1993) present six major strands of political theory:

1. social justice and welfare rights theory
2. democratic theory
3. feminist political theory
4. postmodernism
5. new social movements and society
6. liberalism and communitarianism.

According to Dogan's contribution to Goodin and Klingermann (1996: ch. 3), political science today has open and moving frontiers; its main features are specialisation, fragmentation, and hybridisation. The following hybrid domains are defined: political psychology, political geography, political sociology, politics and economics, political anthropology, political development across natural and social science, and comparative politics.

Goodin in Goodin and Pettit (1995: ch. 6) discusses the contribution of political science to political philosophy. He concentrates on the contribution to political science from mainstream, empirically oriented political science and its ancillary subdisciplines. He discusses the following topics: the operation of democracy, social choice theory, organisation theory as applied to bureaucracy and democracy, power and distributional regimes, rights and liberties in constitutional regimes, and politics in relation to civil society. One conclusion from his survey is that the familiar forms of political constraint may be less constraining than is usually supposed; he gives several examples of this.

The Blackwell Encyclopaedia of Political Science (Bogdanor 1991) clarifies and explains the terms, concepts, and ideas central to the study of politics. Its articles are written by many of the world's leading political experts. A comprehensive reading list is provided for each main topic.

PSYCHOLOGICAL PARADIGMS

Individual Psychology[3]

For a full understanding of political behaviour, it is necessary first to understand human motives, attitudes, and behaviour in general. A study of theoretical and practical psychological paradigms is helpful.

During the twentieth century, psychology has evolved from through several schools of thought, including behaviourism, gestalt psychology, psychoanalysis, humanistic psychology, cognitive psychology, and psychosynthesis.

Behaviourism is the theory that human behaviour is determined by conditioning, rather than by thoughts or feelings, and that disorders of psychology or behaviour are best treated by altering behaviour patterns. The questions of free will, associated with the understanding of behaviour and responsibility, are very important but also very difficult to understand. Honderich (1988) gives an excellent, fairly recent assessment of the philosophy of free will and the possible approaches that can be adopted to this problem; see also Lucas (1970).

Gestalt psychology is a holistic and systems approach to psychology and psychological patterns. It maintains that perceptions and reactions are 'gestalts', that is, wholes that are more than the sum of their parts.

Psychoanalysis explores hidden motivations behind various habits and forms of human behaviour. Its founder, Freud, made major contributions to the exploration of the subconscious mind but overemphasised the role of sex and oversimplified human motivation. Adler developed another version of psychoanalysis, based on the role of urges to power rather than sex. Jung developed what is today probably the most important school of psychoanalysis, based on a much broader understanding of the complexities of human nature. His deep insights included the following. (1) The subconscious mind has higher, creative aspects. (2) The 'collective subconscious', a sort of group mind belonging to the whole human species, contributes much to common strands of human concepts and myths. (3) Human nature is dual, so that people have a 'shadow' side, as well as their benevolent aspects, and both masculine and feminine traits. These insights are especially important for an understanding of political viewpoints and behaviour.

Humanistic psychology has a holistic view of the nature of the whole human being and takes full account of human needs, consciousness, motivation, and personality. Its pioneers included Maslow, whose theory of human needs is outlined earlier in this chapter, and Rogers. It has evolved further into *transpersonal psychology* and the *human growth movement*, described by Woodhouse (1996: ch. 10).

Cognitive psychology addresses the general concepts of mind, intelligence, consciousness, thought, logic, rationality, and knowledge and is strongly influenced by advances in 'artificial intelligence'. Johnson-Laird (1996) presents the concepts of 'cognitive science', which studies mind and intelligence by using a synthesis of ideas from several disciplines. Minsky (1987) develops a theory of mind where each mind is made of many 'agents', smaller process that are linked in 'societies'.

Psychosynthesis, founded by Assagioli,[4] is concerned with realising the more creative and constructive parts of the human mind, and can be viewed as complementary to psychoanalysis. It explicitly recognises the important role of the 'higher self'.

Psychological types were first investigated by Jung, whose classification of types was later developed into the Myers-Briggs Type Indicator (MBTI) of psychological types (Myers and Myers 1995), whose understanding and use can lead to personal fulfillment. The MTBI has many applications to education, training, and the effective running of organisations, business, and industry. Pearson (1991) describes twelve patterns in the human personality that can be developed in a balanced way to help fulfill human potentialities.

Goleman (1996) argues that psychology's view of human intelligence was previously too narrow and that our emotions play a much greater part in thinking, decision making, and individual success than usually admitted. Goleman (1998) applies this concept of 'emotional intelligence' to practical living.

The psychology of human creativity and creative thinking[5] and of risk perceptions and risky behaviour[6] are also very important for politics.

Social Psychology[7]

The principal form of social interaction is between people in everyday life, and this interaction can be rather complex. There are delicate, but very important ways. by which individuals interpret what others say and do in their face-to-face encounters. Zimbardo and Leippe (1991) cover many principles and aspects of major social influences, including those affecting attitudes. Mansbridge (1990) rejects the widespread idea of behaviour as being based mainly on self-interest and argues for a more complex view of individual behaviour and social organisation.

Much can be learned about social behaviour by studying people whose behaviour deviates from generally accepted patterns. What is considered 'normal' or 'deviant' behaviour varies considerably between societies, but women have much lower rates of criminalisation than men. Crime and deviance are mainly socially determined but can also be influenced by genetic[8] and dietary[9] factors. Storr (1991) explores why people can be appallingly destructive and cruel, attempts to throw light on genocide, racial conflict, and other large-scale manifestations of violence, and sees little hope for major changes in human nature.

Psychology and Politics

The application of psychology to politics is discussed in Krieger (1993: 751–754), for example. Throughout human history, political analysts have been interested in the relationships between psychology, personality, attitudes, behaviour, and politics. Various theories have emerged about why rulers and their subjects or governments and their citizens think and act as they do and how their thought influence politics. Krause (1997) provides a modern commentary on the ancient Chinese leadership concepts of Sun Tzu and Confucius. In his famous book *The Prince*, Niccolò Machiavelli (1513) gave much practical advice about the art of political manipulation and urged rulers to study human nature (which he considered unchangeable) so that they could control political action by manipulation. Various forms of psychotechnology have been used during the twentieth century, especially by totalitarian regimes, to exercise undue influence over human minds by such processes as propaganda and brainwashing. Milder forms of these processes are sometimes used by advertisers, political 'image' makers, and 'spin doctors'.

In general, approaches to government depend on perceptions about human nature. Political leaders are interested in political socialisation, because political beliefs and perceptions are learned. Political decisions are shaped by the perceptions, attitudes, viewpoints, and opinions of leaders and other politicians and by the political context at the time. Individual and social psychology can contribute to the understanding of the causes and cures of political conflict and violence and to the development of conflict resolution methods.[10]

SOCIOLOGICAL PARADIGMS

The book *Sociology* (Giddens 1997) aims to combine some originality and accessibility with an analysis of all the basic issues of interest to contemporary sociologists. It covers the background to important advances in theoretical thinking and attempts to understand social institutions. It has especially influenced the discussion in this section. Another very important textbook is *Sociology: Themes and Perspectives* (Haralambos and Holborn 1995). Both these books emphasise the study of distinct problems and fields within sociology and cover the major perspectives in sociology. Abercrombie et al. (1994) provide a good introduction to sociology within the context of social problems in the UK.[11] *The Blackwell Dictionary of Social Thought* (Outhwaite et al. 1994) provides a comprehensive survey of the main themes of social thought, the principal movements and schools of thought, and social institutions. Its coverage includes politics.[12]

Sociology is the systematic study of human societies[13] and attempts to understand their extensive changes during recent centuries. August Comte, Karl Marx, Émile Durkheim, and Max Weber were its most important classical founders, and Michel Foucault and Jürgen Habermas are among its more important contemporary thinkers. Sociology is a science in the sense that it uses scientific method, but it is not as rigorous as the natural sciences due to the complexities and uncertainties of human behaviour. It can contribute to social criticism and practical social reform in several ways (Giddens 1997: 15).

The Problems Studied by Sociology

Sociology systematically studies human societies, especially modern, industrialised societies. Sociologists pose distinct questions that they try to answer by systematic research. These questions may be factual, comparative, developmental, or theoretical. Sociology has links with other social sciences, all of which are concerned with human behaviour, especially with anthropology and history.

Specific problem areas discussed by sociology include:

1. types of society[14] and social interaction[15]

2. modern organisations[16]

3. work and economic life[17]

4. government and political and military power[18]

5. mass media and popular culture[19]

6. education[20]

7. revolutions and other social movements[21]

8. global change and ecological crisis.[22]

Books on political sociology and sociology in relation to political theory include *Research in Political Sociology* (Washburn 1997), the series of books *Research in Politics and Society* (Moore 1985 on), *Civil Society and Political Theory* (Cohen and Arato 1994), and *Politics and Society* (Rush 1992). *Paths of Change* (McWhinney 1997) proposes a new, scientific approach to handling complex problems of organisation and society, based on the assumption that people use different and incompatible concepts of society.

Sociological Theory[23]

Sociology is not a subject based on a body of generally agreed theories but has several differing theoretical traditions. The main theoretical approaches in sociology are as follows. (1) *Functionalism* studies the function of a social practice or institution by analysing its contribution to the continuation of a society as a whole. (2) *Structuralism* is based on concepts about the structure of language and meaning and is useful for exploring communication and culture but less relevant to economics and politics. (3) *Symbolic interactionism* takes special account of active, creative individuals and applies linguistic concepts to face-to-face interaction between people, mainly in everyday life. (4) *Marxism* has developed into several different schools of sociological and political thought and emphasises class divisions, class conflict, power, and ideology. These approaches are partly complementary to each other but also contrasting.

Major theoretical dilemmas in sociology include the following questions. (1) Are we creators of society or created by it? (2) Are societies harmonious and orderly, with much consensus, or marked by persistent conflict? (3) How should sociological analysis handle gender issues? (4) Are processes of change in the modern world shaped mainly by capitalist economic development or by other factors, including noneconomic factors?

ECONOMICS, BUSINESS, AND MANAGEMENT PARADIGMS

Economics, business, and management paradigms all have important impacts on many areas of political policy making and influence the effectiveness of public policies. The two main economic paradigms during the twentieth century have been capitalism and collectivism.

Capitalism and Collectivism

Capitalism[24] is a mode of production and a method of organising economic activity that relies on a free-market system for exchanging goods and services; it is supported by a set of economic and legal institutions making production for private profit the normal course of economic organisation. In practice, it is modified by several forms of state intervention, including restriction of monopolies, regulations and controls, and company taxation. Most national economies worldwide operate under some form of capitalism, as does the international global economy dominated by multinational companies. *Collectivism*[25] is a system whereby a nation-state operates a more or less strict 'command' economy, where it attempts to obtain as much control over national economic activity as is practically feasible. However, Elliott and Atkinson (1998) consider that unrestrained market forces are leading to a 'new command economy', where capital is free, but employees are being coerced, sometimes intimidated. In democratic socialist and social democratic regimes, there are *mixed economies*, where most of a national economy is run by the market, but certain industrial and economic sectors are nationalised or otherwise state-controlled.

By the late 1980s, all the command economies were under considerable strain and reacted in different ways. The contradictions in the Soviet and communist Eastern European economies were so strong that rapid transitions towards capitalism began and were almost complete by the mid- to late 1990s. The Chinese communist regime spontaneously made its economy progressively more capitalist, while maintaining its strong political control. It became evident that collectivism was unworkable as an economic system because of its inefficiencies and unpopularity and also because of the extreme environmental degradation that it caused.

Capitalist economies have had severe crises from time to time, including the Great Depression of the 1930s, from which they recovered fully only in the 1940s because of the vast economic demand created by the military needs of World War II. After the war, capitalist economies, often using Keynesian economic policies,[26] maintained almost full employment for over thirty years, but new waves of unemployment swept over the world from the early 1980s and still occur. These long-term fluctuations of employment levels could have been due to 'economic long waves'.[27]

Capitalism is still the dominant and 'orthodox' economic paradigm,[28] but its intrinsic problems, including instability, rising inequality, and environmental problems, are widely recognised. Brittan (1996) discusses some of its problems, and considers how far it can become more humane. Marquand (1997) addresses the current political questions arising from the capitalist renaissance of recent decades. Armstrong (1996) argues the urgent need for radical economic reform. Thurow (1996), nevertheless, envisages a new form of capitalism emerging to adapt to these problems but seems to be overly optimistic. Naisbitt (1994) is even more optimistic. However, Gray (1998) argues that attempts to impose the Anglo-American type of free-market economy on the world will be as disastrous as Soviet communism was.

'New' and Alternative Economic Paradigms

For over twenty-five years, both capitalism and collectivism have been challenged increasingly by various forms of 'new economics' and 'green' economics, which are based on ethical and environmental principles and go beyond capitalism, socialism, and collectivism.[29] In 1959, the Indian thinker P. R. Sarkar first presented his Progressive Utilisation Theory (PROUT) as a holistic and spiritual socioeconomic philosophy.[30] In his book *Small Is Beautiful*, Schumacher (1974) criticised capitalism's excessive pursuit of profit, argued for a more humane economic system, and proposed a system of 'intermediate technology', based on smaller working units, communal ownership, and regional workplaces using local labour and resources. During the 1980s and 1990s, a series of *The Other Economic Summit* (TOES) conferences has been held, and the New Economics Foundation, founded in the UK, has encouraged further development of new economic thinking. In 1985, ideas were shared between practitioners of both conventional and alternative economics at a conference at Findhorn, Scotland, on *The New Economic Agenda*, whose written version appeared in Inglis and Kramer (1985). Influenced by this conference, I outlined some ideas for a 'world cooperative economy' (Mayne 1986) that would be humane and would attempt to combine the best features of free enterprise, market economics, and a judicious element of planning.

The most notable originators of 'new economic thought' include James Robertson, Herman Daly, Hazel Henderson, Paul Ekins, and Manfred Max-Neef. The books by Robertson (1990, 1998b) advocate a new, worldwide economic order for the twenty-first century, adapted and applied to real human and planetary needs and emphasising the needs to enable people and conserve the Earth.[31] Daly's pioneering work has continued since the early 1970s. Daly et al. (1994) is a penetrating critique of orthodox economics, and offers a new paradigm for sustainable economics, public policy, and social ethics. Daly's later books (1995, 1997) and Daly (ed.) (1995) present 'steady-state economics' as a key to sustainable development and the integration of economics with ecology. Henderson (1993) summarises her own new paradigms, which address broader human goals, including quality of education, health care, and the environment. In this book and in its sequel (Henderson 1997), she offers new directions and possibilities for 'win-win' solutions to a range of global problems. She finds that orthodox economics "is simply politics in disguise" and wants it to cease being "the predominant policy analysis tool of the economic global economic warfare system". In Ekins (1989), leading contributors of new economic thinking analyse the defects of conventional economic theory in the light of contemporary problems and attempt to lay the foundations of a new economic paradigm. Ekins et al. (1992) and Ekins and Max-Neef (1992) also contribute to this new economic synthesis. Douthwaite (1996) advocates the strengthening of local economies to increase security in an unstable world. *Socioeconomics* has emerged as an extension of economics that has a more complex picture of economic reality (Etzioni and Lawrence 1993).

Green economics was discussed by Schumacher (1973) and now covers a range of new approaches. David Pearce and his colleagues have developed an approach to environmental economics as an extension of orthodox economics, in a series of books beginning with Pearce et al. (1989). Dahl (1996) explains why present economic and political systems are not working and integrates economic, ecological, and spiritual aims into a new paradigm for understanding and changing them. Jacobs (1991) presents the central issues involved in creating an environmental economics, together with several practical proposals for linking it with sustainable development and the politics of the future.[32]

In his classic book *Progress and Poverty*, the nineteenth-century American economist Henry George (1879) pioneered an important strand of economic thought that has largely been ignored or underestimated by mainstream economists but has attracted people from most walks of life for over 100 years. This economic paradigm advocates economic justice as a natural law, based on health, symmetry, strength, fraternity, and cooperation. It states that the land should be made public property and that taxation should be based largely on the amounts of land that people hold and use. There now seems to be a significant revival of interest in George's ideas. The book *Land and Taxation* (Tideman 1994) is a good, modern statement of these ideas,[33] including the principle of the classical economists that land is distinct from capital and that land, labour, and capital are the three basic factors of production.[34] Hartzok (1994) shows how to apply these concepts to finance planetary management. In the UK, several organisations and networks are cooperating on the Campaign for Interest-Free Money as a voluntary initiative to promote economic democracy.[35]

Korten (1996) strongly criticises global capitalism's continued quest for economic growth as the organising principle of contemporary public policy, because it is accelerating social and environmental disintegration in almost every country of the world. Its forces have transformed many formerly beneficial corporations and financial institutions, often against their will, into instruments of tyranny. In particular, Korten views the new global World Trade Organization (WTO) as a triumph for corporate libertarianism.[36] However, millions of people worldwide have already begun to reclaim their power, rebuild their communities, and heal the Earth. Korten outlines a citizens' agenda to enhance their efforts, by moving corporations out of politics and creating localised green economies to empower local communities within a framework of global cooperation. There would be a 'community enterprise economy',[37] which would combine the market forces of the money economy with the community forces of the social economy. Dauncey (1988) traces the emergence of a new economy at the grassroots level in many parts of the world.

The authors of Gibson-Graham (1996) explore the possibility of more enlivening modes of thought and action beyond capitalist theory and practice. They argue that capitalism need not be dominant, and outlines a noncapitalist political economy, derived from feminism, that might be able to take root and flourish.

Yamaguchi (1997a) discusses the conditions for an economy to be sustainable, concludes that capitalism is fatally flawed in the sense that it cannot appreciate the most important values for a better life and sustainable development, and outlines a paradigm for a 'MuRatopian'[38] economy. This economy will be adapted to the information age, which we are now entering and which enables the customised production of info-goods, info-services, and knowledge. It will provide an information-sharing network, self-management, participatory democracy, and sustainable development within a cooperative framework. It will be a global village economy.

I developed a preliminary version of a 'resources paradigm for economics' in Mayne (1993a), where I outlined its applications to unemployment and the future of work and constructive activities. Resources can broadly be classified into material resources, both renewable and nonrenewable; human resources; and financial resources, which are essentially keys that make human and material resources available. Due to continuing advances in science and technology, there should, in the long term, be no shortage of the renewable material resources available to all people, but great care is needed with nonrenewable resources and the environmental impacts of material resources during the next few decades. The amount of human resources required to produce sufficient material resources is steadily decreasing, while more human resources need to be applied to fulfilling the educational, service, and caring needs of human beings.

Viewed thus, the appropriate and fair distribution of resources, which includes financing and direct allocation, is a key issue in both politics and economics. Apart from temporary difficulties during the next few decades, there should be no real problem in finding enough material resources. It will be much more important to find sufficient human resources of the right kinds to meet real future human needs. The paradigm urgently needs further development and a mathematical formulation.

Business and Management Paradigms

During recent decades, new paradigms for more human, democratic, and socially accountable forms of business have been emerging. As early as 1896, the German company Zeiss endeavoured to give its workers a stake in its performance, and a few other companies followed suit during subsequent years.[39] From the 1940s on, George Goyder gradually developed his vision of the unity of business, industrial, and social purposes and his proposals for an extension of company law, which would enable a fair balance between the interests of all of a company's stakeholders: shareholders, employees, society, and customers. He presented the latest version of his ideas in the second edition of his book *The Just Enterprise* (Goyder 1993), ideas developed further in the book *The Stakeholder Corporation* (Wheeler and Sillanpää 1997). The Caux Round Table has formulated "Principles for Business"[40] based on general principles of business responsibility and stakeholder principles. During recent years, the idea of *stakeholder partnership* has been carried over from business to politics, at least in the UK.[41]

Similar ideas, combined with the idea that 'people matter most', were used by several groups of businesspeople, including the Business Network[42] and Probono. The Royal Society of Arts in the UK has initiated the important Tomorrow's Company initiative, Redefining Work Project, and Living Systems Group. Business in the Community has been active in the UK for quite a long time "to integrate the social and economic regeneration of communities with business involvement and successful business practice."[43] In this and other ways, the community and social activities of the British business sector are beginning to work with the social and economic regeneration policies of the new British government. In his provocative and passionate personal statement *The Hungry Spirit*, Charles Handy (1998) argues for a responsible individualism, which he calls 'proper selfishness', applied to a more humane 'reinvented capitalism', and 'citizen companies', a different sort of business working more closely with the community.

There has also been a considerable movement for green and sustainable business in many part of the world. During the late 1980s, the green consumer movement and other parts of the green movement were already influencing several large corporations to make their business practice more sustainable, and 'green' entrepreneurs were beginning to emerge.[44] In his book *The Greening of Business*, John Davis (1994), as a businessman, urges business to pursue a new path of discriminating sustainable development, in which the richer countries will have to consume very much less material and energy resources than before[45] to enable decent standards of living and quality of life to be achieved in all parts of the world. The book's final chapter states the need for global sustainable development and a new business philosophy. Hutchinson (1991) is a guide to good environmental performance by businesses. Hawken (1994) argues that only big business worldwide has the power to reverse the Earth's ecological destruction. The commercial system must be more like biological systems by becoming self-sustaining. nonwasteful, and self-replicating.

Frances Cairncross (1992) argues that the right government policies, combined with the innovative powers of industries, can unite ecological aims with industrial needs and innovative targets. She concludes that a truly green economy is unlikely to be badly managed and that a well-managed company can be green relatively easily. The book *Changing Course* (Schmidheiny 1992) presents the global business perspective on development and the environment of the Business Council for Sustainable Development. Here, the expertise of more than fifty leaders of multinational corporations, based in various countries, helped to prepare analyses and case studies showing how ecological imperatives can be introduced into market forces. Its thirty-eight case studies, from business and industry worldwide, show how ways can be found to produce simultaneously both economic development and a cleaner, safer environment.

It is very disheartening to observe that, despite all these encouraging developments, a very large section of big business still adheres to the old economic and business paradigms and continues to threaten the prospects for humanity. One example of this is the way in which the Global Climate Coalition (GCC), representing several big business interests in the United States, has promoted adverse publicity against warnings about the dangers of climate change.[46] The GCC's influence has already led the Clinton-Gore administration to abandon its previous plans to adopt more far-reaching targets for reducing U.S. CO_2 emissions. Korten (1995) has given many other examples of the destructive conduct and damaging influence of many of the world's big corporations. All this throws doubt on how far business and industry intend to adopt more sustainable, longer-term approaches, even in companies that have explicitly expressed willingness to do this in principle.

BIOLOGICAL PARADIGMS

Sociobiology is the study of the social aspects of biological behaviour, but it seems to be more important for its insights into animal life than into human behaviour.[47]

Evolution theory, as originally formulated by Darwin in 1859, emphasised natural selection and the survival of the fittest as one of the major driving forces of biological evolution. Within a few years, social Darwinists, such as Herbert Spencer, already cited Darwinian evolution as a reason for supporting laissez-faire economics. Darwin's theory was later combined with Mendelian genetics, which identifies genes as discrete units of heredity. This led to a Neodarwinist theory, postulating that random mutations of genes cause the genetic variability of individuals, on which natural selection acts, and to molecular biology, which revealed many details of genetic mechanisms.

The resulting reductionist and mechanistic approach contributed to the manipulative and exploitative approach of modern *biotechnology*, including *genetic engineering*. Ho (1998) gives extensive details of the ways in which the effects of genetic engineering, when combined with those of global capitalism, have already become especially damaging and dangerous. She (49–56, ch. 8) outlines a new genetics, which began to emerge in the 1970s, and encourages belief in a similar concept of a dynamic, participatory democratic society.

In 1968, James Lovelock envisaged the *Gaia Hypothesis*, which he formally proposed jointly with Lynn Margulis in 1973.[48] The basic principle of the Gaia Hypothesis is that life on Earth, together with its nonliving environment, closely control the climate and other environmental conditions in such a way that life can flourish and evolve. Planet Earth, Gaia, will probably be able to survive the present global environmental crisis, but will adjust to encourage the evolution of those species that can achieve a better new environment. Nevertheless, Lovelock (1991), applying his concept of *planetary medicine*, gives the diagnosis that Gaia is seriously sick. The survival of the human species is not necessary to the survival of Gaia as a living organism.

Elisabet Sahtouris (1989) explains the Gaia Hypothesis and its wider implications, tracing the history of Earth from its origins to today. She argues that, by understanding Gaia and the true roles of competition and cooperation in biological evolution, we may be able to solve our greatest problems: economic, ecological, political, and spiritual.

Several new medical paradigms are being developed today,[49] especially by those interested in alternative and complementary medicine as well as conventional medicine.[50] The Scientific and Medical Network is an informal, international group of scientists, doctors, and other professionals that aims to deepen understanding in science, medicine, and education through rational analyses and intuitive insights. Several of its members recently formed a very active Energy Medicine Group, which aims to facilitate the integration of different medical approaches and to develop a common model of healing based on science, spirituality, and experience. These emerging new medical paradigms are very significant, because they could indicate new ways of healing the human species.

The Living Systems Paradigm

The living systems paradigm is a possible new paradigm for politics that I have outlined and that provides new insights into the current human and global situation and could provide valuable pointers to its transformation into a new age of human fulfillment and a quantum leap into the next stage of human evolution.

Viewing humankind as a living system, the essential role of politics and governance is to ensure that the necessary products and services are provided to humankind as a whole and to its individual cells (people) and groups of people in the best ways. The essential role of economics and business is to provide these products and services. The essential role of ecology and the environment is to ensure the harmonious relationship between humankind, other living systems, and planet Earth as a whole. These are the ideals, which are at present far from being achieved; our great challenge, as we are about to enter the twenty-first century and the third millennium, is to find feasible ways of moving towards the ideals while overcoming the many threats and crises that face us.

The present situation of humankind is highly unbalanced and unstable; that is why it is also critical. The imbalance includes overwhelming inequalities of power and resources between different individuals and groupings of people in the human 'body', and most of these inequalities are steadily becoming worse.

The escalation of certain global trends, especially the indiscriminate ex-pansion of the global economy at the expense of the global environment, means that the human body shows all the signs of having cancer. But it is not only suffering from cancer; many, if not most of, its inhabitants suffer from lack of purpose and lack of future vision. The root causes of its complex of illnesses and dis-eases include profound faults in human nature and in lack of awareness of the true situation. To address this illness, we need to address its root causes, which, in turn, means reformulating fundamental principles.

These principles include moral principles and ethical values, a true under-standing of human resources, and appropriate paradigms for our times. For example, one aim is to ensure the fulfillment of the potential of each indi-vidual as much as possible, and another aim is to do this within a framework that is a true global community, with all its sections working together in true partnership.

The ultimate aim is to involve as many organisations and individuals as possible, of all different kinds, not only at the national level but also at local and even at neighbourhood levels and upwards at continental and global levels. The organisations would include governments, government depart-ments, businesses, voluntary organisations, educational institutions and, of course, social networks of all kinds. Individuals would be encouraged to participate through many of their different roles, ranging from professional or work skills to social and individual relationships, loving, and caring. This, like other aspects, can be explored best by using both the analogy of a single living organism and also the analogy of a community of living organisms, indeed, when viewed in terms of their environment also, an ecosystem. Detailed explorations there have hardly begun but are urgently needed.

A World Brain/World Mind and a World Heart are both needed. Explora-tion and formulation of the World Brain and World Mind concepts were ably begun by H. G. Wells (1938) in his book *World Brain* and continued by a small, but devoted, group of scholars.[51] To achieve a human brain-plus-nervous system that is effective, a comprehensive, dynamic database is needed, what Wells called the 'World Encyclopaedia', with adequate information and communication functions. All these can be implemented today, vastly more effectively than in Wells' time, by modern multimedia personal computing and information technologies. The World Brain also needs to be intimately linked to a World Mind and closely collaborate with it, as in an advanced living organism, and as Wells himself foresaw. Here, the ideas of the World Brain/World Mind as a learning and teaching system, an education system, come into play. This would act as the main instrument of achieving full global awareness, together with the appropriate purposes, visions, and will to do what needs doing. The implementation of these aspects requires new educational paradigms and ideas for new global curricula and educational networks, now being developed. At the level of global human thinking, generally acceptable human goals need to be formulated, well-considered policies are needed, and a participatory policy-making process within a wider framework of participatory democracy needs to be developed. This would match the processes of human sensory input, transformed by the brain/mind into appropriate motor output in the form of appropriate and effective practical policies and actions. This process needs to be guided by knowledge, understanding, and wisdom, an aspect that Kochen (1972) explored in considerable depth.

The concept of a 'World Heart' was outlined by Richard Kirby and Steven Rosen as a chapter in Kirby and Rossman (1990). The concept envisages that some of the impulses activating the emerging World Brain/World Mind are love (at least of truth and humanity) and the quest for wholeness (as all data and all people are interconnected). This concept urgently needs further development and elaboration, using existing moral philosophies, religious traditions, and ethical movements as some of its starting points. Very recently, the deaths of Diana, Princess of Wales, and of Mother Theresa may have initiated what could become a nationwide, eventually a worldwide 'World Heart Movement', building on the notable love, compassion, caring, and intuition shown by these outstanding people. Such a development needs every encouragement.

PHYSICAL SCIENCES PARADIGMS

At the beginning of this century, classical physics, which many scientists had hitherto considered to provide a 'final' picture of the nature of physical reality, began to be transformed radically by relativity theory and quantum theory. Both these new theories showed that fundamental, widely accepted paradigms can suddenly and rather unexpectedly be challenged by new, alternative paradigms.[52] At the same time, classical physics, relativity theory, and quantum theory still coexist in the sense that each of them has domains of appropriate application inside physics as a whole. Similarly, it is possible to imagine a world where a wide range of social and political paradigms coexist, in what are found to be complementary areas for their appropriate application. Relativity theory and quantum theory also introduced definite roles for the observer inside physics. In relativity, the appropriate frame of reference for describing events depends on the observer's situation, especially his or her velocity relative to that of other observers. Quantum theory introduced the concept that the observer inevitably influences the outcome of scientific measurements, observations, and experiments. Both these aspects of the observer can also be applied in the social and human sciences and in politics.

The book *The Quantum Society* (Zohar and Marshall 1994) argues that the insights of quantum physics can improve our understanding of everyday life and develops a new *quantum psychology*. It addresses contemporary moral and political dilemmas arising from the challenges of today's rapid changes, the inability of conventional societies and politics to cope with this, and the sterile conflict between selfish individualism and restrictive collectivism. We can change our social perceptions, values, and behaviour by drawing our deepest images and metaphors from the nature of the mind and the nature of the physical universe. The book's new theory of cosmic and social evolution could enable us to rediscover the meaning and purpose of our lives and of society, by reinventing ourselves, our relationships, our families, and our communities. Through mutual dialogue we could reach a new consensus that itself richly celebrates diversity.

MATHEMATICAL SCIENCES PARADIGMS

Probability Theory and Statistics

During 1996, the analysis and perception of risk were widely discussed in the UK, as important challenges to the science, engineering, and technology (SET) community. Probability theory can be applied to making quantitative estimates of various types of risk,[53] but it is often difficult to calculate such estimates because of inadequate information and the unquantifiable nature of many types of uncertainty. On 11 September 1996, Ian Taylor, who was then minister for science and technology in the UK government, warned scientists that public concern about risk was leading to increasing skepticism about the advantages of scientific research.[54] He said that it was not enough to inform the public about new discoveries and expect them to react rationally; we must first establish an appropriate system for measuring risk. In his two books, John Adams (1985, 1995) discusses risk mainly from the psychological viewpoint of how people perceive risks and behave in various types of risky situation.

During recent years, there have been increasing public misgivings in the UK about the ability of British courts to give fair verdicts, and a considerable number of convictions for murder and other serious offences have been found to be 'unsafe and insecure' when reviewed by higher courts, usually many years after the original verdict of 'guilty'. Mayne (1994: 25–26) has briefly explored the possibility that one reason for this situation is that judges take insufficient account of probability theory when assessing legal evidence. Sir Richard Eggleston (1983) is one of the few lawyers who have seriously considered probability theory in relation to legal evidence; his book covers various aspects of the legal implications of logic and probability theory.

Politicians' widespread misinterpretation and misuse of statistics, while presenting cases for their particular policies or viewpoints, are so notorious that they have led to the well-known phrase "Lies, damned lies, and statistics!" Champney (1994) gives examples of the applications of statistics to politics.

Nonlinear Mathematics

Recent developments in nonlinear mathematics, especially chaos theory[55] and complexity,[56] have shown that many phenomena studied by science are very much less predictable than had been previously supposed. This is true of the behaviour of market economies, for example. Bak (1996) introduces a concept of 'self-organised criticality' to explain various complex patterns that repeatedly occur in nature and in human affairs. He points out (ch. 11) that economies show various forms of instability, even though the mathematical theory of economics has, until recently, been almost exclusively concerned with 'economic equilibria'. In particular, like many other systems, they are liable to fluctuations of activity that can occasionally be very large. From this point of view, a pure market economy occasionally has depressions as drastic as that of the 1930s, and such depressions could occur in the future. It is still an open question how far financial and economic policies by governments could prevent a major, worldwide depression during the next few years.

The book by Anderla et al. (1997) is "a book to start the new century thinking . . . about optimism. . . . about solutions, creation and understanding".[57] It is entitled *CHAOTICS: An Agenda for Business and Society in the Twenty-first Century*. Its authors strongly feel that human progress does have a future but that we need to redraw our picture of reality, using the perspective provided by 'chaotics' (a combined theory of chaos plus complexity) to give us a truer understanding of the processes of the real world. They suggest various ways of applying it to contribute to the improvement of the human situation.

The book's last chapter sums up some of the key global problems, some of the major areas covered, and some of the pathways towards solutions offered. Although much more work will be needed to find workable, practical applications of chaotics in the areas that the authors address, they make several very brave and interesting initial attempts and provide a wide range of valuable insights in the process. For example, today's world problems require revolutionary new policies; tinkering with the system or relying on gradual evolutionary changes alone will not be enough. Again, microeconomics is becoming much more important than macroeconomics, and it will require an element of mutual cooperation as well as the usual competition. However, I personally feel that the authors somewhat overemphasise what free-enterprise economics can do and underestimate aspects of the generally discredited collectivist, socialist, and planning approaches that could still make an important though limited contribution. They do not mention most of the new economic paradigms emerging during recent decades.

NOTES

1. Paradigms covered by Burrows et al. (1991: pt. 2) include (1) systems thinking and other paradigms related to integrated approaches (ch. 10); (2) paradigms for integrated planning and policies (ch. 11); (3) the Gaia Hypothesis and allied paradigms (ch. 12); (4) Teilhard de Chardin's concept of the noosphere, Wells' 'World Brain' concept, information technology, and computer networking and social networking concepts (ch. 13); (5) paradigms about the human being as a whole (ch. 14); and (6) scientific and holistic paradigms (ch. 15).

2. See Maslow (1987), for example.

3. Recent books on psychology in general include those by Glassman (1995), Gross (1994), Hayes (1994), and Hollin (1995). Banyard and Hayes (1994) discuss the theory and applications of psychology, and Gross (1995) presents themes, issues, and debates in psychology.

4. Books on psychosynthesis include Assagioli (1974, 1993a, b), Russell and Whitmore (1991), and Hardy (1996).

5. Important books on human creativity and creative thinking include Koestler (1964), Boden (1992), Leytham (1990), Buzan (1995), and de Bono (1996). Sternberg and Kalligian (1992) present research on human competence. Majaro (1988) discusses the application of creative thinking to creative management in business.

6. Adams (1985, 1995) presents research on people's perceptions of risk and behaviour in risky situations.

7. Recent books on social psychology include Brown (1996), David Myers (1994), and Hayes (1993). Argyle (1992) discusses some important applications of social psychology to human life.

8. See, for example, Professor Steven Jones' BBC 2 TV programme about genetics and crime on 3 June 1997.

9. See Bryce-Smith (1995) and the references cited there.

10. Conflict resolution is discussed in detail by Tidwell (1998), Vayrynen (1991), Macy (1989), and Barnaby (1988); it is also considered by Felder (1991), Ferencz (1991), and Burrows et al. (1991: 156–160, 165). Otunnu and Doyle (1998) discuss the future of peacemaking and peacekeeping. Gutmann and Thompson (1998) consider how Americans might resolve some of their difficult moral disagreements.

11. Social theories in general are presented by Turner (1995) and by Layder (1994), who provide a general introduction. Turner (1996) covers 'classical' and later theories, and Scott (1995) gives examples of contemporary debates.

12. Goodin and Pettit (1993: ch. 4) discuss the contributions of sociology, especially the ideas of Durkheim and Weber, to political philosophy.

13. See, for example, Giddens (1997: ch. 1). Other major books on sociology and the social sciences include *The Blackwell Companion to Social Theory* (Turner 1996), *The*

Social Science Encyclopedia (Kuper and Kuper 1996), and the reader *Society & Social Science* (Anderson and Ricci 1994). See also Goodin and Pettit (1995: ch. 4).

14. See Giddens (1997: ch. 3).
15. See Giddens (1997: ch. 4).
16. See Giddens (1997: ch. 11).
17. See Giddens (1997: ch. 12).
18. See Giddens (1997: ch. 13).
19. See Giddens (1997: ch. 14).
20. See Giddens (1997: ch. 15).
21. See Giddens (1997: ch. 18).
22. See Giddens (1997: ch. 19).
23. See Giddens (1997: ch. 21).
24. For a brief outline, see Krieger (1993: 112–114).
25. For a brief outline, see Krieger (1993: 157–158).
26. Keynesian theory was based on Keynes' economic 'classic' Keynes (1936). The postwar Keynesian consensus of most British economists lasted until the late 1970s; Cockett (1995) tells how a group of neo-classical 'economic liberals' overturned this consensus after a fifty-year campaign but ends by anticipating a counter-revolution against economic liberalism.
27. Discussions of 'economic long waves' include Freeman et al (1982), Freeman (1986), Barry (1991), and Tylecote (1993). Alesina et al. (1998) discuss political cycles in relation to economic cycles.
28. Leading textbooks on the 'orthodox' theory, practice, and practical applications of capitalist economics include the 'classic' Samuelson et al. (1998), Baumol and Blinder (1997), Lipsey and Chrystal (1995), and Stiglitz (1997), which also discusses economic policy issues. Griffiths and Wall (1997) provide an introductory guide to applied economics. Hunt (1995) reviews the evolution of some of capitalism's most important institutions and analyses ideological defences and radical critiques of capitalism. Perelman (1996) shows how markets have always been subject to many constraints, even in the most capitalist societies. See also *Theory of Games and Economic Behaviour* (von Neumann and Morgenstern 1947).
29. See Burrows et al. (1991: ch. 1) for a fairly detailed discussion of how far 'green' and 'new' economics had developed by 1991.
30. PROUT economics is outlined in Avadhuta (1990: ch. 8) and *New Renaissance* 2(Spring 1990): 10–12 and 3(Summer 1990): 7–10.
31. Robertson (1996) considers some analogies between aspects of contemporary science and economics. Robertson (1998a) contains a collection of Robertson's papers and articles on new economics and allied subjects.
32. See also Prato (1997) and the Group of Green Economists (1992).
33. This book is one of several books in the Georgist Paradigm Series, edited by Fred Harrison.
34. See the paper "Land as a Distinctive Factor of Production" by the American economist Mason Gaffney (Tideman 1994: 38–102).
35. In the Middle Ages, the Christian, Jewish, and Muslim religions all forbade usury, the levying of interest on loans. Islam today, at least in theory, still opposes the use of interest. The German economist Margrit Kennedy (1995) suggests how to devise an interest-free and inflation-free economy.
36. Korten (1995: ch. 13) describes how the WTO emerged quietly on 1 January

1995 during the Uruguay Round of GATT, the General Agreement on Tariffs and Trade. He sees GATT-WTO as de facto the world's highest legislative and judicial body, working to guarantee the corporate rights of big business worldwide without proper democratic accountability. The proposed Multilateral Agreement on Investment (MAI) could be even more sinister, according to Corporate Europe Observatory (1998) and various other commentators.

37. The term 'community enterprise economy' was introduced by Malaysian consumer activist Bishan Singh (1994).

38. The word 'MuRatopian' is derived from the Japanese words 'Mura' (village), 'Mu' (nothingness), and 'Ra' (dispossession) and the Greek word 'topos' (place). The MuRatopian economic paradigm is fully explained in Yamaguchi (1989) and outlined in Yamaguchi (1990). It is extended in Yamaguchi (1999).

39. See Goyder (1993: ix). In the 1960s, Goyder was a policy adviser to the Liberal Party, which proposed the stakeholder company as an alternative to socialist ownership.

40. Copies of this statement are available as a supplement of *Business Ethics* and obtainable by telephoning 612-962-4700 in the United States.

41. See Kelly et al. (1997), the report of the Commission on Public Policy and Big Business (1997), and the end of Chapter 2.

42. Kinsman (1983) gives many examples of the ways in which the climate of thought has been changing in many important British businesses; he was a cofounder of the Business Network.

43. See *Financial Times* (4 December 1997), which includes the 1997 Annual Report of Business in the Community.

44. This trend is discussed by Elkington and Burke (1987) and Elkington et al. (1992).

45. Recently, the book *Factor Four* (von Weizsäcker et al. 1997) has shown many ways in which wealth can by doubled while resource use is halved. The International Factor 10 Club (1997) indicates that even more dramatic savings of resources per unit production can be achieved! It calls on governments, industry, and international and nongovernmental organisations to adopt a factor ten increase in energy and resource productivity as a strategic goal for the twenty-first century; it urges that an immediate start be made on preparations to meet this objective.

46. This news was featured in the BBC 1 television Panorama programme "Greenhouse Wars" on 1 December 1997. In the same programme, John Gummer, who was secretary of state for the environment in the former (Conservative) UK government, expressed extreme concern and dismay about this development.

47. See Giddens (1997: 20–21, 595).

48. Two books by Lovelock (1987, 1994) provide his own exposition of the Gaia Hypothesis.

49. Woodhouse (1996: ch. 11) discusses some new approaches to health and healing. Burrows et al. (1991: 255–259) briefly reviews complementary medicine and holistic medicine.

50. *Medical Marriage* (Featherstone and Forsyth 1997) tells the story of an integrated health care system in the Highlands of Scotland, where doctors collaborate closely with practitioners of complementary therapies; it also has sixty chapters on complementary therapies, written by these practitioners.

51. See the new edition of this book (Wells 1995).

52. Kuhn (1970) describes in considerable detail how and why several major paradigm shifts in the physical sciences actually occurred.

53. The application of probability theory to risk is discussed by Beard et al. (1969), for example.

54. Ian Taylor's speech was part of a discussion about risk at the Festival of Science held by the British Association for the Advancement of Science (BAAS) in September 1996 and reported briefly by Mayne (1997b). On 18 March, the Royal Society held a meeting, "Science, Policy, and Risk", reported by Foxon (1997). The essays in *The Politics of Risk Society* (Franklin 1998) include several about risks associated with scientific and technological advances.

55. Gleick (1998) gives a good, popular exposition of chaos theory.

56. Waldrop (1993) gives a good, popular exposition of complexity theory. His outline of Brian Arthur's economic theory of increasing returns (Waldrop 1993: ch. 1) is especially relevant. Mainzer (1997: ch. 6) discusses complex economic systems and other complex systems in relation to the evolution of human society. Mainzer (1994: ch. 7) considers the relationship between complexity, responsibility, and freedom. In his critique of economics, Ormerod (1995) also considers the relevance of nonlinear mathematics.

57. In an electronic mail message from Jeremy Geelan to members of the UK Futures Group, dated 8 September 1997.

SOME TOPICS FOR FURTHER INVESTIGATION

1. Although lower needs in the 'Maslow hierarchy' must usually be satisfied first, there are many instances when creative people, especially in Third World grassroots movements, are able to achieve much without having those needs fully met. From your own experience or knowledge of such people, discuss how their positive attitudes and motivations are able to overcome their adverse circumstances.

2. Examine how far community spirit is actually achieved in several localities and associations that are well known to you. How often is such community spirit positive, in the sense that all members of the community have good relationships with each other, how often is it negative, in the sense that some members are excluded or bullied, and how often is it present only to a very limited extent? Analyse your findings in terms of communication links between specific pairs or small groups of people.

3. From your experience of different paradigms in political science, how far do you consider that the study of politics can be objective and scientific?

4. Considering politics as 'the constrained use of powers', analyse a political regime that you know at any level from global to local and find out how the actions and policies of some of its leading politicians are actually constrained. Perform the same exercise for corresponding groups of lawyers, business executives, media, and educators and find out the relative amounts exercised by these different groups.

5. Examine a significant political conflict that has already been resolved, apparently successfully, and another that is still continuing. In each case, find out what approaches to conflict resolution were applied and how effectively and what methods were not attempted.

6. Give some examples of how the findings of sociology or other social and human sciences could improve understanding of political ideas and processes.

7. How far does global capitalism, especially the activities of multinational companies, actually restrict the freedom of action of those national governments with which you are familiar? What can national governments do to limit such erosion of their power? What can ordinary citizens and grassroots movements do to limit or transform for the better the influence of global capitalism?

8. Discuss what combinations of 'new economics' thinking and alternative economic paradigms could form the basis for a new economic paradigm that could provide a credible alternative to capitalism and collectivism.

9. After doing the previous exercise, outline how such a new paradigm might be applied to developing effective policies to reduce unemployment and provide everyone with adequate opportunities for constructive and creative work.

10. How would you apply holistic approaches in mainstream and complementary medicine and Lovelock's ideas of 'planetary medicine' to develop concepts of 'healing humanity' and 'healing the planet'? Discuss some implications of these concepts for political theory and practice.

11. Attempt to apply the 'living systems paradigm' to some aspects of politics or some political issues with which you are familiar.

12. Explore some implications of probability theory and statistics and/or of nonlinear mathematics for political practice. For example, do this in relation to risk analysis and prediction and/or chaotics.

11

Spiritual Politics

Like many other words in common use, 'spiritual' has a range of dictionary meanings, so that there is often considerable confusion about what it does or should mean. Sometimes, it refers to the 'nonmaterial', including psychological and mental, side of the human being and human living. At other times, it is more explicitly linked to 'religion', which itself has a variety of meanings and is hard to define. In Burrows et al. (1991: 251), I introduced a threefold concept of the human being as body, mind, and spirit, as a first approximation to what is probably a complex truth. 'Body' does not really need definition, because we all seem to be clear about what it means. 'Mind' is defined as "that part of us that has consciousness and is able to think and decide". 'Spirit' is defined as "that part of us that has values and chooses them; it includes our conscience, which provides our moral imperatives and helps us to make difficult moral judgements, but it is also concerned with truth and beauty". I also use these definitions in this chapter, because I think that they clarify the situation; they have the additional advantage that they are independent of philosophical worldview. They show that people can be 'spiritual', caring deeply for values, without necessarily also being religious; at the same time, the spirituality of those people who *are* religious[1] is closely associated with their religious beliefs and worship.

Wilber (1998) considers that the most urgent political issue today, both in the United States and elsewhere in the world, is to find "a way to integrate the tradition of liberalism with a genuine spirituality" (p. xiii) and discusses how this might be done (xiii–xix). In Wilber's view, liberals have tended to replace salvation by God with salvation by economics. In trying to protect individual liberty, liberalism has been liable to deny religious, spiritual, and other communal values, while conservatism too often has too narrow a religious viewpoint. In this book, he attempts to find a spiritual liberation; although it is not a book about politics, he sees where we locate Spirit as the key issue, which always translates into political agendas that depend on how that question is answered (xix). Indeed, there is *no* place where there is *not* Spirit, and there is *only* Spirit (282).

In this chapter, I define 'spiritual politics' as an approach to politics that is motivated by an altruistic approach to living in general and politics in particular. It always has a strong ethical content and often also has a significant religious component. Therefore, the chapter's first section concerns ethical approaches, and its second section discusses examples of spiritual politics within a religious context. Its third section considers examples of spiritual politics that appear in New Age philosophies of life, whose outlook tends to be 'holistic', by covering all aspects of life, and 'universalist', by drawing on the common ground between different religions.

ETHICAL APPROACHES

'Ethics' provides essential guidance for the actions of every human being, although it can take very different forms in different people. For most religious believers, their religion also provides the foundations for their ethical beliefs and moral codes. For people with an altruistic outlook, whether or not they are religious, their conscience is usually a strong source of moral guidance. Two aspects of ethical approaches to politics are especially important. The first is concerned with how to bring about the higher standards of ethical living and responsibility that are required to improve the quality of citizenship and politics worldwide, in a world where many people have limited moral standards, and a significant minority are obsessed with seeking power and money. The second addresses the problem of how to find systems of global ethics that can attract wide acceptance in a world now split between adherents of different, often conflicting cultures and ideologies. Both these approaches will be needed to make an optimistic political scenario practicable.

Ethical Living

In human affairs, we need to return to the basics of the essential ethics and morality of the great religions, to counter the overwhelming effects of the lust for power, selfishness, and greed that are among the root causes of the present global human crisis.

In his inspiring book *The Seven Habits of Highly Effective People*, Stephen Covey (1992b) presents a much-needed holistic, integrated, principle-centred approach to personal living at home and work. To achieve a more constructive life, with a true sense of purpose, he says that most of us need to understand and then change our maps of life, our paradigms of thinking and living. He advocates a return to the 'Character Ethic', a principle-centred paradigm based on principles of effective living. He defines 'principles' as fundamental guidelines for human conduct that have proven, enduring, permanent value. He identifies the basic principles as fairness, integrity and honesty, human dignity, service, quality and excellence, fulfillment of potential, patience, nurturing, and encouragement, which we require for our personal development. The more closely our paradigms are to these moral principles, the better they will be.

People evolve from dependence in early life, through independence in adolescence, to interdependence in adult life. Covey describes seven primary habits of effectiveness that embody many of the fundamental principles of living. Together with the principle of 'P/PC balance', between production of desired results and ability to produce those results, they help people to improve the process of transition between these successive stages of their evolution. They can be defined as intersections of knowledge (what to do and why), skill (how to do), and desire (wish to do). They can be learned properly only by adopting a principle-centred paradigm. Covey provides a step-by-step pathway for learning them, illustrated by penetrating insights and valuable stories from everyday life.

The first three habits help us to move from dependence to independence. We need to be *proactive* by taking initiative and responsibility for our own lives. We need to *set our goals* clearly and then apply our conscience and efforts to achieve them. We need to *put first things first*, by applying our time and effort effectively to our priorities. The next three habits help us to move from independence to interdependence. We need to *think win-win*[2] by aiming to achieve the best results for others besides ourselves. We need to *understand others and be understood*. We need to *work together with other people* by *synergy*, so that what we do together is greater than the sum of what each of us can achieve separately. The other important habit is to apply the principles of *balanced self-renewal* to all areas of our lives.

These concepts can be generalised to situations involving groups of human beings, all the way from the family to the whole human species. Covey (1992a) has himself applied them to principle-centred leadership and success in business and in work. My own views about this generalisation are as follows. In economics, the approximate analogues of dependence, independence, and interdependence are collectivism, capitalism, and a new form of 'world co-operative economy'[3] whose principles are not yet fully formulated. In business, they correspond approximately to authoritarian styles of management, excessive emphasis on self-reliance and self-employment, and participatory management together with social businesses and cooperative business networks in a 'people matter most' framework. In politics, they correspond approximately to the authoritarian state or the 'nanny state', market-oriented, individualistic regimes, and what could emerge as a worldwide framework of participatory, multilevel democracy. In all these areas of life, the seven habits can be applied directly with immediate advantage for all concerned.

Ervin Laszlo (1989) argues that humanity's really decisive limits are inner, not outer, so that we have been tackling the wrong problems and issues. *We* are the cause of most of our problems and can resolve them only by redesigning our thinking and actions, rather than the world around us. Ways of contributing to human transformation are explored.

Elliott (1995) is a selection of some of the best and most interesting articles on ethics and the environment written during the last twenty years.

Global Ethics

Although there are considerable, occasionally great, divergences between the specific ethical codes of different cultures and religious groups, the basic moral principles are essentially the same for the great religions in their original form. Their basic similarity gives some grounds for hoping for the emergence of a *global ethic*, which can bring together personal, social, national, and international goals.

Laszlo (1977) presents the results of an international survey of national and international goals, conducted for the Club of Rome. Its first part surveys current goals and aspirations worldwide. Its second part considers what long-term international policies could make the world safer and more humane. Its third part examines how people could work together towards these policies. The book as a whole indicates how to change from self-centred, short-term goals to humanity-centred long-term goals in the interest of *all* people.

In 1987, Rushworth Kidder, an American journalist and author, interviewed twenty-two leading global citizens and asked each of them the fundamental question, "What are the half dozen major-intensity issues that will face humanity in the twenty-first century?" While the group generally agreed on a predictable set of problems, such as the nuclear threat, environmental degradation, the population gap, and the need for educational reform, Kidder said that he was unprepared for their pervasive concern about a global breakdown in ethics and morality. They seemed to be saying that a collapse of ethics would doom us just as surely as a nuclear holocaust or a population overrun or an environmental catastrophe. Later, he conducted a series of interviews with twenty-four individuals from sixteen countries,[4] asking the question, "If you could formulate a global code of ethics for the twenty-first century, what would be on it?" Whatever the sex, race, or religion of the interviewee, the values that emerged were very much the same. It was found that many, if not most, people share core values, such as honesty, respect for people, responsibility, fairness, compassion, and respect for life.

In 1990, Kidder founded the Institute for Global Ethics as an independent, nonprofit organisation dedicated to promoting the discussion of ethics in a global context. It responds to the ever-growing need for identifying and describing ethical standards throughout the world. It attempts to help discover what these values actually are and to promote their discussion in ways that are inclusive, do not threaten, and contribute to conflict resolution. The institute began its work in the United States. It helped to formulate the Maine Code of Election Ethics, drawn up between politicians of all viewpoints in Maine, which agreed to the following principles of fair campaign practices: honesty, fairness, respect for opponents, responsibility, and compassion. It now has about 2000 members worldwide and has a small, but active, branch in the UK.

Hans Küng's (1992) book *Global Responsibility* made a powerful plea for a consensus on basic ethical values among those of all religions and none. It was widely influential and led to a Declaration toward a Global Ethic, which was endorsed by the Parliament of the World's Religions held in Chicago in 1993. Here, representatives of the world's great and small religions and of those with no religion signed this statement of a minimal ethic on which all could agree. Küng and Kuschel (1993) present the text of the declaration, which was drafted after a thorough process of interreligious and international consultation.

Its first principle is that there should be no new global order without a new global ethic. Its fundamental demand is that every human being must be treated humanely. Its four irrevocable directives are its commitments to cultures of (1) nonviolence and respect for life; (2) solidarity and a just economic order; (3) tolerance and a life of truthfulness; and (4) equal rights and partnership between men and women. It realised that Earth cannot be changed for the better without transformations in the consciousness of individuals and in public life.

The declaration was only a beginning, and it was realised that much work needed to be done to elaborate its principles and extend its scope. In Küng (1996) the process is taken one stage further by containing the contributions towards the vision of a global ethic by a remarkable group of international figures, including heads of states and world organisations, religious leaders, scholars, and writers. It announced the creation of the Global Ethic Foundation by K. K. von der Groben and Hans Küng. The foundation is based in Germany and will be devoted to intercultural and interreligious research, education, and encounter. See also *Global Ethics for Global Politics and Economics* (Küng 1997).

The emerging 'Gaian ethic' is based on the concept of planet Earth as one living organism and on principles of caring, sharing, mutual cooperation, synergy, and a balance between self-interest and interests outside oneself.

The Report of the Independent Commission on International Humanitarian Issues (Aga Khan 1988) was written by eminent people from twenty-nine countries from all parts of the world. It calls for compassion and conscience but also realistic, timely action by governments and individuals to meet the great humanitarian challenges of our time. It is addressed to both the public and to policy makers and urges us to act, *before* disaster occurs, by placing humanitarian concerns at the centre of national and global policies. Dower (1998) discusses global ethics in general. Elfstrom (1998) examines the moral issues arising from globalisation.

RELIGION AND POLITICS

Giddens (1997: ch. 16) gives a good introduction to the definition, varieties, and theories of religion, together with the role of religion in different societies. Every known society has at least one form of religion, but the variety of religious beliefs and organisations is so large that scholars have found it very difficult to reach a generally accepted definition of 'religion'.

The principal dictionary definition, which reflects the thinking of most people in the West, is that religion is belief in a superhuman, controlling power, especially a personal God or gods entitled to obedience and worship; it also involves the expression of this belief through worship. More generally, it can be defined as a particular system of faith and worship. 'Worship' is homage or respect paid to a deity but can also refer to adoration or devotion, comparable to religious homage, but shown towards a person or principle. Thus, it is possible to have forms of 'religion' and 'worship' that are applied not to a God or god but to the leader of a totalitarian society or to money and wealth. Giddens (1997: 436–437) points out that religion is not necessarily monotheistic (believing in one God) or able to explain how the world came to be as it is or identifiable with the supernatural or with moral commandments. However, religions do seem to involve a set of symbols, invoking feelings of reverence or awe, together with rituals or ceremonies conducted by communities of believers.

In his article in Krieger (1993: 778–782), Ninian Smart discusses several of the ways in which religion relates to politics and gives examples of how it does this in several countries from different parts of the world.[5] Religion interacts in various ways with the nation-state. Many religions affect international arrangements, because they are powerful worldwide. Religious conflicts can intensify divisions within and between nations. Religious values are often used to justify political policies and actions, and the behaviour of political leaders can be influenced by their religious beliefs. Religious institutions sometimes play an important part within nations.

Approaches to politics that are explicitly associated with the world's major religions can broadly be classified into those based on (1) *fundamentalism*, the strict adherence to the fundamental doctrines or scriptures of any religion; (2) the core ethical and spiritual values of *specific religions*; and (3) *universalism*, the core ethical and spiritual values of what is perceived as the common ground of the main religions.

Fundamentalism and Politics

A fundamentalist approach to any given religion emphasises the literal interpretation of the scriptures of that religion. However, it does not necessarily return to the original values and beliefs of the religion's founder and original disciples, because interpretation is liable to error, especially when made after an interval of many centuries. All three of the main theistic religions have fundamentalist adherents who have exerted considerable political influence. The proliferation of fundamentalism in the twentieth century can be seen as slowing down tendencies to secularise the world and as a sign that the process of secularising the world is by no means complete (Krieger 1993: 819–820). Indeed, fundamentalism questions the previously widespread view of history as continuous progress, which secularists especially have tended to adopt.

During the last twenty-five years or so, there has been an especially notable growth of fundamentalist religious organisations in the United States (Giddens 1997: 463–465). Of these, the most influential have been the Southern Baptists, the Assemblies of God, and the Seventh-Day Adventists. They have been among those religious groups making the most extensive use of television and broadcasting. After Pat Robertson, a well-known television evangelist, failed to gain nomination as a Republican presidential candidate in 1988, he founded the Christian Coalition, which has achieved considerable influence as a political movement in the United States. Many Christian fundamentalists believe that the Bible provides practical guidance for politics, government, and, indeed, all human affairs. Many Christian evangelist missionaries have now become active in Russia, other parts of the CIS, and Eastern Europe (Giddens 1997: 459).

Those Jews who insist on a 'hard line' against the Palestinians in Israel and who are especially keen on building Jewish settlements in traditionally Palestinian areas tend to adopt stricter and more fundamentalist versions of the Jewish faith. Shahak and Mezvinsky (1998) discuss Jewish fundamentalism in Israel.

However, Islamic fundamentalism has an especially important influence worldwide (Giddens 1997: 454–459).[6] For many years, Ayatollah Khomeini ran a government organised according to traditional Islamic law, which aimed to make religion the direct basis of all political and economic life. Islamic fundamentalist movements have become influential in North Africa, especially in Algeria, the Middle East, and South Asia during the past ten to fifteen years. In practice, these movements are not wholly religious and are also partly nationalistic and cultural. Indeed, Burgat (1998) questions the usual portrayal of Islamic movements as predominantly fundamentalist, and Halliday (1995) rejects views that there is a clash between Islam and Western civilisation. More radical Islamic movements stress Islam as an expansionist world order (Krieger 1993: 490–491).

The Main Religions and Politics

The Roman Catholic Church[7] has played an important part in politics ever since its foundation, and its headquarters, the Vatican City, is a small independent state within the city of Rome. The church had a strong theocratic influence in Europe during the Middle Ages and in the Catholic countries after that. Its modern diplomatic role began shortly before World War I, and it has been especially important under the present pope, John Paul II. Its influence became broader after the 1962 ecumenical council, Vatican II, which led to its *Declaration on Religious Freedom* and *The Pastoral Constitution of the Church in the Modern World*, both issued in 1965. As a result of the combined influence of Vatican II and John Paul II, the church perceives its religious role as including a broad and varied public ministry to the world. One of the responses to Vatican II was the emergence of liberation theology[8] a new movement that began among several Catholic bishops and priests in Latin America. This movement emphasises Christians' special responsibilities for liberating poor and oppressed people. Gifford (1998) discusses the public role of African Christianity and the church's role in Africa.

The Creation Spirituality movement emerged from the seminal writings of Matthew Fox, who was formerly a Dominican priest. In his book *Original Blessing* (Fox 1996), he presented the four paths of creation-centred spirituality. (1) The Positive Way befriends creation. (2) The Negative Way befriends darkness, letting go, and letting be. (3) The Creative Way befriends creativity and the 'divinity' within us. (4) The Transformative Way befriends new creation, compassion, celebration, and loving justice; it provides a basis for creating a global civilisation and liberating the world's oppressed peoples. His book *Creation Spirituality* (Fox 1991) further develops the theme of the Transformative Way. It uncovers the ancient tradition of a creation-centred spirituality merging Christian mysticism with the contemporary struggle for social justice, feminism, and environmentalism. It encourages action and challenges readers of every religious and political viewpoint to unite in a new vision, through which we learn to honour the Earth and its inhabitants as the gift of a good and just creator. Anne Primavesi (1991) challenges traditional interpretations of the Bible that support a damaging view of human domination over the rest of creation and proposes an ecological paradigm of humankind and nature that expresses the essential wholeness, interrelatedness, and interdependence of all creation. The Religious Education and Environment Programme (REEP) is founded on "the conviction that concern for nature is essential to religion and that religious awareness has a vital contribution to make to respect for nature." In conjunction with Friends of the Centre, it holds important discussion conferences and other events in the UK. Charlene Spretnak (1986) discusses the strong links with spirituality that she has found in the American green movement especially.

Christian Democracy[9] arose in the early twentieth century, as a progressive alternative to the political and socioeconomic conservatism associated with Roman Catholicism from the sixteenth to the nineteenth centuries. It has a substantial following on the European continent and in Latin America and occupies a slightly right-of-centre position on the main spectrum of political ideologies. Christian socialism began to emerge in the UK in the mid-nineteenth century as an alternative to the conservatism of the Church of

England 'establishment', and provided one of several important strands of thinking in the UK's Labour Party.[10] It has been especially concerned with social justice, the removal of poverty, and the reduction of inequalities between the rich and the poor. Its teachings, in effect, provide much-needed practical applications of the Parables of the Good Samaritan, the Sower, and the Talents.

Fowler and Hertzke (1999) discusses religion and politics in America.

The booklets by Jesudoss (1997a, b) give some of the interesting thoughts and reflections of an Indian peace and justice worker for Christian churches during his three-year visit to Milton Keynes, England. The subjects that he covers include justice, development issues, social responsibility and society, Christianity, and spirituality.

Jonathan Sacks, chief rabbi of the Hebrew Congregation of the Commonwealth, presents a challenging political vision in his powerful book *The Politics of Hope* (Sacks 1997). He shows how moral language has largely broken down in the West, resulting in a danger that its citizens cannot properly reflect on the kind of society they hope to make. He argues that liberal democracies currently face the threats of overinstitutionalised political society and underinstitutionalised civil society. Drawing extensively on the Jewish religious tradition, he suggests how to reconstruct civil society by a 'new' type of politics of responsibility in which families, neighbourhoods, communities, voluntary associations, and religious groups have a full part to play in a politics of involvement. This recovers an older vision that used to work well when it was tried.

Sacks (1991) discusses the apparent paradox of deeper secularisation and resurgent religious extremism, including fundamentalism. He sees religion as a major part of contemporary moral and social ecology. He deplores the widespread tendency to treat politics as the only significant vehicle of change in modern societies and considers that their deep-seated problems are cultural, moral, and ultimately religious. He believes that Western society can remain viable only through a broad return to tradition within a context of religious pluralism and tolerance.

Movements founded by several Hindu spiritual teachers have begun to influence politics. In the UK, the Natural Law Party was set up by a group of followers of the Maharishi Mahesh Yogi's technique of Transcendental Meditation. It envisages that every nation can become integrated and strengthen its sovereignty, *without conflict between nations*, by creating coherence in its collective consciousness. It sees this approach bringing about world peace, eliminating stress in society, and progressively solving global problems and preventing new problems from arising. The Indian thinker Shri Prabhat Rainjan Sarkar introduced the new Ananda Marga philosophy in 1955, together with a complementary spiritual practice based on ancient times but suited to present conditions.[11] He was also a notable social thinker, whose PROgressive Utilization Theory (PROUT) closely integrates the principles of economic and social justice with the fulfillment of individual and human potential and spiritual laws.[12] Followers of his teachings have gradually developed a New Renaissance movement, which is active in several parts of the world and publishes *New Renaissance* as an excellent international journal of new paradigms and progressive thinking along spiritual lines.

A new monastic and lay Buddhist leadership is emerging that combines Buddhist spirituality, rooted in meditation and other personal disciplines, with a Buddhist social ethic that addresses specific economic, social, and political issues (Krieger 1993: 92–93). This international 'engaged Buddhist movement', in which the Dalai Lama plays a prominent part, has criticised the West's exploitation of the Third World and argues for more balanced and humane approaches to development that have greater respect for indigenous religious, cultural, and natural environments.

The globalisation of institutions has led to a trend to form worldwide groups representing the traditional religions (Krieger 1993: 782). For example, the World Council of Churches has had considerable political influence, and there are also the Organization of the Islamic Conference and the World Fellowship of Buddhists.

Universalism and Politics

Several of the progressive applications of religion to politics, described earlier, are already moving closer and closer to the true spirit of universalism, which believes in mutual cooperation between adherents of different religious faiths. This spirit has already been expressed well in the movement for global ethics discussed at the beginning of this chapter.

A further good example can be found in the work of the Brahma Kumaris World Spiritual University, an international, nongovernmental organisation that works closely with the United Nations as a Peace Messenger Initiative and is committed to its broader objectives. It works for people's inner peace of mind through meditation and for world peace. With the support of many other people, it coordinated a worldwide effort to collect visions of a better world from both children and adults and from many schools and a wide variety of other groups. It organised workshops, conferences, seminars, festivals, drama productions, and exhibitions. Ideas and viewpoints about a better world were shared by creative groups formed in many parts of the world. The Global Cooperation Bank was established as a database to receive and store details of all ideas and actions from over sixty countries. Early in 1989, the National Coordinators of Brahma Kumaris prepared a synopsis of the ideas and visions most often expressed. These formed the basis for the Mount Abu Declaration in February 1989, which included a one-page statement, The Peoples' Vision, a set of principles of cooperation, and a programme of action to articulate a more detailed Global Vision. Project activities had expanded to over 120 countries by 1990. The book *Visions of a Better World* (Hassija and

Panjabi 1993) presents the work done during the early 1990s and includes the Global Vision Statement, covering twelve aspects of life in some detail, some visions of leaders, plans and actions, and principles of cooperation.

Baha'i emerged as a world religion in the late nineteenth century as a result of the teachings of its founder, Baha'ullah. Esslemont (1923) outlines the main concepts of the Baha'i faith, one of whose principles is the unity between science and religion and another of which is the evolution of a new world order of brotherhood. As a result, followers of Baha'i have always been interested in the possibility of a democratic federal world government. In his book, Arthur Dahl (1996) introduces the concept of 'eco'[13] and uses it as the foundation for his proposed integration of ecology and economics. Here, he has been deeply influenced by his Baha'i religion and by his extensive, practical experience of biological ecology, the environment, and economic development in the Third World. He explains why present economic and political systems are not working and applies the 'eco' concept to integrate economic, environmental, and spiritual ideas and aims into a new paradigm for changing them. He shows how human institutions can be understood better and how they are shaped by our values and understanding. This opens the way to a more integrated view of the solutions required for human and global problems.

NEW AGE SPIRITUAL POLITICS

New Age Philosophies and Ideals

What are now known as New Age philosophies and ideals have their roots in unified religious, spiritual, and esoteric philosophies, influenced by the advances of science, that have been emerging for nearly 150 years. The first of these worldviews to appear was theosophy in the mid-nineteenth century. It was followed, for example, by the Baha'i faith, Rudolf Steiner's anthroposophy, modern Hindu mystical philosophy, the Alice Bailey teachings, and John Williamson's neometaphysics of the mid-twentieth century. Steiner's thought shows a remarkable blend of science, art, spiritual philosophy, mysticism, education, and practical living. The Alice Bailey teachings have led to the World Goodwill movement, which has taken considerable interest in the human situation and held many conferences and published many papers about it, including those in its magazine *World Goodwill*. The contributions of neometaphysics to holistic politics are discussed briefly in Chapter 12.

These New Age paradigms could be forerunners of an emerging major new paradigm that several modern thinkers, including Willis Harman (1998), have called 'the consciousness paradigm'.[14] This paradigm would view the ultimate, primary substance of the universe as consciousness-mind, from which matter-energy would arise in some way. The physical world would be to the greater mind as a dream image is to the individual mind. In another variant of the paradigm, 'physical reality' would be the 'virtual reality', corresponding to some 'higher reality', and a series of such 'realities' might even be nested within each other like Chinese boxes.[15] A consciousness paradigm would also be able to conceive of mind existing without matter, so that concepts of survival after bodily death[16] and even reincarnation[17] would at last make scientific sense; they have been prevalent in many religious beliefs for thousands of years and are also held by many New Agers.

Similarly, many New Agers believe in the enhanced human faculties of 'extrasensory knowing', 'channeling', 'cosmic consciousness', and healing, which would also be natural in terms of the new paradigm. Quite a lot of them also believe in the reality of intervention in human affairs by extraterrestrial civilisations or by spiritual beings from higher realms of 'reality'. New Agers have such a wide range of different individual viewpoints that some of them seem bizarre or even utterly fantastic to more orthodox people. In addition, empirical evidence is accumulating for a variety of strange and complex phenomena, such as 'synchronicities',[18] whose exploration would go *beyond* the contemporary scientific conceptual framework and require a new 'mathematics of pattern'.[19]

What *is* clear is that a future acceptance of any form of consciousness paradigm will bring with it radical changes in some contemporary assumptions about the nature of the human being and the human environment, comparable to the changes that were made in the transition between medieval and modern civilisations. This would include some radical changes in the assumptions to be made about future political possibilities, although it is too early yet to do more than guess what these changes might be. This situation should be borne in mind when reading some of the formulations of New Age political ideas that have already appeared and when developing future political paradigms or even policies.

Examples of New Age Approaches to Politics

Mark Satin's (1978) book *New Age Politics* is a survey of New Age and spiritual politics in its earlier stages. It arose out of the ideas of the feminist, men's liberation, spiritual, human potential, environmental, appropriate technology, simple living, and nonviolent action movements of the 1970s, together with the ideas of social scientists and others who shared these concerns. At that time, the common strand of New Age politics in those movements was mostly implicit and hard to perceive. The book aimed to make this politics explicit by presenting in some detail its analysis, worldview, goals, economics, and strategy. See also Mark Satin (1991).

In his book *The Dance of Change*, Michael Lindfield (1986) discusses the present critical stage of the evolution of human society, where many institutions and structures of governance, economy, education, and social welfare face crisis, if not collapse. To create a future that adequately supports all life on Earth, he says, we individually and collectively need to learn to harness our inner creative abilities and translate them into practical, everyday life. To practice the new 'politics of consciousness', we need to focus the inner world of spirit so that it can meet human needs effectively. Lindfield (1986: ch. 9) describes what this politics is like. Its important concepts include spirit in action, the ecology of peace, the wise investment of money, and the power of choice.

In their book *Spiritual Politics*, Corinne McLaughlin and Gordon Davidson (1994) introduce and develop some contemporary concepts of 'spiritual politics'. They present ways to develop a new, spiritual approach to creating a happier, more peaceful world, starting from the present human situation. They were radical political activists in the United States in the 1960s but then turned to the inner side of life: personal growth, humanistic psychology, and spiritual teachings. They explored the 'Ageless Wisdom', which is often called the 'Perennial Philosophy' or the 'Sacred Science', and were especially drawn to the teachings of Alice Bailey, although they were brought up as Christians. They met at Findhorn, Scotland, and then married. In 1978, they founded Sirius, a spiritual community and ecological village similar to Findhorn, at Shutesbury, Massachusetts. They have also been working with several groups that have experimented with a new political and economic paradigm.

Spiritual Politics represents the authors' understanding of the practical application of the Ageless Wisdom tradition to world events. Although most people view 'politics' as a 'partisan power struggle', which they often deplore, politics is "really the art of governance, a science that synthesizes opposing views into a higher level of understanding." Thus, spiritual politics focuses on the next step in the evolution of individuals and groups. The authors believe that the time has come to unite politics and spirituality, which have been separated for so long. Thus, local, national, and global politics must address the greatest good of the greatest number. The book addresses the division in the social change movement between political activists and people who are more spiritually inclined and tries to bridge the gap between them. It seeks to transform the world from inside out rather than outside in.

It has five parts. (1) "The Book of Life" outlines its philosophical framework. (2) "Evolutionary Governance" explores a new type of political process, outlines a new political paradigm based on the Ageless Wisdom, and describes successful examples of political groups using this paradigm. (3) "The Hidden Causes of World Events" outlines how world events have been shaped by various esoteric causes. (4) "The Divine Hand behind Human Affairs" explores more universal influences, including the forces of Light and Darkness and the 'invisible' spiritual guidance being given to humanity. (5) "Creating a New Planetary Order" grounds spiritual people in the world by outlining a new planetary economics and providing practical applications for new economic ideas emerging from the inner side; it also outlines many techniques that we can each apply on inner and outer levels to help the world, including meditation, visualisation, thought-form building, and practical activities.

The book's true purpose is to encourage us to begin examining events in our world from a spiritual perspective. It will help us to discover for ourselves even deeper understanding of how things really are. It is the best presentation that I have found so far about the nature of a new political paradigm, based on spiritual principles, and about its theory and practice. It contains a remarkable combination of systems thinking and Ageless Wisdom. Its win-win approach,[20] also used by writers like Hazel Henderson and Willis Harman, is a welcome, long overdue counterbalance to the prevailing confrontational conflict of most contemporary party politics. The authors rightly point out that contrasting political approaches, such as 'conservatism', 'liberalism', and 'socialism', all have some good ideas, which can usefully be brought together into a new synthesis. Thus, people of all political ideologies can and should learn from each other. Above all, the book's altruistic approach is like a searchlight that will help to sweep away the selfish and power-seeking attitudes that pervade too much contemporary politics, even in 'democracies'.

When I read *The Celestine Prophecy*, a remarkable book by James Redfield (1994) and its sequel, *The Tenth Insight* (Redfield 1996b),[21] in summer 1997, I immediately realised their relevance to this chapter, especially the importance of their Ten Insights. They present these important spiritual principles for transforming life on Earth in the twenty-first century in striking fictional form. The First Insight is that a new spiritual awakening is occurring in human culture, brought about by a 'critical mass' of individuals who experience their lives as a spiritual unfolding, in which they are led forward by mysterious 'coincidences' or 'synchronicities'. The Second to Seventh Insights enable us to live more spiritual lives and prepare for the individual transformations that are needed. The Eighth Insight brings a new interpersonal ethic; as people begin to interact with each other in consciously spiritual ways, human culture will develop more and more rapidly into a completely spiritual form. The Ninth Insight brings awareness of how human culture will continue to transform, as more and more people learn to stay connected to divine energy within, while actively pursuing a sense of spiritual mission. The Tenth Insight will bring an expansion of human consciousness into awareness of the long span of human history and the special mission that we will all share to bring humanity through the next stage of human evolution.

NOTES

1. See the beginning of the section on religion and politics for a discussion of possible definitions of 'religion'.

2. Compare the 'win-win' of Hazel Henderson (1993, 1997), mentioned in Chapter 10's subsection on 'new economics'.

3. See Chapter 10's subsection on 'new economics'.

4. The results were published in the first book by Kidder on global ethics.

5. See Krieger (1993: 778–782). More extensive discussions of religion and politics include those by Haynes (1998), Perry (1997), Benavides and Daly (1989), Merkl and Smart (1983), and Rubinstein (1987).

6. Books on Islamic fundamentalism include Hoveyda (1998), Moussalli (1998), Choueiri (1997), and Faksh (1997).

7. Krieger (1993: 745–747) surveys the political roles of the Roman Catholic Church since its foundation, and Krieger (1993: 491–493, 952–953) describes some specific aspects.

8. For brief descriptions of liberation theology, see, for example, Ball and Dagger (1995b: 219–224) and Krieger (1993: 542–544). I discuss liberation theology briefly in the section on liberation ideologies in Chapter 9.

9. Krieger (1993: 136–137) gives a brief description of Christian Democracy as a political movement.

10. Christian socialists, such as William Temple (a former archbishop of Canterbury) and R. H. Tawney, were especially influential in the 1930s and 1940s. Bryant (1997) relates the history of Christian socialism.

11. The booklet *The Wisdom of Yoga* (Avadhuta 1990) presents Sarkar's Ananda Marga philosophy and the extension of this philosophy into solving the social and economic problems of today. It includes a fairly detailed description of PROUT (ch. 8).

12. See also the references to PROUT, as a form of 'new economics', made in Chapter 10.

13. The concept of 'eco' is similar to the concept of 'holon' introduced by Koestler (1978) and elaborated by Wilber (1996: ch. 1).

14. I summarise the first (1988) edition of Harman (1998) in *New Paradigms Newsletter*, no. 7 (June 1989: 15). *New Paradigms Newsletter*, no. 13 (October 1991) has the theme 'Mind and Consciousness' and includes some suggestions about how humanity may be moving towards a new 'consciousness paradigm'. During recent years, there has been rapidly increasing scientific interest in research about consciousness from various viewpoints.

15. Dukes (1988) explores the analogy between the perceived physical universe and a virtual reality computer display and introduces the concept of universes within universes within universes and so on. This book is summarised in *New Paradigms Newsletter*, no. 12 (July 1991: 5–6).

16. Lorimer (1984) examines speculations on the nature of life after death, ranging from those of indigenous cultures to those of modern scientists and philosophers, and presents many interesting case histories of psychic experiences strongly indicating the possibility of such survival.

17. Stevenson (1997) presents scientific research on apparent memories of previous lives.

18. One of the most striking groups of phenomena of this type was investigated by the biologist Paul Kammerer, who claimed to have observed a 'law of series'. They were then studied by the psychoanalyst Carl Jung and the physicist Wolfgang Pauli, who developed the concept of 'synchronicity' or 'meaningful coincidence' during the 1920s and 1930s and presented it in their book *The Interpretation of Nature and the Psyche* (Jung and Pauli 1955). This subject has been extensively explored in recent years by several scientists and various other people; see, for example, Peat (1987). Several of my friends and I have personally experienced many such 'synchronicities', which sometimes occur in very striking 'coincidence clusters'.

19. John W. Campbell, Jr., mentioned this possibility to me at an international science fiction conference many years ago.

20. The win-win approach is also advocated by Covey (1992a, b) and Henderson (1993, 1997), for example.

21. Redfield (1996a) summarises the first nine Insights in a compact form. Redfield and Adrienne (1995, 1996) provide an experiential guide to the development of the Ten Insights. Redfield (1997) explores more directly the new experiences that many of us are having and examines more closely the specific challenges of living this new way of life.

SOME TOPICS FOR FURTHER INVESTIGATION

1. After studying the views of religious leaders on global ethics, as outlined by Küng and Kuschel (1993) and Küng (1996), consider what further developments could be made to an evolving global ethic, in the light of your own moral outlook.

2. How far had your own religious approach influenced your political views before you started reading this chapter? In what ways has your reading of this chapter begun to modify your political viewpoint?

3. If you have been involved in any form of religious and spiritual politics, how does it relate to the forms of religious and political politics discussed in this chapter? How far is your reading of this chapter likely to change the nature of your involvement?

4. What form of spiritual approach to politics do you consider most appropriate to your own spiritual and religious viewpoints? How would you expect to develop this approach further, and how would you apply it to change your own lifestyle and way of life for the better?

5. If you and a group of your friends have answered Question 4 individually, try developing a joint spiritual approach through mutual discussion and meditation. You may, alternatively, find that you can work better by following complementary approaches in different subgroups that mutually cooperate and compare notes from time to time.

6. If you find that the Celestine Prophecies and Ten Insights appeal to you personally follow them up for yourself, in your own way, or in a group of friends to whom they appeal.

7. What new insights have you gained into the theory and practice of spiritual politics as a result of reading this chapter and some of the literature cited there and answering your own selection of Questions 1 to 6?

12

Towards a New Political Paradigm

The world situation is so complex and has become so critical that repeated application of conventional thinking and conventional approaches alone will not resolve it but will usually only make matters worse. New, creative, lateral thinking is needed—not only that, but unified, integrated, systems thinking that will address human problems and global problems as an interconnected, coherent, and meaningful whole. There is now an urgent need for a new form of politics that is *holistic* in several different ways. It must address the world as a whole, consider the whole human and global problematique and resolutique, examine the whole range of existing ideologies and paradigms for ideas that they could usefully contribute, and draw on all relevant fields of human knowledge.

This chapter provides a preliminary formulation of a possible way to develop and evolve holistic politics. It covers some of the essential concepts and components, which include a strong methodological basis, the formulation of appropriate human and global goals, the clarification of problems and issues, the policy-making process, the development of cooperative politics and adaptive political systems, the concept of unity in diversity, and the combination of all these essential elements into a political synthesis.

HOLISTIC POLITICS

From 1987 on, I began to draw together various ideas that could form the basis for a holistic politics of cooperation. Several articles that I wrote at the time in *New Paradigms Newsletter* endeavoured to formulate how to achieve a cooperative form of politics that would build on a broad consensus of basic altruistic values, social justice, and decent standards for all and attempt to unite peoples both nationally and internationally. Here, I was influenced by the Findhorn Foundation Conference "The Individual and the Collective— Politics as if the Whole World Mattered", held at Findhorn, Scotland, from 15–22 October 1988. A later, complementary formulation of some of these ideas appeared in Burrows et al. (1991: pt. 2).

The approach that I proposed starts by considering the true basis for democracy and seeking common values and aims. It needs to have an adequate conceptual framework, which would be provided by a holistic political philosophy based on a *unified, practical philosophy*, which is now emerging as the result of the convergence of many complementary ideas and paradigms from many different thinkers, scientists, and practical people.[1] The principles of this philosophy should be applied worldwide, not only in one country or group of nations.

The following objectives would arise out of such a philosophy and already represent a wide range of existing human aspirations: (1) unite people with a common sense of purpose; (2) care for all people, share resources fairly, and provide everyone with a decent quality of life; (3) develop and use constructively the abilities of all citizens and enable them to fulfill their creative talents; (4) establish a just society, with a proper framework of human rights and human responsibilities; (5) build up a strong, effective, well-balanced, sustainable, world cooperative economy, conserving planet Earth; (6) provide public services of a high quality at reasonable cost and accessible to all citizens; (7) promote law and order, reduce conflict and confrontation, and work for peace worldwide; and (8) carry out political functions at whatever scale or level is appropriate; decentralise, devolve, and avoid bureaucracy wherever possible.

Holistic politics needs to provide people with a basis for living and working together, peacefully and with the minimum of conflicts, with full recognition of their rights to individuality and individual differences of personal characteristics, abilities, personalities, values, motivations, beliefs, and outlooks. It recognises the value of unity arising out of diversity. Similarly, the new emerging political paradigm will combine the best features of all existing political paradigms and ideologies. At the same time, it should not attempt to impose uniformity of political or other thinking and values. Instead, it should provide a common framework within which the different political ideas, values, aims, and aspirations of almost all people in the future will be naturally and comfortably located.

THE NEED FOR A HOLISTIC APPROACH

Conventional decision making and more 'orthodox' political approaches tend to tackle individual problems one at a time or in small groups, often on an ad hoc and piecemeal basis. They have not sufficiently considered the complex web of interactions between different problems and problem areas or paid enough attention to long-term considerations and policies. Contemporary political leaders are often aware of intricate interactions between problem areas and of the complexity of the situations facing them, but they rarely have much idea of how to cope effectively with these situations. Therefore, there is a very urgent need for a holistic approach to politics.

This need has been partially recognised by many politicians and political thinkers. For example, the Third Way debate in the UK, discussed near the end of Chapter 2, has been paralleled by similar debates in the United States and many other countries, not only today but on many earlier occasions during the twentieth century. Some participants in the debate, such as Giddens (1998a, b) and White (1998), view the Third Way as a broad emerging framework for new political thinking, within which there will be many interpretations and variants.[2] It could be one of the forerunners of the even more fundamental new, holistic political approach that is so urgently needed and could appear early in the twenty-first century.

Several political books present various other strands of thought that could eventually contribute to this paradigm, perhaps after some modification. For example, Ophuls (1998) argues that the 'modern' parliamentary paradigm, the body of political concepts and beliefs formulated in the eighteenth- century Enlightenment, is no longer intellectually tenable or practically viable and advocates an alternative, ecological approach. Cohen et al. (1995) propose an innovative scheme for rejuvenating democratic states; it is part of the Real Utopias Project. Miliband (1973) advocates a radical alternative to the pluralist, democratic, capitalist view of society. Mulgan (1997) is a collection of new political thinking, oriented to the twenty-first century, that outlines some of the best work of the independent think tank Demos and includes contributions from important thinkers of various political viewpoints; it assesses the current situation, states future objectives, and discusses how to attain them. Riemer (1996) discusses some possible political breakthroughs that could move political science forward from 'Cold War mentality' towards more future-oriented, 'prophetic' politics.

REQUIREMENTS FOR A HOLISTIC APPROACH

This common framework would move towards an integrated approach that would take due account of the interconnections and interactions between different problems. An essential part of this approach would be *systems thinking*, reviewed by Burrows et al. (1991: ch. 10), and including general systems theory,[3] cybernetics,[4] and operational research.[5] Systems thinking can view complicated systems and processes as a unified whole and begin to make sense of intricate networks of problems and events that it would be hopeless to tackle in a piecemeal fashion. For example, it reveals common principles, laws, and patterns that apply to many sciences and many different areas of life.

Jervis (1997) shows how to apply systems thinking to address complexity in political and social life.

One consequence of the systems approach would be *integrated planning and policies*, discussed by Burrows et al. (1991: ch. 11), which should preserve the best of the past, act effectively in the present, and plan for a sustainable future, taking a long-term view. There would also need to be a whole range of *holistic thinking*, ranging from unified, practical philosophies and integrated world-views[6] to comprehensive pictures and theories of the whole human being,[7] the human and natural environments, and planet Earth viewed as a whole.

To achieve an adequate holistic approach, we need an open-mind and an integrated perspective, including especially various forms of systems thinking and scientific method.[8] Decision making and policy formulation need, not only need this unified methodology, but should also be set in a cooperative rather than confrontational framework of policy development, with a firm foundation of spiritual values, as discussed in Chapter 11.

Deming (1995) presents his System of Profound Knowledge, the knowledge needed for transformation to a new, improved system of management. Its four interrelated parts are:

1. systems thinking and appreciation for a system and its emphasis on the emergent properties of new 'wholes'
2. the ability to distinguish significant variations from ordinary variations that are the result of normal system changes
3. using a useful, though not strictly correct, theory to guide policies and actions, especially system changes
4. understanding human behaviour.

These four parts can be viewed as four principles of effective learning, both in business and in wider aspects of life, including politics.

The applications of *neometaphysics* to human affairs, which are now being developed, will be especially vital and timely for developing this holistic approach. In its principles of human living, neometaphysics views the individual as the basic human unit but does not endorse selfish individualism. Indeed, it is essential to strive for mutual harmony, respect, and consideration between individuals. All aspects of human living should be integrated, with each supporting and reinforcing the other. Education should start in the family and be broad-based to fulfill individual human potential and support cooperative social living, citizenship, and altruistic social purpose. In business, there should be good ethics, right human relationships, and responsibilities for the community as well as the company; neometaphysics has pioneered the concept of *social business*, the conduct of business with social benefits in mind. The neometaphysical approach to economics avoids the conceptual limitations of most academic economics and goes beyond the extremes of pure capitalism and pure collectivism to a 'new economics' that combines the best features of different approaches to economics, and aims for a 'world cooperative economy' of the type outlined in Chapter 10. In this approach, the market is viewed as a good servant but not as a master or a panacea.

Neometaphysics could play a very important part in showing how to transform politics along the lines advocated in this book, which are based on the principle of mutual aid. In particular, it points out the need for a 'new politics', combining the best features of the different political ideologies and viewpoints. It believes that there is a need to work towards a true participatory democracy by studying the real meaning of Abraham Lincoln's definition of democracy: "government of the people, by the people, for the people", as discussed in Chapter 7. It would promote both human rights and responsibilities, full social justice, cooperation rather than confrontation, and win-win human situations.[9] It could help humanity to achieve a better human future by enabling people to become more aware and encouraging them to become much better motivated and more strongly committed than they are now. It could help people to transform themselves so that they can meet the tremendous challenge of achieving a good future.

The integrated approach to policy-making, outlined earlier, also requires a built-in procedure for reviewing existing policies and decisions and learning from their mistakes. There is an urgent need for the sufficient briefing and proper education of politicians, executives, managers, and other decision makers and professionals.

GOAL FORMULATION

Human and political goals need to be formulated that have a good chance of gaining very wide, if not universal, acceptance among humankind. The whole hierarchy of human needs, first recognised by Abraham Maslow (1987), represents a set of individual needs that should be satisfied as far as possible. They are listed in Chapter 10.

Although different human nations, cultures, societies, communities, and organisations often have very different specific goals, ideally all of them should have an overriding aim that the basic needs of all individuals throughout the world should be met as far as possible. In practice, great difficulties arise from mutual conflicts between individual aims and needs, which can be resolved only by placing certain limitations on individual drives and wants, to achieve the common good. In any human society or community and also worldwide, there needs to be an appropriate balance between freedoms and responsibilities, which need to be provided in all areas of life: economics, work, politics, social services, education, science, technology, culture, the arts, religion, and spirituality.

Nevertheless, there are considerable hopes that common aims, goals, and objectives can be formulated that would be concerned with meeting the basic needs and would be accepted by most people and communities of people. Due allowance would have to be made for various individual adaptations and choices. In his book *The Goals of Mankind*, Ervin Laszlo (1977) presented the results of an international survey of national and international goals, which shows remarkable common ground despite the great differences between regimes in different countries. It indicates how to move from self-centred, short-term goals to humankind-centred, long-term goals in the interest of all people. The extensive work towards the development of a global ethic, reviewed in the first section of Chapter 11, will make very important contributions in this direction.

Nevertheless, ways need to be found for addressing conflicting goals and exploring possibilities for 'adaptive compromise' that will meet real needs as much as possible, without sacrificing too many other individual needs. As far as possible, policy-makers for a government or business need to have a core of shared values, preferably shared also by their constituents. These core values should include the common set of basic values found in the teachings of the world religions, which also form the basis of a global ethic.[10] They include individual and social responsibility, mutual respect, treating humanity as one family, peace, and justice. We should aim to abandon violence as a means of settling our differences. We should strive for a fair economic and social order, where everyone has an equal chance to fulfill his or her full potential.

At any given time, the decision-makers' and policy-makers' stated objectives should be consistent with their values and directed towards their constituents' needs. They need to identify the issues, for which policies are required to meet these objectives and needs.

The greatest difficulty here is to overcome the present dominance of many parts of the world's national and business leadership by selfish, power-seeking, and often fanatical vested interests. Current prospects for this do not seem good, but this situation might change through an eventual recognition that it will be in nobody's interest to continue with the old self-centred approaches to life, especially if this was seen to risk the survival of humanity. The more that the human nature and awareness of ordinary people can be transformed and improved through education and good moral example, the less influence and power the vested interests are likely to have.

CLARIFYING PROBLEMS AND ISSUES

It is vitally important for both decision makers and policy-makers to have really clear initial perceptions of the issues, with which their constituents and the whole of humanity are faced. Thus, it is essential that they should consult the people and discuss the issues with them as much as possible during the early stages of policy formulation. This can be done in several ways, each of which should be used. Elected representatives of the people are continually listening to their constituents to find out about their problems and grievances and discuss possible solutions with them. In this way, they gain a good idea about what many of the real problems and issues are and how important they are perceived to be. To an increasing extent, the governments of at least some democracies, including the UK, issue consultation documents about proposed policies in specific areas. From the responses received, the governments are able to obtain a better perception of the relevant problems and issues, as well as indications of some possible approaches to solutions. Citizens of democracies are also free to communicate their opinions directly to their political leaders, as well as to the media. Again, this process provides important information about perceived problems, issues, and possibilities for solution. It is very important, at this stage, to identify areas of agreement and disagreement about different possible policies in each problem area. It is also very important to develop more effective two-way communication systems between politicians and citizens.[11]

THE POLICY-MAKING PROCESS[12]

Social invention is an essential part of the process of finding the large and varied stock of ideas on which policy-making should be based. Here, the Institute for Social Inventions (ISI) has done valuable pioneering work.[13] Areas for which social inventions are currently being proposed include politics, neighbourhood and community, international affairs, war and peace, welfare, social problems, relationships, family life and children, health and therapy, quality of life, spirituality, education, work and employment, business, economics, taxation, housing, the environment, transport, communications, information, science and technology, the arts, leisure, and the promotion of social inventions.

For each identified issue, policy options should be formulated in relation to available facts, interactions between different issues, and public perceptions of issues. As the complexity of the world situation increases, so does the need for more detailed, factual information about its events and problems, about the increasing number and complexity of interactions between them, and about possible ways of improving the situation.[14] No collection of policies can even begin to be adequate without an extensive database of such information. At the top levels of decision making, in international and national government, the extent of this information is already enormous and is expanding rapidly. At more local levels of government, only a relatively small proportion of that information is needed. In addition, policy makers need access to extensive collections of statistical data, covering a very wide variety of facts but all too often not available in sufficient detail and not sufficiently up to date.

The likely consequences, benefits, and risks of each policy option must be assessed. For each issue, the 'best' policy option needs to be chosen by evaluating and comparing the available options in relation to values and objectives. Policy makers need many case histories of the impacts of their policies on groups of people and on individuals. They need to know the results of various policy options carried out by a variety of governments and authorities around the world. They also need to find out how far the results of these policies will be applicable in their own policy-making environments and how far they may need to be modified first.

For each chosen policy option, specific, detailed policies need to be formulated and implemented. This is not always easy to do. In more complicated situations, it may involve a process of research and development, often including the formulation of mathematical models.[15] The successful construction of such models can be more of an art than a science, because much depends on the validity of the assumptions made and the accuracy of the data used. Information about future trends is very important to policy-makers but notoriously difficult to obtain. Extrapolation from existing trends is usually dangerous for more than a few months ahead. During recent decades, the technique of *scenario planning* has evolved for projecting different possible futures, with some indication of their relative probabilities and of what steps can be taken to make preferred futures more likely. This technique should be combined with other forecasting techniques.

Continual feedback on the results of policies as executed should be obtained and evaluated. This should use policy-making networks rather than rigid hierarchies. The inner part of the network would include not only policy makers and decision makers and their immediate professional advisers but also generalists and holistic thinkers. The outer part of the network would include links with members of the general public.

Public reactions to the policies should then be assessed. The best way to do this is to place generalists in policy and *ideas clearinghouses* that would collect, indeed, seek out the relevant ideas and information.[16] The clearinghouses would also bring together many kinds of creative talent and skilled individuals. They would apply understanding and wisdom to sift, transform, and re-present the ideas submitted into a form that policy-makers and decision-makers could manage to handle. At the same time, well-informed replies would be sent back from the clearinghouses to those who suggested the ideas, so that they could feel that they were really participating in the policy-making process and that their contributions were being appreciated. Governments and their advisers would take people into their confidence and value them as people. They would fully encourage what practical contributions they can make, in any aspect of life. Thus, they should actively seek creative and altruistic people, enable them to do what they need to do, provide them with adequate resources and opportunities for this purpose, and praise them in public whenever they succeed.

Policy-makers face various information problems (Mayne 1992: 36–37). They need far more detailed, factual information about world events and problems and about possible solutions. Information about future trends and events is very important for policy-makers but also very difficult to obtain. Policy-makers and their advisers are at present usually ill equipped to be aware of, or fully appreciate, the emerging new ideas and new paradigms that will be essential for the solution of their problems in the future. Their education is generally not broad enough, so that they are usually too specialised and rarely have the required holistic outlook. Many if not most policy-makers and senior decision makers are overworked, usually because they are overloaded with information that they feel to be potentially relevant. For example, this problem is known to be especially severe in the new British government elected in May 1997. This situation could be greatly relieved by applying up-to-date scientific methods and advances, especially those from information science and technology, futures studies, systems thinking, and new paradigms studies.

Policy-makers should *review the whole policy-making cycle* fairly often, in the light of feedback and other relevant experience. These principles and several others provide a valuable basis for the *new paradigm for policy-making* in government and business that is now emerging. In such a paradigm, problems and issues would be viewed as a whole and handled in relation to each other, taking full account of their interactions. Policy-makers would need a broad, up-to-date, unified conceptual framework based on adequate education and experience; without this, their perception of specific problems, situations, and issues could be dangerously limited. A unified, long-term approach to human and global problems would be adopted, in place of the prevailing preoccupation with 'ad hoc' and short-term policies and issues. As far as possible, cooperative approaches, leading to 'win-win' situations and solutions for all, would be adopted in place of the presently dominant approaches of confrontation and competition. Policy-making would be decentralised as far as possible and conducted within a multilevel framework ranging from global, through continental, national, regional, and urban, to local. It would be participatory, with full consultation between policy makers and their constituents.

COOPERATIVE POLITICS

Looking at the world situation today and in the past, it is only too clear that the dominant confrontational approach to politics has not worked. Its defects are all too obvious. If human prospects are to improve significantly, it is essential that we move towards a cooperative approach as soon as possible. Indeed, there are signs, though still too few, that this is beginning to happen. There is an especial need for democracy to become more participatory, so that people would have more of a say in policy-making and in how they are governed, instead of just voting at relatively infrequent intervals. There are various ways in which the evolving new approaches to policy-making and politics, discussed earlier in this chapter, could help to bring this about and help to develop *a new paradigm for cooperative politics*.

In general, it is important for a political system to be sufficiently unified, yet diverse enough to cater to the very varied needs and aspirations of all its people. It will be easier to achieve this aim when it has become possible to develop *adaptive political systems*. In particular, there is a need for methods whereby regimes could adapt to people's responses to them, become more flexible, and make really determined efforts to try to meet their very varied individual needs. There is a need to develop the concept of 'variants within a regime', so that people living within a given regime could have considerable choice about their way of life and about what sorts of policies are applied to them.

HOLISTIC GOVERNMENT

Perri 6 (1997) suggests how a new approach to 'holistic government' could help governments to deliver more effective results with better quality and value for money and within stable budgets. In his view, the core problem for government is that it has inherited a nineteenth-century model of organ- isation, based on functions and services rather than problem solving. Budgets are divided into separate sections for specific departments, each of which is based on one or more functions. Vertical links between departments and pro- fessional groups in their field are strong, but horizontal cross-links are weak or do not exist.

To solve complex problems cutting across departmental boundaries, gov- ernment needs to adopt a holistic approach with more integration across the public sector. As problems are solved, it needs to shift its main effort from cure towards prevention of further problems. It also needs to become oriented to outcomes and change cultures. In practice, Perri 6 says, this process of change will take about a decade to implement and require twelve major changes of policy and management style in government:

1. Holistic budgeting
2. Organisations defined around outcomes
3. Integrated information systems
4. Cross-departmental caseworkers
5. Outcome-based contracts
6. Audits for preventive activities
7. Enhancement of the status of preventive work
8. The provision of early warning systems with safeguards
9. More skillful purchasing by managers
10. Audits on the cultural dimensions of key problems
11. The incorporation of information and persuasion into budgets
12. Cross-functional outcome measures.

TOWARDS A POLITICAL SYNTHESIS

In this chapter and elsewhere in this book, I have endeavoured to identify the essential elements of a political synthesis that include the best features of existing political regimes, ideologies, and policies. These elements need to be combined in the 'best' possible ways, appropriate for each level of governance and government from global to neighbourhood. Such a synthesis, when achieved, will make a vital contribution to that unified conceptual framework for politics, that new holistic political paradigm within which many different specific forms of government, social organisation, political viewpoint, and creative and constructive way of life will be able to flower.

I hope very much that what I have said in this book will encourage many of its readers to play their part in developing this paradigm and applying its emerging principles to those areas of practical politics in which they choose to be involved. I would welcome the opportunity to exchange ideas with them from time to time.[17]

NOTES

1. The best approximation that I have yet seen to a workable unified, practical philosophy is neometaphysics, which is outlined by Mayne and Williamson (1997). The philosophical approach of the American thinker Ken Wilber is, in many ways, similar; Wilber (1996), especially in Chapters 1 and 5, gives a good introduction, and Wilber (1995) provides a fuller exposition. Wilber (1997) introduces additional aspects, some of which are especially relevant to politics; see the introduction to Chapter 11. Burrows et al. (1991: ch. 15) provide a general discussion of various strands of holistic thinking that would contribute to such a philosophy.

2. Anthony Giddens expressed this viewpoint during a public debate on the Third Way held in London on 20 May 1998. His opinion was sharply challenged by Liberal Democrat peer Lord Dahrendorf, who distrusts comprehensive theoretical systems and prefers a much more pragmatic approach to politics, oriented to addressing and attempting to solve important actual problems. Both sides of this controversy have some validity, and a truly holistic approach to politics requires both a sound theoretical framework and an effective methodology for practical problem solving.

3. General systems theory was originated in the 1940s by Ludwig von Bertalanffy, whose formulation is presented in von Bertalanffy (1969) and developed further by members of the Society for General Systems Research especially. Klir (1972, 1991) gives later surveys of the state of the art of general systems theory as it later evolved. A 1995 conference discussed some of its critical theoretical and practical issues (Ellis et al. 1995).

4. Cybernetics was founded by Norbert Wiener, who defined it as "the science of communication and control in the animal and the machine". Its original formulation is Wiener (1948), its human and social implications are discussed in Wiener (1950), and a useful, nonspecialist introduction is given in Pask (1961). Beer (1994) provides a broad perspective of its approach, including its applications to government and the achievement of social change.

5. Operational research, called 'operations research' in the United States, originated during World War II as the application of scientific method to military decision-making and was extended after the war to business and management decision making. It has, even now, apparently been applied relatively little to government policy-making and decision-making. Moder and Elmagrabhy (1978) provide a comprehensive survey of the state of its art in the late 1970s.

6. See, for example, Lemkow (1995) and Wilber (1996).

7. Theories of the whole human being are surveyed by Burrows et al. (1991: ch. 12), for example.

8. Kuhn (1970) gave a classic exposition of how scientific method is used by scientists in practice and how new paradigms emerge in science from time to time. The philosophy of scientific method has evolved considerably since that book was written. For example, Solo (1991) discusses the method and philosophy of science in relation to economics, social sciences, and value judgments.

9. See Henderson (1993, 1997) and Covey (1992a, b), for example.

10. See the introductory statement in Küng (1996: 9–11), prepared by an Editorial Committee of the 'Council' of the 1993 Parliament of the World's Religions in Chicago.

11. Blumler and Gurevitch (1995) provide an extensive analysis of systems of political communication and discuss the present crisis of public communication and how to resolve it.

12. For more detailed discussions of my approach to various aspects of policy-making, see Mayne (1992) and my critical introduction to the new edition of *World Brain* (Wells 1995: 47–56). That introduction also refers to the very important related 'WISE' ideas of the late Manfred Kochen (Wells 1995: 52–54). Castles (1989) is a comparative history of public policy in eight leading democracies, including the United States, the UK, Japan, and three continental European countries. Olson and Mezey (1991) reassess the role of legislatures in the public policy-making process and present some significant advances in research on the influence of legislatures. Kim (1984) takes an alternative, policy-oriented approach to the study of world politics, in response to increasing dissatisfaction with the state of the world and with research on international relations.

13. The most recent compilations of ideas, collected by the Institute for Social Inventions, are Albery (1992) and Albery et al. (1993 to 1998).

14. The *Encyclopedia of World Problems and Human Potential* (Judge 1995) provides a remarkable and extensive survey of human and global problems and their mutual interactions and approaches to their possible solution. For more details, see the last two sections of Chapter 1.

15. Burrows et al. (1991: ch. 16) survey many possible approaches to modeling, forecasting, and scenario planning, as applied to global human futures. Similar principles can be applied to specific problem areas and aspects of policy-making.

16. Such clearinghouses would generalise and enhance the national networks of coordinated suggestion schemes originally proposed by P. Clavell Blount (1962). Compare also the idea of a 'Global Suggestion Box' (Wright and Pokras 1990).

17. Readers are invited to send messages or transfer files to my electronic mail address: new_paradigm@compuserve.com.

SOME TOPICS FOR FURTHER INVESTIGATION

1. Formulate a set of about eight basic objectives, fairly similar to those presented in this chapter's section on holistic politics, that you would use as a basis for your own holistic political philosophy.

2. If you have had any experience of any form of systems thinking, how has it influenced your approach to politics? How would you apply this experience to develop your approach further?

3. Take a problem area with which you are reasonably familiar and discuss how you would use the approach to policy-making presented in this chapter to develop new policies in this area. What potential candidates for new policies do you see emerging in this area? Which ones do you consider most promising and why?

4. Discuss with some politicians whom you know personally how seriously they are affected by pressures like information overload and other pressures of work and try to work out together some ways of improving this situation.

5. 'Shortage of resources' is often cited as a reason for making 'painful choices' between different beneficial political programmes, with the result that some sections of the population lose out. Discuss with some politicians who are faced with such choices how you could use existing resources more efficiently and effectively to enable more of these beneficial programmes to be put into effect. Better still, use creative thinking to find out how to create, at minimal cost, additional resources that could be applied to bring additional benefits and thus bring nearer the time when win-win for all people becomes possible.

6. Taking Northern Ireland or some other part of the world where there are serious conflicts between different communities within a nation-state, try to work out some form of 'adaptive political' system that would lead to an improved situation for all its people.

7. After studying the Demos pamphlet *Holistic Government* (Perri 6 1997), try to work out how you would apply its ideas to government at some given level in the country in which you live.

8. Outline some theoretical and practical contributions that you could make, which would contribute to the development of a form of holistic world politics of benefit to all humanity and planet Earth.

III

POLITICS IN THE
TWENTY-FIRST CENTURY

13

A Pessimistic Scenario— Armageddon

This chapter indicates the sort of future that could happen if most of the present trends in the world situation have some of the worst of their possible outcomes. There would be relatively little change in present policies and approaches to decision making, and the major power-seeking interests of the world would steadily increase their power. At least some of the major world problems, especially some of the new problems that have arisen as a result of rapid advances in science and technology, would become worse and perhaps lead to catastrophic events, any one of which could happen all too easily. Eventual planetary disaster, following one particular crisis or, more likely, several crises together, would probably become inevitable. Such a disaster would include the extinction of the human species and perhaps also of many, if not most, of the higher animals and plants. Planet Earth would have to make another of its gigantic adaptations, comparable to what occurred when the dinosaurs became extinct about 60 million years ago. These events are illustrations of what could happen, not predictions.

The chapter ends with an assessment of whether something like the Pessimistic Scenario is a genuine threat. Later chapters show how it could be countered.

THE SHORT-TERM FUTURE

Terrorism becomes more widespread and becomes a serious problem in the affluent countries as well as in other parts of the world. Early in 1999, internationally collaborating 'left-wing' gangs emerge that gain considerable public sympathy by purporting to represent the interests of the underprivileged and the cause of social justice. A little bit later, they show their true colours by committing acts of terrorism. In one terrible day, several of their well-placed bombs in London[1] destroy Buckingham Palace, Parliament, Whitehall, the Law Courts, and the City, and their infiltration of powerful computer viruses[2] paralyses much of the UK's national administration and financial transaction networks. Similar attacks within a few days devastate the Channel Tunnel, the European Union headquarters in Brussels, the White House and Congress in Washington, the Wall Street area in New York, and government and financial offices in Tokyo. Authoritarian governments take over in many of the affluent countries by declaring a state of emergency to counter the terrorist threat. They are soon given an additional excuse for ruling by the collapse of the global financial and commercial system in many parts of the world.

One consequence is that the affluent countries are no longer able to use their influence to restrain the already unstable situation in the Middle East. All-out war between the Israelis and Palestinians is soon followed by a new revival of Iraqi power, armed with nuclear, chemical, and biological weapons,[3] as leader of a new, more powerful Arab Alliance. By the end of 1999, a full-scale 'Armageddon War' has broken out in the whole of the Middle East. A few terrorist nuclear bombs, acquired from former USSR stockpiles explode high in the air above the North Sea, the north eastcoast of the United States, and the southeast coast of Japan, and emit electromagnetic pulses that put large sections of the world's computers and computer networks out of action. China 'waits in the wings' for an opportunity to become the world's leading power, with increasing economic as well as military strength.

INTO THE TWENTY-FIRST CENTURY

Once well established in power, the authoritarian regimes of the First World, together with the Russian Mafia regime in Moscow, form a new alliance with the big business interests of the world, which realise that it is in their interests to collaborate with them. By this time, they have made considerable progress in countering the left-wing terrorists, who have largely been driven 'underground' for the time being. Thus, there is a resurgence of multinational businesses in all parts of the world, except the Middle East, which has been devastated beyond recovery. A massive, new economic boom begins, which is fueled by very extensive developments in optical computing and information technology (which have bypassed the destructive effects of the electromagnetic pulses), biotechnology, industrialised agriculture, the car industry, and a variety of consumer goods industries. Many of these industries also flourish in parts of the Third World due to their extensive supplies of cheap labour, which are quickly trained to become sufficiently skilled. However, the effects of the boom prosperity do not trickle down to the poorest sections of the industrialised countries; this expanded 'underclass', which has grown to over 30% of their population, is kept largely unemployed, on a bare subsistence income, while those of its members who are 'in work' have jobs with very low pay, which range from insecure, part-time work to full-time employment with very long hours. The expanded middle classes and upper working classes, now numbering over 60%, live in affluence again, though often not at the peak high incomes that they experienced before. As before, they spend much of their income on extravagant consumer goods, stimulated by even more massive advertising campaigns. Those who are in executive jobs often have very long working hours. The richest 5% to 10% become much wealthier than ever before. All these developments accentuate trends in the global economy already evident in the late 1990s.

In the Third World, a considerable proportion of countries, especially in Asia and Latin America, successfully make the transition to rapid economic growth and rising standard of living, paralleling the development of the East Asian 'tiger economies' in the late 1990s. However, a hard core of Third World countries, especially in Africa, is pushed deeper and deeper into poverty, locked in eternal debt cycles. There, things go from bad to worse, as the polarisation between the richest and poorest countries, as well as between the richest and poorest within countries, becomes worse and worse. Poverty, malnutrition, infant mortality, and chronic ill health become even more endemic, as a sharp decline in world agricultural production begins; the effects of years of agribusiness, together with environmental degradation in many parts of the world, have begun to reduce soil fertility drastically in many parts of the world. Even among the richer people, various illnesses begin to escalate, as virulent strains of viruses and bacteria, resistant to all antibiotics, begin to become dominant.

World population is still expanding rapidly, though not so fast as in earlier decades; by 2000, it has already exceeded 6 billion, and growth rates are as high as ever in the poorest countries. It is already becoming increasingly difficult to feed people in these countries, and massive famines occur from time to time. Excessive pressure on some of the more marginal agricultural land causes its overfarming, followed by its degeneration to semidesert. Global warming, now beginning to be felt to a marked extent, has made the previously highly productive prairies of North America and the Ukraine much more subject to drought and therefore no longer reliable granaries for the world. More farmland crops are blighted by unwanted ultraviolet light, penetrating more and more through the thinning ozone layer. Global sea level rises, still only 'slightly' on average, but with much greater vulnerability to some surges. Eventually, a massive tidal surge sweeps over many of the rice lands of Bangladesh, putting them out of action for ever and drowning millions of people. Man-made pollution becomes worse, especially in many parts of the Third World.

THE MID–TWENTY-FIRST CENTURY

As the twenty-first century unfolds, most of the crises become steadily worse. After relative peace early in the century, major wars break out later, as shortages in the poorest countries become even more acute, and impoverished populations, in desperation, begin to revolt. In a few cases, aided by terrorists, they manage to seize stocks of chemical and biological weapons and apply them with devastating effectiveness. By 2040, terrorist scientists and technologists[4] begin to develop an 'ultimate superweapon', a group of genetically engineered organisms that are able to cause a worldwide plague, thus fulfilling the potential of biotechnology to be a veritable 'Pandora's box'.

Soon after 2050, an escalating spiral of rising population, food shortage, global warming, vanishing ozone layer, ever-increasing pollution, and ever more incurable disease, aggravated by new, genetically engineered microorganisms, rapidly brings the world situation to a 'Big Crunch'. The population explosion is quickly replaced by a massive decline to a level near zero. For a while, less than a million superrich people try to hang on in their isolated citadels, but even they find the going hard and are forced to live underground to find a tolerable environment; their numbers continue to decline. Finally, before 2070, Homo sapiens, extinguisher of many other species, is itself made extinct by a plague of particularly virulent mutants of the genetically engineered microorganisms. By that time, polluted by a now terrible environment on the Earth's surface, almost all the higher animals on land and in the sea have become extinct, too. So have most of the higher plants.

ASSESSMENT

This scenario is intended to be a sharp warning about what could go wrong if several contemporary trends continue and happen to have exceptionally unfavourable outcomes. This may seem far-fetched, but is it? As far back as 1991, an official Organization for Economic Cooperation and Development (OECD) report, *The State of the Environment*[5] warned that the world's massive pollution problems must be solved by the end of the 1990s, that ever more affluent consumption would worsen pollution, and that there would be serious problems unless there were fundamental shifts of economic policy towards the achievement of sustainable growth. By late 1997, there were already increased concerns about the seriousness of global warming[6] and about the dangers of genetic engineering and other forms of biotechnology. Lister (1996) warns that the conflicts emerging since the Cold War could threaten the survival of civilisation because of the increasing availability of a whole range of lethal weapons.

NOTES

1. This is feasible, assuming a large, international terrorist organisation. The Irish Republican Army (IRA), which is based on the British Isles only, although it had some support from Americans of Irish descent, succeeded in devastating quite large parts of the commercial areas of London and Manchester with single bombs.

2. This assumes that the terrorist organisation has some members with good professional and technological skills, again quite possible, as it could appeal to intellectuals with communist or other far-left views. In contrast, the IRA has been rather *un*sophisticated but, nevertheless, very dangerous on occasion.

3. This is not altogether improbable, considering Iraq's considerable success in preventing United Nations inspectors from fully investigating its stocks of these weapons.

4. Many aspects of the sometimes extremely dangerous potential misapplications of genetic engineering, especially, are very clearly discussed by Mae-Wan Ho (1998).

5. The report *The State of the Environment* (OECD 1991) was prepared for a conference of environment ministers from the twenty-four countries then in the OECD. It was widely reviewed in the British national press and doubtless also by newspapers and periodicals in other OECD countries.

6. Global warming and other aspects of climate change were discussed at an international conference, the Climate Change Convention Meeting, in Kyoto, Japan, in December 1997. Some concerned British scientists from Scientists for Global Responsibility (SGR), with colleagues from several other countries, traveled on a special 'Climate Train' across Siberia, en route to Kyoto, to publicise the increased threat of global warming from various causes, including the rapid expansion of air travel.

SOME TOPICS FOR FURTHER INVESTIGATION

1. Study carefully any recent report on the global state of the environment. Combining its information and recommendations with other ideas and information, formulate some policies that could usefully be applied globally, internationally, in your country, and in your locality to minimise the future effects of pollution.

2. Apply an analysis, similar to that of Topic 1, to at least one other vitally important world problem.

3. Outline a combination of constructive measures that could be taken to minimise the probability of occurrence of a Pessimistic Scenario.

14

A Piecemeal Scenario— The End of History?

This chapter describes an example of the sort of future that could easily happen if different world problems and human problems are tackled separately, with little regard for the complex interactions between them. It indicates a combination of possibilities that could occur if most uncertainties about future trends are neither especially unfavourable nor specially favourable. With this type of scenario, the breakdown of world civilisation would almost certainly be averted, but probably at a very high price, with a low quality of life for many perhaps most people. Conditions might also favour authoritarian regimes, at least in some localities and possibly even worldwide. However, the desperate poverty of large parts of the Third World might eventually be abolished. These events are illustrations of what could happen, not predictions.

The chapter ends with an assessment of whether something like the Piecemeal Scenario is a genuine threat and how it could be countered.

THE SHORT-TERM FUTURE

A major slump is triggered by excessive financial speculation and by the failure of several leading Third World countries to service their debts. The banking system partly collapses in some affluent countries and is damaged in others. The average proportion of unemployed typically exceeds 20% in most developed countries, but is much higher in many impoverished parts of the Third World. There is also considerable social unrest, even rioting, from groups of unemployed people and other impoverished people, as the recession bites deeper. This, in turn, leads to an upsurge of terrorism in developed countries, as well as in other parts of the world. The authorities contain it by introducing some emergency regulations, often gradually becoming authoritarian.

Many businesses run by progressive entrepreneurs and also a considerable number run by smart profiteers and by Mafia and drug gangs manage to thrive through the depression. Several multinational companies do well, including a few more public-spirited companies. However, most of them continue to exploit the Third World and the 'underclass' in the First and Second Worlds and to have an unhealthy influence on many political leaders.[1] Because of the slump and because of limited applications of anti-pollution measures, pollution emissions from most of the industrialised countries decline somewhat. However, there is a substantial increase of pollution from China, which is by now rapidly developing its coalfields and fossil-fuel power stations. Despite recent renewed warnings about the dangers of global warming,[2] the level of CO_2 is still rising. The rate of destruction of the tropical and temperate forests decreases but is still high. Endemic poverty and chronic malnutrition in most parts of Africa become somewhat worse, due to a continued lack of appropriate, integrated, international aid programmes.

As the basic problems of the Middle East remain unsolved, the usual pattern of fierce local conflicts, separated by uneasy truces, continues; in particular, full-scale war breaks out between the Israelis and Palestinians. There are also extensive wars in parts of Central Africa. Relations between the most powerful countries are somewhat uneasy, and there are no further major arms reduction agreements; on the other hand, the arms race between them is not resumed, despite some increase in tension. World arms expenditure stays about level, and the 'peace dividend' seems to have been forgotten.

INTO THE TWENTY-FIRST CENTURY

The slump in the developed countries gradually gives way to a boom, which is stimulated by very extensive developments in computing and information technology, nanotechnology,[3] biotechnology, industrialised agriculture, the car industry, and a variety of consumer goods industries. Many of these industries also flourish in parts of the Third World due to their extensive supplies of cheap labour, which are quickly trained to become sufficiently skilled. However, the effects of the boom prosperity do not trickle down to the poorest sections of the industrialised countries; this expanded 'underclass', which has grown to over 20% of their population, is kept largely unemployed, on a bare subsistence income, while those of its members who are 'in work' have jobs with very low pay, which range from insecure, part-time work to full-time employment with very long hours. The expanded middle classes and upper working classes, numbering about 70% to 75%, are again well-off, sometimes affluent again, though often not at the peak high incomes that they experienced before. As before, they spend much of their income on extravagant consumer goods, stimulated by even more massive advertising campaigns.

Those who are in executive jobs often have very long working hours. The richest 5% to 10% become much wealthier than ever before. All these developments accentuate trends in the global economy already evident in the late 1990s.

In the Third World, a considerable proportion of countries, especially in Asia and Latin America, successfully make the transition to rapid economic growth and rising standard of living, paralleling the development of the East Asian 'tiger economies' in the late 1990s. However, a hard core of Third World countries, especially in Africa, remains impoverished, despite a gradual easing of their debt burdens. The polarisation between the richest and poorest countries, as well as between the richest and poorest within countries, becomes somewhat worse. Poverty, malnutrition, infant mortality, and chronic ill health remain endemic, as world agricultural production begins to pass its peak; the effects of years of agribusiness, together with environmental degradation in many parts of the world, have begun to reduce soil fertility in many parts of the world. Even among the richer people, various illnesses begin to increase, as virulent strains of microorganisms, resistant to all antibiotics, become more widespread.

World population is still expanding rapidly, though not so fast as in earlier decades; by 2000, it has already exceeded 6 billion, and growth rates are almost as high as ever in the poorest countries. It is already becoming increasingly difficult to feed people in these countries, and serious famines occur from time to time. Excessive pressure on some of the more marginal agricultural land causes its overfarming. Global warming, now beginning to be felt to a marked extent, has made the previously highly productive prairies of North America and the Ukraine more subject to drought and therefore less reliable granaries for the world. More farmland crops are damaged by unwanted ultraviolet light, now penetrating more through the thinning ozone layer. Global sea level rises, still only 'slightly' on average, but with greater vulnerability to some surges. Eventually, a large tidal surge sweeps over some of the rice lands of Bangladesh, putting them out of action forever and drowning a million people. Man-made pollution becomes worse, especially in many parts of the Third World.

THE MID–TWENTY-FIRST CENTURY

By about 2020, the world's decision makers become increasingly aware of the impending ecological crises, but their responses are at first still relatively limited and inflexible. Most of the world's by now numerous authoritarian regimes become concerned about their ability to survive the forthcoming crises. Eventually, they decide to collaborate to take decisive action against them. They constitute the United States of the World (USW), as a federation of their governments. The USW is set up in 2025 as an authoritarian world state, with decisive powers in various key areas. It contains the organs of central world government, both legislature and executive. Its World Police Force soon has such overwhelming military power that no national armed forces can stand for long against it; it gradually brings under control the endemic wars and terrorist activities that have continued to plague the world. Its World Environmental Authority strictly controls the use of energy and material resources, industrial processes, and all other sources of pollution. Its World Population Ministry imposes birth control and family planning rules and regulations for all people under USW jurisdiction. Food rationing ensures at least a minimal subsistence diet for everyone, meager as that is for most people. The World Labour Directorate assigns people throughout the USW to work of its own choosing, under working conditions that it lays down. Its network of planning authorities collaborates with many multinationals to control most of the industrial and commercial operations within the USW, even though a judicious measure of private enterprise and competition is allowed, as they are considered important for promoting productivity and innovation.

When the USW is set up, it by no means rules the whole world. There are still some nominally democratic countries, led by the United States, and many powerful multinationals operating outside the USW. A sort of uneasy truce, the 'New Cold War', develops between these countries and companies and the USW. None of them want to bring their differences to an armed conflict, as it would be devastating and ecologically extremely damaging, even though the USW would win it fairly decisively, due to its technological lead in weapons systems. Because of this, no arms race is attempted, and the proportion of resources devoted to military preparations is too small to upset the new eco-logical balance.

The USW has set up a sustainable planned economy, with a carefully limited element of free enterprise, which coexists with the United States and the other democracies, which remain capitalist, though by now with almost sustainable economies. The USW has a low standard of living for most people, and the United States is much less affluent than it was, because that is all that the available material resources can support at the time. Environmental degradation no longer escalates, and global warming gradually begins to be brought under control. The deterioration of the ozone layer has been halted, and agriculture is gradually being made much more sustainable worldwide. Firm international health measures have halted the spread of new plagues, partly aggravated by genetically engineered microorganisms originally devel-oped on behalf of big business.[4] Although most people, especially within the USW, live drab, unexciting lives, most of them survive at a minimal physical standard of living, appreciably above subsistence level. In several respects, the USW's way of life is not unlike that of the USSR in the early 1980s, while that of the United States parallels that of the New Deal period of the late 1930s. For the very long-term future, there are prospects of a considerable increase in standards of living, as almost limitless solar energy resources would eventually be harnessed.[5]

ASSESSMENT

Although becoming more open than previously to new approaches, present types of government thinking and policies are still predominantly orthodox, too often focusing on single problem areas and issues and mostly short-term and dominated by the advice of specialist 'experts'. To a limited extent, some governments are willing to consider unorthodox ideas; sometimes, they address situations where several problem areas interact and devote some attention to longer-term issues. Most governments today probably think flexibly enough to avoid viewing the continuance of all major trends without question; thus they should be able to avoid situations that would lead them into a Pessimistic Scenario. It seems much more probable that their policies will move them towards a Piecemeal Scenario, unless it becomes possible to influence them into more holistic, generalist, longer-term ways of thinking.

In the long run, it is quite possible that governments will become naturally holistic in their approach, perhaps between 2010 and 2020, because by then they will be ruled by members of the present younger generation, who are more open-minded and receptive to new ideas. But can we wait that long for a fundamental change? The next chapter shows how it may become possible to influence events much more positively much sooner, to minimise the risk of a Piecemeal Scenario's occurring.

NOTES

1. A recent *New Statesman* (Richards 1997a) interview with Ken Livingstone, a Labour MP in the House of Commons, quotes his opinion that many unpleasant people, with their own agenda, are advising the UK's prime minister. Similar people could be advising many other democratic governments, and the 'hidden agenda' could often be that of the multinationals and other big business vested interests. Their overall influence would help to perpetuate a Piecemeal Scenario.

2. Global warming and other aspects of climate change were discussed at an international conference, the Climate Change Convention Meeting, in Kyoto, Japan, in December 1997. Some concerned British scientists from Scientists for Global Responsibility (SGR), with colleagues from several other countries, traveled on a special 'Climate Train' across Siberia, en route to Kyoto, to publicise the increased threat of global warming.

3. 'Nanotechnology', the construction of machines of minute size with many potential applications was foreseen by Drexler (1992) as being one of the revolutionary new technologies of the twenty-first century.

4. Many aspects of the applications of genetic engineering, including especially their potential dangers and abuses, especially by big business, are very clearly discussed by Mae-Wan Ho (1998).

5. Scheer (1994) outlines a feasible route to the eventually almost limitless use of solar energy and other forms of renewable energy ultimately deriving from natural solar power. Scheer (1997) urges politicians to embark on such a path as soon as possible.

SOME TOPICS FOR FURTHER INVESTIGATION

1. Study carefully any recent report on the global state of the environment. How far do you think that its recommendations meet the need to address pollution problems in conjunction with other major world problems? How would you strengthen them to do this more effectively?

2. Formulate some policies for a world problem area of your choice. First attempt to formulate them by considering that problem area in isolation. Then modify your formulation by taking account of interactions with other problem areas. How extensive are the changes?

3. Outline a combination of constructive measures that could be taken to shift current trends in decision making and policy-making beyond a Piecemeal Scenario. How quickly do you expect them to become effective?

15

An Optimistic Scenario— Towards Human Fulfillment

This chapter indicates the sort of future that could easily happen if we could achieve the clarity of vision to improve the human situation and transform our consciousness and morality.[1] Then we could really work together towards the development of a holistic approach to human and planetary evolution. This would provide real hope for the future of planet Earth and reach out beyond Earth into the wider universe. Although the chapter indicates a combination of possibilities that could happen if most of the uncertainties about likely trends are generally favourable, it includes setbacks as well as advances. It also includes some unexpected, though not entirely unpredictable, dramatic events and 'breakthroughs', any of which could happen under these circumstances. These events are illustrations of what could happen, not predictions.

With this type of scenario, a new social order would evolve that would have a balanced economy and ecology and a participatory democracy, providing a good quality of life for all people and fulfillment of their potentialities. There could be a true world community.

The chapter ends with an assessment of the probability that something like the Optimistic Scenario will occur. It shows how its achievement could be made much more likely by reacting constructively to many positive projects, initiatives, and activities that are already in progress and are becoming more and more numerous, despite the difficult, complex, unpredictable, and turbulent times in which we live. Thus, in spite of today's crises and disasters, this chapter ends on a note of real hope for the future.

THE SHORT-TERM FUTURE

The UK begins a remarkably constructive phase of social, political, and cultural evolution, which is made easier by the more community-oriented approach of the Labour government, elected in May 1997, and the upsurge of more altruistic feeling around the funeral of Diana, Princess of Wales, on 6 September 1997. It is enhanced by the emergence of more effective social networking for creative and constructive purposes, combined with new grassroots and professional movements arising from the Local Agenda 21 processes. A new sense of national unity and purpose emerges after the formation of a non-party clearinghouse for new ideas about the reform of all aspects of political life, contributed by members of the public. Helped by the success of the Internet, this movement soon becomes international and becomes especially strong in Europe, North America, Australasia, and Japan.

Encouraged by this climate of opinion, the British government is moderately successful at clearing up pockets of unemployment, improving the economy and the environment, promoting energy efficiency and conservation, upgrading public transport, and beginning to develop high-quality, broadband communications networks. However, its progress is seriously hampered by adherence to overly cautious spending policies and reluctance to apply higher taxation to the rich.

A People's Europe movement among European citizens begins to demand renegotiation of the European Treaties, leading to a new, gentler form of European Union, which is less bureaucratic, more democratically accountable, and more responsive to national, regional, and local public opinion throughout Europe.

The United States begins to use its influence to soften the rough edges of global capitalism, reduce the burden of Third World debt, and work more openly for sustainable economic development and environment protection. A serious threat of famine in several African countries is averted. A new programme of aid, donated directly by people from many countries to African farmers and villagers via relief agencies and charities, is shown to be far more effective than almost all the costly government-administered Third World aid programmes since 1945.

INTO THE TWENTY-FIRST CENTURY

In 2000, millennium celebrations worldwide bring in a new mood of optimism and altruism, with a determination that the twenty-first century should at last bring humanity into a new era of fulfillment. This widespread feeling begins to transform politics, society, economics, and business worldwide.

In 2001, the new U.S. administration under President Al Gore introduces radical reforms on a scale not known since President Roosevelt's New Deal of the 1930s. His proposals for a 'Global Marshall Plan'[2] are at last implemented.

This transforms the prospects for the Third World, especially the most impoverished countries in Africa, in the same way that the Marshall Plan of 1948 transformed the prospects of Western Europe.

In the UK general election in 2002, no party obtains an overall majority, and negotiations for a Coalition government begin. A Coalition 'Government of All the Talents' is formed, which includes nonparty members as well as representatives of different political parties. It becomes a genuine government of national unity, which begins to apply long-term thinking to the development of holistic policies addressing several problem areas simultaneously. This is the beginning of an era of cooperative, progressive, green politics, evolving into a fully participatory democracy.

In Europe, popular pressure leads to a complete rethinking of the future of the European Union and eventually to renegotiation of the previous European treaties. In 2003, the Treaty of Brussels is signed, establishing the European Union as a genuinely democratic confederation of nations and regions, with the principle of subsidiarity properly applied. Its Parliament now has equal powers with its Council of Ministers, and its 'government' has only strictly limited powers to pass legislation affecting all its member states. By this time, most of the countries of Eastern as well as Western Europe belong to the European Union.

In 2002, the Third World debt problem is finally solved, partly as a result of the Global Marshall Plan, partly because of an international conference called to design a totally new, fair system of world trade, combining free trade with international subsidies. The New Treaty of Rome is signed, which sets up an International Compensation Fund, to which all wealthy countries contribute many billions of dollars according to their means. This fund is used to repay all outstanding Third World debt immediately and to complement the development and investment programmes of the Global Marshall Plan.

As a result, a dramatic transformation of economies towards sustainability proceeds in all parts of the world. This is accompanied by further political reforms in more progressive and democratic directions, leading to the acceptance of a United Nations Declaration of Human Rights and Responsibilities[3] in 2005. because of this greening of capitalism, democratic politics, and public opinion, dramatic advances are made in environmental protection and energy conservation worldwide. The share of renewable energy, based especially on solar energy,[4] rises faster than previously expected. Pollution is dramatically decreased, as the impacts of heavy industry and transport on the environment decrease. Both global warming and the deterioration of the ozone layer proceed much less rapidly than had been feared. Only very slight rises in sea level are noticed.

In the developed countries and even in some of newly industrialised countries in the Third World, the transition to a postindustrial society proceeds rapidly. The nature of manufacturing industry is transformed, with much less heavy industry and much more light industry, mostly highly localised and decentralised. Dramatic advances in personal computing and communication equipment and in information science and technology lead to the development of national, multipurpose, multimedia telecommunications networks, soon merged into a similarly versatile global communication system, a highly enhanced version of the Internet, which was already expanding very rapidly during the late 1990s. The World Brain/World Mind has truly arrived![5]

Although local wars, guerrilla fighting, and terrorist attacks still continue in various parts of the world, their level falls gradually at first, then more and more rapidly, as the economic, political, and social climate of the world improves steadily, and as alienation of large sections of the population declines. Due to the further decrease in international tension, military spending continues to be reduced significantly. In 2005, an international 'peace dividend' is officially declared, which is assigned to the International Compensation Fund and to many other projects for peaceful development, at all levels ranging from the global to the local.

By 2010, the incidence of poverty in the Third World has fallen really dramatically. Indeed, all the major world problems are well on the way to solution. In almost all parts of the world, population growth rates have decreased to well under 1% per year. The world economy is sustainable and becoming progressively more cooperative; operating within an international framework of fair free trade and effective resource planning, it has now achieved a balanced pattern of growth. World agriculture is now on a sustainable basis, with widespread multicropping. Chronic hunger has been eliminated. The planetary environment is at last adequately protected and conserved.

THE MID–TWENTY-FIRST CENTURY

These beneficial trends continue throughout the century. There is a gradual convergence between the standards of living in the developed and developing countries, although many people in the Third World express a preference for maintaining a simple lifestyle. At the same time, economic, political, social, and cultural evolution is proceeding well. Material standards of living, though rarely affluent, are decent worldwide and sufficient to allow a wide diversity of cultures to flower.

By 2030, a new global order has been achieved, predominantly through the will of the people and their voluntary cooperation. Most people are now motivated by altruism, public spirit, moderation, tolerance, love, and mutual cooperation. The major obstacles to achieving a true planetary civilisation have been removed. There is a minimal world 'government' at the apex of a whole range of organic governmental structures at different levels. All government is based on social networking rather than hierarchical organisation and administration and makes more use of democratic participation than of representation. A genuine human organism is emerging, with the noosphere[6] as its World Brain/World Mind/World Heart.

By 2050, there has been a gradual increase in prosperity, as almost unlimited sources of solar energy could now be tapped for heating and electricity generation. People no longer have to work on tasks not of their choice for more than a few weeks a year on average, because almost all routine, boring, and dangerous work has been handed over to robots and computers. Fuller attention can be devoted to personal living and the development of significant human relationships. Very many opportunities are emerging for an immense new range of creative expression and adventurous living, and almost every person achieves fulfillment of most of his or her talents and potentialities. Before the end of the century, there is regular, meaningful communication with intelligent beings from other planets, and prospects open up for peaceful collaboration between planet Earth and a wider Interplanetary Confederation.[7]

ASSESSMENT

Most of the more publicly evident contemporary trends suggest that the most likely future will be something like a Piecemeal Scenario. The many good trends apparent today are still too closely matched by too many bad trends to make anything different seem likely.

This is good news in the sense that a Pessimistic Scenario, which would probably involve the extinction of the human species, seems unlikely, although it cannot be ruled out. But it is not such good news in the sense that very formidable obstacles need to be overcome before an Optimistic Scenario can become practicable. Since my original presentation of versions of all three scenarios in 1991 in the book *Into the 21st Century* (Burrows et al. 1991), which I coauthored with two of my friends, the relative probabilities of the three scenarios have not changed very much. *A tremendous effort by many very committed people will be needed to bring about an Optimistic Scenario.* Gurtov (1994) considers that the future of our planet depends on individuals whose example of courage and self-sacrifice will help to empower others.[8]

History has already shown that some very sudden changes, *not* predicted before the event, have happened during recent years. The most notable examples are the overthrow of the communist regimes in the former USSR and Eastern Europe and the apartheid regime in South Africa, by revolutions that were almost entirely peaceful. However, the overthrow of Soviet communism led to many further problems in the former USSR, so much so that the situation there remains very critical. Thus, there is a need to be cautious even when apparently very beneficial 'breakthroughs' occur.

Several such breakthroughs, especially in the area of effective social networking, seem to be required before an Optimistic Scenario can become likely. One of them could result from the explosion of global communication associated with the Internet, which is itself still expanding very rapidly worldwide.

Further breakthroughs could result from the ever-increasing emergence of new paradigms, some of which were discussed extensively in Part II. Some of them will provide a new framework of participatory democracy and an effect-ive system of planetwide governance and planetary management.[9] Others will provide a basis for a unified, holistic, practical philosophy and lifestyle, which are also sustainable. Most important of all, others again could lay the founda-tions for a true moral and spiritual renaissance.

For some years, there has been a succession of significant conferences where spiritual leaders, politicians, professionals, and other leaders have met together to discuss future prospects for humankind and planet Earth. The Epilogue shows what we can do, in many different ways, to help bring about an Optim-istic Scenario. It gives many illustrative examples of positive initiatives already in progress.

NOTES

1. Blumenfeld (1997) presents "a focused picture of our spectrum of potentialities" and shows that "the seeds for positive change are scattered all around us".

2. Al Gore presents his proposals for a 'Global Marshall Plan' in Chapter 15 of his book *Earth in the Balance* (Gore 1992).

3. The InterAction Council began its search for universal ethical standards in 1987 and, in 1996, requested a report on these standards by a high-level expert group. In April 1997, this group presented its draft of "A Universal Declaration of Human Responsibilities", which is intended as a complement to the "Universal Declaration of Human Rights", adopted by the United Nations in 1948. This work was summarised in a presentation by Helmut Schmidt to a public meeting of the One World Trust in London on 7 October 1997. In my Optimistic Scenario, I envisage that the texts of these two declarations are eventually merged into one, after the citizens of the world have engaged in worldwide moral dialogues. Etzioni (1996: 236) considers that this sort of declaration can have compelling moral power among humanity as a whole *only* after such dialogues have occurred; that is one reason I have imagined them to take place. The other reason is the right of citizens to participate in discussions of important issues affecting their future.

4. Scheer (1994) outlines a feasible route to the eventually almost limitless use of solar energy and other forms of renewable energy ultimately deriving from natural solar power. Scheer (1997) urges politicians to embark on such a path as soon as possible.

5. Many of these developments were foreseen by the mid-1990s. See, for example my Critical Introduction to the new edition of H. G. Wells' book *World Brain* (Wells 1995).

6. The concept of 'noosphere', as a sphere of evolving human mental activity and growing human self-consciousness around the Earth, was originated by Teilhard de Chardin and published in his book *The Phenomenon of Man* (Teilhard de Chardin 1965). See also Burrows et al. (1991: ch. 13).

7. In the current state of scientific knowledge, it is not known how many other civilisations there are in our galaxy; the number could be anything between very many and none at all. It seems much more likely than not that there are at least some; indeed, many New Agers and unidentified flying object (UFO) enthusiasts claim that com-munications and contacts with such civilisations are already occurring. I personally believe that, at least through telepathic communication, they will also have broken the

apparent barrier to 'faster than light' space travel, which is required by contemporary relativity theory. Therefore, there will be no real obstacles to effective communication across the galaxy or even between galaxies!

8. Gurtov (1994) presents the approach of 'global humanism', which combines two approaches: (1) a set of human values and norms that enables the examination of all aspects of politics from the viewpoint of our planet, considered as a human community and an ecological system, and (2) a focus of political economy on how systems, such as global capitalism and imperialism, and structures, such as transnational corporations and military-industrial complexes, aggravate inequalities in the distribution of wealth and power within and between nations.

9. For a full discussion of planetary management, see Burrows et al. (1991: ch. 20).

SOME TOPICS FOR FURTHER INVESTIGATION

1. Outline a combination of constructive measures and policies that could be applied, at levels ranging from global through national to local, to make an Optimistic Scenario more likely.

2. Describe how you would envisage a 'Government of All the Talents' operating in your own country.

3. Discuss the feasibility of the proposals for the 'Global Marshall Plan', as formulated by Al Gore (1992: ch. 15). In particular, consider how you would modify them in the light of circumstances that have changed since then.

4. Discuss the feasibility of the 'International Compensation Fund' and other reforms for world trade in the 'New Treaty of Rome', as outlined in the Optimistic Scenario. Try to formulate some of their details.

5. Present your own vision for an Optimistic Scenario, describe the successive stages in which you envisage that it might be achieved, and estimate the approximate probability of its occurrence.

16

Conclusions

This chapter sums up my assessments of the contemporary global political situation, current world problems, new paradigms that could contribute to their possible solutions, and the future prospects for humanity. It presents my conclusion that a properly formulated and sufficiently well developed holistic approach to politics and other aspects of life could lead to an Optimistic Scenario for the the future evolution of humankind and planet Earth. This scenario would include a worldwide participatory democracy, genuinely meeting the needs and aspirations of the people.

POLITICS TODAY

My conclusions about the contemporary global political situation are as follows:

1. Human problems and world problems cannot be solved in isolation, They must be addressed as a unified whole, the human problematique, taking full account of their complex mutual interactions, which are now beginning to be mapped. The complex web of mutually interacting possible solutions, the human resolutique, is also beginning to be mapped. Both problematique and resolutique need to be considered together as a unified whole, which is beginning to be understood better. A valuable strategy is to identify the most important feedback loops there and attempt to eliminate those that are 'vicious circles' and reinforce those that are 'virtuous circles'.

2. The United Kingdom (UK) has been very important during the last three centuries and could continue to play a key part in the politics of the twenty-first century. With the election of a Labour government in May 1997, the UK is at a critical turning point, with a potential for steady, further political

progress and development of the creative talents of its people. However, such progress is not yet assured and will require much skillful and dedicated work by many of its politicians and citizens.

3. Having been the leading world power during most of the twentieth century, the United States has similar potential and similar opportunities to those of the UK, but, again, its progress is by no means assured. The Clinton administration has so far been severely hampered by a largely hostile Congress, but this situation could have changed by the end of the year 2000, when prospects of a really effective, progressive Gore administration could open up.

4. Recent trends in Western Europe have been towards the development of a European Union (EU) that is a confederation of mutually collaborating nations but not fully accountable democratically. While feeling that they belong to Europe, most European citizens feel that they are becoming increasingly remote from the EU's institutions. In response to this situation, a new movement for a People's Europe has begun to emerge, so that the EU could become more democratic and responsive to the needs and aspirations of its peoples. New treaties could be negotiated in consultation with them, to make the European Union more flexible, while including many, if not most, countries from Eastern Europe and giving more autonomy to regions.

5. 'Democratic' regimes are gradually spreading to more and more countries of the world, so that there are now not very many nation-states that have authoritarian or dictatorial regimes. However, almost all 'democracies' are probably less than 50% democratic, so that there is a tremendous need for further progress towards full democracy.

6. The collapse of Soviet communism in the former USSR and Eastern Europe has by no means always been followed by reasonably smooth transitions towards democracy. In many respects, the situation in many of these countries is even more critical than it was in the last days of communism. Several countries in the former Soviet Union could become authoritarian or even dictatorial, and this possibility cannot be ruled out in Russia itself, especially if its economy collapses.

7. The range and variety of significant political movements are wider than ever before in most countries of the world. Nationalism has tended to become stronger, although there are also appreciable movements for international and even global federation. People are tending to become more and more disillusioned with party politics and often favour special-issue movements and seek alternative ideologies. There are now important constitutional reform, economic reform, green, feminist, religious, and spiritual political movements.

POLITICAL PARADIGMS

The following conclusions refer to existing and new political paradigms and integrated, new political thinking, some of which will make vitally important contributions to the development of feasible and practical approaches for resolving the human and planetary crises.

1. Dictatorships and authoritarian regimes, which were quite widespread during the middle decades of the twentieth century, now seem to be dying out, and there are not very many remaining. Democratic paradigms are well developed in many countries and beginning to be established in many others. In most countries, there are democratic, free elections at fairly regular intervals, which are more or less 'representative' of their citizens. There is some controversy over which electoral systems are most fairly representative. There are strong trends towards making democracy more participatory, responding better to the needs of its people and consulting them more.

2. A paradigm of multilevel worldwide democracy is gradually emerging, based on the principle of subsidiarity, where different functions of governance would be conducted at the 'most appropriate' levels. The top level would be global, and the bottom level would be the local neighbourhood community. In between, there would be continental, national, regional, conurbation, urban, county, and other levels. This could lead to a very loose form of global federation or to a worldwide network of interlocking confederations.

3. The conventional, 'mainstream' spectrum of political ideologies ranges from right to left as follows: 'far Right' or 'fascist', conservative, liberal, social democratic, socialist, and 'far Left' or 'communist'. The other mainstream ideologies are nationalism, anarchism, communitarianism, and the green ideologies. In practice, there are no firm boundaries between these ideologies, and they often overlap so much that the 'ideology' for which a person votes often has rather little correlation with his or her real political views and values. Alternative political ideologies include basic needs ideologies, nonviolence ideologies, and liberation ideologies, such as feminism.

4. Political paradigms are strongly influenced by paradigms in other fields, such as political science, sociology, psychology, economics, business, biology, medicine, physics, nonlinear mathematics, philosophy, and religion. Chapter 10 gives many illustrative examples, and several other examples are given in Chapters 11 and 12.

5. Spiritual politics covers a wide range of political ideas and viewpoints, including those that are based on specific religions and those that are oriented to spirituality with little or no specific religious association. Among religious movements, Islamic, Christian, and Judaic fundamentalist movements are especially important and are becoming more influential. There also are examples of 'gentler' religious movements, such as 'Christian socialism', community-oriented Judaism, Sufism, Baha'i, and some modern forms of Hinduism and Buddhism. At the other end of the spectrum, New Age spiritual politics is rapidly becoming more important; notable examples include the outlook of the Findhorn Community and the 'Celestine Vision'.

6. There is now an urgent need for a new form of politics which is *holistic* in several different ways and partly based on the best ideas in twentieth-century

political thought. Ideally, it should be based on a 'unified, practical philosophy', towards which several contemporary streams of holistic thinking are already converging. Holistic politics must adequately address goal formulation, clarification of problems and issues, the policy-making process, cooperative politics, the need for adaptation in political systems, and a synthesis of ideologies and paradigms as 'unity in diversity'. Chapter 12 outlines significant progress that is being made in all these directions.

POLITICS IN THE TWENTY-FIRST CENTURY

Some indications can be obtained about possible futures for humankind and planet Earth by applying scenario analysis. It is important to realise that a scenario is not a prediction of the future but that it provides a picture of what types of events and trends could occur in the more distant future if certain assumptions are made about what will happen in the near future.

In attempting to assess the future, a range of scenarios can be used, corresponding to a range of possible futures. Chapters 13 to 15 present three scenarios, representing qualitatively different possible futures.

1. The Pessimistic Scenario assumes that existing trends will continue basically as at present, but with exceptionally unfavourable outcomes. It ends with the extinction of the human species, probably some time in the latter half of the twenty-first century. The probability of this scenario seems to be less than 5%.

2. The Piecemeal Scenario assumes that there will gradually be a considerable modification to existing trends but that world problems will usually continue to be solved separately, with little or no regard for their complex mutual interactions. Its result during most of the twenty-first century is an authoritarian United States of the World (USW), coexisting uneasily, though peacefully, with relatively few democratic countries, including the United States. For most people, the quality of life is much lower than that of the wealthy countries today, though appreciably above subsistence level. In the course of time, as the use of solar energy becomes more widespread, the standard of living and quality of life rise very gradually. A scenario of this type seems to have a probability of about 90%, *unless* many more people than at present make committed and well-informed positive efforts for a better future.

3. The Optimistic Scenario assumes that that there will be radical modifications to existing trends in sufficiently positive directions, that a holistic approach to resolving human and planetary problems will be adopted, and that there will be a dramatic raising of human consciousness and improvement to human morality, probably arising from a worldwide spiritual movement. Its eventual outcome, by the middle of the twenty-first century, is a resolution of even the most intractable of the present world problems, a good quality of life for at least almost all people, and the start of a positive new stage of evolution

for humankind and planet Earth. If present trends continue to change only slowly, the probability of something like an Optimistic Scenario's occurring seems to be somewhere between 5% and 10%. However, there is a good chance of achieving something like this future *if* enough people start to raise their consciousness and commitment, become more unselfish, and improve their lifestyles, and *if* various positive initiatives, more and more of which are now emerging, actually succeed.[1]

The Epilogue outlines various possible ways in which we can help to make the occurrence of an Optimistic Scenario more likely.

NOTE

1. This process probably requires a 'critical mass' of people adopting this approach, although the number of people required is not yet known. It would be best if *everybody* who reads this message decides to act on it positively!

SOME TOPICS FOR FURTHER INVESTIGATION

1. Having read this book and several of the references that it cites, write your own outline assessment of the future of politics, both in your own country and worldwide. Repeat this exercise every year or at any other interval that you think appropriate. Note carefully the direction in which your successive assessments change.

2. Do a similar set of assessments of the future prospects for humankind and planet Earth.

3. Outline some important problem areas and other aspects of the world political situation and of the human and planetary situation in general that, in your opinion, have not been sufficiently discussed in this book or, perhaps, have not been mentioned there at all.

4. Send me a list of exceptionally important additional references and items of further reading that should have been included in this book but were omitted, probably because I was unable to locate them with the limited time and resources at my disposal.

5. Write to me, or e-mail me at new_paradigm@compuserve.com, indicating any specific ways in which you could support or participate in any continuation of the project on which I embarked when writing this book. Indicate any organisations, societies, networks, or individuals, not already mentioned in the book, that might help.

6. If you are a qualified researcher, undertake some research project relevant to the themes of this book and send summaries of your findings to other researchers and to me at suitable intervals, perhaps about once a year.

Epilogue—What We Can Do

There are many things that we can do to help bring about an Optimistic Scenario, a really positive future for humanity and Planet Earth. We should and can become aware of the total human and global situation, complex as it is. We should and can adopt a positive attitude to life and living, well grounded in altruism and spirituality. We should and can form effective social networks[1] to discuss with each other what to do for the best. In this way, we should and can identify what we should and can do, both individually and collectively. In our collective constructive work and action, we should and can form effective groups and teams to do what we need to do. We should and can have the ideals, ideas, awareness, will, and commitment needed to achieve this.[2]

We urgently need a sudden surge of understanding, positive thinking, and altruistic attitudes, combined with wisdom and a genuine will to act, to make good the current shortage of effective leadership and overcome the widespread apathy and general feeling of helplessness. A dramatic change of heart and personal transformation, among sufficient people with ability, goodwill, and awareness, is needed so suddenly that its occurrence may be almost a miracle. This could happen soon, because a heartening number of individuals have shown by their achievements that they have already at least partly taken that great step forward.[3]

Within this broad framework, there are many specific ways in which we can participate in politics. If we live in a more or less democratic country, we can all vote whenever there is an election, communicate with our political representatives and meet them to exchange our views, and write to the local press or, if fortunate, appear on the broadcast media to express our political and other viewpoints. Increasingly, government bodies are calling for citizens' and experts' viewpoints when preparing new policies in specific areas of life, and this provides many of us with new opportunities for democratic participation. Local Agenda 21 discussions are occurring in many communities in many parts of the world, and considerable numbers of citizens are participating in them. Many urban areas and some rural communities have rich networks of voluntary organisations addressing issues at more or less practical levels. In the Third World especially, grassroots movements and nongovernmental organisations are becoming increasingly important and involving more and more people. However, in First World countries, most people are still relatively inactive politically and often lack good understanding of more than a few problems and issues. Therefore, a very important task that politically aware people can do is to pass on some of their awareness to as many as possible of their neighbours and those whom they meet in their everyday life.

There are additional opportunities for those of us who have special knowledge or special skills. There is a wide range of social networks,[4] discussion forums,[5] associations,[6] learned societies, professional associations, university research departments, think tanks,[7] and other organisations where significant contributions can be made to political discussions, researches, and policy formulation. There are many relevant conferences and meetings. The Internet has an increasing number of online political discussion groups and forums, covering many topics.[8]

NOTES

1. Effective networking requires effective teamwork throughout all subnetworks of a social network. Effective networking of networks that are becoming more effective is better still. Fairtlough (1994) discusses 'creative compartments' of a few hundred people each, that are emerging in many business and other organisations and that have the opportunity to generate great creative energy, are nonhierarchical, and generally have mutually networking, small, effective teams within them. Lipnack & Stamps (1997) presents the principles of *virtual teams*, which are formed across social networks, reaching across boundaries of space and time and organisation. They have been made possible by recent advances in information and communication technology and provide an antidote to the high failure rate of many face-to-face teams.

2. Hazel Henderson (1993: 9) expresses a similar view. In her book, she points to many hopeful new developments that could largely counteract the many harmful and dangerous trends that are also occurring. Especially important, she offers new directions and possibilities for 'win-win' solutions that will benefit *all*.

3. Michael Pegg (1993) offers practical tools that people can use to encourage future generations and build a better world. It gives many inspiring examples of how people can make positive contributions.

4. For example, the Scientific and Medical Network (SMN), which began in the UK but now has over 2,000 members in different parts of the world. Its book reviews especially cover a wide range of subjects, including, but going well beyond, science and medicine.

5. For example, the UK Futures Group, which is a leading forum for future-

oriented people in the UK, and covers wide range of topics, some of them relevant to politics.

6. For example, the British Association for the Club of Rome (BriCoR), which holds fairly regular discussion meetings and is also a networking interface between the Club of Rome and various networks, associations, and groups in the UK. Scientists for Global Responsibility (SGR) addresses many ethical and political issues, arising from science and technology and their applications.

7. For example, in the UK, the Institute for Public Policy Research, the Policy Studies Institute, Demos, the Centre for Policy Studies, and the Adam Smith Institute. The United States has very many think tanks.

8. For example, in the UK, UK Citizens Online Democracy (UKCOD), UK Communities Online, Nexus, and Cambridge Online. There are many such forums in the United States, including Democracies Online and Minnesota E-Democracy.

SOME TOPICS FOR FURTHER INVESTIGATION

1. Describe what you are already doing to help achieve an optimistic scenario and discuss what additional contributions you hope to make.

2. Have you already joined any effective teams or 'creative compartments' that could contribute to the achievement of an optimistic scenario? Which additional teams or compartments do you expect to join or consider that you could help to create?

Annotated Bibliography

This Annotated Bibliography is selective and includes only items in the English language. It contains entries for considerably more than 200 of the many thousands of books that have been written on various aspects of politics and other relevant areas. It emphasises very recent books, although it also includes many earlier books. Although I consider that every book listed here is currently important, I make no claim that all currently important political books have been cited. Many additional references, up to and including 1992, are given in *Resources for the Future* (Mayne 1993b), and many more will be given in my forthcoming book *Multimedia Resources for the Future* (Mayne 1999) and associated computer databases.

The Bibliography's citations are complementary to the references given in the text and notes of the chapters; all references are listed in alphabetical author order in the References at the end of the book. The Bibliography lists many titles not cited in the chapters and does not include most of the chapter references. It can provide a useful guide to those readers who wish to obtain a bird's-eye view of some of the most important literature on different aspects of politics, even before they start reading the chapters.

Most of its entries refer to books and contain only basic title, author, and date information, but an indication of content is sometimes included; their full citations are given in the References chapter. The entries for books are classified into the following sections: reference books, political dictionaries and glossaries, textbooks, classics, problems and issues, history and current events, regimes, parties and movements, democracy, government and governance, comparative politics, political science and political theory including political ideas and paradigms, ideologies, other paradigms, and human futures. Where appropriate, a specially important book is cited in several sections. A list of political periodicals is also given. There is no section on non-print media, because they will be covered thoroughly in Mayne (1999) and some earlier examples have been reviewed in Mayne (1993b).

POLITICAL REFERENCE BOOKS

The *Oxford Companion to Politics of the World* (Krieger 1993) and *Blackwell Encyclopedia of Political Science* (Bogdanor 1991) are comprehensive guides to all aspects of politics, with entries in alphabetical subject or name order; they are still very useful although now several years out of date. *Political Systems of the World* (Derbyshire and Derbyshire 1996) compares systems of government throughout the world, covers social and economic data and key political figures, and outlines political histories of different countries. *The Statesman's Yearbook* (Hunter 1997) has detailed descriptions of the regimes in all countries of the world and gives many other details including statistics and summaries of recent events. Note also its new edition (Turner 1998) with a somewhat modified arrangement. A *Companion to Contemporary Political Philosophy* (Goodin and Pettit 1995) has three parts, whose essays cover the contributions of other disciplines to political theory, major ideologies, and a wide range of important special topics. *A New Handbook of Political Science* (Goodin and Klingermann 1998) surveys developments in political science. *The Social Science Encyclopedia* (Kuper and Kuper 1996) includes many entries on government and political theory. *The Oxford Companion to Philosophy* (Honderich 1995) includes many articles on aspects of philosophy relevant to politics; its 'maps of philosophy' Appendix is especially useful for locating articles on relevant subjects.

Relevant atlases include *Atlas of World Affairs* (Boyd 1998), *The State of the World Atlas* (Kidron and Segal 1995), and *The Gaia Atlas of Planet Management* (Norman Myers 1994).

World Databases in Government and Politics (Armstrong and Fenton 1998) provides detailed evaluations of the huge range of online databases available on politics and government.

POLITICAL DICTIONARIES AND GLOSSARIES

Dictionaries of politics in general include *Concise Oxford Dictionary of Politics* (McLean 1996) and *The Penguin Dictionary of Politics* (Robertson 1993). More specialised political dictionaries include *The American Political Dictionary* (Plano and Greenberg 1997), *A Dictionary of Political Thought* (Scruton 1996), *The Routledge Dictionary of Twentieth Century Political Thinkers* (Benewick and Green 1997), *The A–Z Guide to Modern Social and Political Theorists* (Sim and Parker 1997), *A Dictionary of Political Biography*

(Kavanagh 1998), and *The Oxford Dictionary of Political Quotations* (Jay 1997).

Other relevant dictionaries include *The Development Dictionary* (Sachs 1992), *The Global Village Companion* (Levinson and Christensen 1998), and *Blackwell Dictionary of Social Thought* (Outhwaite et al. 1994).

Books containing glossaries of political terms and other relevant terms include *Politics* (Heywood 1997), *World Politics* (Kegley and Wittkopf 1997), *The British Polity* (Norton 1994), and *Sociology* (Giddens 1997).

POLITICAL TEXTBOOKS

Introductory textbooks on politics include *Politics: An Introduction* (Axford et al. 1997), *Politics* (Heywood 1997), *An Introduction to Politics* (Ponton and Gill 1993), *World Politics: Trend and Transformation* (Kegley and Wittkopf 1997), *Modern Politics and Government* (Ball 1993), and, at a relatively elementary level, *Teach Yourself Politics* (Joyce 1996) and *Politics* (Minogue 1995).

Textbooks on political science, political theories, and political ideas include *An Introduction to Political Science* (Jacobsohn 1998), *Principles of Politics and Government* (Coulter 1997), *Political Science: An Introduction* (Roskin 1996), *An Introduction to Modern Political Theory* (Barry 1995), *Power and Choice: An Introduction to Political Science* (Shively, 1996), *An Introduction to Political Ideas* (Stirk and Weigall 1995), *Political Ideas and Concepts: An Introduction* (Heywood 1994), *Theories and Concepts of Politics: An Introduction* (Bellamy 1993), *The Concepts and Theories of Modern Democracy* (Birch 1993), and *Modern Political Thought* (Plant 1991). See also *The Modern State* (Christopher Pierson 1996).

Textbooks on comparative politics include: *Comparative Government and Politics* (Hague et al. 1998), *Understanding the Political World: A Comparative Introduction to Political Science* (Danziger 1998), *Comparative Political Economy* (Lane and Ersson 1997), *Comparative Politics* (Palmer 1997a), *Comparative Politics* (Lane and Ersson 1994), and *An Introduction to Comparative Politics* (Calvert 1993).

Textbooks on politics and society include *The State in Contemporary Society: An Introduction* (Schwarzmantel 1994) and *Politics and Society: An Introduction to Political Sociology* (Rush 1992).

POLITICAL CLASSICS

The earliest political classics include *The Republic* (Plato c. 400 B.C.) and the writings of Sun Tzu, presented by Teck (1997). Renaissance classics include *The Prince* (Machiavelli 1513) and *Utopia* (More 1516). The best-known nineteenth-century classics are the *Communist Manifesto* (Marx and Engels

1848), *Capital* (Marx 1864); see also the *Collected Works* (Marx and Engels 1998 ed.). *News from Nowhere* (Morris 1890) is a famous democratic socialist classic, and *Progress and Poverty* (George 1879) is still the basis for the thought of one modern school of thought in political economy.

Modern political classics include *Capitalism, Socialism, and Democracy* (Schumpeter 1947), *The Origins of Totalitarian Democracy* (Talmon 1952), *A Theory of Justice* (Rawls 1973), and *Anarchy, State, and Utopia* (Nozick 1978).

Ideals and Ideologies: A Reader (Ball and Dagger 1995a) quotes passages from many political classics. Ball (1995) includes appraisals of classic work in political theory, and Brown (1990) includes discussions of Marx, Rawls, Nozick, and some other classical political thinkers. *The Way of the Leader* (Krause 1997) discusses the contemporary relevance of the ideas of Sun Tzu and Confucius on leadership.

POLITICAL, HUMAN, AND GLOBAL PROBLEMS AND ISSUES

Global and human problems and their possible solutions are identified in great detail in the *Encyclopedia of World Problems and Human Potential* (Judge 1995) and discussed in an introductory way in *Unravelling Global Apartheid: An Overview of World Politics* (Alexander 1996) and *The First Global Revolution* (King and Schneider 1991). For general guides to global problems and issues, see *Issues in World Politics* (White et al. 1997) and *The World Affairs Companion* (Segal 1996). *The State of the World Atlas* (Kidron and Segal 1995) presents some of them in graphic form. *A Global Agenda* (Tessitore and Woolfson 1997) discusses the issues considered by the fifty-second UN General Assembly. *Third World Politics* (Haynes 1996) explores and analyses the most important political issues in the Third World.

Series of books on global issues include the annual *State of the World* reports, of which the latest is Brown et al. (1998); *Understanding Global Issues*, published by Understanding Global Issues, Cheltenham, England, which already has over fifty titles in print; and *Foundations*, published by Weidenfeld & Nicolson, London, some of whose books discuss future aspects of specific issues.

The Public and the National Agenda (Wayne 1997) shows how people learn about important issues. Books about politics and the media include *Global Information and World Communication* (Mowlana 1997), *Global Communications, International Affairs and the Media since 1945* (Taylor 1997), *Political Communication Today* (Watts 1997), and *Beyond Cultural Imperialism* (Golding and Harris 1996). The relevant influence of new media, including those based on information technology, is addressed by *Media* (Barwise 1998), *Politics and the Press: News Media and Its Influence* (Norris 1997), and *Politics on the Net: Wiring the Political Process* (Rash 1997).

Books on global environmental problems and issues include *Earth Summit II: Outcomes and Analysis* (Osborn and Bigg 1998), *Global Politics of the Environment* (Elliott 1997), *The World at the Crossroads: Towards a Sustainable, Equitable and Liveable World* (Smith et al. 1994), and *Earth in the Balance* (Gore 1992). *Tomorrow's World: Britain's Share in a Sustainable Future* (McLaren et al. 1998) argues the need for Britain to make deep cuts in resource consumption for the benefit of sustainability and humanity as a whole; it sets targets for reduced consumption levels. Manchester University Press publishes the *Issues in Environmental Politics* series.

Global Change: Regional Response to the New International Context of Development (Stallings 1995) provides a valuable survey of global and 'regional' trends in development, offers a new perspective on the study of contemporary development, and reintroduces the international dimension. The *Development Dictionary* (Sachs 1992) contains articles about many aspects of development. *Masters of Illusion: The World Bank and the Poverty of Nations* (Caufield 1998) shows how the World Bank has impoverished many people in the Third World, even though its business is development, and its declared aim is poverty reduction.

The Human Rights Reader (Ishay 1997) contains extracts from major political essays, speeches, and documents on human rights from ancient times to the present. *Human Rights Watch: World Report 1998* (Human Rights Watch 1998) assesses the current status of human rights in different parts of the world. *The Three Pillars of Liberty* (Klug et al. 1996) introduces (13–25) the concept of a Human Rights Index, which can measure political freedom in any country against international standards. *Contemporary Political Philosophy: An Anthology* (Goodin and Pettit 1996) includes essays on state and society, democracy, justice, rights, liberty, equality, and oppression. See also *Human Rights Fifty Years On* (Evans 1998), *Human Rights and Comparative Politics* (Bouandel 1997), and *Alternatives to Freedom* (Miller 1995). Leading books on distributive justice include *Theories of Distributive Justice* (Roemer 1998), *Toward a Just Social Order* (Phillips 1986), and *Social Justice* (Commission on Social Justice 1994). See also *The Economic of the Welfare State* (Barr 1998), *The Welfare State* (Paul et al. 1997), *Dismantling the Welfare State* (Paul Pierson 1996), and *Beyond the Welfare State?* (Pierson 1998).

Recent books on international politics and international relations include *Issues in International Relations* (Salmon 1998), *International Relations and World Politics* (Viotti and Kauppi 1996), *International Politics* (Berridge 1996), and *World Politics: Trend and Transformation* (Kegley and Wittkopf 1997). *International Politics* (Art and Jervis 1996) is a reader. *Global Information and World Communication: New Frontiers in International Relations* (Mowlana 1997) considers the effects of media on international relations. *World Orders, Old and New* (Chomsky 1996) offers a devastating critique of conventional definitions of the 'new world order'. *The New World Order's Defining Crises* (Jacobsen 1996) discusses the clash between the promise and essence of the 'new world order' and considers that the United Nations must become more democratic if it is to become more powerful. *The Global Trap* (Martin and Schumann 1997) explores the spread of globalisation and its possible threat to democracy.

HISTORY AND CURRENT EVENTS

Age of Extremes (Hobsbawm 1996) is a wide-ranging, widely praised history of the world from 1914 to 1991. *World Politics since 1945* (Calvocoressi 1996) is one of the most comprehensive and up-to-date histories of the world since the end of World War II. *The World System* (Frank and Gills 1996) builds on Immanuel Wallerstein's 'world system' concepts and takes a step towards a theory of history in terms of 'communication nets'. *The Hinge of History* (Waterlow 1995) discusses the history of humanity from traditional civilisations into modern times and outlines the enormous problems now confronting us as the clash between modernity and tradition releases the stored emotions and aspirations of centuries but finds hope with organisations, such as the United Nations, that contribute to a sense of world community.

Political Systems of the World (Derbyshire and Derbyshire 1996) outlines recent political histories of different countries, and *The Statesman's Yearbook* (Hunter 1997) summarises recent events there. *Quiet Cataclysm: Reflections on the Recent Transformation of World Politics* (Mueller 1994) and *The World after Communism* (Skidelsky 1996) examine some of the fundamental changes to the world situation during recent years. *Along the Domestic-Foreign Frontier* (Rosenau 1997) explores the enormous changes now transforming world affairs and argues that world trends, such as globalisation and technological advances are clashing with equally powerful local forces. See also *Re-Imagining Political Community* (Archibugi et al. 1998). *The Changing Global Order* (Gardels 1997) includes conversations with world leaders. *The Clash of Civilizations and the Remaking of the World Order* (Huntington 1998) covers contemporary global politics and its future and argues that an international order based on civilisations is the best protection against war.

The World Affairs Companion (Segal 1996) provides information on key political, economic, and social trends. See also *Atlas of World Affairs* (Boyd 1998). *Modernization and Postmodernization* (Inglehart 1997) assesses the political, economic, and cultural changes in forty-three countries. *Megatrends Asia* (Naisbitt 1997) assesses eight major trends in Asia. *Asia's Deadly Triangle* (Calder 1997) shows how arms, energy and growth threaten to destabilise the Asia-Pacific 'region'. *Hidden Agendas* (Pilger 1998) reveals the hidden histories of contemporary events in the UK, Australia, Southeast Asia, South Africa, and so on and presents an extensively researched journalist's view. He argues that contemporary holders of power have their own agendas, celebrates the eloquent defiance and emergence of those who resist oppression, and gives us hope for the future. *The Third World Handbook* (Arnold 1994) covers the emerging problems of the Third World since 1945, the mutual collaboration between its countries, and their common problems.

POLITICAL REGIMES

Political Systems of the World (Derbyshire and Derbyshire 1996) compares systems of government and key political figures of different countries throughout the world. *The Statesman's Yearbook* (Hunter 1997) has detailed descriptions of the regimes in all countries of the world. The *Oxford Companion to Politics of the World* (Krieger 1993) includes articles on most political regimes as they were until the early 1990s, and *States in a Changing World* (Jackson and James 1993) makes a similar survey of regimes in different parts of the world.

Comparative Politics: Nations and Theories in a Changing World (Mayer et al. 1996) combines theoretical and comparative introductions to Western democracies, less developed emerging democracies, and modern autocracies. *Prospects of Democracy* (Vanhanen 1997) studies how far democracy has progressed in 172 different countries. See also *European Democracies* (Steiner 1997) and *Third World Politics: A Comparative Introduction* (Cammack et al. 1993).

POLITICAL PARTIES AND MOVEMENTS

General surveys of political parties include: *Party Systems* (Wolinetz 1997a), *Political Parties* (Wolinetz 1997b), *Political Parties and Democracy* (Lipow 1996), which also covers other voluntary associations, and *Parties, Policies, and Democracy* (Klingemann et al. 1994). *Political Systems of the World* (Derbyshire and Derbyshire 1996: ch. 7) briefly surveys political parties throughout the world. *Changing Party Systems in Western Europe* (Broughton and Donovan 1998) and *Politics and Society in Western Europe* (Lane and Ersson 1998: ch. 3–5) discusses political parties and party systems in Western Europe. *Third World Politics* (Cammack et al. 1993: pt. 3) considers political parties in developing countries.

One Hundred Years of Socialism: The West European Left in the Twentieth Century (Sassoon 1997) presents the history of European socialist organisations from 1889 on. For a current assessment of the European green movement, see *Green Parties and Political Change in Contemporary Europe* (O'Neill 1997).

Books on other aspects of political parties include *Party System Change: Approaches and Interpretations* (Mair 1997), *Party Organizations* (Katz and Mair 1992), and *A Social Psychology of Party Behaviour* (Triandafyllidou 1996).

The *Oxford Companion to Politics of the World* (Krieger 1993) includes articles on selected political movements. For liberation movements associated with 'liberation ideologies' see *Political Ideologies and the Democratic Ideal* (Ball and Dagger 1995b: ch. 8). Other literature on political movements is cited in Chapter 6.

DEMOCRACY

Models of Democracy (Held 1996) reviews the varieties of democratic theory, explores ten major models of democracy, and defines a new concept of democracy. *Prospects for Democracy* (Held 1993) assesses the debate about the meaning and future of democracy through wide-ranging theoretical considerations and a variety of case studies. *Democracy and the Global Order* (Held 1995) describes the changing meaning of democracy in the changing world. *Theories of the State* (Dunleavy and O'Leary 1987) analyses contemporary Western democracies in terms of five theories of the state. *Democracy* (Weale 1998) considers the main arguments about democracy and the wide range of conceptions of democracy. *Engendering Politics* (Phillips 1991) reconsiders the dominant strands in democratic thinking from a feminist perspective.

Democracy's Victory and Crisis (Hadenius 1997) addresses questions central to the development and survival of democratic government. *Comparative Constitutional Engineering* (Sartori 1996) examines the merits, failures, and problems of various forms of democratic government. See also *Liberal Democracy and Its Critics* (Carter and Stokes 1998). *Constitutional Democracy* (Mueller 1996) considers what political institutions an 'ideal' democratic constitution would contain. *Associative Democracy* (Hirst 1993) and *From Statism to Pluralism* (Hirst 1997) present a proposed model, 'associative democracy' that could address major obstacles to democratic theory. *Western Political Theory in the Face of the Future* (Dunn 1993) presents some of the challenges facing democracy. *Civil Society, Democracy and the Muslim World* (Ozdalga and Persson 1998) explores how the growth of a 'civil society' affects the development of democracy.

Democracy and Democratization: Processes and Prospects in a Changing World (Sørensen 1997) and *Democratization* (Potter 1997) explore and explain in some detail the process of democratisation in the modern world. *Establishing Democracies* (Fischer 1996) gives case studies of transitions to democracy from the seventeenth century to the late twentieth century. *Sustainable Democracy* (Przeworski 1995) discusses the choices and prospects for new democracies in Eastern Europe and Latin America. See also *Democracy and Its Alternatives: Understanding Post-Communist Societies* (Rose et al. 1998) and *Political Change in Eastern Europe: Prospects for Liberal Democraccy and Market Economies* (Zuzowski (1998). *The Elite Connection* (Etzioni-Halevy 1993) explores the role of elite relations as a key to understanding democracy.

Other important recent books on democracy include *Democracy in Dark Times* (Isaac 1997), *Understanding Democracy: Economic and Political Perspectives* (Breton et al. 1997), *Democracy: The Challenges Ahead* (Shain and

Klieman 1997), *Reinventing Democracy* (Hirst and Khilnani 1996), *Radical Democracy* (Lummis 1997), *The Dark Side of Liberalism: Elitism vs Democracy* (Hollinger 1996), and *Education for Citizenship: Ideas and Innovations in Political Learning* (Roeher and Cammarano 1997).

Rethinking Democracy (Gould 1990) argues that democracy should apply to economics and social life as well as to politics. *The Waning of the Welfare State* (Zijderveld 1998) views democracy as a system where state, market, and civil society are carefully balanced. *Democracy and Development* (Leftwich 1996) is a comprehensive introduction by experts to the best literature on democracy and development and considers whether democracy is a necessary condition for economic development or an outcome of it. *Democracy in Capitalist Times* (Dryzek 1996) discusses the challenge that capitalism presents to democracy. *Re-Imagining Political Community* (Archibugi et al. 1998) and *The Transformation of Democracy?* (McGrew 1997) consider how the process of globalisation is transforming the conditions of liberal democratic government and critically evaluates the prospects for democratising global forces influencing current events. *Democracy in the Digital Age* (Freeman 1997) assesses the impact of information technology on democracy.

GOVERNMENT AND GOVERNANCE

Textbooks on government and governance include *Principles of Politics and Government* (Coulter 1997), *The Modern State* (Christopher Pierson 1996), *The State in Contemporary Society: An Introduction* (Schwarzmantel 1994), *Modern Politics and Government* (Ball 1993), and *Comparative Government and Politics* (Hague et al. 1998).

Political Systems of the World (Derbyshire and Derbyshire 1996) compares systems of government throughout the world. Ashgate publishes the *International Library of Politics and Comparative Government*. See also *Comparing Government Authority* (Imbeau and McKinley 1996) and *Political Authority and Bureaucratic Power: A Comparative Study* (Page 1992).

Constitutional Reform Now (Blackburn and Plant 1998) reviews and analyses various aspects of constitutional reform. *Designs for Democratic Stability* (Baaklini and Desfosses 1997) discusses how to obtain viable democratic constitutions. *Debating the Constitution* (Barnett et al. 1993) provides new perspectives on constitutional reform. See also *Constitutions in Democratic Politics* (Bogdanor 1988).

Bringing the State Back In (Evans et al. 1985) discusses government and state with respect to economic development, transnational relations, social redistribution, and social conflict. See also *Modern Government: New Government–Society Interactions* (Kooiman 1993). *The Principle of Liberty* (Sartorius 1994) examines the basic purpose of government, scans the history of policies during the last 100 years, states a natural 'Principle of Liberty' that grants freedom to all as long as it does not interfere with the freedom of others, and applies it to legislation in several areas of policy. *Associations and Democracy* (Cohen and Rogers 1995) proposes an innovative scheme for rejuvenating the democratic state. *On Humane Governance* (Falk 1995) presents the World Order Models Project of the Global Civilization Initiative, which aims to find a way of replacing inhumane governance by humane governance. *The State under Stress* (Foster and Plowden 1996) argues that there has been a general decline in the ability to deliver good government.

The Politics of Bureaucracy (Peters 1995) provides a comprehensive, comparative evaluation of the political and policy-making roles of public bureaucracies in many countries around the world. *Politics and Administration at the Top: Lessons from Down Under* (Dunn 1997) examines high-level relationships between politicians and government departments in Australia and offers insights into issues of accountability and responsibility in democratic governments in general. See also *Bureaucrats and Politicians in Western Democracies* (Aberbach et al. 1983). *Reinventing Government* (Osborne and Gaebler 1993) and *Banishing Bureaucracy* (Osborne and Plastrik 1997) present case histories of a third way of government, different from both bureaucratic and laissez-faire approaches, that aims to combine positive and caring government with high efficiency and productivity and has already been tried extensively at federal, state, and local levels of government in the United States.

Books on leadership in government include *Leaders and Leadership: An Appraisal of Theory and Research* (Rejai and Phillips 1997) and *Leading Minds: An Anatomy of Leadership* (Gardner 1996). *Governance and Environmental Quality* (Hanf and Jansen 1998) shows how ten West European countries have reorganised their administrative systems to implement environmental policies.

Books on public policy analysis include *Public Policy: An Introduction to the Theory and Practice of Policy Analysis* (Parsons 1997), *Super Optimising Policy Analysis* (Nagel 1998b), *Analysing Public Policy* (John 1997), *Public Policy Analysis* (Dunn 1992), and *Rational Techniques in Policy Analysis* (Corley 1980). *Comparative Politics* (Almond and Powell 1996a) discusses government and policy-making (ch. 7) and public policy (ch. 8). *The Comparative History of Public Policy* (Castles 1998) compares public policies in the UK, the United States, West Germany, the Netherlands, Sweden, Australia, Israel, and Japan. *Power and Policy in Liberal Democracies* (Harrop 1992) examines power and policy in the UK, the United States, France, and Japan; it integrates policy studies with traditional approaches to government. *Political Economy of Modern Capitalism* (Crouch and Streeck 1997) analyses the public policy choices facing governments and businesses worldwide. *Democracy and Welfare Economics* (van den Doel and van Velthoven (1993) presents an economic theory of political decision making.

Other books on public policy include *Governing in the Information Age* (Bellamy and Taylor 1997) and other books in the *Public Policy and Management Series* published by the Open University Press, *Understanding Governance: Policy Networks, Governance, Responsibility and Accountability* (Rhodes

1997), *The Policy Process in the Modern State* (Hill 1997a), *The Policy Process: A Reader* (Hill 1997b), *The Policy Implementation Process in Developing Nations* (Nagel 1998a), and *Games Real Actors Play: Actor-Centred Institutionalism in Policy Research* (Scharpf 1997). *The Social Science Encyclopedia* (Kuper and Kuper 1996) includes many entries on government and public policy.

COMPARATIVE POLITICS

Introductions to comparative politics include *Comparative Government and Politics* (Hague et al. 1998), *Understanding the Political World: A Comparative Introduction to Political Science* (Danziger 1998), *Comparative Political Economy* (Lane and Ersson 1997), *Comparative Politics* (Palmer 1997a), *Comparative Politics* (Lane and Ersson 1994), and *An Introduction to Comparative Politics* (Calvert 1993). See also *Political Systems of the World* (Derbyshire and Derbyshire 1996: pt. 1)

Other books on comparative politics in general include *Comparative Politics: A Theoretical Framework* (Almond and Powell 1996a), *Comparative Politics Today: A World View* (Almond and Powell 1996b), *Understanding Comparative Politics: A Framework for Analysis* (Kamrava 1995), *Comparative Politics* (Mayer et al. 1996), *Concepts and Issues in Comparative Politics* (Frank Wilson 1996), and *Comparative Politics: New Directions in Theory and Method* (Keman 1993).

Political Systems of the World (Derbyshire and Derbyshire 1996) compares systems of government throughout the world. Ashgate publishes *The International Library of Politics and Comparative Government*. Other books on comparative government include *Comparing Government Authority* (Imbeau and McKinley 1996), *Comparing Constitutions* (Finer et al. 1995), *The Politics of Bureaucracy* (Peters 1995), and *Political Authority and Bureaucratic Power: A Comparative Study* (Page 1992).

Power and Policy in Liberal Democracies (Harrop 1992) and *The Comparative History of Public Policy* (Castles 1998) compare public policies in the UK, the United States, and several other democracies.

Books on specific aspects of comparative politics include *Human Rights and Comparative Politics* (Bouandel 1997), *Courts, Law, and Politics in Comparative Perspective* (Jacob et al. 1996), *Political and Economic Liberalization: Dynamics and Linkages in Comparative Perspective* (Nonneman 1996), and *Third World Politics: A Comparative Introduction* (Cammack et al. 1993).

POLITICAL SCIENCE, POLITICAL THEORY, POLITICAL IDEAS AND PARADIGMS

Introductions to political science, political theories, and political ideas include *An Introduction to Political Science* (Jacobsohn 1998), *Principles of Politics and Government* (Coulter 1997), *Political Science: An Introduction*

(Roskin 1996), *An Introduction to Modern Political Theory* (Barry 1995), *Power and Choice: An Introduction to Political Science* (Shively, 1996), *An Introduction to Political Ideas* (Stirk and Weigall 1995), *Political Ideas and Concepts: An Introduction* (Heywood 1994), *Theories and Concepts of Politics: An Introduction* (Bellamy 1993), *The Concepts and Theories of Modern Democracy* (Birch 1993), and *Modern Political Thought* (Plant 1991).

A New Handbook of Political Science (Goodin and Klingermann 1998) surveys developments in political science and analyses its progress since the early 1970s in the context of historical trends. The *Oxford Companion to Politics of the World* (Krieger 1993) and *Blackwell Encyclopedia of Political Science* (Bogdanor 1991) contain many relevant articles. The *Social Science Encyclopedia* (Kuper and Kuper 1996) includes many entries on government and political theory. *The Oxford Companion to Philosophy* (Honderich 1995) includes many articles on aspects of philosophy relevant to politics; its 'maps of philosophy' Appendix is especially useful for locating articles on relevant subjects. Relevant dictionaries include *A Dictionary of Political Thought* (Scruton 1996), *The Routledge Dictionary of Twentieth Century Political Thinkers* (Benewick and Green 1997), *The A–Z Guide to Modern Social and Political Theorists* (Sim and Parker 1997), and *Blackwell Dictionary of Social Thought* (Outhwaite et al. 1994).

Books on political theory include: Macmillan's *Issues in Political Theory Series, Thinking Politics: Perspectives in Ancient, Modern, and Postmodern Political Theory* (Thiele 1997), *Political Theory: Tradition and Diversity* (Vincent 1997), *Contemporary Empirical Political Theory* (Monroe 1997), *Twentieth Century Political Thought: A Reader* (Bronner 1996), *Theory and Methods of Political Science* (Marsh and Stoker 1995), *Political Theory Today* (Held 1991), *Modern Political Analysis* (Dahl 1990), and *Theories of Political Economy* (Caporaso and Levine 1992).

Political Theory and Ecological Values (Hayward 1998) shows how political theory can allow for environmental issues, while *The Politics of the Earth: Environmental Discourses* (Dryzek 1997) and *Debating the Earth: The Environmental Politics Reader* (Dryzek and Scholsberg 1998) present the wide range of political responses to these issues.

Books on topics allied to political theory include *The Research Process in Politics and International Studies* (Burnham 1997), *Political Development: Dilemmas and Challenges* (Palmer 1997b), *Contemporary Political Philosophy: An Anthology* (Goodin and Pettit 1996), *Contemporary Political and Social Philosophy* (Paul et al. 1995), and *Political Obligation* (Horton and Jones 1992).

Polity and Society: Philosophical Underpinning of Social Science Paradigms (Haas 1992) is a critique of theoretical and conceptual literature on political science and the social sciences in general, and it has an extensive bibliography.

Books on political thought include: *European Political Thought, 1815–1989* (Di Scala and Mastellone 1998), *Political Thought and Political Thinkers* (Shklar 1998), *Liberal Democracy and Its Critics: Perspectives in Contemporary*

Political Thought (Carter and Stokes 1998), *Post-Liberalism: Studies in Political Thought* (Gray 1996), *A History of Western Political Thought* (McClelland 1998), *Ideological Voices: An Anthology in Modern Political Ideas* (Schumaker et al. 1996), *Postmodernism and the Other: The New Imperialism of Western Culture* (Sardar 1997), and *Political and Economic Forms of Modernity* (Allen et al. 1992). *Life after Politics: New Thinking for the Twenty-First Century* (Mulgan 1997) is a selection of the best work published by the independent British think tank Demos. *Connexity: How to Live in a Connected World* (Mulgan 1998) discusses the implications for politics of 'connexity', the increasing interconnectedness and interdependence of contemporary life. *Paradise Dreamed* (Neville-Sington and Sington 1993) discusses how utopian thinkers have changed the modern world.

POLITICAL IDEOLOGIES

Discussions of ideology include those in *Ideology and Utopia* (Mannheim 1936) and *Identity, Interest and Ideology: An Introduction to Politics* (Needler 1996). 'Systematic ideology' provided the first major classification of ideologies and is presented in *Ideologies and Their Functions: A Study in Systematic Ideology* (Walford 1979) and *Beyond Politics: An Outline of Systematic Ideology* (Walford 1990). Recent surveys of ideologies include those in *New Political Thought: An Introduction* (Lent 1998), *The Age of Ideology: Political Ideologies from the American Revolution to Post-Modern Times* (Schwarzmantel 1997), *Ideology and Politics in Britain Today* (Adams 1998), *Political Ideologies and the Democratic Ideal* (Ball and Dagger 1995b), *A Companion to Contemporary Political Philosophy* (Goodin and Pettit 1995: pt. 2), and *Political Systems of the World* (Derbyshire and Derbyshire 1996: ch. 3). *The Oxford Companion to Philosophy* (Honderich 1995) includes several articles on political ideologies and related political polarities; see p. 943 for a 'map' indicating their locality. *Ideals and Ideologies: A Reader* (Ball and Dagger 1995a) quotes passages representing different political ideologies. *Left and Right* (Bobbio 1996) considers the significance of the political distinction between 'left' and 'right', and *Beyond Left and Right* (Giddens 1994) proposes a framework for a radical politics that draws on philosophical 'conservatism' but preserves some 'socialist' core values.

OTHER PARADIGMS

Most of the references to paradigms in subjects outside politics are cited in Chapter 10. This section cites a few additional references. The essays in *A Companion to Contemporary Political Philosophy* (Goodin and Pettit 1995: pt. 1) cover the contributions of philosophy, history, sociology, economics, and law to political theory. *The Social Science Encyclopedia* (Kuper and

Kuper 1996) includes entries on anthropology, business, communication and media, culture, demography, economics, education, geography, history, law, linguistics, philosophy, psychiatry, psychology, social administration, social research methods, and sociology. *The Oxford Companion to Philosophy* (Honderich 1995) includes various articles on nonpolitical ideas and paradigms relevant to philosophy. The *Blackwell Companion to Social Theory* (Turner 1995) and *Blackwell Dictionary of Social Thought* (Outhwaite ett al. 1994) include entries on sociology, social theory, and social thought. *The Icon Critical Dictionary of Postmodern Thought* (Sim 1998) also contains relevant entries.

Introductions to political sociology include *The State in Contemporary Society: An Introduction* (Schwarzmantel 1994) and *Politics and Society: An Introduction to Political Sociology* (Rush 1992). Important texts on sociology in general include *Sociology* (Giddens 1997), *Sociology: A Global Introduction* (Macionis and Plummer 1997), and *Sociology* (Haralambos and Holborn 1995); much of their content is relevant to politics.

HUMAN FUTURES

Preparing for the Twenty-First Century (Kennedy 1993) projects future general trends in world affairs and their impact in different parts of the world. It argues that demography and technology will drive the world into the twenty-first century, confronting us with much greater force than before. It considers how far we are as yet unprepared for the new millennium. *The World in 2020: Power, Culture and Prosperity: A Vision of the Future* (McRae 1995) draws on available research to develop a radical new vision of the political, social, and economic changes in Europe, America, and East Asia during the next generation. *Social Futures: Global Visions* (Hewitt de Alcantára 1996) presents the future global visions of ten distinguished people. *After Liberalisation* (Gentle 1996) presents a vision of Europe in the global economy of the twenty-first century.

The End of History and the Last Man (Fukuyama 1993) argues that the twenty-first century will see 'the end of history', with a 'permanent' domination of 'liberal' market economics worldwide; *Francis Fukuyama and the End of History* (Williams et al. 1997) argues for the fundamental importance and contemporary relevance of Fukuyama's ideas, controversial as they are. *Millennium: Towards Tomorrow's Society* (Kinsman 1990) considers three possible scenarios for the UK and for the world as a whole in the light of changes in the proportions of major social groupings. *Anticipating the Future* (Segal and Buzan 1998) is partly history, partly about current affairs, and partly a 'science fiction' view of the future.

In Weidenfeld & Nicolson's new *Predictions* series, academics and other writers attempt to forecast the future. Some of these books make predictions about what will happen in different parts of the world, and others project future trends relating to specific problems and issues.

The *21st Century Studies* series of Adamantine Press is an especially notable group of future-oriented books, many of whose authors are well known as leading thinkers. Its titles include: *Into the 21st Century* (Burrows et al. 1991), *Visions for the 21st Century* (Moorcroft 1992), *Paradigms in Progress* (Henderson 1993), *The Destiny Choice: Survival Options for the 21st Century* (Laszlo 1993), *Creative Compartments: A Design for Future Organisation* (Fairtlough 1994), *Small Is Powerful* (Papworth 1995), *CHAOTICS: An Agenda for Business and Society in the 21st Century* (Anderla et al. 1997), *Sustainable Global Communities in the Information Age: Visions from Future Studies* (Yamaguchi ed. 1997), *Culture: Beacon of the Future* (Schafer 1998), and *Creating Public Philosophies for Future Generations* (Kim and Dator 1999).

The *Chalice and the Blade: Our History, Our Future* (Eisler 1998) sees humanity at a crossroads. Humanity can either continue to live by the 'blade', according to a 'dominator model' of society, risking global annihilation, or it can rediscover the 'partnership model' of society and a spirit of cooperation and use the 'chalice' to transform our culture and our future for the better. The viewpoint presented there is similar to my own in the sense that its scenarios match those presented here; the Pessimistic Scenario of Chapter 13 and the Piecemeal Scenario of Chapter 14 are like different versions of the 'blade scenario', and the Optimistic Scenario is similar to the 'chalice scenario'.

POLITICAL PERIODICALS

A selection of important political periodicals is listed in suitable groups by title only; full details of all of them, except for those few marked with an asterisk (*), can be obtained from *Ulrich's International Periodicals Directory*, published by R. R. Bowker, New Providence, Rhode Island, and available in almost every large library. Most of them can be found in the Political Sciences section of the Directory, but some are listed in the Literary and Political Reviews section.

The quarterly *World Review: New Books for a New Century*, published by New European Publications, London, draws attention to twelve significant new books per issue and contains articles on these books by their own authors. Many of the books are on politics and other aspects of the human and global situation.

Abstracts and bibliographic journals on politics include:

Political Science Abstracts

International Bibliography of the Social Sciences. Political Science

United States Political Science Documents

Peace Research Abstracts

Academic periodicals on political science and politics, mostly with general coverage, include:

American Academy of Arts and Sciences. Annals
American Journal of Political Science
American Politics Quarterly
British Journal of Political Science
Canadian Journal of Political Science
Developments in Politics (an annual review)
European Journal of Political Research
Harvard Political Review
International Journal of Political Economy
Journal of Politics
Journal of Social, Political and Economic Studies
Journal of Theoretical Politics
Major Concepts in Politics and Political Theory
Michigan Journal of Political Science
New Perspectives Quarterly
Perspectives on Political Science
Political Quarterly
Political Research Quarterly
Political Science
Political Science Quarterly
Political Studies
Political Theory
Politics (Blackwell)
Politics and Society
Polity
Review of Political Economy
Review of Politics
Schools of Thought in Politics

More specialist academic periodicals include:

Current History
East European Politics and Society
Governance
History of Political Thought
Journal of Common Market Studies
Journal of Democracy

Journal of Political Ideologies
Nations and Nationalism
Pacific Affairs
Party Politics
Peace Review
Philosophy and Public Affairs
Political Affairs
Political Analysis
Political Behaviour
Political Communication
Political Crossroads
Political Geography
Political Psychology
Problems of Post-Communism
Public Opinion Quarterly
QJI (Quarterly Journal of Ideology)
Russian Briefing
Science and Society
Studies in American Political Development
Studies in East European Thought
Women & Politics (Haworth Press, Binghamton, New York)
Women & Politics (Praeger)

Ulrich's International Periodicals Directory also has subsections on Civil
Rights and International Relations in its section on Political Science.
   Periodicals on policy studies, policy making, and policies include:

Journal of Policy Modeling
National Journal (Washington, D.C.)
Policy Review (Washington, D.C.)
Policy Sciences
Policy Studies
Policy Studies Journal
Policy Studies Review

   Periodicals for keeping up-to-date with current affairs include:

Intelligence Digest: A Review of World Affairs
Keesing's Record of World Events
World Press Review

Country Forecasts, *Country Profiles*, and *Country Reports*.

The latter three titles are published by the Economist Intelligence Unit (London and New York) for many if not most countries.
   Annual political reference books include:

Political Handbook of the World
Political Parties of the World
Statesman's Year Book, The

   Many publishers publish series of books on specific political themes. Some of these series are listed earlier in this Annotated Bibliography. The series published by Praeger are:

Political Communication
Political Economy
Presidential Studies
Transformational Politics and Political Science

The present book is in the last series.
   Besides the national press, American magazines with a political content include:

American Spectator
Atlantic Monthly, The
Critical Review
Democratic Left (left)
Forward Motion (left)
Harper's Magazine
Monthly Review (New York, left)
National Review (New York, right)
New Politics (New York, left)
New Republic, The
Progressive (left)
Radical America (left)

   Besides the national press, British magazines with a political content include:

Contemporary Review, The
Demos Papers (left)
Demos Quarterly (left)

Ecologist, The (environmental)
Fabian Review (left)
*Freedom Today (right)
Fourth World Review (alternative)
New Economy (left)
New Ground (left, environmental)
New Humanity, The (spiritual)
New Internationalist, The
New Left Review (left)
New Statesman (left)
Peace News
Politics Today (right)
*Progress (left)
*Red Pepper (left)
*Renewal (left)
Resurgence (environmental, spiritual)
*Right Now! (right)
Spectator, The (right)

World Goodwill is a magazine that applies a spiritual approach to human affairs and world affairs; it is distributed in several countries, including the United States and the UK. *New Renaissance* is an internationally distributed forum for progressive and holistic discussion on both local and global issues; it is published by New Renaissance in Mainz, Germany. *Nexus* provides an interesting selection of alternative and unorthodox viewpoints; it is published in Australia and also distributed in the United States and the UK.

References

Aberbach, Joel D., Putnam, Robert D., & Rockman, Bert A. (1983). *Bureaucrats & Politicians in Western Democracies*. 2d ed. Cambridge, MA, & London: Harvard University Press.

Abercrombie, Nicholas, et al. (1994). *Contemporary British Society: A New Introduction to Sociology*. Cambridge & Oxford: Polity Press.

Aberle, David F. (1991). *The Peyote Religion Among the Navaha*. 3d ed. Norman & London: University of Oklahoma Press.

Adams, Iain. (1998). *Ideology and Politics in Britain Today*. Manchester: Manchester University Press; New York: St. Martin's Press.

Adams, John. (1985). *Risk and Freedom: The Record of Road Safety Regulation*. London: Transport Publishing Projects.

———. (1995). *Risk*. London: UCL Press; Bristol, PA: Taylor & Francis.

Aga Khan, Sadruddin, et al. (1988). *Winning the Human Race? The Report of the Independent Commission on International Humanitarian Issues*. London & New York: Zed Books.

Albery, Nicholas (ed.). (1992). *The Book of Visions: An Encyclopaedia of Social Innovations*. London: Institute for Social Inventions.

Albery, Nicholas, Evans, Stephen, & Wienrich, Stephanie (eds.). (1998). *World's Best Ideas: A Global Ideas Bank Compendium*. London: Institute for Social Inventions.

Albery, Nicholas, Irvine, Lindesay, & Evans, Stephen (eds.). (1997). *Creative Speculations: A Compendium of Social Innovations*. London: Institute for Social Inventions.

Albery, Nicholas, Irvine, Lindesay, Buckley, Philip, & Pieau, Stephanie (eds.). (1996). *DIY Futures—People's Ideas & Projects for a Better World*. London: Institute for Social Inventions.

Albery, Nicholas, & Mezey, Matthew (eds.). (1994). *Reinventing Society—A Bumper Book of Best Ideas, Schemes, & Speculations*. London: The Institute for Social Inventions.

Albery, Nicholas, Mezey, Matthew, McHugh, Mary, & Papworth, Marie (eds.). (1995).

Best Ideas—A Compendium of Social Innovations. London: The Institute for Social Inventions.

Albery, Nicholas, Mezey, Matthew, & Ratcliffe, Peter (eds.). (1993). *Social Innovations: A Compendium*. London: Institute for Social Inventions.

Alexander, Titus. (1996). *Unravelling Global Apartheid: An Overview of World Politics*. Cambridge: Polity Press; Cambridge, MA: Blackwell.

Alesina, Alberto, et al. (1997). *Political Cycles and the Macroeconomy*. Cambridge, MA, & London: MIT Press.

Allen, John, et al. (eds.). (1992). *Political and Economic Forms of Modernity*. Cambridge: Polity Press.

Almond, Gabriel A., & Powell, Bingham, Jr. (1996a). *Comparative Politics: A Theoretical Framework*. 2d ed. New York: Harper Collins College.

————. (1996b). *Comparative Politics Today: A World View*. 6th ed. New York: Harper Collins College.

Alter, Peter. (1994). *Nationalism*. 2d ed. London: Arnold; New York: Oxford University Press.

Anderla, Georges, Dunning, Anthony, & Forge, Simon. (1997). *CHAOTICS: An Agenda for Business and Society in the 21st Century*. London: Adamantine Press; Westport, CT: Praeger.

Anderson, James, & Ricci, Paul. (1994). *Society & Social Science: A Reader*. 2d ed. Milton Keynes, England: The Open University.

Anderson, Paul, & Mann, Nyta. (1997). *Safety First: The Making of New Labour*. London: Granta Books.

Andrews, George Reid, & Chapman, Herrick (eds.). (1995). *The Social Construction of Democracy: 1870–1990*. London: Macmillan.

Anton, Thomas J. (1989). *American Federalism and Public Policy*. New York: Random House.

Archer, Clive, & Butler, Fiona. (1996). *The European Union: Structure and Process*. London: Pinter Publishers; New York: St. Martin's Press.

Archibugi, Daniele, et al. (1998). *Re-Imagining Political Community*. Cambridge: Polity Press.

Argyle, Michael. (1992). *The Social Psychology of Everyday Life*. London & New York: Routledge.

Armstrong, Alan. (1996). *To Restrain the Red Horse: The Urgent Need for Radical Economic Reform*. Dunoon, Scotland: Towerhouse Publishing.

Armstrong, C., & Fenton, R. (1998). *World Databases in Government and Politics*. London & New York: Bowker-Saur.

Armstrong, David, Lloyd, Lorna, & Redmond, John. (1996). *From Versailles to Maastricht: International Organisation in the Twentieth Century*. London: Macmillan.

Arnold, Guy. (1994). *The Third World Handbook*. 2d ed. London: Cassell.

Art, Robert C., & Jervis, Robert (eds.). (1996). *International Politics*. 4th ed. New York: Harper Collins College.

Assagioli, Roberto. (1974). *The Act of Will*. London: Wildwood House.

————. (1993a) *Psychosynthesis: A Collection of Basic Writings*. New York: Viking Penguin.

————. (1993b). *Psychosynthesis: A Manual of Principles and Techniques*. London: Aquarian Press.

Avadhuta, Ac Vedaprajinánanda. (1990). *The Wisdom of Yoga: An Introduction to Ananda Marga Philosophy.* 3d ed. Singapore: Ananda Marga.

Avineri, Shlomo, & de-Shalit, Avner (eds.). (1992). *Communitarianism and Individualism.* Oxford & New York: Oxford University Press.

Axford, Barrie, et al. (1997). *Politics: An Introduction.* London & New York: Routledge.

Baaklini, Aldo I., & Desfosses, Helen (eds.). (1997). *Designs for Democratic Stability: Studies in Viable Constitutionalism.* Armonk, NJ, & London: M. E. Sharpe.

Babcock, Robert, & Thompson, Kenneth (eds.). (1992). *Social and Cultural Forms of Modernity.* Cambridge: Polity Press.

Bagehot, Walter. (1867). *The English Constitution.* London: Fontana, 1963.

Bailey, Alice. (1996). Quoted in *World Goodwill Newsletter* 3: 7.

Bainbridge, Timothy, & Teasdale, Anthony. (1998). *The Penguin Companion to the European Union.* 2d ed. London & New York: Penguin Books.

Bak, Per. (1996). *How Nature Works: The Science of Self-Organized Criticality.* New York, Copernicus, Springer-Verlag; Oxford: Oxford University Press.

Ball, Alan R. (1993). *Modern Politics & Government.* 5th ed. London: Macmillan; Chatham, NJ: Chatham House.

Ball, Terence. (1994). *Reappraising Political Theory: Revisionist Studies in the History of Political Thought.* Oxford & New York: Oxford University Press.

Ball, Terence, & Dagger, Richard. (1995a). *Ideals and Ideologies: A Reader.* 2d ed. New York & London: Harper Collins College.

Ball, Terence, & Dagger, Richard. (1995b). *Political Ideologies and the Democratic Ideal.* 2d ed. New York & London: Harper Collins College.

Banyard, Philip, & Hayes, Nicky. (1994). *Psychology: Theory and Application.* London & New York: Chapman & Hall.

Baratta, Joseph Preston (ed.). (1987). *Strengthening the United Nations: A Bibliography on U.N. Reform and World Federalism.* New York, Westport, CT, & London: Greenwood.

Barberis, Peter (ed). (1997). *The Civil Service in an Era of Change.* Aldershot, England, & Brookfield, VT: Dartmouth.

Barker, Rodney. (1997). *Political Ideas in Modern Britain: In and after the 20th Century.* 2d ed. London & New York: Routledge.

Barnaby, Frank (ed.). (1988). *The Gaia Peace Atlas: Survival into the Third Millennium.* London: Pan Books: New York: Doubleday.

Barnett, Anthony. (1997). *This Time: Our Constitutional Revolution.* London: Vintage.

Barnett, Anthony, Ellis, Caroline, & Hirst, Paul (eds.). (1993). *Debating the Constitution: New Perspectives on Constitutional Reform.* Cambridge: Polity Press.

Barr, Nicolas A. (1998). *The Economics of the Welfare State.* 3d ed. Oxford & New York: Oxford University Press.

Barry, Brian J. L. (1991). *Long-Wave Patterns in Economic Development and Political Behaviour.* Baltimore & London: Johns Hopkins University Press.

Barry, Norman P. (1995). An Introduction to Modern Political Theory. 3d ed. London: Macmillan; New York: St. Martin's Press.

Barwise, Paddy. (1998). *Media.* London: Weidenfeld & Nicolson.

Baum, Michael J. (1995). *The New European Union: The Maastricht Treaty and European Integration after the Cold War.* Boulder, CO, & Oxford: Westview Press.

Baumol, William J., & Blinder, Alan S. (1997). *Economics: Principles and Policy.* 7th ed. New York & London: Harcourt Brace Jovanovich.

Beard, R. E., Pentikäinen, T., & Pesonen, E. (1969). *Risk Theory*. London: Methuen; U.S. Distributor Barnes & Noble.

Beckerman, Wilfred. (1995). *Small Is Stupid: Blowing the Whistle on the Greens*. London: Duckworth.

Beer, Stafford. (1994). *Platform for Change*. New ed. Chichester & New York: Wiley.

Begg, D., et al. (1993). *Making Sense of Subsidiarity: How Much Centralization for Europe*. London: Centre for Economic Policy Research; Washington, D.C.: Brookings Institution Press.

Bell, Daniel. (1993). *Communitarianism and Its Critics*. New York & Oxford: Oxford University Press.

Bellamy, Christine, & Taylor, John A. (1997). *Governing in the Information Age*. Buckingham, England: Open University Press; Bristol, PA: Taylor & Francis.

Bellamy, Richard (ed.). (1993). *Theories and Concepts of Politics: An Introduction*. Manchester: Manchester University Press; New York: St. Martin's Press.

Beloff, Nora, with Beloff, Bruno. (1997). *Yugoslavia: An Avoidable War*. London: New European.

Benavides, Gustavo, & Daly, Martin W. (eds.). (1989). *Religion and Political Power*. Albany: State University of New York Press.

Benewick, Robert, & Green, Philip (eds.). (1997). *The Routledge Dictionary of Twentieth Century Political Thinkers*. London & New York: Routledge.

Berridge, Geoffrey R. (1996). *International Politics: States, Power and Conflict since 1945*. 3d ed. London & New York: Prentice-Hall & Harvester Wheatsheaf.

Berrington, Hugh. (1998). *Britain in the Nineties: The Politics of Paradox*. London: Frank Cass.

Bethell, Leslie (ed.). (1996). *Ideas and Ideologies in Twentieth-Century Latin America*. Cambridge & New York: Cambridge University Press.

Birch, Anthony H. (1993). *The Concepts and Theories of Modern Democracy*. London & New York: Routledge.

————. (1998). *British System of Government*. 10th ed. London & New York: Routledge.

Blackburn, Robert, & Plant, Raymond. (1998). *Constitutional Reform Now*. London: Blackstone Press.

Blackstone, Tessa, & Plowden, William. (1988). *Inside the Think Tanks: Advising the Government 1971–1983*. London: Heinemann.

Blair, Tony. (1996). *New Britain: My Vision of a Young Country*. London: Fourth Estate; Boulder, CO: Westview Press.

————. (1998). *The Third Way: New Politics for the New Century*. London: Fabian Society.

Blecher, Marc. (1997). *China against the Tide: Restructuring through Revolution, Radicalism and Reform*. London: Pinter; Herndon, VA: Books International.

Blount, P. Clavell. (1962). *Ideas into Action*. London: Clair Press.

Blumenfeld, Yorick. (1997). *Towards the Millennium: Optimistic Visions for Change*. London: Chimera Press.

Blumler, Jay G., & Gurevitch, Michael. (1995). *The Crisis of Public Communication*. London & New York: Routledge.

Bobbio, Roberto. (1996). *Left and Right: The Significance of a Political Distinction*. Cambridge: Polity Press.

Boden, Margaret. (1992). *The Creative Mind: Myths and Mechanisms*. 2d ed. London: Abacus.

Body, Richard. (1990). *Europe of Many Circles: Constructing a Wider Europe*. London: New European.

——. (1998). *The Breakdown of Europe*. London: New European.

Bogdanor, Vernon. (1979). *Devolution*. Oxford & New York: Oxford University Press.

——. (1981). *The People and the Party System: The Referendum and Electoral Reform in British Politics*. Cambridge & New York: Cambridge University Press.

——. (1985). *Representatives of the People? Parliamentarians and Constituents in Western Democracies*. Aldershot, & Brookfield, VT, England: Gower.

——. (1996). *Politics and the Constitution: Essays on British Government*. Aldershot, England, & Brookfield, VT: Dartmouth.

——. (1997a). *The Monarchy and the Constitution*. 2d ed. Oxford & New York: Oxford University Press.

——. (1997b). *Power and the People: A Primer of Constitutional Reform*. London: Gollancz.

Bogdanor, Vernon. (ed.). (1988). *Constitutions in Democratic Politics*. Aldershot, England: Gower.

——. (1991). *Blackwell Encyclopedia of Political Science*. Oxford & Cambridge, MA: Blackwell.

Bogdanor, Vernon, & Butler, David. (1983). *Democracy and Elections: Electoral Systems and Their Political Consequences*. Cambridge & New York: Cambridge University Press.

Bohm, David, & Peat, F. David. (1987). *Science, Order and Creativity*. New York: Bantam Books; London: Routledge.

Bohman, James, & Rehg, William. (eds.). (1998). *Deliberative Democracy: Essays on Reason and Politics*. Cambridge, MA, & London: MIT Press.

Bok, Derek. (1998). *The State of the Nation: Government and the Quest for a Better Society*. 2d ed. Cambridge, MA, & London: Harvard University Press.

Bouandel, Youcef. (1997). *Human Rights and Comparative Politics*. Aldershot, England, & Brookfield, VT: Dartmouth.

Bowles, Nigel. (1998). *The Government and Politics of the United States*. 2d ed. London: Macmillan; New York: St. Martin's Press.

Boyd, Andrew. (1998). *Atlas of World Affairs*. 10th ed. London & New York: Routledge.

Bradbury, Jonathan, & Mawson, John. (eds.). (1997). *British Regionalism and Devolution: The Challenges of State Reform and European Integration*. London: Jessica Kingsley; Bristol, PA: Taylor & Francis.

Bramwell, Anna. (1989). *Ecology in the Twentieth Century: A History*. New Haven, CT, & London: Yale University Press.

——. (1994). *The Fading of the Greens: The Decline of Environmental Politics in the West*. New Haven, CT, & London: Yale University Press.

Breton, Albert, et al. (1997). *Understanding Democracy: Economic and Political Perspectives*. Cambridge & New York: Cambridge University Press.

Brittan, Samuel. (1996). *Capitalism with a Human Face*. 2d ed. London: Fontana Press; Cambridge, MA: Harvard University Press.

Bronner, Stephen Eric (ed.). (1996). *Twentieth Century Political Thought: A Reader*. New York & London: Routledge.

Brook, Peter. (1972). *Pacifism in Europe to 1914*. Princeton, NJ: Princeton University Press.

Broughton, David & Donovan, Mark. (1998). *Changing Party Systems in Western Europe*. London: Pinter.

Brown, Alan. (1990). *Modern Political Philosophy: Theories of the Just Society*. 2d ed. London: Penguin Books; New York: Viking Penguin.

Brown, Archie. (1997). *The Gorbachev Factor*. 2d ed. Oxford & New York: Oxford University Press.

Brown, Lester R., et al. (1998). *State of the World 1998: A Worldwatch Institute Report on Progress Toward a Sustainable Society*. New York: W. W. Norton; London: Earthscan.

Brown, Roger. (1996). *Social Psychology*. 2d ed. New York & London: Free Press.

Browne, Anthony. (3 May 1998). "All for a Handful of Change". *The Observer, Business*, p. 4.

Bryant, Christopher. (1997). *Possible Dreams: A Personal History of the British Christian Socialists*. 2d ed. London: Hodder & Stoughton.

Bryant, Raymond L., & Bailey, Sinéad. (1997). *Third World Political Ecology*. London & New York: Routledge.

Bryce-Smith, Derek. (1995). "Crime and Nourishment". *Network, the Scientific & Medical Network Review* 59(December): 3–6.

Budge, Ian. (1996). *The New Challenge of Direct Democracy*. Cambridge: Polity; Cambridge, MA: Blackwell.

Budge, Ian, & Newton, Kenneth. (1997). *Politics of the New Europe*. London & New York: Addison Wesley Longman.

Budge, Ian, et al. (eds.). (1998). *The New British Politics*. London & New York: Addison Wesley Longman.

Burgat, François. (1998). *Face to Face with Political Islam*. London: Tauris.

Burgess, Adam. (1997). *Divided Europe: The New Domination of the East*. London: Pluto Press; Milford, CT: LPC In/Book.

Burnham, Peter. (ed.). (1997). *The Research Process in Politics and International Studies*. London: Pinter; Herndon, VA: Books International.

Burrows, Brian C., Mayne, Alan J., & Newbury, Paul A. R. (1991). *Into the 21st Century: A Handbook for a Sustainable Future*. London: Adamantine Press.

Butler, David, & Butler, Gareth. (1994). *British Political Facts 1900–1994*. 7th ed. London: Macmillan; New York: St. Martin's Press.

Butler, David, & Kavanagh, Peter. (1997). *The British General Election of 1997*. London: Macmillan New York: St. Martin's Press.

Butler, David, & Ranney, Austin (eds.). (1994). *Referendums Around the World: The Coming Age of Direct Democracy*. 2d ed. London: Macimillan.

Button, John. (1995). *The Radicalism Handbook: A Complete Guide to the Radical Movement in the Twentieth Century*. London: Cassell.

Buzan, Barry, & Segal, Gerald. (1998). *Anticipating the Future*. London: Simon & Schuster.

Buzan, Tony, with Buzan, Barry. (1995). *The Mindmap Book*. 2d ed. London: BBC Books.

Byrne, Liam. (1997). *Redesigning the State: Information Age Government: Delivering the Blair Revolution*. London: Fabian Society.

Cairncross, Frances. (1992). *Costing the Earth: What Governments Must Do; What*

Consumers Need to Know; How Businesses Can Profit. 2d ed. Boston: Harvard Business School Press.

Calder, Kent E. (1997). *Asia's Deadly Triangle: How Arms, Energy and Growth Threaten to Destabilise Asia-Pacific.* London & Santa Rosa, CA: Nicholas Brealey Publishing.

Calhoun, Craig. (1997). *Nationalism.* Buckingham, England: Open University Press; Minneapolis: University of Minnesota Press.

Calvert, Peter. (1993). *An Introduction to Comparative Politics.* London: Harvester Wheatsheaf.

Calvocoressi, Peter. (1996). *World Politics Since 1945.* 7th ed. London & New York: Longman.

Cammack, Paul, Pool, David, & Tordoff, William. (1993). *Third World Politics: A Comparative Introduction.* 2d ed. London: Macmillan; Baltimore: Johns Hopkins University Press.

Canovan, Margaret. (1996). *Nationhood and Political Theory: Do Internationalists Need Nations?* Cheltenham, England, & Lyme, NH: Elgar.

Caporaso, James M., & Levine, David P. (1992). *Theories of Political Economy.* 2d ed. Cambridge & New York: Cambridge University Press.

Carter, April, and Stokes, Geoff. (1998). *Liberal Democracy and Its Critics: Perspectives in Contemporary Political Thought.* Cambridge: Polity Press.

Castles, Francis G. (1998). *The Comparative History of Public Policy: Patterns of Post-War Transformation.* Cheltenham, England, & Lyme, NH: Elgar.

Caufield, Catherine. (1998). *Masters of Illusion: The World Bank and the Poverty of Nations.* 3d ed. London: Pan Books.

Centeno, Miguel Angel, & Font, Mauricio (eds.). (1996). *Toward a New Cuba: Legacies of Revolution.* Boulder, CO, & Oxford: Rienner.

Champney, Leonard. (1994). *Introduction to Quantitative Political Science.* London & New York: Harper Collins College.

Chapman, David. (1997a). "Preference-Score Representation," Democracy Design Forum paper.

———. (1997b). "The Role of Electoral Systems in the Resolution of Electoral Conflict," Democracy Design Forum paper, prepared for the Third International Conference of the Ethnic Studies Network, Londonderry, 26–29 June 1997.

———. (1997c). "The Territorial Additional-Member System," Democracy Design Forum paper, also in pp. 225–231 of Albery et al. (1997).

———. (1997d). "Three New Electoral Systems," Democracy Design Forum paper.

Chehabi, V. E., & Linz, Juan J. (eds.). (1998). *Sultanistic Regimes.* Baltimore & London: Johns Hopkins University Press.

Childers, Erskine. (1993). *In a Time beyond Warnings: Strengthening the United Nations System.* London: Catholic Institute for International Relations (CIIR) & Pax Christi.

Childers, Erskine, ed. (1994). *Challenges to the United Nations: Building a Safer World.* London: Catholic Institute for International Relations (CIIR); New York: St. Martin's Press.

Childers, Erskine with Urquhart, Brian. (1994). *Renewing the United Nations System.* Uppsala, Sweden: Dag Hammarskjöld Foundation.

Childs, David. (1997). *Britain Since 1945: A Political History.* 4th ed. London & New York: Routledge.

Chomsky, Noam. (1996). *World Orders, Old and New.* 2d ed. New York: Columbia University Press; London: Pluto Press.

Choueiri, Youssef. (1997). *Islamic Fundamentalism*. 2d ed. London: Pinter; Herndon, VA: Books International.

Church, Clive H., & Phinnemore, David. (1994). *European Union and European Community: A Handbook and Commentary on the Post-Maastricht Treaties*. London & New York: Prentice Hall.

Clark, Bruce. (1995). *An Empire's New Clothes: The End of Russia's Liberal Dream*. London: Vintage.

Clinton, President Bill. (1997). *Between Hope and History: Meeting America's Challenges for the 21st Century*. 2d ed. New York: Random House.

Close, Paul. (1994). *Citizenship Europe and Change*. London: Macmillan.

Cockett, Richard. (1995). *Thinking the Unthinkable: Think-Tanks and the Economic Counter-Revolution, 1931–1983*. London: Fontana Press.

Cohen, Jean L., & Arato, Andrew. (1994). *Civil Society and Political Theory*. 2d ed. Cambridge, MA, & London: MIT Press.

Cohen, Joshua, & Rogers, Joel (ed. Wright, Erik Olin). (1995). *Associations and Democracy*. London & New York: Verso.

Cole, Ken. (1998). *Cuba Development Strategy: The Options*. London: Pinter; Herndon, VA: Books International.

Coleman, John. (1999). *The Council of Europe as the Conscience of Europe*. London: New European Publications.

Collins, Richard, & Murroni, Cristina. (1996). *New Media, New Policies*. Cambridge: Polity Press; Cambridge, MA: Blackwell.

Colomer, Josep M. (ed.). (1996). *Political Institutions in Europe*. London & New York: Routledge.

Commission on Global Governance. (1995). *Our Global Neighbourhood: The Report of the Commission on Global Governance*. New York & Oxford: Oxford University Press.

Commission on Public Policy and Big Business. (1997). *Promoting Prosperity: A Business Agenda for Britain*. London: Vintage.

Commission on Social Justice. (1994). *Social Justice: Strategies for National Renewal*. London: Vintage.

Connolly, Bernard. (1998). *The Rotten Heart of Europe: The Dirty War for Europe's Money*. 2d ed. London & Boston: Faber & Faber.

Connor, Walter. (1993). *Ethnonationalism: The Quest for Understanding*. Princeton, NJ, & Chichester: Princeton University Press.

Cook, Chris. (ed.). (1995). *The World Political Almanac*. 3d ed. New York & Oxford: Facts on File.

Corera, Gordon. (1998). "More by Default than Design: The Clinton Experience and the Third Way". *Renewal* 6(April): 6–16.

Corley, Michael. (1980). *Rational Techniques in Policy Analysis*. Aldershot, England, & Brookfield, VT: Gower.

Corporate Observatory Europe (CEO). (1998). "MAIgalomania: The Multilateral Agreement in Investment". *Nexus* 5 (April–May): 25–30, 36–37.

Cortada, James N., & Cortada, James W. (1997). *Can Democracy Survive in Europe?* Westport, CT, & London: Praeger.

Coulter, Edwin M. (1997). *Principles of Politics and Government*. 6th ed. Madison, WI, & London: Brown & Benchmark.

Covey, Stephen R. (1992a). *Principle-Centred Leadership*. New York & London: Simon & Schuster.

Covey, Stephen R. (1992b). *The Seven Habits of Highly Effective People: Powerful Lessons in Personal Change.* New York & London: Simon & Schuster.

Cox, Michael (ed.). (1997). *Soviet Collapse and the Post-Communist World: A Critical Reassessment.* Herndon, VA: Books International; London: Pinter.

Coxall, Bill, & Robins, Lynton. (1997). *British Politics since the War.* London: Macmillan.

———. (1998). *Contemporary British Politics.* 3d ed. London: Macmillan.

Cranna, Michael (ed.). (1994). *The True Cost of Conflict.* London: Earthscan.

Crewe, Ivor, et al. (eds.). (1998). *Political Communities: The General Election Campaign of 1997.* London: Frank Cass.

Croft, Stuart, & Redmond, John. (1998). *The Enlargement of Europe.* Manchester: Manchester University Press.

Crouch, Colin, & Marquand, David (eds.). (1995). *Reinventing Collective Action: From the Global to the Local.* Oxford & Cambridge, MA: Blackwell.

Crouch, Colin, & Streeck, Wolfgang (eds.). (1997). *Political Economy of Modern Capitalism: Mapping Convergence and Diversity.* London & Thousand Oaks, CA: Sage.

Dahbour, Omar, & Ishay, Micheline R. (1995). *The Nationalism Reader.* Atlantic Highlands, NJ: Humanities Press.

Dahl, Arthur Lyon. (1996). *The Eco Principle: Ecology and Economics in Symbiosis.* New York: St. Martin's Press; London: Zed Books.

Dahl, Robert A. (1990). *Modern Political Analysis.* 5th ed. New York & London: Prentice-Hall.

Dale, Iain (ed.). (1998). *Directory of Think Tank Publications: The Definitive Guide to UK Policy Think Tanks and a Bibliography of Their Publications.* London: Politico's.

Daly, Herman E. (1995). *Steady-State Economics: The Economics of Biophysical Equilibrium and Moral Growth.* 4th ed. New York: W. H. Freeman.

———. (1997). *Beyond Growth: The Economics of Sustainable Development.* 2d ed. Boston & London: Beacon Press.

——— (ed.). (1995). *Economics, Ecology, Ethics: Essays toward a Steady State Economy.* New York: W. H. Freeman.

Daly, Herman E., Cobb, John B., Jr., & Cobb, Clifford W. (1994). *For the Common Good: Redirecting the Economy toward Community, the Environment and a Sustainable Future.* 2d ed., Boston: Beacon Press; 1st ed. London: Green Print.

Danenberg, R. V. (1996). *Understanding American Politics.* London: Fontana Press.

Danziger, James N. (1998). *Understanding the Political World: A Comparative Introduction to Political Science.* 4th ed. New York & London: Addison Wesley Longman.

Dauncey, Guy. (1988). *After the Crash: The Emergence of the Rainbow Economy.* Basingstoke, England: Green Print; New York: Bootstrap Press.

Davis, John. (1994). *Greening Business: Managing for Sustainable Development.* Oxford & Cambridge, MA: Blackwell.

Daws, Sam, & Taylor, Paul (eds.). (1997). *The United Nations.* Aldershot, England; Ashgate.

de Bono, Edward. (1995). *Serious Creativity: Using the Power of Lateral Thinking.* 2d ed. New York & London: Harper Collins Business.

de Lourdes Pintaçilgo, Maria, et al. (1996). *Coping for the Future: Making the Next Decade Provide a Life Worth Living.* Oxford & New York: Oxford University Press.

De Marco, Guido, & Bartolo, Michael. (1996). *A Second Generation United Nations: For Peace in Freedom in the 21st Century*. Niwot: University of Colorado Press; London: Kegan Paul International.

De Smijter, E. (ed.). (1997). *The Future of the European Union in the Light of the 1996 Intergovernmental Conference*. Leuven, Belgium, & London: Leuven University Press; Eagle Point, OR: Coronet Books.

Deegan, Heather. (1996). *Third Worlds: The Politics of the Middle East and Africa*. London & New York: Routledge.

————. (1998). *South Africa Reborn: Building a New Democracy*. London: UCL Press.

Deming, W. Edwards. (1995). *The New Economics for Industry, Government, Education*. 2d ed. Cambridge, MA: MIT Center for Advanced Engineering; Salisbury, England: British Deming Association.

Denham, Andrew. (1998). *Think Tanks and British Politics*. London: UCL Press.

Derbyshire, J. Denis, & Derbyshire, Ian. (1996). *Political Systems of the World*. 2d ed. Oxford: Helicon; New York: St. Martin's Press.

Di Scala, Spencer M., & Mastellone, Salvo. (1998). *European Political Thought, 1815–1989*. Boulder, CO, & Oxford: Westview Press.

Diamond, Larry, & Plattner, Marc F. (eds.). (1994). *Nationalism, Ethnic Conflict, and Democracy*. Baltimore & London: Johns Hopkins University Press.

Dickson, Malcolm. (1996). *British Political Culture*. New York & London: Prentice-Hall & Harvester Wheatsheaf.

Dixon, Patrick. (1996). *The Truth about Westminster: Can We Change the Heart of British Politics?* Eastbourne, England: Kingsway.

————. (1998). *Futurewise: Six Faces of Global Change*. London: Harper Collins.

Dobson, Andrew. (1995). *Green Political Thought*. 2d ed. London & New York: Routledge.

Dobson, Andrew, & Lucardie, Paul. (1995). *The Politics of Nature: Explorations in Green Political Theory*. 2d ed. London & New York: Routledge.

Dodds, Felix (ed.). (1997). *The Way Forward: Beyond Agenda 21*. London: Earthscan; Washington, DC: Island Press.

Doherty, Brian, & de Geus, Marius. (1996). *Democracy and Green Political Thought: Subsidiarity, Rights and Citizenship*. London & New York: Routledge.

Donald, James, & Hall, Stuart (eds.). (1986). *Politics and Ideology: A Reader*. Milton Keynes, England: Open University Press; Bristol, PA: Taylor & Francis.

Douthwaite, Richard. (1996). *Short Circuit: Strengthening Local Economies for Security in an Unstable World*. Totnes, England: Green Books; Charter Spring, PA: Dufour.

Dower, Nigel. (1998). *World Ethics: The New Agenda*. Edinburgh: Edinburgh University Press.

Doxiadis, Constantinos. (1968). *Ekistics: An Introduction to the Science of Human Settlements*. London & New York: Hutchinson.

————. (1977). *Ecology and Ekistics*. London: Elek.

Drexler, K. Eric. (1992). *Engines of Creation: The Coming Era of Nanotechnology*. Oxford & New York: Oxford University Press.

Driver, Stephen, & Martell, Luke. (1998). *New Labour Politics after Thatcherism*. Cambridge: Polity Press.

Drucker, Henry M., & Brown, Gordon. (1980). *Politics of Nationalism and Devolution*. London & New York: Longman.

Drucker, Peter. (1994). *Post-Capitalist Society*. 2d ed. Oxford & Boston: Butterworth-Heinemann; Bellevue, WA: Harper Business.

Dryzek, John S. (1996). *Democracy in Capitalist Times: Ideals, Limits, and Struggle*. New York & Oxford: Oxford University Press.

———. (1997). *The Politics of the Earth: Environmental Discourses*. New York & Oxford: Oxford University Press.

Dryzek, John S., and Scholsberg, David (eds.). (1998). *Debating the Earth: The Environmental Politics Reader*. New York & Oxford: Oxford University Press.

Duff, Andrew, Pinder, John, & Pryce, Roy (eds.). (1994). *Maastricht and Beyond: Building the European Union*. London & New York: Routledge.

Dukes, Ramsey. (1988). *Words Made Flesh or Information in Formation: Artificial Intelligence, Humanity, and the Cosmos*. Winchester, England: Mouse That Spins.

Dummett, Michael. (1997). *Principles of Electoral Reform*. Oxford & New York: Oxford University Press.

Dunleavy, Patrick, & O'Leary, Brendan. (1987). *Theories of the State: The Politics of Liberal Democracy*. London: Macmillan; Franklin, NY: New Amsterdam Books.

Dunn, Delmer. (1997). *Politics and Administration at the Top: Lessons from Down Under*. Pittsburgh & London: University of Pittsburgh Press.

Dunn, John. (1993). *Western Political Theory in the Face of the Future*. 2d ed. Cambridge & New York: Cambridge University Press.

Dunn, William N. (1992). *Public Policy Analysis: An Introduction*. 2d ed. London & New York: Prentice-Hall.

Dutton, David. (1997). *British Politics Since 1945*. 2d ed. Oxford & Cambridge, MA: Blackwell.

East, Roger F., & Pontin, Jolyon. (1997). *Revolution and Change in Central and Eastern Europe*. London: Pinter; Herndon, VA: Books International.

Eatwell, Roger, & Wright, Anthony. (1993). *Contemporary Political Ideologies*. London: Pinter; New York: St. Martin's Press.

Eccleshall, Robert et al. (1994). *Political Ideologies: An Introduction*. 2d ed. London & New York: Routledge.

Eckersley, Robin. (1992). *Environmentalism and Political Theory*. London: UCL Press; Albany: State University of New York Press.

Edwards, Geoffrey, & Pijpers, Alfred (eds.). (1997). *Politics of European Union Reform: The 1996 Intergovernmental Conference and Beyond*. London: Pinter; Herndon, VA: Books International.

Edwards, George C., III, Wattenberg, Michael P., & Lineberry, Robert B. (1998). *Government in America: People, Politics, and Policy*. 8th. ed. New York & London: Addison Wesley Longman.

Eggleston, Richard. (1983). *Evidence, Proof and Probability*. London: Weidenfeld & Nicolson.

Eisler, Riane. (1998). *The Chalice and the Blade: Our History, Our Future*. New ed. San Francisco: Harper San Francisco: London: Thorsons.

Ekins, Paul. (1992). *A New World Order: Grassroots Movements for Social Change*. London & New York: Routledge.

——— (ed.). (1989). *The Living Economy: A New Economics in the Making*. 2d ed. London & New York: Routledge.

Ekins, Paul, Hillman, Mayer, & Hutchinson, Robert. (1992). *Wealth Beyond Measure:*

An Atlas of the New Economics. London: Gaia Books; New York: Anchor Books, Doubleday, with title *The Gaia Atlas of Green Economics*.

Ekins, Paul, & Max-Neef, Manfred (eds.). (1992). *Real-Life Economics: Understanding Wealth Creation*. London & New York: Routledge.

Elazar, Daniel J. (1987). *Exploring Federalism*. Tuscaloosa & London: University of Alabama Press.

Elfstrom, Gerard. (1998). *International Relations: Contemporary Ethical Issues*. Oxford: ABC-CLIO.

Elkington, John, & Burke, Tom. (1987). *The Green Capitalists: Industry's Search for Environmental Excellence*. London: Gollancz.

Elkington, John, & Knight, Peter, with Hailes, Julia. (1992). *The Green Business Guide: How to Take Up—and Profit From—the Environmental Challenge*. London: Gollancz.

Elliott, Larry, & Atkinson, Dan. (1998). *The Age of Insecurity*. London & New York: Verso.

Elliott, Lorraine. (1997). *Global Politics of the Environment*. London: Macmillan; New York: New York University Press.

Elliott, Robert (ed.). (1995). *Environmental Ethics*. Oxford & New York: Oxford University Press.

Ellis, Keith, et al. (eds.). (1995). *Critical Issues in Systems Theory and Practice*. New York & London: Plenum Press.

Escobar, Arturo, & Alvarez, Sonia E. (1992). *The Making of Social Movements in Latin America: Identity, Strategy, and Democracy*. Boulder, CO, & Oxford: Westview Press.

Esler, Gavin. (1998). *The United States of Anger: The People and the American Dream*. 2d ed. London & New York: Penguin Books.

Esslemont, J. E. (1923). *Bah'ullah and the New World Era*. 4th ed. London: Baha'i Publishing Trust, 1974.

Etzioni, Amitai. (1995). *The Spirit of Community: Rights, Responsibilities and the Communitarian Agenda*. London: Fontana Press.

———. (1996). *The New Golden Rule: Community and Morality in a Democratic Society*. New York: Basic Books; London: Profile Books.

——— (ed.). (1998). *The Essential Communitarian Reader*. Lanham, MD & Oxford: Rowman & Littlefield.

Etzioni, Amitai, & Lawrence, Paul R. (eds.). (1993). *Socio-Economics: Towards a New Synthesis*. 2d ed. Armonk, NY: M. E. Sharpe.

Etzioni-Halevy, Eva. (1993). *The Elite Connection: Problems and Potential of Western Philosophy*. Cambridge: Polity Press; Cambridge, MA: Blackwell.

Evans, Peter B., Ruschemeyer, Dietrich, & Skocpol, Theda (eds.). (1985). *Bringing the State Back In*. Cambridge & New York: Cambridge University Press.

Evans, Tony. (1998). *Human Rights Fifty Years On: A Reappraisal*. Manchester: Manchester University Press; New York: St. Martin's Press.

Fairtlough, Gerard. (1994). *Creative Compartments: A Design for Future Organisation*. London: Adamantine Press.

Faksh, Mahmud A. (1997). *The Future of Islam in the Middle East: Fundamentalism in Egypt, Algeria, and Saudi Arabia*. Westport, CT, & London: Praeger.

Falk, Richard. (1995). *On Humane Governance: Toward a New Global Politics*. Cambridge: Polity Press; University Park: Pennsylvania State University Press.

Farrell, David M. (1996). *Comparing Electoral Systems.* London & New York: Prentice-Hall & Harvester Wheatsheaf.

Featherstone, Cornelia, & Forsyth, Lori. (1997). *Medical Marriage: The New Partnership between Orthodox and Complementary Medicine.* Forres, Scotland: Findhorn Press.

Feld, Werner J. (1998). *The Integration of the European Union and Domestic Political Issues.* Westport, CT, & London: Praeger.

Felder, David W. (1991). *How to Work for Peace.* Gainesville & London: University Press of Florida.

Fenby, Jonathan. (1998). *On the Brink: The Trouble with France.* London: Little, Brown (UK).

Ferencz, Benjamin B. (ed.). (1991). *World Security for the 21st Century: Challenges and Solutions.* London: Adamantine Press.

Field, Frank, et al. (1996). *Stakeholder Welfare.* London: IEA Health & Welfare Unit.

Financial Times. (4 December 1997). *Business in the Community* Supplement. London: FT Surveys, Financial Times.

Finer, S. E., Bogdanor, Vernon, & Rudden, Bernard. (1995). *Comparing Constitutions.* 2d ed. Oxford & New York: Oxford University Press.

Fischer, Mary Ellen (ed.). (1996). *Establishing Democracies.* Boulder, CO, & Oxford: Westview Press.

Fisher, Justin. (1996). *British Political Parties.* London & New York: Prentice-Hall & Harvester Wheatsheaf.

Fishkin, James S. (1993). *Democracy and Deliberation: New Directions for Democratic Reform.* 2d ed. New Haven, CT, & London: Yale University Press.

———. (1997). *The Voice of the People: Public Opinion and Democracy.* 2d ed. New Haven, CT, & London: Yale University Press.

Fitzmaurice, John. (1996). *The Politics of Belgium: A Unique Federation.* London: Hurst.

Flood, Christopher, & Bell, Laurance (eds.). (1997). *Political Ideologies in Contemporary France.* London: Pinter; Herndon, VA: Books International.

Foster, Christopher D., & Plowden, Francis J. (1996). *The State under Stress: Can Hollow State Be Good Government?* Buckingham, England: Open University Press; Bristol, PA: Taylor & Francis.

Fowler, Robert Booth, & Hertzke, Allen D. (1999). *Religion and Politics in America: Faith, Culture, and Strategic Choices.* 2d ed. Boulder, CO, & Oxford: Westview Press.

Fox, Matthew. (1991). *Creation Spirituality: Liberating Gifts for the Peoples of the Earth.* San Francisco: Harper San Francisco; London: Harper Collins.

———. (1996). *Original Blessing: A Primer in Creation Spirituality.* 3d ed. Santa Fe, NM, & London: Bear.

Foxon, Tim. (1997). "Science, Policy and Risk: Report on Royal Society Meeting," *Scientists for Global Responsibility Newsletter*, 15(May): 4–5.

Frank, Andre Gunder, & Gills, Barry K. (eds.). (1996). *The World System: Five Hundred Years or Five Thousand?* 2d ed. London & New York: Routledge.

Franklin, Jane (ed.). (1997). *Equality.* London: Institute for Public Policy Research.

———. (1998). *The Politics of Risk Society.* Cambridge: Polity Press.

Freeman, Christopher (ed.). (1986). *Design, Innovation and Long Cycles in Economic Development.* London: Pinter.

Freeman, Christopher, Clark, John, & Soete, Luc. (1982). *Unemployment and Technical Innovation: A Study of Long Waves and Economic Development.* London: Pinter.

Freeman, Roger. (1997). *Democracy in the Digital Age*. London: Demos.

Friedrich, C. J. (1965). *Totalitarian Dictatorship and Autocracy*. Cambridge, MA, & London: Harvard University Press.

Fukuyama, Francis. (1993). *The End of History and the Last Man*. London: Penguin Books; New York: Avon.

Funderburk, Charles, & Thobaben, Robert G. (1994). *Political Ideologies*. 2d ed. New York & London: Harper Collins College: New York: Addison Wesley Education.

Galbraith, Kenneth. (1993). *The Culture of Contentment*. 2d ed. New York: Houghton Mifflin; London: Penguin Books.

Gardels, Nathan (ed.). (1997). *The Changing Global Order: World Leaders Reflect*. Cambridge: Polity Press; Cambridge, MA, Blackwell.

Gardner, Howard. (1996). *Leading Minds: An Anatomy of Leadership*. 2d ed. New York: Basic Books; London: Harper Collins.

Garner, Robert. (1995). *Environmental Politics: An Introduction*. London & New York: Prentice-Hall & Harvester Wheatsheaf.

Gellner, Ernest. (1994). *Encounters with Nationalism*. Oxford & Cambridge, MA: Blackwell.

———. (1998a). *Nationalism*. 2d ed. London: Phoenix, Orion Books; 1st ed. New York: New York University Press, 1997.

———. (1998b). *Nationalism Observed*. London: Weidenfeld & Nicolson.

Gentle, Christopher J. S. (1996). *After Liberalisation: A Vision of Europe in the Global Economy of the Twenty-First Century*. London: Macmillan; New York: St. Martin's Press.

George, Henry. (1879). *Progress and Poverty: An Inquiry into the Cause of Industrial Depressions and of Increase of Want with Increase of Wealth . . . The Remedy*. 3d ed. New York: Robert Schalkenbach Foundation, 1996; London: Shepheard-Walwyn.

Ghai, Dharam, & Vivian, Jessica M. (eds.). (1995). *Grassroots Environmental Action: People's Participation in Sustainable Development*. 2d ed. London & New York: Routledge.

Gibson, Tony. (1984). *Counterweight: The Neighbourhood Option*. London: Town and Country Planning Association.

———. (1996). *The Power in Our Hands: Neighbourhood Based—World Shaking*. Charlbury, Oxfordshire, England: Jon Carpenter; Concord, MA: Paul.

Gibson-Graham, J. K. (1996). *The End of Capitalism (as We Knew It): A Feminist Critique of Political Economy*. Oxford & Cambridge, MA: Blackwell.

Giddens, Anthony. (1994). *Beyond Left and Right: The Future of Radical Politics*. Cambridge: Polity Press; Stanford, CA: Stanford University Press.

———. (1997). *Sociology*. 3d ed. Cambridge: Polity Press.

———. (1998a). "After the Left's Paralysis," *New Statesman* (1 May): 18–20.

———. (1998b). *The Third Way: The Renewal of Social Democracy*. Cambridge: Polity Press.

Gifford, Paul. (1998). *African Christianity: Its Public Role*. London: Hurst.

Glassman, William E. (1995). *Approaches to Psychology*. 2d ed. Buckingham, England: Bristol, PA: Taylor & Francis.

Gleick, James. (1998). *Chaos: Making a New Science*. New ed. London: Minerva.

Glennerster, Howard. (1995). *British Social Policy since 1945*. Oxford & Cambridge, MA: Blackwell.

Golding, Peter, & Harris, Phil. (1996). *Beyond Cultural Imperialism: Globalization, Communication and the New International Order.* London & Thousand Oaks, CA: Sage.

Goldsmith, James. (1994). *The Trap.* London: Macmillan. New York: Carroll & Graf.

———. (1995). *The Response.* London: Macmillan.

Goleman, Daniel. (1996). *Emotional Intelligence: Why It Can Matter More than IQ.* 2d ed. London: Bloomsbury; New York: Bantam.

———. (1998). *Emotional Intelligence at Work.* Bloomsbury; New York: Bantam, with title *Working with Emotional Intelligence.*

Goodin, Robert E. (1992). *Green Political Theory.* Cambridge: Polity Press; Cambridge, MA: Blackwell.

Goodin, Robert E., & Klingermann, Hans-Dieter (eds.). (1998). *A New Handbook of Political Science.* 2d ed. Oxford & New York: Oxford University Press.

Goodin, Robert E., & Pettit, Philip (eds.). (1995). *A Companion to Contemporary Political Philosophy.* Oxford & Cambridge, MA: Blackwell.

———. (1996). *Contemporary Political Philosophy: An Anthology.* Oxford & Cambridge, MA: Blackwell.

Goodwin, Barbara. (1997). *Using Political Ideas.* 4th ed. Chichester & New York: Wiley.

Gorbachev, Mikhail. (1987). *Perestroika: New Thinking for Our Country and the World.* London: Collins.

———. (1997). *Memoirs.* 2d ed. London & New York: Bantam Books.

Gore, Al. (1992). *Earth in the Balance: Ecology and the Human Spirit.* London: Earthscan; New York: NAL-Dutton.

Gould, Carol. (1990). *Rethinking Democracy: Freedom and Social Cooperation in Politics, Economy, and Society.* 2d ed. Cambridge & New York: Cambridge University Press.

Gowan, Peter, & Anderson, Perry. (1997). *The Question of Europe.* London & New York: Verso.

Goyder, George. (1993). *The Just Enterprise.* 2d ed. London: Adamantine Press.

Grant, Alan. (1997). *The American Political Process.* 6th ed. Aldershot, England & Brookfield, VT: Dartmouth.

Gray, John. (1996). *Post-Liberalism: Studies in Political Thought.* 2d ed. London & New York: Routledge.

———. (1998). *False Dawn: The Delusions of Global Capitalism.* London: Granta Books.

Gray, John, & Willetts, David. (1997). *Is Conservatism Dead?* London: Profile Books.

Greenberg, Stanley B., & Skocpol, Theda (eds.). (1997). *The New Majority: Toward a Popular Progressive Politics.* New Haven, CT, & London.

Greenstein, F. I., & Polsky, N. W. (eds.). (1975). *Handbook of Political Science.* 8 vols. Reading, MA: Addison-Wesley.

Griffiths, Alan, & Wall, Stuart (eds.). (1997). *Applied Economics: An Introductory Guide.* London & New York: Longman.

Gross, Richard. (1994). *Key Studies in Psychology.* 2d ed. London: Hodder & Stoughton.

———. (1995). *Themes, Issues and Debates in Psychology.* London: Hodder & Stoughton.

Group of Green Economists, The. (1992). *Ecological Economics: A Practical Programme for Global Reform.* London: Zed Books.

Grubb, Michael et al. (1993). *The 'Earth Summit' Agreements: A Guide and Assessment*. London: Earthscan; Washington, DC: Brookings Institution Press.

Gurtov, Mel. (1994). *Global Politics in the Human Interest*. Boulder, CO, & Oxford: Rienner.

Gutmann, Amy, & Thompson, Dennis. (1998). *Democracy and Disagreement: Why Moral Conflict Cannot Be Avoided in Politics and What Should Be Done about It*. 2d ed. Cambridge, MA, & London: Harvard University Press.

GVN. (1996). *Life on Earth: A True Civilisation*. Video documentary about the "State of the World Forum," San Francisco, October 1996, London: GVN.

Haas, Michael. (1992). *Polity and Society: Philosophical Underpinning of Social Science Paradigms*. Westport, CT, & London: Praeger.

Hackett, Clifford. (1990). *The Cautious Revolution: The European Union Arrives*. Westport, CT, & London: Praeger.

Hadenius, Axel (ed.). (1997). *Democracy's Victory and Crisis: Nobel Symposium No. 93*. Cambridge & New York: Cambridge University Press.

Hague, Rod, Harrop, Martin, & Breslin, Shaun. (1998). *Comparative Government and Politics: An Introduction*. 4th ed. London: Macmillan.

Hailsham, Lord. (1976). *Elective Dictatorship*. London: BBC.

Hain, Peter. (1986). *Proportional Misrepresentation: The Case against PR in Britain*. Aldershot, England: Wildwood House.

Hall, Gardner. (1997). *Dangerous Crossroads: Change, Russia, and the Future of NATO*. Westport, CT, & London: Praeger.

Hall, Stuart, Massey, Doreen, & Rustin, Michael (eds.). (1997). *The Next Ten Years: Key Issues for Blair's Britain*. London: Lawrence & Wishart; New York: New York Unversity Press.

Halliday, Fred. (1995). *Islam and the Myth of Confrontation: Religion and Politics in the Middle East*. London: Tauris; New York: St. Martin's Press.

Halsey, A. H. (1995). *Change in British Society from 1900 to the Present Day*. 4th ed. Oxford & New York: Oxford University Press.

Hames, Tim, & Nicol, Rae. (1996). *Governing America: History, Culture, Institutions, Organisation, Policy*. Manchester: Manchester University Press.

Hancock, M. Donald & Conradt, David P. (1998). *Politics in Western Europe: United Kingdom, France, Germany, Italy, Sweden and the European Community*. 2d ed. London: Macmillan; Chatham, NJ: Chatham House Press.

Handelman, Stephen. (1997). *Comrade Criminal: Russia's New Mafiya*. 2d ed. New Haven, CT, & London: Yale University Press.

Handy, Charles. (1998). *The Hungry Spirit: Beyond Capitalism—A Quest for Purpose in the Modern World*. 2d ed. London: Arrow Books; 1st. ed. New York: Broadway BDD.

Hanf, Kenneth, & Jansen, Alfe-Inge. (1998). *Governance and Environmental Quality: Environmental Politics, Policy and Administration in Western Europe*. London & New York: Addison Wesley Longman.

Haralambos, Michael, & Holborn, Martin. (1995). *Sociology: Themes and Perspectives*. 3d ed. London: Collins Educational, Harper Collins.

Hardy, Jean. (1996). *A Psychology with a Soul: Psychosynthesis in Evolutionary Context*. Torquay, England: Woodgrange Press.

Hargreaves, Ian, & Christie, Ian (eds.). (1998). *Tomorrow's Politics: The Third Way and Beyond*. London: Demos.

Harman, Willis. (1998). *Global Mind Change: The Promise of the Last Years of the Twentieth Century.* 2d ed. San Francisco: Berrett-Koehler.

Harris, Errol. (1993). *One World or None: Prescription for Survival.* Atlantic Highlands, NJ, & London: Humanities Press.

Harrop, Martin (ed.). (1992). *Power and Policy in Liberal Democracies.* Cambridge & New York: Cambridge University Press.

Hartzok, Alanna. (1994). *Financing Planet Management: Sovereignty, World Order and the Earth Rights Imperative.* New York: Robert Schalkenbach Foundation.

Hassija, Jagdish Chander, & Panjabi, Mohini (eds.). (1993). *Visions of a Better World.* London: Brahma Kumaris World Spiritual University.

Hawken, Paul. (1994). *The Ecology of Commerce: A Declaration of Sustainability.* 2d ed. Belleview: WA: Harper Business; London: Phoenix, Orion Books.

Hayes, Nicky. (1993). *Principles of Social Psychology.* London: Lawrence Erlbaum Associates.

———. (1994). *Foundations of Psychology: An Introductory Text.* 2d ed. London & New York: Routledge.

Haynes, Jeff. (1996). *Third World Politics.* Oxford & Cambridge, MA: Blackwell.

———. (1998). *Religion in Global Politics.* London & New York: Addison Wesley Longman.

Hayward, Tim. (1995). *Ecological Thought: An Introduction.* Cambridge: Polity Press; Cambridge, MA: Blackwell.

———. (1998). *Political Theory and Ecological Values.* Cambridge: Polity Press; Cambridge, MA: Blackwell.

Held, David. (1995). *Democracy and the Global Order: From the Modern State to Cosmopolitan Governance.* Cambridge: Polity Press.

———. (1996). *Models of Democracy.* 2d ed. Cambridge: Polity Press.

Held, David (ed.). (1991). *Political Theory Today.* Cambridge: Polity Press.

———. (1993). *Prospects for Democracy: North, South, East, West.* Cambridge: Polity Press.

Held, David, & Pollitt, Christopher (eds.). (1986). *New Forms of Democracy.* London & Newbury Park, CA: Sage.

Henderson, Hazel. (1993). *Paradigms in Progress: Life Beyond Economics.* London: Adamantine Press.

———. (1997). *Building a Win-Win World: Life Beyond Global Economic Warfare.* 2d ed. San Francisco & London: Berrett-Koehler Publishers.

Henderson, Karen, & Robinson, Neil. (1997). *Post-Communist Politics: An Introduction.* London & New York: Prentice-Hall Europe.

Hennessy, Peter. (1990). *Whitehall.* 2d ed. London: Fontana Press.

———. (1996). *The Hidden Wiring: Unearthing the British Constitution.* 2d ed. London: Indigo, Gollancz; North Pomfret, VT: Trafalgar.

———. (1997). *Muddling Through: Power, Politics, and the Quality of Government in Postwar Britain.* 2d ed. London: Indigo, Gollancz.

———. (1998). *The Prime Minister: The Office and Its Holders since 1945.* London: Harper Collins.

Hewitt de Alcantára, Cynthia (ed.). (1996). *Social Futures: Global Visions.* Oxford & Cambridge, MA: Blackwell.

Heywood, Andrew. (1994). *Political Ideas and Concepts: An Introduction.* London: Macmillan; New York: St. Martin's Press.

Heywood, Andrew. (1997). *Politics*. London: Macmillan.

———. (1998). *Political Ideologies*. 2d ed. London: Macmillan.

Hill, Michael. (1997a). *The Policy Process in the Modern State*. 3d ed. New York & London: Prentice-Hall & Harvester Wheatsheaf.

———. (1997b). *The Policy Process: A Reader*. 3d ed. New York & London: Prentice-Hall & Harvester Wheatsheaf.

Hirst, Paul. (1993). *Associative Democracy: New Forms of Economic and Social Governance*. Amherst: University of Massachusetts Press; Cambridge: Polity Press.

———. (1997). *From Statism to Pluralism: Democracy, Civil Society and Global Politics*. London: UCL Press; Bristol, PA: Taylor & Francis.

Hirst, Paul, & Khilnani, Sunil (eds.). (1996). *Reinventing Democracy*. Oxford & Cambridge, MA: Blackwell.

Ho, Mae-Wan. (1998). *Genetic Engineering Dreams or Nightmares? The Brave New World of Bad Science and Big Business*. Bath, England: Gateway Books: Grawn, MI: Access Publishers Network.

Ho, Mae-Wan, Miller, Henry, & Wynne, Brian. (1997). "Biotechnology, Friend or Foe?" *Science & Public Affairs* (Winter): 38–44.

Hobsbawm, Eric. (1996). *Age of Extremes: The Short Twentieth Century 1914–1991*. 3d ed. New York: Random House; 2d ed. London: Abacus.

Hogwood, Brian W. (1992). *Trends in British Public Policy: Do Governments Make Any Difference?* Buckingham, England: Open University Press; Bristol, PA: Taylor & Francis.

Hollin, Clive R. (ed.). (1995). *Contemporary Psychology: An Introduction*. Bristol, PA, & London: Taylor & Francis.

Hollinger, Robert. (1996). *The Dark Side of Liberalism: Elitism vs Democracy*. Westport, CT, & London: Praeger.

Holman, Kay. (12 November 1997). "Day of the Gurus". *Guardian Society*, p. 9.

Holmes, Leslie. (1997). *Post-Communism: An Introduction*. Cambridge: Polity Press.

Holtham, Gerald. (Spring 1998). "IPPR's Third Way" In *IPPR in Progress* pp. 1–2. London: Institute for Public Policy Research.

Honderich, Ted. (1988). *A Theory of Determinism*. Oxford & New York: Oxford University Press.

——— (ed.). (1995). *The Oxford Companion to Philosophy*. Oxford & New York: Oxford University Press.

Horton, John, & Jones, Peter (eds.). (1992). *Political Obligation*. London: Macmillan.

Hoveyda, Fereydoun. (1998). *The Broken Crescent: The "Threat" of Militant Islamic Fundamentalism*. Westport, CT, & London: Praeger.

Hoyt, Katharine. (1997). *The Many Faces of Sandinista Democracy*. Columbus & London: Ohio University Press.

Human Rights Watch. (1998). *Human Rights Watch: World Report 1998*. London: Human Rights Watch; New Haven, CT; Yale University Press.

Hunt, E. K. (1995). *Property and Prophets: The Evolution of Economic Institutions and Ideologies*. 7th ed. New York: Harper Collins College.

Hunter, Brian (ed.). (1997). *The Statesman's Yearbook: A Statistical, Political and Economic Account of the States of the World for the Year 1997–98*. 134th ed. London: Macmillan.

Huntington, Samuel. (1998). *The Clash of Civilizations and the Remaking of the World Order*. 2d ed. London: Simon & Schuster.

Hutchinson, Colin. (1991). *Business and the Environmental Challenge: A Guide for Managers*. Reading, England: Conservation Trust.

Hutchinson, John, & Smith, Anthony D. (eds.). (1994). *Nationalism*. Oxford & New York: Oxford University Press.

———. (1996). *Ethnicity*. Oxford & New York: Oxford University Press.

Hutton, Will. (1996). *The State We're In*. 2d ed. London: Vintage.

———. (1997). *The State to Come*. London: Vintage.

———. (1998). *Salvos and Skirmishes: The State of Our Country*. Cambridge: Polity Press.

Icke, David. (1996). *I Am Me, I Am Free: The Robots' Guide to Freedom*. Ryde, Isle of Wight, England: Bridge of Love Publications; San Diego, CA: Truth Seeker.

Ignatieff, Michael. (1994). *Blood and Belonging: Journeys into the New Nationalism*. 2d ed. London: Vintage; New York: Farrar, Straus, & Giroux.

———. (1998). *The Warrior's Honour: Ethnic War and the Modern Consciousness*. London: Chatto & Windus; New York: Holt.

Imbeau, Louis M., & McKinley, Robert D. (eds.). (1996). *Comparing Government Authority*. London: Macmillan; New York: St. Martin's Press.

Inglehart, Renold. (1997). *Modernization and Postmodernization: Cultural, Economic, and Political Change in 43 Societies*. Princeton, NJ, & Chichester: Princeton University Press.

Inglis, Mary, & Kramer, Sandra (eds.). (1985). *The New Economic Agenda 1985*. Forres, Scotland: Findhorn Press.

International Factor 10 Club, The. (1997). *Statement to Government and Business Leaders*. Carnoules, France: Factor 10 Institute.

Isaac, Jeffrey C. (1997). *Democracy in Dark Times*. Ithaca, NY, & London: Cornell University Press.

Ishay, Micheline R. (ed.). (1997). *The Human Rights Reader: Major Political Essays, Speeches and Documents from the Bible to the Present*. New York & London: Routledge.

Ishiyama, John T., & Breuning, Marijke. (1998). *Ethnopolitics in the "New Europe"*. Boulder, CO, & Oxford: Rienner.

Itoh, Makito. (1995). *Political Economy for Socialism*. London: Macmillan.

Jackson, Peter M., & Lavender, Michaela (eds.). (1996). *Public Services Yearbook 1996–97*. London: Pitman.

Jackson, Robert, & James, Alan (eds.). (1993). *States in a Changing World: A Contemporary Analysis*. New York & Oxford: Oxford University Press.

Jacob, Herbert, et al. (1996). *Courts, Law, and Politics in Comparative Perspective*. New Haven, CT, & London: Yale University Press.

Jacobs, Michael. (1992). *The Green Economy: Environment, Sustainable Development and the Politics of the Future*. 2d ed. London: Pluto Press; Milford, CT: LPC In/Book.

———. (1996). *The Politics of the Real World*. London: Earthscan.

———. (ed.). (1998). *Greening the Millennium: The New Politics of the Environment*. Oxford & Cambridge, MA: Blackwell.

Jacobsen, Carl G. (1996). *The New World Order's Defining Crises: The Clash of Promise and Essence*. Aldershot, England, & Brookfield, VT: Dartmouth.

Jacobsohn, Gary A. (1998). *An Introduction to Political Science*. Belmont, CA: Wadsworth; London: West.

James, Simon. (1992). *British Cabinet Government*. London & New York: Routledge.
———. (1997). *British Government: A Reader in Policy Making*. London & New York: Routledge.
Jay, Anthony (ed.). (1997). *The Oxford Dictionary of Political Quotations*. 2d ed. Oxford & New York: Oxford University Press.
Jenkins, Lindsay. (1998). *Britain Held Hostage: The Coming Euro Dictatorship*. 2d ed. Washington, DC: Orange State Press; London: June Press.
Jenkins, Simon. (1996). *Accountable to None: The Tory Nationalization of Britain*. 2d ed. London: Penguin Books.
Jervis, Robert. (1997). *System Effects: Complexity in Political and Social Life*. Princeton, NJ, & Chichester: Princeton University Press.
Jesudoss, Johnson S. (1997a). *Here, We Are . . .* Milton Keynes: Milton Keynes Peace & Justice Centre.
———. (1997b). *Thoughts on Justice, Peace and Integrity of Creation*. Milton Keynes: Milton Keynes Peace & Justice Centre.
John, Peter. (1997). *Analysing Public Policy*. Herndon, VA: Books International; London Leicester University Press.
Johnson-Laird, P. N. (1996). *The Computer and the Mind: An Introduction to Cognitive Science*. 2d ed. London: Fontana; 1st. ed. Cambridge, MA: Harvard University Press, 1986.
Johnston, Larry. (1996). *Ideologies: An Analytic and Contextual Approach*. Peterborough, ONT, Canada: Broadview Press.
Jones, Bill (ed.). (1994). *Political Issues in Britain Today*. 4th ed. Manchester: Manchester University Press; New York; St. Martin's Press.
Jones, Bill, et al. (1998). *Politics UK*. 3d ed. London & New York: Prentice-Hall.
Jones, Bill, & Kavanagh, Dennis. (1998). *British Politics Today*. 6th ed. Manchester: Manchester University Press.
Joyce, Peter. (1996). *Teach Yourself Politics*. London: Teach Yourself; Lincoln Wood, IL: NTC/Contemporary.
Judge, Anthony (ed.). (1995). *Encyclopedia of World Problems and Human Potential*. Volume 1, *World Problems*; Volume 2, *Human Potential—Transformation and Values*; Volume 3, *Actions—Strategies—Solutions*. Munich, London, & New York: K. G. Saur.
Jung, C. G., & Pauli, W. (1955). *The Interpretation and Nature of the Psyche*. New York: Pantheon.
Kamrava, Mehran. (1995). *Understanding Comparative Politics: A Framework for Analysis*. London & New York: Routledge.
Kandiah, Michael David, & Seldon, Anthony (eds.). (1996). *Ideas and Think Tanks in Contemporary Britain*. 2 vols, 2nd vol. 1997. London & Portland, OR: Frank Cass.
Katz, Ellis, & Tarr, G. Alan. (1995). *Federalism and Rights*. Oxford & Lanham, MD: Rowman & Littlefield.
Katz, Richard S. (1997). *Democracy and Elections*. Oxford & New York: Oxford University Press.
Katz, Richard S., & Mair, Peter (eds.). (1992). *Party Organizations: A Data Handbook on Party Organizations in Western Democracies, 1960–1990*. London & Newbury Park, CA: Sage.
———. (1994). *How Parties Organize: Change and Adaptation in Party Organizations in Western Democracies*. London & Newbury Park, CA: Sage.

Kaufman, Gerald. (1997). *How to Be a Minister*. 2d ed. London & Boston: Faber and Faber.

Kautz, Stephen. (1997). *Liberalism and Community*. 2d ed. Ithaca, NY & London: Cornell University Press.

Kavanagh, Dennis. (1990). *Thatcherism and British Politics*. Oxford & New York: Oxford University Press.

———. (1995). *Election Campaigning: The New Marketing of Politics*. Oxford & Cambridge, MA: Blackwell.

———. (1997). *The Reordering of British Politics: Politics after Thatcher*. Oxford & New York: Oxford University Press.

——— (ed.). (1992). *Electoral Politics*. Oxford & New York: Oxford University Press.

———. (1998). *A Dictionary of Political Biography: Who's Who in Contemporary World Politics*. Oxford & New York: Oxford University Press.

Kedourie, Elie. (1993). *Nationalism*. 4th ed. Oxford & Cambridge, MA: Blackwell.

Keen, Linda, & Scase, Richard. (1997). *Local Government Management: The Rhetoric and Reality of Change*. Buckingham, England: Open University Press; Bristol Park, PA: Taylor & Francis.

Kegley, Charles W., Jr., & Wittkopf, Eugene R. (1997). *World Politics: Trend and Transformation*. 6th ed. New York: St. Martin's Press; London: Macmillan.

Kelly, Gavin, Kelly, Dominic, & Gamble, Andrew. (1997). *Stakeholder Capitalism*. London: Macmillan; New York: St. Martin's Press.

Keman, Hans (ed.). (1993). *Comparative Politics: New Directions in Theory and Method*. Amsterdam: VU University Press; Concord, MA: Paul.

Kennedy, Margrit. (1995). *Interest and Inflation-Free Money: Creating an Exchange Medium that Works for Everybody and Protects the Earth*. 2d ed. Branford, CT, & London: New Society.

Kennedy, Paul. (1993). *Preparing for the Twenty-First Century*. London: Harper Collins; New York: Random House.

Keynes, John Maynard. (1936). *The General Theory of Employment, Interest and Money*. 3d ed. Cambridge & New York: Cambridge University Press, 1978; New ed. Amherst, NY: Prometheus Books, 1997.

Kidron, Michael, & Segal, Ronald. (1995). *The State of the World Atlas*. 5th ed. London: Penguin Books; New York: Viking Penguin.

Kim, Samuel S. (1984). *The Quest for a Just World Order*. Boulder, CO, & Oxford: Westview Press.

Kim, Tae-Chang, & Dator, Jim (eds.). (1999). *Creating Public Philosophies for Future Generations*. London: Adamantine Press.

King, Alexander, & Schneider, Bertrand. (1992). *The First Global Revolution*. 2d ed. London & New York: Simon & Schuster.

King, Desmond, & Stoker, Gerry (eds.). (1996). *Rethinking Local Democracy*. London: Macmillan.

Kinsman, Francis. (1983). *The New Agenda: Business in Society*. London: Spencer Stuart Management Consultants.

———. (1990). *Millennium: Towards Tomorrow's Society*. London: W. H. Allen.

Kirby, Richard, & Rossman, Parker (eds.). (1990). *Christians and the World of Computers: Professional and Social Excellence*. Harrisburg, PA: Trinity Press International; London: SCM Press.

Klingemann, Hans-Dieter, Hofferburt, Richard L., & Budge, Ian. (1994). *Parties, Policies, and Democracy*. Boulder, CO, & Oxford: Westview Press.

Klir, George J. (ed.). (1972). *Trends in General Systems Theory*. London & New York: Wiley.

———. (1991). *Facets of Systems Science*. New York & London: Plenum Press.

Klug, Francesca, Starmer, Keir, & Weir, Stuart. (1996). *The Three Pillars of Liberty: Political Rights and Freedoms in the United Kingdom*. London & New York: Routledge.

Knop, Karen (ed.). (1995). *Rethinking Federation: Citizens, Markets and Governments in a Changing World*. Victoria, BC, Canada, & London: University of British Columbia Press.

Kochen, Manfed. (1972). "WISE, a World Information Synthesis and Encyclopedia". *Journal of Documentation* 28(4): 322–343.

Koestler, Arthur. (1964). *The Act of Creation*. New ed. London: Penguin, 1989; New York: Viking Penguin.

———. (1978). *Janus: A Summing Up*. London: Hutchinson.

Kohr, Leopold. (1978). *The Breakdown of Nations*. 2d ed. London: E. P. Dutton.

Kooiman, Jan (ed.). (1993). *Modern Government: New Government–Society Interactions*. London & Thousand Oaks, CA: Sage.

Korten, David C. (1996). *When Corporations Rule the World*. 2d ed. West Hartford, CT: CoPublications & Kumarian Press; London: Kumarian Press & Earthscan.

Kourvetaris, George A., & Moschonas, Andreas (eds.). (1996). *The Impact of European Integration: Political, Sociological and Economic Changes*. Westport, CT, & London: Praeger.

Kramer, Hilton, & Kimball, Roger (eds.). (1997). *The Future of the European Past*. London & Chicago: Ivan R. Dee.

Krause, Donald G. (1997). *The Way of the Leader*. New York: Berkley; London: Nicholas Brealey.

Krieger, Joel (ed.). (1993). *The Oxford Companion to Politics of the World*. New York & Oxford: Oxford University Press.

Kuhn, Thomas. (1970). *The Structure of Scientific Revolutions*. 3d ed. Chicago: University of Chicago Press, 1996.

Küng, Hans. (1992). *Global Responsibility: In Search of a New World Ethic*. London: SCM Press; New York: Continuum.

———. (1997). *Global Ethics for Global Politics and Economics*. London: SCM Press; New York: Oxford University Press.

——— (ed.). (1996). *Yes to a Global Ethic*. London: SCM Press.

Küng, Hans, & Kuschel, Karl-Josef. (1993). *A Global Ethic: The Declaration of the Parliament of the World's Religions*. London: SCM Press.

Kuper, Adam, & Kuper, Jessica. (1996). *The Social Science Encyclopedia*. 2d ed. London & New York: Routledge.

Kymlicka, Will. (1991a). *Contemporary Political Philosophy: An Introduction*. 2d ed. Oxford & New York: Oxford University Press.

———. (1991b). *Liberalism, Community, and Culture*. 2d ed. Oxford & New York: Oxford University Press.

Lake, David A., & Rothchild, Donald (eds.). (1998). *The International Spread of Ethnic Conflict: Fear, Diffusion, and Isolation*. Princeton, NJ, & Chichester: Princeton University Press.

Lane, Jan-Erik. (1996). *Constitutions and Political Theory*. Manchester: Manchester University Press; New York: St. Martin's Press.

Lane, Jan-Erik, & Ersson, Svante. (1994). *Comparative Politics: An Introduction and New Approach*. 3d ed. Cambridge: Polity Press; Cambridge, MA: Blackwell.

———. (1996). *European Politics: An Introduction*. London & Thousand Oaks, CA: Sage.

———. (1997). *Comparative Political Economy: A Developmental Approach*. 2d ed. London: Pinter; Herndon, VA: Books International.

———. (1998). *Politics and Society in Western Europe*. 4th ed. London & Thousand Oaks, CA: Sage.

Lasser, William. (1996). *Perspectives on American Government: A Comprehensive Reader*. 2d ed. Lexington, MA: D. C. Heath.

Laszlo, Ervin. (1977). *The Goals of Mankind: A Report to the Club of Rome*. London: Hutchinson.

———. (1993). *The Destiny Choice: Survival Options for the 21st Century*. London: Adamantine Press.

———. (1994). *The Inner Limits of Mankind: Heretical Reflections on Today's Values, Culture and Politics*. 2d ed. Oxford & Bostoon: Oneworld.

———. (1997). *Third Millennium: The Challenge and the Vision: The Club of Budapest Report on Creative Paths of Human Evolution*. Stroud, England: Gaia Books.

Laughland, John. (1998). *The Tainted Source: Undemocratic Origins of the European Idea*. 2d ed. London: Warner Books.

Laurent, Pierre-Henri, & Maresceau, Marc (eds.). (1997). *The State of the European Union: The Deepening and Widening Exercise*. Boulder, CO, & Oxford: Rienner.

Lawson, Kay, & Merkl, Peter H. (eds.). (1988). *When Parties Fail: Emerging Alternative Organizations*. Princeton, NJ, & Guildford, England: Princeton University Press.

Layard, Richard. (1997). *What Labour Can Do*. London: Warner Books.

Layder, Derek. (1994). *Understanding Social Theory*. London & Thousand Oaks, CA: Sage.

Le Grand, Julian. (1998). "The Third Way Begins with Cora". *New Statesman* (6 March): 26–27.

Leach, Robert. (1996). *British Political Ideologies*. London & New York, NJ: Prentice-Hall Europe.

Leach, Steve. (1998). *Local Government Reorganisation: The Review and Its Aftermath*. London: Frank Cass.

Leadbeater, Charles. (1998a). "A Hole at the Heart of the Third Way". *New Statesman* (8 May): 32–33.

———. (1998b). "I Think I've Found It". *The Observer* (10 May): 23.

Leftwich, Adrian (ed.). (1996). *Democracy and Development*. Cambridge: Polity Press; Cambridge, MA: Blackwell.

Lemkow, Anna F. (1995). *The Wholeness Principle: Dynamics of Unity within Science, Religion & Society*. 2d ed. Wheaton, IL: Theosophical Publishing House; London: Quest Books.

Lent, Adam (ed.). (1998). *New Political Thought: An Introduction*. London: Lawrence & Wishart; New York: New York University Press.

Leonard, Dick. (1998). *Rediscovering Europe*. London: Demos.

Levinson, David, & Christensen, Karen. (1998). *The Global Village Companion: A–Z to Understanding Current Affairs*. Oxford: ABC-CLIO.

Leytham, Geoffrey. (1990). *Managing Creativity*. Dereham, Norfolk, England: Peter Francis.

Li, Cheng. (1996). *Rediscovering China: Dynamics and Dilemmas of Reform*. Lanham, MD, & Oxford: Roman & Littlefield.

Lijphart Arend. (1995). *Electoral Systems and Party Systems: A Study of Twenty-Seven Democracies*. 2d ed. Oxford & New York: Oxford University Press.

———— (ed.). (1992). *Parliamentary versus Presidential Government*. Oxford & New York: Cambridge University Press.

Lindfield, Michael. (1986). *The Dance of Change: An Eco-Spiritual Approach to Transformation*. London & New York: Arkana, Routledge & Kegan Paul.

Lipnack, Jessica, & Stamps, Jeffrey. (1997). *Virtual Teams: Reaching across Space, Time and Organizations with Technology*. New York & Chichester: Wiley.

Lipow, Arthur. (1996). *Political Parties and Democracy: Explorations in History and Theory*. London: Pluto Press; Milford, CT: LPC In/Book.

Lipsey, Richard, & Chrystal, K. Alec. (1995). *An Introduction to Positive Economics*. 8th ed. Oxford & New York: Oxford University Press.

Lister, Frederick K. (1996). *The European Union, the United Nations, and the Revival of Confederal Governance*. Westport, CT, & London: Greenwood.

Little, Adrian. (1998). *Post-Industrial Socialism: Towards a New Politics of Welfare*. London & New York: Routledge.

Lloyd, John, & Bilefsky, David. (1998). "Transatlantic Wonks at Work". *New Statesman* (27 March): 33–34.

Longley, Lawrence D., & Davidson, Roger H. (1998). *The New Roles of Parliamentary Committees*. London: Frank Cass.

Longworth, Philip. (1997). *The Making of Eastern Europe: From Prehistory to Postcommunism*. 2d ed. London: Macmillan; New York: St. Martin's Press.

Lorimer, David. (1984). *Survival? Body, Mind and Death in the Light of Psychic Experience*. London: Routledge & Kegan Paul.

Lovelock, James E. (1987). *Gaia: A New Look at Life on Earth*. Oxford & New York: Oxford University Press.

————. (1991). *Gaia: The Practical Science of Planetary Medicine*. London: Gaia Books.

————. (1994). *The Ages of Gaia: A Biography of Our Living Earth*. New York: W. W. Norton; Oxford: Oxford University Press.

Lowenthal, Abraham F., & Treverton, Gregory F. (1994). *Latin America in a New World*. Boulder, CO, & Oxford: Westview Press.

Lucas, J. R. (1970). *Freedom of the Will*. Oxford & New York: Oxford University Press.

Lummis, C. Douglas. (1997). *Radical Democracy*. 2d ed. Ithaca, NY, & London: Cornell University Press.

Machiavelli, Niccolò. (1513). *The Prince*. New Haven, CT, & London: Yale University Press. 1997.

Macionis, John J., & Plummer, Ken. (1997). *Sociology: A Global Introduction*. New York & London: Prentice-Hall.

Macy, Mark (ed.). (1989). *Solutions for a Troubled World*. 2d ed. London: Adamantine Press.

Maidment, Richard, & Goldblatt, David (eds.). (1998). *Governance in the Asia-Pacific*. London & New York: Routledge.

Mainzer, Klaus. (1997). *Thinking in Complexity: The Complex Dynamics of Matter, Mind, and Mankind*. 3d ed. New York & London: Springer-Verlag.

Mair, Peter. (1997). *Party System Change: Approaches and Interpretations*. Oxford & New York: Oxford University Press.

Majaro, Simon. (1988). *The Creative Gap: Managing Ideas for Profit*. London: Longman.

Mandelson, Peter, & Liddle, Roger. (1996). *The Blair Revolution: Can New Labour Deliver?* London & Boston: Faber and Faber.

Mannheim, Karl. (1936). *Ideology and Utopia*. London: Routledge & Kegan Paul; New ed. London & New York: Routledge, 1991.

Mansbridge, Jane J. (ed.). (1990). *Beyond Self-Interest*. Chicago: University of Chicago Press.

Markoff, John. (1996). *Waves of Democracy: Social Movements and Political Change*. Thousand Oaks, CA, & London: Pine Forge Press, Sage.

Marquand, David. (1997). *The New Reckoning: Capitalism, States and Citizens*. Cambridge: Polity Press; Cambridge, MA, Blackwell.

Marr, Andrew. (1995). *Ruling Britannia: The Failure and Future of British Democracy*. 2d ed. London: Penguin Books.

Marsh, David, & Stoker, Gerry (eds.). (1995). *Theory and Methods of Political Science*. London, Macmillan; (1997) New York: St. Martin's Press.

Martin, Hans-Peter, & Schumann, Harold. (1997). *The Global Trap: Globalization and the Assault on Prosperity and Democracy*. London: Zed Books; New York: St. Martin's Press.

Marx, Karl. (1864). *Capital*. Ed. Mark Cowling. Edinburgh: Edinburgh University Press, 1998.

Marx, Karl, & Engels, Friedrich. (1848). *The Communist Manifesto*. The latest editions are published by Edinburgh: Edinburgh University Press, 1998, ed. Mark Cowling; London & New York: Verso (Hobsbawm, Eric, ed.).

———. (1998). *Collected Works* (including vol. 3, *Capital*). London: Lawrence & Wishart.

Maslow, Abraham. (1987). *Motivation and Personality*. New York & London: Harper & Row.

Mathews, Russel (ed.). (1976). *Making Federalism Work: Towards a More Efficient, Effective and Responsive Federal System*. Canberra, Australia: Centre for Research on Federal Financial Relations, Australian National University.

Mayer, Lawrence C., et al. (1996). *Comparative Politics: Nations and Theories in a Changing World*. 2d ed. New York & London: Prentice-Hall & Harvester Wheatsheaf.

Mayhew, Alan. (1998). *Recreating Europe: The EU's Policy towards Central and Eastern Europe*. Cambridge & New York: Cambridge University Press.

Mayne, Alan J. (1986). "The Vision of a World Cooperative Economy". *New Paradigms Newsletter* 1(November): 6.

———. (1992). "Policy Making for the 21st Century". *The Intelligent Enterprise* 1(January): 33–37.

———. (1993a). "Ending the Recession". *New Paradigms Newsletter* 15(June): 3–8.

———. (1993b). *Resources for the Future: An International Annotated Bibliography for the 21st Century*. London: Adamantine Press; Westport, CT: Greenwood.

———. (1994). "Probability and Provability". *NeoMetaphysical Digest* 6(June): 21–26.

Mayne, Alan J. (1995). Review of Wakeford & Walters (1995), *Scientists for Global Responsibility Newsletter* 11(February): 11–12.

———. (1997a). "Politics and Living Systems". Presentation to Royal Society of Arts Living Systems Group, 22 September, London.

———. (1997b). "Risk Analysis and Risk Perception," *Scientists for Global Responsibility Newsletter* 15(May): 1, 4.

———. (1999). *Multimedia Resources for the Future: A Global Directory of Web- and Print-Based Reference Sources.* London: Adamantine Press.

Mayne, Alan J., & Williamson, John J. (1997). "The Neometaphysical Bridge". *NeoMetaphysical Digest* 8(July): 18–28.

Mayor, Federico, with Forstenzer, Tom. (1995). *The New Page.* Paris: UNESCO; Aldershot, England, & Brookfield, VT: Dartmouth.

McClelland, J. S. (1998). *A History of Western Political Thought.* 2d ed. London & New York: Routledge.

McCloughry, Roy. (1996). *Belief in Politics.* London: Hodder & Stoughton.

McCormick, John. (1995a). *The European Union: Politics and Policies.* Boulder, CO, & Oxford: Westview Press.

———. (1995b). *The Global Environmental Movement: Reclaiming Paradise.* 2d ed. Chichester & New York: Wiley.

McGrew, Anthony (ed.). (1997). *The Transformation of Democracy?* Cambridge: Polity Press; Cambridge, MA: Blackwell.

McKay, David. (1997). *American Politics and Society.* 4th ed. Oxford & Cambridge, MA: Blackwell.

McKenna, George. (1997). *The Drama of Democracy: American Government and Politics.* 3d ed. New York: McGraw Hill; Andover, England: W. C. Brown.

McKinstry, Leo. (1997). *Turning the Tide: A Personal Manifesto for Modern Britain.* London: Michael Joseph.

McLaren, Duncan, Bullock, Simon, & Youssouf, Nusrat. (1998). *Tomorrow's World: Britain's Share in a Sustainable Future.* London: Earthscan; Washington, DC: Island Press.

McLaughlin, Corinne, & Davidson, Gordon. (1994). *Spiritual Politics: Changing the World from the Inside Out.* Findhorn, Forres, Scotland: Findhorn Press.

McLean, Iain (ed.). (1996). *Concise Oxford Dictionary of Politics.* Oxford & New York: Oxford University Press.

McNaughton, Neil. (1998). *Local and Regional Government in Britain.* London: Hodder & Stoughton.

McNulty, W. Kirk. (1989). "The Paradigm Perspective". *Futures Research Quarterly* 5(3): 35–54.

McRae, Hamish. (1995). *The World in 2020: Power, Culture and Prosperity: A Vision of the Future.* 2d ed. London: Harper Collins; Boston: Harvard Business School Press.

McSmith, Andy. (1998). "Inside the Workathon". *The Observer* (10 May): 23.

McWhinney, Will. (1997). *Paths of Change: Strategic Choices for Organizations and Society.* 2d ed. Newbury Park, CA, & London: Sage.

Mellor, Mary. (1992). *Breaking the Boundaries: Towards a Feminist Green Socialism.* London: Virago Press.

Merchant, Carolyn. (1992). *Radical Ecology: The Search for a Livable World.* London & New York: Routledge.

Merchant, Carolyn. (1995). *Earthcare: Women and the Environment*. New York & London: Routledge.

Merkl, Peter, & Smart, Ninian (eds.). (1983). *Religion and Politics in the Contemporary World*. New York: New York University Press.

Middlemas, Keith. (1995). *Orchestrating Europe: The Informal Politics of European Union 1973–1995*. London: Fontana Press.

Mies, Maria, & Shiva, Vandana. (1993). *Ecofeminism*. London & Atlantic Highlands, NJ: Zed Books.

Miliband, Ralph. (1973). *The State in Capitalist Society: The Analysis of the Western System of Power*. 2d ed. London & New York: Quartet Books.

Miller, William N. (ed.). (1995). *Alternatives to Freedom: Arguments and Opinions*. London & New York: Longman.

Milne, A. J. M. (1997). *Ethical Frontiers of the State: An Essay in Political Philosophy*. London: Macmillan; New York: St. Martin's Press.

Minogue, Kenneth. (1995). *Politics: A Very Short Introduction*. Oxford & New York: Oxford University Press.

Minsky, Marvin. (1987). *The Society of Mind*. London: Heinemann; New York: Simon & Schuster.

Moder, Joseph J. & Elmagrabhy, Salah E. (eds.). (1978). *Handbook of Operations Research*. New York & London: Van Nostrand Reinhold.

Monroe, Kristen Renwick (ed.). (1997). *Contemporary Empirical Political Theory*. London & Berkeley: University of California Press.

Moorcroft, Sheila (ed.). (1992). *Visions for the 21st Century*. London: Adamantine Press.

Moore, Gwen (ed.). (1985 on). *Research in Politics and Society*. Series. Greenwich, CT, & London: JAI Press.

More, Thomas. (1516). *Utopia*. New York & London: W. W. Norton, 1975.

Morgan, Ivan W. (1994). *Beyond the Liberal Consensus: A Political History of the United States since 1965*. London: Hurst; New York: St. Martin's Press.

Morrice, David. (1996). *Philosophy, Science and Ideology in Political Thought*. London: Macmillan; New York: St. Martin's Press.

Morris, William. (1890). *News from Nowhere*. Ed. Krishan Kumar. Cambridge & New York: Cambridge University Press, 1995.

Moss, Robert. (1977). *The Collapse of Democracy*. London: Sphere Books.

Moussalli, Ahmad S. (1998). *Islamic Fundamentalism: Myths and Realities*. Reading, England: Ithaca Press; Milford, CT: LPC In/Book.

Mowlana, Hamid. (1997). *Global Information and World Communication: New Frontiers in International Relations*. 2d ed. London & Thousand Oaks, CA: Sage.

Mueller, Dennis C. (1996). *Constitutional Democracy*. Oxford & New York: Oxford University Press.

Mueller, John. (1994). *Quiet Cataclysm: Reflections on the Recent Transformation of World Politics*. London: Harper Collins; New York: Addison Wesley.

Mulgan, Geoff. (1998). *Connexity: How to Live in a Connected World*. 2d ed. London: Vintage; Boston: Harvard Business School Press.

——— (ed.). (1997). *Life after Politics: New Thinking for the Twenty-First Century*. London: FontanaPress.

Muller, Robert. (1991). *The Birth of a Global Civilization with Proposals for a New Political System for Planet Earth*. Anacortes, WA: World Happiness and Cooperation.

Myers, David G. (1994). *Exploring Social Psychology*. 2d ed. New York & London: McGraw-Hill.

Myers, Isobel Briggs, with Myers, Peter B. (1995). *Gifts Differing*. 2d ed. Palo Alto, CA: Consulting Psychologists Press; Lancaster, England: Davies-Black.

Myers, Norman. (1994). *The Gaia Atlas of Planet Management for Today's Caretakers of Tomorrow's World*. 3d ed. London: Gaia Books; New York Doubleday.

Naess, Arne. (1990). *Ecology, Community, and Lifestyle: Outline of an Ecosophy*. 2d ed. Cambridge & New York: Cambridge University Press.

Nagel, Stuart S. (1998a). *The Policy Implementation Process in Developing Nations*. London: JAI Press.

———. (1998b). *Super Optimising Policy Analysis*. London: JAI Press.

Nairn, Tom. (1997). *Faces of Nationalism: Janus Revisited*. London & New York: Verso.

Naisbitt, John. (1994). *Global Paradox: The Bigger the World Economy, the More Powerful Its Smallest Players*. London: Nicholas Brealey; New York: Avon.

———. (1997). *Megatrends Asia: The Eight Asian Megatrends That Are Changing the World*. 2d ed. London: Nicholas Brealey; New Yotk: Simon & Schuster.

Needler, Martin C. (1996). *Identity, Interest and Ideology: An Introduction to Politics*. Westport, CT, & London: Praeger.

Nelson, Barbara J., & Chowdhury, Najma (eds.). (1994). *Women and Politics World-wide*. New Haven, CT, & London: Yale University Press.

Neville-Sington, Pamela, & Sington, David. (1993). *Paradise Dreamed: How Utopian Thinkers Have Changed the Modern World*. London: Bloomsbury.

New Economy. (June 1998). Feature: "A 'Third Way' for the Welfare State", pp. 69–108.

The New Internationalist. (1997). Special Issue 287(January/February) *State of the World Report*.

———. (1998). Special Issue 288(May) *Cuba*.

Nolan, Patrick, & Lenski, Gerhard. (1998). *Human Societies: An Introduction to Macrosociology*. 8th ed. New York & London: McGraw-Hill.

Nonneman, Gerd (ed.). (1996). *Political and Economic Liberalization: Dynamics and Linkages in Comparative Perspective*. Boulder, CO, & Oxford: Rienner.

Norris, Pippa (ed.). (1997). *Politics and the Press: News Media and Its Influence*. Boulder, CO, & Oxford: Rienner.

North, Richard D. (1995). *Life on a Modern Planet: A Manifesto for Progress*. Manchester: Manchester University Press; New York: St. Martin's Press.

Northcott, Jim. (1995). *The Future of Britain and Europe*. London: Policy Studies Institute; Washington, D.C.: Brookings Institution Press.

Norton, Philip. (1994). *The British Polity*. 3d ed. New York & London: Longman.

Nozick, Robert. (1978). *Anarchy, State, and Utopia*. Oxford: Blackwell; New York: Basic Books.

Nye, John S., Jr., Zelikov, Philip D., & King, David C. (eds.). (1997). *Why People Don't Trust Government*. Cambridge, MA, & London: Harvard University Press.

O'Neill, Michael. (1997). *Green Parties and Political Change in Contemporary Europe*. Aldershot, England, & Brookfield, VT: Ashgate.

——— (ed.). (1996). *The Politics of European Integration: A Reader*. London & New York: Routledge.

OECD (Organization for Economic Cooperation and Development). (1991). *The State of the Environment*. Paris: OECD.

Olson, David M., & Mezey, Michael L. (eds.). (1991). *Legislatures in the Policy Process:*

The Dilemmas of Economic Policy. Cambridge & New York: Cambridge University Press.

OMRI (Open Media Research Institute, Prague). (1997). *The OMRI Annual Survey of Eastern Europe and the Former Soviet Union: Forging Ahead, Falling Behind: 1996*. Armonk, NY; London: M. E. Sharpe.

Ophuls, William. (1998). *Requiem for Modern Politics: The Tragedy of the Enlightenment and the Challenge of the New Millennium*. Boulder, CO, & Oxford: Westview Press.

Ormerod, Paul. (1995). *The Death of Economics*. London; Faber and Faber; New York: St. Martin's Press; New York, Wiley, 1997.

Osborn, Derek, & Bigg, Tom. (1998). *Earth Summit II: Outcomes and Analysis*. London: Earthscan.

Osborne, David, & Gaebler, Ted. (1993). *Reinventing Government: How the Entrepreneurial Spirit Is Transforming the Public Sector*. 2d ed. New York: Plume, Penguin Books USA; London: Plume, Penguin Books.

Osborne, David, & Plastrik, Peter. (1997). *Banishing Bureaucracy: The Five Strategies for Reinventing Government*. New York & London: Addison Wesley Longman.

Ostrom, Vincent. (1997). *The Meaning of Democracy and the Universality of Democracies: An Answer to de Tocqueville's Challenge*. Ann Arbor & London: University of Michigan Press.

Ottaway, Marina (ed.). (1997). *Democracy in Africa: The Hard Road Ahead*. Boulder, CO, & Oxford: Rienner.

Otunnu, Olara A., & Doyle, Michael W. (1998). *Peacemaking and Peacekeeping for the Next Century*. Lanham, MD, & Oxford: Rowman & Littlefield.

Outhwaite, William, et al. (1994). *The Blackwell Dictionary of Political Thought*. 2d ed. Oxford & Cambridge, MA: Blackwell.

Ozdalga, Elisabeth, & Persson, Sune (eds.). (1998). *Civil Society, Democracy and the Muslim World*. London: Curzon Press.

Paehlke, Robert C. (1991). *Environmentalism and the Future of Progressive Politics*. 2d ed. New Haven, CT: Yale University Press.

Page, Edward C. (1992). *Political Authority and Bureaucratic Power: A Comparative Study*. 2d ed. London & New York: Harvester Wheatsheaf.

Palmer, Monte. (1997a). *Comparative Politics: Political Economy, Political Culture, and Political Independence*. Itasca, IL, & London: F. E. Peacock.

———. (1997b). *Political Development: Dilemmas and Challenges*. Itasca, IL, & London: F. E. Peacock.

Panitch, Leo, & Leys, Colin (eds.). (1998). *The Communist Manifesto Now: Socialist Register 1998*. Woodbridge, Suffolk, England: Merlin Press; New York: Monthly Review Press.

Pankin, Boris. (1995). *The Last Hundred Days of the Soviet Union: Choosing the Road to Its Future*. London: Tauris; New York: St. Martin's Press.

Papworth, John. (1995). *Small Is Powerful: The Future as If People Really Mattered*. London: Adamantine Press.

Parenti, Michael. (1996). *Democracy for the Few*. 7th ed. New York: St. Martin's Press.

Parsons, Anthony. (1995). *From Cold War to Hot Peace: UN Interventions 1947–95*. London & New York: Penguin Books.

Parsons, Wayne. (1997). *Public Policy: An Introduction to the Theory and Practice of Policy Analysis*. 2d ed. Cheltenham, England, & Lyme, NH: Elgar.

Pask, Gordon. (1961). *An Approach to Cybernetics*. London: Hutchinson.

Pateman, Carole. (1990). *Participation and Democratic Theory*. New ed. Cambridge & New York: Cambridge University Press.

Patten, Chris. (1998). *East and West*. London: Macmillan.

Patterson, Thomas E. (1997). *We the People: A Concise Introduction to American Politics*. 2d ed. New York & London: McGraw-Hill.

Paul, Ellen Frankel, Miller, Fred D., Jr., & Paul, Jeffrey (eds.). (1995). *Contemporary Political and Social Philosophy*. New York & Cambridge: Cambridge University Press.

————. (1997). *The Welfare State*. New York & Cambridge: Cambridge University Press.

Pearce, David, Markandya, Anil, & Barbier, Edward B. (1989). *Blueprint for a Green Economy*. London: Earthscan.

Pearce, Fred. (1990). *Green Warriors: The People and Politics behind the Environmental Revolution*. London: Bodley Head.

Pearson, Carol S. (1991). *Awakening the Heroes Within: Twelve Archetypes to Help Us Find Ourselves and Transform Our World*. San Francisco: Harper San Francisco; London: Harper Collins.

Peat, David. (1987). *Synchronicity: The Bridge between Matter and Mind*. New York & London: Bantam Books.

Peele, Gillian. (1995). *Governing the UK*. Oxford & Cambridge, MA: Blackwell.

Pegg, Mike. (1993). *The Positive Planet: People Who Work to Build a Better World*. Leamington Spa, Warwickshire: Enhance.

Pei, Minxin. (1998). *From Reform to Revolution: The Demise of Communism and China and the Soviet Union*. 2d ed. Cambridge, MA & London: Harvard University Press.

Pepper, David. (1993). *Eco-Socialism: From Deep Ecology to Social Justice*. London & New York: Routledge.

Perelman, Michael. (1996). *The End of Economics*. London & New York: Routledge.

Perri 6. (1997). *Holistic Government*. London: Demos.

Perry, Michael J. (1997). *Religion in Politics: Constitutional and Moral Perspectives*. New York & Oxford: Oxford University Press.

Perryman, Mark (ed.). (1996). *The Blair Agenda*. London: Lawrence & Wishart; New York: New York University Press.

Peters, B. Guy. (1995). *The Politics of Bureaucracy*. 4th ed. New York & London: Longman.

Petrie, Ruth (ed.). (1997). *The Fall of Communism and the Rise of Nationalism: The Index Reader*. London & Washington, DC: Cassell.

Petro, Nicolai N. (1997). *The Rebirth of Russian Democracy: An Interpretation of Political Culture*. 2d ed. Cambridge, MA, & London: Harvard University Press.

Phillips, Anne. (1991). *Engendering Politics*. Cambridge: Polity Press.

Phillips, Derek L. (1986). *Toward a Just Social Order*. Princeton, NJ: Princeton University Press.

————. (1993). *Looking Backward: A Critical Appraisal of Communitarian Thought*. Princeton, NJ, & Chichester: Princeton University Press.

Pierson, Christopher. (1995). *Socialism after Communism: The New Market Socialism*. Cambridge: Polity Press.

————. (1996). *The Modern State*. London & New York: Routledge.

Pierson, Christopher. (1998). *Beyond the Welfare State?* 2d ed. Cambridge: Polity Press; University Park: Pennsylvania University Press.

Pierson, Paul. (1996). *Dismantling the Welfare State: Reagan, Thatcher, and the Political Retrenchment.* Cambridge & New York: Cambridge University Press.

Pilger, John. (1998). *Hidden Agendas.* London & New York: Viking.

Pinder, John. (1995). *European Community: The Building of a Union.* 2d ed. New York & Oxford: Oxford University Press.

Pinkney, Robert. (1993). *Democracy in the Third World.* Buckingham, England: Open University Press; Bristol, PA: Taylor & Francis; Boulder, CO: Rienner.

Plano, Jack, & Greenberg, Milton. (1997). *The American Political Dictionary.* 10th ed. Fort Worth, TX, New York, & London: Harcourt Brace College.

Plant, Judith, & Plant, Christopher. (1992). *Putting Power in Its Place: Create Community Control.* Philadelphia & Gabriola Island, BC, Canada: New Society.

Plant, Raymond. (1991). *Modern Political Thought.* Oxford & Cambridge, MA: Blackwell.

Plato. (c. 400 B.C.). *The Republic.* Ed. Robin Waterfield. Oxford: Oxford University Press, 1998.

Pogany, Istvan. (1998). *Righting Wrongs in Eastern Europe.* Manchester: Manchester University Press.

Polychroniou, Chris, & Targ, Harry R. (eds.). (1996). *Marxism Today: Essays on Capitalism, Socialism, and Social Change.* Westport, CT, & London: Praeger.

Ponton, Geoffrey, & Gill, Peter. (1993). *An Introduction to Politics.* 3d ed. Oxford & Cambridge, MA: Blackwell.

Porritt, Jonathon, & Winner, David. (1988). *The Coming of the Greens.* London: Fontana-Collins.

Potter, David, et al. (eds.). (1997). *Democratization.* Cambridge: Polity Press; Cambridge, MA: Blackwell.

Prato, Tony. (1997). *Natural Resource and Environmental Economics.* Des Moines & London: Iowa State University Press.

Primavesi, Anne. (1991). *From Apocalypse to Genesis: Ecology, Feminism and Christianity.* Tunbridge Wells, England: Burns & Oates.

Przeworski, Adam (ed.). (1995). *Sustainable Democracy.* Cambridge & New York: Cambridge University Press.

Radice, Giles. (1996). *What Needs to Change: New Visions for Britain.* London: Harper Collins.

Ramphal, Sridath. (1994). *Global Governance in the Global Neighbourhood.* Santa Barbara, CA: Nuclear Age Peace Foundation.

Rash, Wayne, Jr. (1997). *Politics on the Net: Wiring the Political Process.* New York & Basingstoke, England: W. H. Freeman.

Rawls, John. (1973). *A Theory of Justice.* 2d ed. Oxford & New York: Oxford University Press.

———. (1996). *Political Liberalism.* 2d ed. New York: Columbia University Press.

Red-Green Study Group. (1995). *What On Earth Is to Be Done? A Red-Green Dialogue.* Manchester: Red-Green Study Group.

Redfield, James. (1994). *The Celestine Prophecy: An Adventure.* New York & London: Bantam Books.

———. (1996a). *The Celestine Prophecy: A Pocket Guide to the Nine Insights.* New York & London: Bantam Books.

Redfield, James. (1996b). *The Tenth Insight: Holding the Vision: Further Adventures of the Celestine Prophecy*. New York & London: Bantam Books.

———. (1997). *The Celestine Vision: Living the New Spiritual Awareness*. New York & London: Bantam Press.

Redfield, James, & Adrienne, Carol. (1995). *The Celestine Prophecy: An Experiential Guide*. New York & London: Bantam Books.

———. (1996). *The Tenth Insight: An Experiential Guide*. New York & London: Bantam Books.

Redington, Thomas F. (ed.). (1994). *Parliaments in Transition: The New Legislative Process in the Former USSR and Eastern Europe*. Boulder, CO, & Oxford: Westview Press.

Redmond, John, & Rosenthal, Glenda G. (eds.). (1997). *The Expanding European Union: Past, Present, Future*. Boulder, CO, & Oxford: Rienner.

Rees, Judith. (1997). "And Now the Global Water Crisis". *Science & Public Affairs* (Winter): 20–23.

Reinicke, Wolfgang H. (1998). *Global Public Policy: Governing without Government?* Washington, D.C., & Plymouth, England: Brookings Institution Press.

Rejai, Mostafa, & Phillips, Kay. (1997). *Leaders and Leadership: An Appraisal of Theory and Research*. Westport, CT & London: Praeger.

Rhodes, P. A. W. (1997). *Understanding Governance: Policy Networks, Governance, Responsibility and Accountability*. Buckingham, England; Open University Press; Bristol, PA: Taylor & Francis.

Richards, Steve. (1997a). "Interview: Ken Livingstone". *New Statesman* (10 October): 20–21.

———. (1997b). "Interview: William Hague". *New Statesman* (19 December): 18–20.

Richardson, Jeremy N. (ed.). (1993). *Pressure Groups*. Oxford & New York: Oxford University Press.

Riddell, Carol. (1990). *The Findhorn Community: Creating a Human Identity for the 21st Century*. Forres, Scotland: The Findhorn Press; Oakland, CA: Words Distribution.

Riddell, Peter. (1998). *Parliament under Pressure*. London: Gollancz; North Pomfret, VT: Trafalgar.

Riemer, Neal. (1996). *Creative Breakthroughs in Politics*. Westport, CT, & London: Praeger.

Roberts, David, et al. (eds.). (1997). *British Politics in Focus*. Ormskirk, Lancashire, England: Causeway Press.

Robertson, David (ed.). (1993). *The Penguin Dictionary of Politics*. 2d ed. London & New York: Penguin Books; London, Europa.

Robertson, James. (1990). *Future Wealth: A New Economics for the 21st Century*. London: Cassell; New York: Bootstrap Press.

———. (1996). "New Models in Science and Economics: The Scope for Mutual Learning," *Network, the Scientific and Medical Network Review* 62(December): 21–22.

———. (1998a). *Beyond the Dependency Culture: People, Power and Responsibility*. London: Adamantine Press.

———. (1998b). *Transforming Economic Life: A Millennial Challenge*. Totnes, Devon, England: Green Books.

Robins, Lynton, Blackmore, Hilary, & Pyper, Robert (eds.). (1994). *Britain's Changing*

Party System. London: Leicester University Press; Herndon, VA: Books International.

Robins, Lynton, & Jones, Bill (eds.). (1997). *Half a Century of British Politics*. Manchester: Manchester University Press; New York: St. Martin's Press.

Robins, Robert S., & Post, Jerrold M. (1997). *Political Paranoia: The Psychopolitics of Hatred*. New Haven, CT, & London: Yale University Press.

Robinson, Mike. (1992). *The Greening of British Party Politics*. Manchester: Manchester University Press.

Roeher, Grant, & Cammarano, Joseph (eds.). (1997). *Education for Citizenship: Ideas and Innovations in Political Learning*. Lanham, MD, & Oxford: Rowman & Littlefield.

Roemer, John E. (1998). *Theories of Distributive Justice*. Cambridge, MA, & London: Harvard University Press.

Rose, Richard, & Davies, Philip L. (1994). *Inheritance in Public Policy: Change without Choice in Britain*. New Haven, CT, & London: Yale University Press.

Rose, Richard, et al. (1998). *Democracy and Its Alternatives: Understanding Post-Communist Societies*. Cambridge: Polity Press.

Rosenau, James N. (1997). *Along the Domestic–Foreign Frontier: Exploring Governance in a Turbulent World*. Cambridge & New York: Cambridge University Press.

Roskin, Michael, et al. (1996). *Political Science: An Introduction*. 6th ed. London & New York: Prentice-Hall.

Rowell, Andrew. (1996). *Global Subversion of the Environmental Movement*. London & New York: Routledge.

Rubinstein, Richard L. (ed.).(1987). *Spirit Matters: The Worldwide Impact of Religion on Contemporary Politics*. New York: Paragon House.

Rüdig, Wolfgang (ed.). (1990). *Green Politics One*. Edinburgh: Edinburgh University Press.

———. (1992). *Green Politics Two*. Edinburgh: Edinburgh University Press.

———. (1995). *Green Politics Three*. Edinburgh: Edinburgh University Press.

Rush, Michael. (1992). *Politics and Society: An Introduction to Political Sociology*. London & New York: Harvester Wheatsheaf.

Russell, Margo, & Whitmore, Diana. (1991). *Psychosynthesis Counselling in Action*. London & Newbury Park, CA: Sage.

Sachs, Wolfgang (ed.). (1992). *The Development Dictionary: A Guide to Knowledge as Power*. New York: St. Martin's Press; London: Zed Books.

Sacks, Jonathan. (1991). *The Persistence of Faith: Religion, Morality and Society in a Secular Age*. London: Weidenfeld & Nicolson.

———. (1997). *The Politics of Hope*. London: Jonathan Cape.

Sahtouris, Elisabet. (1989). *Gaia: The Human Journey from Chaos to Cosmos*. New York & London: Simon & Schuster.

Sakwa, Richard. (1996). *Russian Politics and Society*. London & New York: Routledge.

Salmon, Trevor (ed.). (1998). *Issues in International Relations*. London: UCL Press.

Samuelson, Paul A., & Nordhaus, William D., with Mandel, Michael J. (1998). *Economics: An Introductory Analysis*. 16th ed. New York & London: McGraw-Hill.

Sandel, Michael J. (1998). *Democracy's Discontent: America in Search of a Public Philosophy*. 2d ed. Cambridge, MA, & London: Harvard University Press.

Sardar, Ziauddin. (1997). *Postmodernism and the Other: The New Imperialism of Western Culture*. London: Pluto Press; Milford, CT: LPC In/Book.

Sargent, Lyman Tower (ed.). (1997). *Political Thought in the United States: A Documentary History*. New York & London: New York University Press.

Sartori, Giovanni. (1996). *Comparative Constitutional Engineering: An Inquiry into Structures, Incentives and Outcomes*. 2d ed. London: Macmillan; New York University Press.

Sartorius, Michael. (1994). *The Principle of Liberty*. Ringmer, Sussex, England: Aston.

Sassoon, Donald. (1997). *One Hundred Years of Socialism: The West European Left in the Twentieth Century*. 2d ed. London: Fontana Press.

Satin, Mark. (1978). *New Age Politics: Healing Self and Society*. West Vancouver, BC, Canada: Whitecap Books.

———. (1991). *New Options for America: The Second American Experiment Has Begun*. 2d ed. Carbondale: University of South Illinois Press.

Saward, Michael. (1998). *The Terms of Democracy*. Cambridge: Polity Press.

Schaeffer, Robert K. (1997). *Power to the People: Democratization around the World*. Boulder, CO, & Oxford: Westview Press.

Schafer, D. Paul. (1998). *Culture: Beacon of the Future*. London: Adamantine Press.

Scharpf, Fritz W. (1997). *Games Real Actors Play: Actor-Centered Institutionalism in Policy Research*. Boulder, CO, & Oxford: Westview Press.

Schacter, Oscar, & Joyner, Christopher C. (eds.). (1995). *The United Nations Legal Order*. Cambridge & New York: Cambridge University Press.

Schedler, Andrew. (1997). *The End of Politics? Explorations into Modern Antipolitics*. London: Macmillan; New York: St. Martin's Press.

Scheer, Hermann. (1994). *A Solar Manifesto: The Need for a Total Solar Energy Supply . . . and How to Achieve It*. London: James & James; Herndon, VA: Books International.

———. (1997). "A Place for the Sun: Politicians Must Back Renewable Energy and They Must Do So Now". *New Statesman* (17 October): 18.

Schmidheiny, Stephan, with the Business Council for Sustainable Development. (1992). *Changing Course: A Global Business Perspective on Development and the Environment*. Cambridge, MA, & London: MIT Press.

Schumacher, E. F. (1973). *Small Is Beautiful: A Study of Economics as If People Mattered*. New ed. London: Vintage, 1993.

Schumaker, Paul, Kiel, Dwight C., & Heilke, Thomas W. (eds.). (1996). *Ideological Voices: An Anthology in Modern Political Ideas*. New York & London: McGraw-Hill.

Schumpeter, J. A. (1947). *Capitalism, Socialism, and Democracy*. 6th ed. London & New York: Routledge, 1994.

Schwarzmantel, John. (1994). *The State in Contemporary Society: An Introduction*. London & New York: Harvester Wheatsheaf.

———. (1997). *The Age of Ideology: Political Ideologies from the American Revolution to Post-Modern Times*. London: Macmillan; New York: New York University Press.

Scientific American. (September 1989). Special Issue, *Managing Planet Earth*.

Scott, John. (1995). *Sociological Theory: Contemporary Debates*. Aldershot, England, & Brookfield, VT: Edward Elgar.

Scruton, Roger. (1996). *A Dictionary of Political Thought*. 2d ed. London: Macmillan.

Searing, Donald D. (1994). *Westminster's World: Understanding British Political Roles*. Cambridge, MA, & London: Harvard University Press.

Segal, Gerald. (1996). *The World Affairs Companion: The Essential One-Volume Guide to Global Issues*. London & New York: Simon & Schuster.

Segal, Gerald, & Buzan, Barry. (1998). *Anticipating the Future*. London: Simon & Schuster.

Service, Robert. (1998). *A History of 20th Century Russia*. London & New York: Penguin/Allen Lane.

Shahak, Israel, & Mezvinsky, Norton. (1998). *Jewish Fundamentalism in Israel*. London: Pluto Press.

Shain, Yossi, & Klieman, Aharon (eds.). (1997). *Democracy: The Challenges Ahead*. London: Macmillan; New York: St. Martin's Press.

Shapiro, Ian. (1996). *Democracy's Place*. Ithaca, NY, & London: Cornell University Press.

Shapiro, L. B. (1972). *Totalitarianism*. London: Pall Mall.

Shively, W. Phillips. (1996). *Power and Choice: An Introduction to Political Science*. 5th ed. London & New York: McGraw-Hill.

Shklar, Judith M. (Hoffman, Stanley, ed.). (1998). *Political Thought and Political Thinkers*. Chicago & London: University of Chicago Press.

Silk, Paul, & Walters, Rhodri. (1998). *How Parliament Works*. 4th ed. London & New York: Addison Wesley Longman.

Sim, Stuart (ed.). (1998). *The Icon Critical Dictionary of Postmodern Thought*. Cambridge: Icon.

Sim, Stuart, & Parker, Noel. (1997). *The A–Z Guide to Modern Social and Political Theorists*. London & New York: Prentice-Hall Europe.

Singh, Bishan. (1994). "A Social Economy: The Emerging Scenario for Change". In *Civil Society and Sustainable Livelihoods Workshop Report*, ed. Tina Liamzon, pp. 29–37. Rome: Society for International Development.

Sked, Alan. (1997). *Intelligent Person's Guide to Post-War Britain*. London: Duckworth.

Sked, Alan, & Cook, Chris. (1993). *Post-War Britain: A Political History: 1945–1992*. 4th ed. London: Penguin Books; New York: Penguin Books USA.

Skidelsky, Robert. (1996). *The World after Communism: A Polemic for Our Times*. London: Macmillan.

Skolimowski, Henryk. (1992). *Living Philosophy: Eco-Philosophy as a Tree of Life*. London & New York: Arkana Penguin.

Smith, Anthony D. (1995). *Nations and Nationalism in a Global Era*. Cambridge: Polity Press; Cambridge, MA: Blackwell.

———. (1998a). *The Ethnic Origins of Nations*. Oxford & Cambridge, MA: Blackwell.

———. (1998b). *Nationalism and Modernism*. London & New York: Routledge.

Smith, Cyril. (1996). *Marx at the Millennium: Humanity and Inhumanity*. London: Pluto; Milford, CT: LPC In/Book.

Smith, Graham (ed.). (1995). *Federalism: The Multi-Ethnic Challenge*. London & New York: Longman.

Smith, Philip B. et al. (eds.). (1994). *The World at the Crossroads: Towards a Sustainable, Equitable and Liveable World: A Report to the Pugwash Council*. London: Earthscan; Washington, D.C.: Island Press.

Solo, Robert A. (1991). *The Philosophy of Science and Economics*. Armonk, NJ, & London: M. E. Sharpe.

Sørensen, Georg. (1997). *Democracy and Democratization: Processes and Prospects in a Changing World*. 2d ed. Boulder, CO, & Oxford: Westview Press.

Spencer, Sarah, & Bynoe, Ian. (1998). *A Human Rights Commission: The Options for Britain and Northern Ireland*. London: Institute for Public Policy Research.

Spretnak, Charlene. (1986). *The Spiritual Dimension of Green Politics.* Santa Fe, NM, & London: Bear.

Stallings, Barbara (ed.). (1995). *Global Change: Regional Response to the New International Context of Development.* New York & Cambridge: Cambridge University Press.

Stavridis, Stelios, et al. (eds.). (1996). *New Challenges to the European Union: Policies and Policy-Making.* Aldershot, England, & Brookfield, VT: Dartmouth.

Steiner, Jürg. (1997). *European Democracies.* 4th ed. New York & London: Addison Wesley Longman.

Sternberg, Robert J., & Kalligian, John, Jr. (1992). *Competence Considered.* 2d ed. New Haven, CT, & London: Yale University Press.

Stevenson, Ian. (1997). *Where Reincarnation and Biology Interact.* Westport, CT, & London: Praeger.

Stiglitz, Joseph E. (1996). *Whither Socialism?* 2d ed. Cambridge, MA & London: MIT Press.

———. (1997). *Economics.* 2d ed. New York & London: W. W. Norton.

Stirk, Peter M. R., & Weigall, David. (1995). *An Introduction to Political Ideas.* London: Pinter; New York: St. Martin's Press.

Storr, Anthony. (1991). *Human Destructiveness: The Roots of Genocide and Human Cruelty.* London & New York: Routledge.

Switzer, Jacqueline Vaughn. (1996). *Green Backlash: The History and Politics of the Environmental Opposition in the U.S.* Boulder, CO, & Oxford: Rienner.

Talmon, J. L. (1952). *The Origins of Totalitarian Democracy.* New ed. Boulder, CO: Westview Press.

Tam, Henry. (1998). *Communitarianism: A New Agenda for Politics and Citizenship.* London: Macmillan; New York: New York University Press.

Taylor, Paul, et al. (1997). *Documents on Reform of the United Nations.* Aldershot, England & Brookfield, VT: Dartmouth.

Taylor, Philip. (1997). *Global Communications, International Affairs and the Media since 1945.* London & New York: Routledge.

Teck, Foo Check. (1997). *Reminiscences of an Ancient Strategist: The Mind of Sun Tzu.* Aldershot, England, & Brookfield, VT: Gower.

Teichman, J. (1986). *Pacifism and the Just War: A Study in Applied Philosophy.* Oxford & Cambridge, MA: Blackwell.

Teilhard de Chardin, Pierre. (1956). *The Phenomenon of Man.* New ed. New York: Harper Collins.

Tessitore, John, & Woolfson, Susan. (1997). *A Global Agenda: Issues before the 52nd General Assembly of the United Nations, 1997–1998.* 52d ed. Lanham, MD, & London: Rowman & Littlefield.

Thiele, Leslie Paul. (1997). *Thinking Politics: Perspectives in Ancient, Modern, and Postmodern Political Theory.* Chatham, NJ, & Oxford: Chatham House Press.

Thomas, Graham. (1998). *Prime Minister and Cabinet Today.* Manchester: Manchester University Press; New York: St. Martin's Press.

Thurow, Lester. (1997). *The Future of Capitalism: How Today's Economic Forces Shape Tomorrow's World.* 2d ed. New York: Viking Penguin; London: Nicholas Brealey.

Tideman, Nicolaus (ed.). (1994). *Land and Taxation.* London: Shepheard-Walwyn; Concord, MA: Paul.

Tidwell, Alan C. (1998). *Conflict Resolved? A Critical Assessment of Conflict Resolution*. London: Pluto; Herndon, VA: Books International.

Tilly, Charles. (1978). *From Mobilization to Revolution*. New York & London: McGraw-Hill.

Time. (27 October 1997). *Special Report: Renewed Britannia.*

Time. (11 May 1998). Feature "What's behind EMU?" Vol. 151, no. 19, pp. 26–40.

Tismaneanu, Vladimir. (1998). *Fantasies of Salvation: Nationalism and Myth in Post-Communist Europe*. Princeton, NJ, & Chichester: Princeton University Press.

Tough, Allen. (1995). *Crucial Questions About the Future*. 2d ed. London: Adamantine Press.

Triandafyllidou, Anna. (1996). *A Social Psychology of Party Behaviour*. Aldershot, England, & Brookfield, VT: Dartmouth.

Turner, Barry (ed.). (1998). *The Statesman's Yearbook: A Statistical, Political and Economic Account of the States of the World for the Year 1998–99*. 135th ed. London: Macmillan.

Turner, Bryan S. (ed.). (1995). *The Blackwell Companion to Social Theory*. Oxford & Cambridge, MA: Blackwell.

Turner, Stephen (ed.). (1996). *Social Theory and Sociology: The Classics and Beyond*. Oxford & Cambridge, MA: Blackwell.

Tylecote, Andrew. (1993). *The Longwave in the World Economy: The Present Crisis in Historical Perspective*. 2d ed. London & New York: Routledge.

Udovicki, Jasminka, & Ridgeway, James (eds.). (1998). *Burn This House: The Making and Unmaking of Yugoslavia*. Durham, NC, & London: Duke University Press.

van den Doel, Hans, & van Velthofen, Ben. (1993). *Democracy and Welfare Economics*. 2d ed. Cambridge & New York: Cambridge University Press.

Van Parijs, Philippe. (1993). *Marxism Recycled*. Cambridge & New York: Cambridge University Press.

Vanhanen, Tatu. (1997). *Prospects of Democracy: A Study of 172 Countries*. London & New York: Routledge.

Vankin, Jonathan, & Whelan, John. (1997). *60 Greatest Conspiracies of All Time: History's Biggest Mysteries, Coverups, and Cabals*. Distributed by East Grinstead, England, & Kempton, IL: Nexus.

Vayrynen, Raimo (ed.). (1991). *New Directions in Conflict Theory: Conflict Resolution and Conflict Transformation*. London & Newbury Park, CA: Sage.

Vile, M. J. C. (1973). *Federalism in the U.S., Canada and Australia*. London: HMSO.

Vincent, Andrew. (1995). *Modern Political Ideologies*. 2d ed. Oxford & Cambridge, MA: Blackwell.

———. (1997). *Political Theory: Tradition and Diversity*. Cambridge & New York: Cambridge University Press.

Viotti, Paul R., & Kauppi, Mark V. (1996). *International Relations and World Politics: Security, Economy, Identity*. New York & London: Prentice-Hall.

von Bertalanffy, Ludwig. (1969). *General System Theory*. 2d ed. New York, Braziller; London: Allen Lane.

von Neumann, John, & Morgenstern, Oscar. (1947). *Theory of Games and Economic Behaviour*. Princeton, NJ, & Oxford: Princeton University Press; 3d ed. New York & London: Wiley, 1953.

von Weizsäcker, Ernst, Lovins, Amory B., and Lovins, L. Hunter. (1997). *Factor Four:*

Doubling Wealth—Halving Resource Use: The New Report to the Club of Rome.
London: Earthscan.

Wainwright, Hilary. (1994). *Arguments for a New Left: Answering the Free-Market
Right*. 2d ed. Oxford & Cambridge, MA: Blackwell.

Wakeford, Tom, & Walters, Martin (eds.). (1995). *Science for the Earth: Can Science
Make the World a Better Place?* Chichester & New York: Wiley.

Waldrop, M. Mitchell. (1993). *Complexity: The Emerging Science at the Edge of Order
and Chaos*. 2d ed. New York: Simon & Schuster; London: Penguin Books.

Walford, George. (1979). *Ideologies and Their Functions: A Study in Systematic
Ideology*. London: Villiers.

———. (1990). *Beyond Politics: An Outline of Systematic Ideology*. London: Calabria
Press.

Walker, Martin. (1998). "The Third Way International". *New Statesman* (27 March):
30–32.

Wall, Derek. (1993). *Green History: A Reader in Environmental Literature, Philosophy
and Politics*. London & New York: Routledge.

Wallace, Helen, & Wallace, William. (1996). *Policy-Making in the European Union*. 3d
ed. Oxford & New York: Oxford University Press.

Wallace, William. (1997). *Why Vote Liberal Democrat?* London: Penguin Books; New
York: Penguin USA.

Waterlow, Charlotte. (1995). *The Hinge of History*. London: One World Trust.

Watts, Duncan. (1997). *Political Communication Today*. Manchester: Manchester
University Press.

Wayne, Wanta. (1997). *The Public and the National Agenda: How People Learn about
Important Issues*. Mahwah, NJ, & London: Lawrence Erbaum Associates.

Weale, Albert. (1998). *Democracy*. London: Macmillan.

Wells, H. G. (1928). *The Open Conspiracy: Blue Prints for World Revolution*. London:
Gollancz.

———. (1931a). *What Are We to Do with Our Lives?* London: Heinemann.

———. (1931b). *The Work, Wealth and Happiness of Mankind*. New York: Doubleday,
Doran; 3d ed. London: Heinemann, 1934.

———. (1938). *World Brain*. London: Methuen.

———. (1942). *The Outlook for Homo Sapiens*. London: Secker & Warburg.

———. (Mayne, Alan, ed.). (1995). *World Brain: H. G. Wells on the Future of World
Education*. New ed. London: Adamantine Press.

———. (Wagar, Warren, ed.). (1998). *The Open Conspiracy: H. G. Wells on World
Revolution*. London: Adamantine Press.

Wheare, K. C. (1963). *Federalism*. Oxford: Oxford University Press.

Wheeler, David, & Sillanpää, Maria. (1997). *The Stakeholder Corporation: A Blueprint
for Maximizing Stakeholder Value*. London: Pitman; Alexandria, VA: FT Pitman.

White, Brian, Little, Richard, & Smith, Michael. (1997). *Issues in World Politics*.
London: Macmillan; New York: St. Martin's Press.

White, N. D. (1996). *The Law of International Organisations*. Manchester: Manchester
University Press; New York: St. Martin's Press.

White, Stephen, et al. (1997). *Developments in Russian Politics*. 4th ed. London:
Macmillan; Durham, NC: Duke University Press.

White, Stuart. (1998). "Interpreting the 'Third Way': Not One Road, but Many",
Renewal 6(Apr): 17–30.

Whittaker, David S. (1997). *The United Nations in the Contemporary World*. London & New York: Routledge.

Wicker, Hans-Rudolf (ed.). (1997). *Rethinking Nationalism and Ethnicity: The Struggle for Meaning and Order in Europe*. Oxford: Berg; New York: New York University Press.

Wiener, Norbert. (1948). *Cybernetics: The Science of Communication and Control in the Animal and the Machine*. 2d ed. Cambridge, MA: MIT Press, 1961.

———. (1950). *The Human Use of Human Beings*. New ed. New York: De Capo, 1988.

Wilber, Ken. (1995). *Sex, Ecology, Spirituality: The Spirit of Evolution*. Boston & London: Shambhalla.

———. (1996). *A Brief History of Everything*. Boston & London: Shambhalla; Dublin: Gill & Macmillan.

———. (1998). *The Eye of the Spirit: An Integral Vision for a World Gone Slightly Mad*. 2d ed. Boston & London: Shambhalla.

Willetts, David. (1997). *Why Vote Conservative?* London: Penguin Books; New York: Penguin USA.

Willetts, Peter. (1995). *'The Conscience of the World': The Influence of Non-Governmental Organisations in the U.N. System*. London: Hurst.

Williams, Howard, Sullivan, David, & Matthews, Gwyn. (1997). *Francis Fukuyama and the End of History*. Cardiff: University of Wales Press; Concord, MA: Paul.

Williams, Robert. (1998). *Political Scandals in the USA*. Edinburgh: Keele University Press.

Williams, Shirley. (1998). "Interview". *Progress* 7(Winter): 4–6.

Wilson, Dick. (1996). *China the Big Tiger: A Nation Awakes*. London: Little, Brown (UK).

Wilson, Frank L. (1996). *Concepts and Issues in Comparative Politics: An Introduction to Comparative Analysis*. New York & London: Prentice-Hall & Harvester Wheatsheaf.

Wolinetz, Steven B. (ed.). (1997a). *Party Systems*. Aldershot, England, & Brookfield, VT: Ashgate.

———. (1997b). *Political Parties*. Aldershot, England, & Brookfield, VT: Ashgate.

Woodhouse, Mark B. (1996). *Paradigm Wars: Worldviews for a New Age*. Berkeley, CA, & London: Frog.

Wright, Gregory, & Pokras, Stan. (1990). "Linking the World's Idea-Gathering Organizations to Create an Electronic/Print 'Global Suggestions Box'". Unpublished paper available from 14161 Riverside Drive, No. 3, Sherman Oaks, CA 91423.

Wright, Tony. (1997). *Why Vote Labour?* London: Penguin Books; New York: Penguin USA.

——— (ed.). (1996). *Socialisms Old and New*. 2d ed. London & New York: Routledge.

Yamaguchi, Kaoru. (1990). "Fundamentals of a New Economic Paradigm in the Information Age". *Futures* 22(October): 1023–1036.

———. (1997). "Sustainability and a MuRatopian economy". In *Sustainable Global Communities in the Information Age: Visions from Future Studies*, ed. Kaoru Yamaguchi, ch. 5. London: Adamantine Press.

———. (1999). *New Scientific-Visionary Paradigm: Non-Linear and Complex Thinking in the 21st Century*. London: Adamantine Press; Westport, CT, Praeger.

——— (ed.). (1989). *Beyond Walras, Keynes and Marx: Synthesis in Economic Theory toward a New Social Design*. New York: Peter Lang.

Yamaguchi, Kaoru (ed.). (1997). *Sustainable Global Communities in the Information Age: Visions from Future Studies*. London: Adamantine Press.

Yergin, Daniel, & Gustafson, Thane. (1994). *Russia 2010 and What It Means for the World*. London: Nicholas Brealey; New York: Random House.

Yoder, John. (1971). *Nevertheless: A Meditation on the Varieties and Shortcomings of Religious Pacifism*. Scotdale, PA: Herald Press.

Young, Ralph A., et al. (1993). *Introducing Government: A Reader*. Manchester: Manchester University Press.

Zijderveld, Anton C. (1998). *The Waning of the Welfare State*. New Brunswick, NJ & London: Transaction.

Zimbardo, Philip G., & Leippe, Michael R. (1991). *The Psychology of Attitude Change and Social Influence*. 3d ed. New York: McGraw-Hill.

Zirakzadeh, Cyrus Ernesto. (1997). *Social Movements in Politics: A Comparative Study*. London & New York: Longman.

Zohar, Danah, & Marshall, Ian. (1994). *The Quantum Society: Mind, Physics and a New Society*. 2d ed. London: Flamingo; New York: Morrow.

Zolo, Danilo. (1997). *Cosmopolis: Prospects for World Government*. Cambridge: Polity Press.

Zuzowski, Robert. (1998). *Political Change in Eastern Europe: Prospects for Liberal Democracy and Market Economies*. Westport, CT, & London: Praeger.

Index

Geography, political, 146
George, Henry, 153
German Democratic Republic (GDR),
57, 58, 66–67
German Federal Republic, 41–42, 66
German Green Party, 42, 81
German politics and government, 41–42
Germany, 41–42, 75, 91, 97 n.1, 103, 105,
107, 155; East, 57, 58, 126; Nazi, 11,
41, 45, 51, 53, 54, 56, 81, 88, 97 n.1,
122–123; reunification of, 41, 67
Gestalt psychology, 147
Gibson-Graham, J. K., 154
Giddens, Anthony, 37, 149, 172, 173,
185, 193 n.2
Gifford, Paul, 174
Gilman, Robert, xi
Glasnost (public openness), 63–65, 72 n.2
Gleick, James, 165 n.55
Global awareness, 159, 225
Global capitalism, 153
Global Challenges Network, 78
Global change, 150
Global Climate Coalition (GCC), 156
Global community, 143, 158
Global cooperation, 154
Global Cooperative Bank, 176
Global ethic, 111, 170, 188
Global Ethic Foundation, 171
Global ethics, 168, 170–171, 180 n.4, 222
*Global Ethics for Global Politics and
Economics*, 171
Global goals, 183
Global governance, approaches to,
108–114
'Global humanism', 217 n.8
'Global Marshall Plan', 202–203, 216 n.2
Global politics, 115 n.12
Global problems and issues. *See*
Problems and issues
Global Responsibility, 171
Global Suggestion Box, 194 n.16
Global village economy, 154
Global Vision, 176
Global Vision Statement, 177
Global warming, 7, 202, 203 n.8, 209 n.2
Globalisation, 171, 217 n.8
Glorious Revolution (UK), 24

Goal formulation, 169, 187–188, 222
Goals, 159, 170, 183, 188; differences and
conflicts between, 178
Goals of Mankind, 188
Goleman, Daniel, 148
Goodin, Robert, 145, 146, 162 n.12
Gorbachev, Mikhail, 13, 39, 55, 56–57,
59, 63–66, 71, 72 nn.2–8
Gore, Al, 12, 126, 212, 216 n.12
Gore administration, 212, 220
Governance. *See* Government
Government, 4, 141, 158; books on,
237–239; British, 18–19, 24–32;
entrepreneurial paradigm of, 40–41,
46 n.20; essential role of, 157–158;
forms of, Ch. 7, 10; German, 81;
holistic, 192; levels of, Ch. 8, 96, 221;
local, 29, 103–104; multilevel, Ch. 8,
96, 221; policies, 156, 209; problems
and issues, 4, 10–11; regional, 105;
Russian, 66; structures of, 10; U.S., 38,
40–41; world, 12, 108–114
Government departments, 10, 26–27, 29,
31, 158, 192
Governments, 145, 158, 209; need to
listen, 11
Governments' perception of problems
and issues, 189
Goyder, George, 155, 164 n.39
Grassroots movements, 43, 75, 79–81,
82 n.1, 136, 154, 226
Gray, John, 152
Great Depression, 6, 39, 54, 157
Great Leap Forward (China), 58
Great Society programme (United
States), 39
Greece, 5, 42, 53, 95
Greed, 168
Green audits, 113–117
Green business, 87, 155–156
Green consumer movement, 84, 155
Green economics, 152–154, 163 n.29
Green entrepreneurs, 155
Green ideologies, 135–137, 139 n.14, 211;
critiques of, 139 n.14
Green movements, 75, 80–81, 82,
83 n.27, 155, 174
Green political parties, 23, 42, 81, 136

About the Author

ALAN J. MAYNE is a consultant and independent author–information provider.
He is Honorary Secretary of the British Association for the Club of Rome and the
author or editor of several books on information technology and the future, including *Resources for the Future* (Greenwood Press, 1993).

ISBN 0-275-96151-6

90000>

EAN

9 780275 961510

HARDCOVER BAR CODE